Charles Herrold, Inventor of Radio Broadcasting

Charles Herrold, Inventor of Radio Broadcasting

Gordon Greb *and* Mike Adams

With a Foreword by Christopher H. Sterling

McFarland & Company, Inc., Publishers
Jefferson, North Carolina, and London

LIBRARY OF CONGRESS CATALOGUING-IN-PUBLICATION DATA

Greb, Gordon.
Charles Herrold, inventor of radio broadcasting /
Gordon Greb and Mike Adams ;
with a foreword by Christopher H. Sterling.
p. cm.
Includes bibliographical references and index.

ISBN-13: 978-0-7864-1690-5
softcover : 50# alkaline paper ♾

1. Herrold, Charles.
2. Radio broadcasters—United States—Biography.
I. Adams, Mike, 1943–
II. Title.
PN1991.4.H39G74 2003 791.44'028'092—dc21 2003013981

British Library cataloguing data are available

Cover portrait: Charles Herrold (Stephen True Collection);
background: 1915 patent for water-cooled microphone
(Clark Papers, Smithsonian Institution);
1930s San Francisco Bay area radio station
(Perham Foundation Electronics Museum)

Manufactured in the United States of America

McFarland & Company, Inc., Publishers
Box 611, Jefferson, North Carolina 28640
www.mcfarlandpub.com

To our wives,
Darlene
and
Barbara

Acknowledgments

The individual who helped inspire our research more than anyone else was the late Clyde Arbuckle, San Jose historian, teacher, and museum curator. He was a true lover of history, known to both of us. Thanks to Arbuckle's collected documents, artifacts and photographs on the Herrold station, our early tentative inquiries were confirmed and encouraged. When we made further inquiries, we were welcomed by a host of radio pioneers, their relatives and acquaintances. If we had more space on these pages, we could specify in great detail the kindness and cooperation each of the following persons gave: Harry Engwicht, Mrs. Charles D. Herrold (Sybil True), Robert True, Stephen True, Ray Newby, Lee de Forest, Simpson Reinhard, Leonard D. Fairfield, Douglas and Connie Perham, Ira L. Smith, Robert Stull, Joseph D. Cappa, Gene Wilson, Terry Hansen, Frank Quement, Roy Grandey, Lee Kopp, Evelyn Clark, Ken Ackerman, Don Mozley, P. D. Worth, Thorn Mayes, Dick Barrett, Bill Spendlove, and Joseph E. Baudino. Since Herrold's station had become KCBS, owned and operated by the Columbia Broadcasting System in San Francisco, there was complete support given to plans to publish and celebrate Herrold's achievement from the CBS network and its executives Maurie Webster, Jules Dundes, and Arthur Hull Hayes.[1]

Those students at San Jose State University (SJSU) who helped encourage our research and subsequent honoring of Herrold also deserve special thanks, particularly Anthony Taravella, William F. Knowles and James Curry. Sixteen members of the campus chapter of Sigma Delta Chi, now the Society of Professional Journalists, helped make possible the 1959 event we called the 50th Anniversary of Broadcasting. The celebration owed much of its success to the enthusiasm and devotion of the chapter's co-adviser, assistant professor Kenneth Roed, together with the active participation of journalism professors Pearce Davies, Charles V. Kappen, Joe Swan, and Dolores Spurgeon. Thanks also are due to SJSU journalism head Dwight Bentel and Publications Director Lowell Pratt, without whose support our project never could have been launched. All the facilities of the college were made available to us by college President John T. Wahlquist, giving us more than normal service in the library, photography labs, and audio-visual center so that we could collect and preserve necessary documents and photographs. We appreciate, too, the help given us by various others in the San Jose State academic community, including Walt Fox and Glen Pensinger, both of whom Director Richard B. Lewis authorized to give us audio-visual services as needed; graduate student Jack Ashworth, who used Greb as host in a TV documentary about Herrold for classroom instruction, an idea conceived and supervised by Professor Clarence Flick; San Francisco State College Professor Charles H. Smith, who donated an audio cassette copy of the 1945 radio documentary *The KQW Story* to our files; and San Francisco State graduate student John F. Schneider, whose master's thesis was invaluable in detailing many of Herrold's radio contemporaries of the 1920s and 30s.

In addition, we wish to thank the non-profit organizations that endeavored to partially underwrite our expenses. Preservation of documentary evidence was greatly assisted by a grant from the Sourisseau Academy of San Jose State University. The collection of old and new evidence for the 1995 PBS television documentary *Broadcasting's Forgotten Father: The Charles Herrold Story* was funded by KTEH (PBS), the SJSU Foundation, and the Perham Foundation Electronics Museum, the repository for the surviving pieces of Herrold technology. Our appreciation must also be expressed to Robert E. Summers, editor, for publishing Herrold's first station claim in the *Journal of Broadcasting*.

Our search took us to many locations. We extend thanks to Elliot Sivowitch of Division of Electricity, National Museum of American History, at the Smithsonian Institution; the late Bruce Kelley of the Antique Wireless Association; the employees in charge of special radio collections or exhibits of the Perham Foundation; History San Jose; the Tech Museum of Innovation in downtown San Jose; the Library of Congress; the New York Public Library; the San Francisco Public Library; the Oakland Public Library; and the libraries of San Jose State University, Stanford University and the University of California. Special thanks also must go to the press in the San Francisco Bay Area whose librarians made newspaper collections available to us or searched for particular information on our behalf, particularly, the *San Jose Mercury News*, the *San Francisco Chronicle*, the *San Francisco Examiner*, and the *Oakland Tribune*. Many collections of radio memorabilia kept by private individuals and associations were made available to us, the most significant of which is owned by Herrold's grandson, Stephen True. Other important archival information was made available to us by John F. Schneider, Dick Barrett, Bart Lee, Jim Maxwell, George Durfey, Don Koijane, Jim Kreuzer, William Byron, Leonard McKay, and Ron Gordon.

Last, but not least, we wish to thank many of our academic colleagues who encouraged us to write this book, especially those specialists in broadcast history who recognized its importance and graciously read our manuscript. Their critiques were valuable in helping us seek to achieve the highest scholarly standards. The two persons most helpful in this regard are well known for their own publications in this field. They are Dr. John Michael Kittross, retired communications professor and former Provost of Emerson College, Boston, who now is managing director of K\E\G Associates, an academic consulting firm and editor of *Media Ethics* magazine; and Dr. Christopher H. Sterling, Professor of Media and Public Affairs and Director of the Graduate Telecommunication Program at George Washington University, Washington, D.C.

Original, unpublished source materials used in this book, such as letters, affidavits, recorded interviews, typescript, and other materials are identified in our bibliography under Special Collections and their particular locations are letter-coded in our endnotes.[2] None but the authors who wrote this book are responsible for whatever factual errors or judgments may appear, and it goes without saying that the book's merits and defects are our own.

Contents

Foreword: Discovering Broadcasting's Birthplace

by Christopher H. Sterling

An hour south of San Francisco, the San Jose metropolitan area lies in the middle of what has, in recent decades, become known to the world as Silicon Valley. Back in the late 19th century it was fast developing into acres of prosperous fruit orchards dotted with small market towns. Early in the 1900s, the area began to develop as a technology and communications center. The military needs of two world wars hastened the creation of electronic innovations and new companies to produce them, especially during and after World War II. Since the 1950s the area has been transformed into seemingly endless square miles of one computer chip or software manufacturing facility after another. The few remaining fruit trees are purely decorative.

As the Bay Area grew into an important technical center, it became famous for its garages— not for the lowly buildings themselves, but for the often-unwashed yet brilliant pioneers who began their careers there. An early pioneer was Lee de Forest, who developed applications of his Audion three-element vacuum tube in a Palo Alto garage while working with Cyril Elwell of the Federal Telegraph Co. Later pioneers included David Packard and William Hewlett in the 1930s to the "two Steves"— Jobs and Wozniak — in the 1970s, and certainly unknown others fiddling with circuits in yet other garages as you read these words. There was something about central California — the wonderful weather and scenery, the location near a major port and numerous military bases, a cosmopolitan city (who could *not* like San Francisco?), and the world-class universities (Stanford and Berkeley, to name two of the oldest and largest) to help encourage scientific research and industrial start-ups— the list of reasons why this region has been such a technological hot spot could go on.

But too often ignored in this parade of progress is yet another "first" for the San Jose area — the very beginning of what has grown into the modern electronic media business. For it was right in downtown San Jose, then still best known for shipping fruit, that the world's first radio broadcasting station took to the air in 1909 and broadcast regularly for five years, from 1912 until April 1917. Unlike some other claims for early radio broadcasting, this one is well-documented in contemporary sources. What follows is the story of how that happened, why it happened in San Jose, and why by a man largely forgotten even before his death more than a half century ago. For out of his efforts developed the thousands of radio and later television stations operating today. Yet almost nobody in the business has ever heard of Charles David Herrold or what he accomplished.

As you will learn in more detail in the pages that follow, Herrold moved to California with his family in 1890 when he was 15. He soon entered Stanford University, studying astronomy, and switching to electrical engineering a year later. Forced by ill health to drop out, Herrold turned to tinkering with various electrical inventions until he lost everything in the San Francisco earthquake of 1906. After that he turned to teaching at a technical school in Stockton, California. He probably first considered what is now called broadcasting while in Stockton, sometime before 1908.

The pace of this story quickens with Herrold's return to San Jose and the formation at the start of 1909 of his own College of Wireless and Engineering. It was a commercial training school rather than a liberal arts based college, and Herrold moved quickly to develop the laboratory facilities needed for practical wireless telegraphy training. Out of that laboratory and the experience his students required came his radio transmitter.

Herrold was most certainly not alone. Hundreds and probably thousands of other amateur or "ham" operators across the nation and in many other countries were working the airwaves on a daily basis, most as a hobby, a few as a means of earning a living. Several government and commercial wireless telegraphy stations, primarily operated by or for the navy and shipping companies, were located in the Bay Area by this time. A few local manufacturers were also turning out wireless equipment. These stations and companies needed trained workers and thus indirectly supported the formation of local training programs. What was different at Herrold's college, however, was his early focus on wireless *telephony*, or the transmission of voice rather than coded (telegraphy) signals. Attempting to combine his own arc phone transmitter innovation with the desire to send out "clear" signals of voice (and even music) led Herrold and his assistants to begin experimental transmissions in 1910. These could be heard by any amateur operator because they were purposely *broadcast* to anyone who cared to tune them in and had the equipment to do so. To that point, wireless had generally meant point-to-point communication, paralleling and often competitive with wired telegraphy or telephony services.

What happened over the next several years is the focus of the chapters that follow. What became the world's first broadcasting station had to make all of its own equipment, develop its own "programs" (the very idea was totally new), construct a schedule, and promote what it was doing as best it could. Herrold's wife was one of the first women involved in experimental radio and most assuredly one of the first heard on the air. Had World War I not intervened in 1917, the story might not have gotten lost. In April of that year the government required that most wireless transmitters (including virtually all amateur operations) cease transmissions for the duration of the war and continuity of the Herrold station ground to a halt. From 1917 until 1920, Herrold helped to train military radio operators. In late 1919 or early 1920, he returned to the air with an experimental transmitter, eager to resume where he had left off. But as the authors relate, this was not to be. Lacking funds and overtaken by technology, Herrold was swept to radio's sidelines. He soon lost his station and spent the remainder of his life in a series of ever more menial jobs. He died unknown and little mourned in July 1948.

How this story came to light a decade after the inventor's death is told in this volume's fascinating penultimate chapter, "Herrold: Lost and Found." The scholarly research reads a bit like a mystery story, from some initial lucky breaks followed by decades of perseverance by Gordon Greb, who later enlisted the interest and help of San Jose State University colleague Mike Adams. Together they dug wide and deep to find the vital first-person accounts, contemporary documents and reports, and long-ago interviews and photographs needed to do the story justice. They have overcome both the passage of time and seeming lack of documentation that had prevented earlier publication — and thus wider knowledge — of Herrold's role. Applying all of their finds, they reveal events that are often poignant, always interesting and absolutely important.

Greb and Adams highlight the vital, innovative spark of a seminal individual. Broadcast history remains heavily dominated by stories of large corporations and organizations. Some are both true and valuable, but too many are misleading and claim too much. And the commercial promotion often obscures the important contributions of those who never enjoyed corporate backing and promotion. Herrold is one of those who, despite the lack of corporate support, made a difference.

Thanks to the authors, Herrold's inspiring and important role has been rescued from history's dustbin. Telling what Herrold accomplished in no way diminishes the role of others, but rather fills in important context. Charles Herrold's primacy and innovations are finally given the historical attention they have long deserved.

Christopher H. Sterling,
George Washington University

Preface

One of the first descriptions of what is now known as radio broadcasting is found in this notarized statement in an advertisement for radio parts in the 1910 catalogue of the Electro Importing Company of New York: "We have given wireless phone concerts to amateur wireless men throughout the Santa Clara Valley."[1] The statement describes the broadcasting of entertainment by radio to a known audience. Its author was Charles Herrold. This is his story.

It is not widely known that broadcasting's early beginnings were nearly lost to recorded history and that its first major practitioner was Charles David Herrold of San Jose, California. To remedy this situation is the purpose of this book. Here we tell the fascinating story of a number of early experimenters and the various avenues they took before broadcasting came into being, and explain why those important pioneering years of broadcasting have remained in the shadows for far too long.

Many believe that American radio arrived fully developed one day in 1920, completely equipped and ready to go, the date and inventor being absolutely certain.[2] The existence of broadcasting prior to World War I is not widely known, and accounts of its gradual development during the first two decades of the 20th century are difficult to find. Small town San Jose in the far West, after all, was not a radio manufacturing center or important part of the entertainment industry. Therefore, the authors carefully examine the records from the East Coast, where it has been assumed for far too long that radio had its beginnings, and add to that account those elements of the Herrold West Coast broadcasting story which are backed by evidence. By shedding new light on "the lost years of broadcasting," we believe a case can be made that an obscure California inventor, teacher, and experimenter — working in the far West in what is today called Silicon Valley — should be called America's first broadcaster.

Rediscovering Herrold[3]

Charles Herrold was largely forgotten when he died penniless and alone in 1948.[4] His reputation as a pioneer broadcaster was unknown outside of his immediate area and what he had accomplished lay virtually dormant until 1958, when Herrold's

114 *The Electro Importing Co., N. Y., Mfrs.* 1/1910

90 MILES WITH AN E. I. Co. COIL

WORLD'S RECORD BROKEN

SPECIAL AEROGRAM SENT AS TEST OF NEW AERIAL

On the 17th of April, 1910 at 5:15 P. M., Ray Newby operating for the school of Wireless, broke all previous records for the most efficient transmission, sending to Mare Island a distance of nearly **70 MILES** from San Jose, with an expenditure of not more than **15 WATTS OF ENERGY.** Further tests were carried on the following day the Farallon Island registering interference showing that the earth's potential had been disturbed at this distance ABOUT 90 MILES.

The current was supplied by a small storage battery actuating a **1 INCH E. I. CO. COIL.** The spark gap used was a small E. I. Co. Zinc gap set at about 3 millimeters. The (apparent) wave length was about 500 meters, the frequency 600,000 cycles per second. Following is a copy of the message sent at that time:

1 FN RA Ck Dh Fn

REAR ADMIRAL H. OSTERHAUS,
Mare Island, Calif.

Congratulations from the Soldier boy whose gun your honored Father shot in rifle pits at Spanish Forts.

W. G. HAWLEY, Postmaster.

3/26/10

SCHOOL OF WIRELESS

Garden City Bank Building
San Jose, Calif., June 23, 1910.

The Electro Importing Co.,
233 Fulton St., New York City.

Gentlemen:—

We have transmitted messages from our station to the Government Stations at Mare Island and the Farallon Island, A DISTANCE OF 90 MILES, and also to the U. W. T. Co. Station in the Crocker Tract, San Francisco, USING ONE OF YOUR ONE INCH (1") coils and a small portable storage battery. We have made some of our best of the above tests at midday USING THE SAME ONE INCH COIL. We have given wireless phone concerts to amateur wireless men throughout the Santa Clara Valley. USING THE SAME ONE INCH COIL and an Ericsson Dust Transmitter.

(Signed) CHAS. D. HERROLD.

STATE OF CALIFORNIA,
ss.:
COUNTY OF SANTA CLARA.

I, Chas. D. Herrold, being duly sworn deposes and says that the above matter to which my signature is attached is true to my best knowledge and belief.

CHAS. D. HERROLD.

Subscribed and sworn to before me this 24th day of June, 1910.

WESLEY PIAPA,
Notary Public in and for County of Santa Clara, State of California.

San Jose, Calif., June 23, 1910.

TO WHOM IT MAY CONCERN:

Mr. Raymond Newby and I USING AN E. I. CO.'S ONE INCH COIL, and E. I. Co.'s zinc gap set at about 1/16 inch, and the antenna of the School of Wireless in the Garden City Bank Bldg. called up operator RH of Mare Island Station getting an immediate response. He gave us time from the standard clock and told us that we came in strong.

I have also heard Operator Newby talk to PH, the big U. W. T. Co.'s Station in the Crocker Tract, San Francisco, and also heard the Farallon Island Station tell us "Keep out." In every case we used the **SAME ONE INCH COIL.** I have also, using the same set, talked with PH myself two different times.

(Signed) THAD STEVENS.

STATE OF CALIFORNIA,
ss.:
SANTA CLARA CO.

I, THAD STEVENS, being duly sworn, deposes and says that the above facts as therein set forth are true to my best knowledge and belief.

THAD STEVENS.

Subscribed and sworn to before me this 25th day of June, 1910.

WESLEY PIAPA,
Notary Public in and for County of Santa Clara, State of California.

San Jose, Calif., June 23, 1910.

TO WHOM IT MAY CONCERN:

I transmitted the message from Major Hawley to Admiral Osterhaus using a one inch E. I. Co.'s (1") COIL actuated by a small portable storage battery. The energy used was LESS THAN 15 WATTS, the distance covered being that between San Jose, Calif., and Mare Island. I used the system of the School of Wireless, designed and built by Chas. D. Herrold, the Electrical Engineer for the Company. I also talked with Operator Ludwig of the Farallon Islands and PH United Wireless Station in San Francisco using the same hook-up and using the same one inch coil. Mr. Thad Stevens was present at several of the tests and himself talked with the last named station.

(Signed) RAY NEWBY.

STATE OF CALIFORNIA,
ss.:
COUNTY OF SANTA CLARA.

I, Ray Newby, being duly sworn deposes and says that the above is true to my best knowledge and belief.

(Signed) RAY NEWBY.

Subscribed and sworn to before me this 24th day of June, 1910.

WESLEY PIAPA,
Notary Public in and for County of Santa Clara, State of California.

In the author's opinion, this is the "smoking gun" document proving Charles Herrold was broadcasting to a known audience as later claimed. It appeared in the 1910 catalogue of New York–based Electro Importing Company, a mail order electric parts company. In a notarized statement, Herrold says: "We have given wireless concerts to amateur wireless men throughout Santa Clara County." The provision of radio entertainment regularly to wireless audiences this early in the century clearly supports Herrold's claim he was the first broadcaster (courtesy Perham Foundation Electronics Museum).

work was accidentally rediscovered, documented and given national attention. Why was Herrold's accomplishment neglected and almost forgotten? Why has much of broadcasting history prior to the 1920s remained virtually unknown? These are some of the questions the authors examine in this book, hoping to put the Herrold story into its place in history and to focus attention on the neglected years of broadcasting.

Interest in Herrold was revived with the publication of an article about his "first station" in a professional journal by one of the authors of this book.[5] This led to renewed interest in what Herrold had done and set off a long chain of events which finally led to this work. What follows is the collaborative effort of professors Gordon Greb and Mike Adams of San Jose State University, who became acquainted after Adams read what Greb had published and suggested they work together to produce a book.

In creating this volume, we hope new light will be shed on the origins of one of the major forms of mass communications in the 20th century and to recover for posterity a period of radio history which deserves more attention. Our goal has been to reveal, as accurately as possible, the life and accomplishments of Charles Herrold as biography and as an important part of radio's fascinating history.

Before and After Licensing

As no licenses were required when Herrold first transmitted voice and music from his San Jose wireless school from 1909 to 1912, listeners who heard his programs and students who helped run the station remembered him saying, "This is Charles Herrold in the Garden City Bank in San Jose." Fortunately, we found many of these people still living within close proximity to San Jose when our research began. After 1912, when all wireless amateurs were required to obtain government licenses, a colleague who was in San Jose said that Herrold picked his call sign out of the sky and used the signature FN.[6] We were fortunate enough to get this important detail, as well as a lot of other first-hand knowledge, from Herrold's former station announcers, program producers, or engineers. Their information was supplemented by official government documents or other publications which gave us more specific dates and places as well as context. A few years after 1912, Herrold got an experimental license (6XE) from the government and used it to conduct his broadcasting as an "experimenter," until a government shutdown resulting from World War I silenced his operation in April 1917. With the coming of peace, Herrold received experimental license 6XF on March 9, 1920, and on Sept. 24, 1920, authorities relicensed his old portable transmitter, 6XE. When the Commerce Department began licensing commercial stations in the 1920s, Herrold's station became KQW on Dec. 9, 1921, and his station was authorized to use 50 watts of power, unlimited time, at 360 meters.[7] These are undisputed facts because they are all part of the public record.

To understand Herrold the broadcaster, it is important to first consider Herrold as a teacher, an inventor, and a human being. We know much about Herrold the teacher and the person from the eyewitness accounts of former students, friends and family. To help piece together Herrold the inventor, a wireless technical expert was asked to study the Herrold patents. The authors also asked several other broadcast historians to answer the question, "Who was first?" This was done using the most modern means of connecting with informed opinions worldwide — an Internet radio history discussion forum. The opinions gleaned from this Web site provided an interesting counterpoint and perspective for the authors in reaching their conclusions.

Method and Scope

In seeking to prove that Charles Herrold began radio broadcasting experiments in 1909 in San Jose, California, and continued to operate his station over the years, we used a variety of methods to validate the claim. At the outset, Greb located a large repository of original documents, records, affidavits, and photographs which had been kept by Herrold himself and preserved by his son. The publication of Greb's research in 1959 led to a 50th anniversary of broadcasting celebration, and alerted acquaintances, station alumni and former listeners, who contacted him at San Jose State College (later University) and provided him with further information. On joining the faculty at San Jose State and learning about Herrold, Adams took up the research, reviewed Greb's collection and added important new documents, fresh interviews and photographs. In the earliest stages Greb had the cooperation of KCBS, the descendant of the station Herrold founded, and used their airwaves to locate listeners who could contribute information about the man and his work. They were interviewed and sometimes donated additional printed materials and photographs to the authors' growing archive. After deciding to collaborate on a book, Greb and Adams searched the literature in libraries from coast to coast, including the archives of the Smithsonian Institution, and sought all of the original witnesses to Herrold's work they could locate.

The importance of eyewitnesses cannot be underestimated. History books tell us that in 1876 when Alexander Graham Bell invented the telephone, his first words after spilling the battery acid were, "Mr. Watson, come here. I need you." If we are to demand documented proof that he actually said this, our search will be difficult indeed because a recording apparatus did not exist at that time to prove it. The fact is that we accept this account and put it in our history books because there was a witness to the event and Bell recorded it in his own lab notebooks the same day. Just as Watson witnessed Bell's accomplishment, Ray Newby was on hand for Herrold's earliest broadcasts. By interviewing Newby, who was there in 1909, we have the kind of data available nowhere else. Recorded interviews constitute a substantial portion of our information and we have contributed some of these to such oral history collections as that of Columbia University. As new tools became available for our research activities, we adapted them to our needs. They ranged from our using Internet search engines to the myriad ways of electronically recording, reproducing and preserving what we found using computer technology, or recording it on tape or film.

Admired for His Work

What has impressed us about Herrold the man is the admiration and respect he earned as a teacher when he ran his small wireless college, which may account for his being so well remembered by those we talked to years later. Students nicknamed him "Prof" or "Doc" because they held him in high regard, and they continued to do so throughout their lifetimes. This is not a surprising heritage for men who are gifted teachers. Such talented men dazzle, exhibit superior intellects and inspire generations of students. A great Harvard philosopher, Alfred North Whitehead, said in the *Atlantic Monthly* more than 70 years ago:

> In every faculty you will find that some of the more brilliant teachers are not among those who publish. Their originality requires for its expression direct intercourse with their pupils in the form of lectures, or of personal discussion. Such men exercise an immense influence; and yet, after the generation of their pupils has passed away, they sleep among the innumerable unthanked benefactors of humanity. Fortunately one of them is immortal — Socrates.

Students of Plato were attentive and wrote down what they learned about Socrates from their teacher's dialogues. These students' notes were saved and have been passed on in printed books, preserving what were originally oral lectures. But until our own time the advantage of preserving the thoughts and actions of men with things to say has all gone to the writer, not the sayer, of the word. Fortunately, we were able to find and interview Herrold's former students, friends, and acquaintances, as well as his former wife, who reached back in time to tell us what Herrold was like. Hans Frederik Dahl two decades ago observed that too many writers of radio history tend to focus on the sender, ignoring the receiver, and said, "The social situation arising through the encounter between receiver and programme is so evasive that it can hardly be subject to methodic treatment. In spite of the difficulties, this encounter is indeed the main point of the activity."[8] He complimented British historian Asa Briggs for seeing this interrelationship in his multi-volume history of the BBC.[9] Although several Europeans successfully experimented with voice and music, the authors could find no radio broadcasting abroad on a regular basis prior to that in America. Thus no attempt was made to chronicle foreign broadcasting developments in this book.[10]

Major Questions

How Charles Herrold began regularly scheduled broadcasts before anyone else and how his wife Sybil became the first woman to do regular weekly radio programs is the principal story of this book. What led Herrold to start a scheduled broadcasting station in 1909? What prompted Mrs. Herrold to play phonograph records for anyone who wanted to listen? Did her advertising of a phonograph store make her the first commercial announcer? Was Herrold's assistant, Ray Newby, truly America's first radio disc jockey? Was Herrold the founder of the first network when he linked two stations together, San Jose and San Francisco, in 1912? Answers to these and other questions are what we wanted to know. With the information we have uncovered, we believe the work of these radio pioneers should no longer be considered "the lost years of broadcasting" but be recognized as true contributions to radio's history.

Just as radio developed out of the work of many, so did this book. Recovering the lost years of broadcasting required the help and assistance of many generous people. We owe thanks to more individuals than we can possibly credit and apologize to those not mentioned. In trying to learn what Charles Herrold did as a broadcaster, a large number of people were interviewed during the many years of our research.[11] In questioning Ray Newby, the first operator of Herrold's station in 1909, author Greb decided in advance to employ the technique of non-suggestive interrogation; that is, to acquire information without divulging what he had learned from other sources. We started by asking Newby questions to test the accuracy of his recall and measured his answers against the factual record in Greb's possession, which showed that Newby could be believed on nearly all major points and that he could become an invaluable primary source. Newby not only got all of the initial questions right but he contributed further interesting details about each of the incidents. In subsequent interviewing, he proved his memory of events so exceptionally well that he confirmed what Herrold said in his own collection of papers in nearly every major detail.[12] Furthermore, when additional printed materials became available, they verified Newby's statements.

Boxes of documents obtained from Herrold's son, Robert Herrold True,[13] and later his grandson, Stephen True, provided a vast survey of original source material: correspondence, notarized statements, partnership arrangements, testimonials, news accounts, texts of speeches, articles, and the like. There also were many photographs and even some rare motion picture films. In addition to spending long hours talking to Newby, Greb was able to find and interview many participants in or witnesses to early San Jose radio. Some of them, like former program director Ira L. Smith, had saved Herrold's correspondence. Records and photographs turned up. People who personally witnessed, audited, or participated in Herrold's work as a broadcaster in the first and second decades of this century, and whose papers and memories were mined for this book included the following:

1908 Ray Newby became assistant to Prof. Herrold in setting up a radio laboratory. W. J. Erich, who said Newby "helped me build my first ham station" (W6AL), became one of the first Herrold College students to hear the programs.

1909 Simpson Reinhard played the first violin solo on Herrold's station. Doug Perham and Clyde Arbuckle remembered listening to Herrold's first programs.

1910 Terry Hansen, Harley Corey, and Clifford Berry were radiotelephone listeners.

1911 George Ninnis and Frank Lindsay heard Herrold radio concerts.

1912 Joseph Cappa, a regular listener as a boy, said the station operated on a schedule. He enrolled in Herrold's College when he was older.

1912 Ken Sanders was heard on the air as one of Herrold's operator-announcers.

1913 Sybil M. Paull (as Mrs. Herrold) recalled how she produced a weekly radio show for "Little Hams" every Wednesday night. She took requests and was loaned phonograph records to play from a local music store. Her baby, Robert, cried over the air.

1915 Herrold students Willis Clayton, Gene Wilson, and Maurice Dee heard the station. Armond Higgins and Hall Berringer recalled programs broadcast to the 1915 San Francisco World's Fair; W. C. Sartorette heard the station that year. Dr. S. C. Maynard, knew about Herrold's work, as his office was nearby.

1916 Al Pearce, a 1930s network radio star, first appeared on the Herrold station as a singer with brother Cal. They sold newspapers outside the station. Robert Stull studied under Herrold in San Jose and then went to the University of California at Berkeley where he demonstrated to engineering professors how a Herrold radiotelephone operated.

1919 Stull, now an electrical engineer, helped Herrold return his San Jose station to the air with a new transmitter located on South First Street. Joe Cappa came to help.

Amateur radio operators Frank Quement, Tony Bauer, and Harry Engwicht, Herrold wireless students knew the station first-hand and helped with its operation. Other resource material was provided by station staff and management:

1920s KQW managers Fred Hart and Ira L. Smith began celebrating their "first station" anniversaries and helped Herrold collect documents of proof. Harry Saine installed the new transmitter for the First Baptist Church.

1930s KQW owner Ralph Brunton and manager E. L. McCarthy arranged anniversary celebrations and honored Herrold as the founder of America's pioneer station. Staffer Theron Fox was the station's first sportscaster.

1940s KQW staff announcer Ken Ackerman and newsman Don Mozley recalled the station's joining the CBS network, and producer Roy Grandey summed up the history of the station by writing and directing *The KQW Story* for airing in 1945.

Gordon Greb
Mike Adams

1

Introduction to Broadcasting

Once the work of the mind of man had become a source of power and wealth, every addition to knowledge, every fresh discovery, and every new idea became a germ of power within reach of the people ... all things scattered broadcast by heaven, were a profit to democracy....

Alexis de Tocqueville (1835)[1]

Broadcasting was in the womb of development long before anyone even knew its name. Hugh G. Aitken, in his book *The Continuous Wave* (1985) notes that broadcasting was not originally intended but arose unexpectedly out of the work of early experimenters:

> The development in the 1920s and 1930s of broadcasting in the popular sense — that is, the transmission of news, entertainment, and advertising to the general public by radio — would have been impossible without previous advances in continuous wave technology that had originally been made with quite different objectives in view ... the rise of radio broadcasting is a classic example of the unanticipated consequences of technological change.[2]

While the peculiar phenomenon which ultimately led to broadcasting was noted by inquisitive minds many centuries ago, dating back to the ancient Greeks and Romans, our understanding and use of radio's scientific principles had to wait until recent times. Broadcasting never would have occurred had there not been an inventive use of electricity shortly before the mid–19th century. By using electricity to send signals rapidly from place to place along a wire, Samuel F.B. Morse introduced a new communications system known as the telegraph — meaning "tele" (distance) and "graph" (word). The wire carried electrical sounds rapidly over great distances and these simple dots and dashes were organized into a common code which both the sender and receiver could learn and understand as a special language. Morse, whose name was given to the code, had refined the telegraph (1838) and patented it (1854). The invention of the telephone, which was patented later by Alexander Graham

Charles Herrold, formal portrait, circa 1920 (Stephen True Collection).

Bell (1876), made it possible for individuals to engage in two-way communication without the need for telegraph operators relaying messages in code. However, both of these technologies required linking the sender and receiver by wires and were limited by terrain and economics. What was needed was a system enabling people to communicate reliably over great distances without wires. Although a number of inventors were conducting experiments around this time, the person who finally did this was Guglielmo Marconi in 1895. He and others called it "wireless."

Wireless started out as the "radiotelegraph," a recorded form of communication — written rather than spoken — which, in today's usage, means communicating written matter without wires as in data transmissions by commerce, industry, and government. Wireless then evolved into the radiotelephone, leading to its current manifestations in point-to-point cellular telephones and other wireless personal communication systems. And then — at the time of our story — it evolved into transmitting from one source to many receivers, or "broadcasting" (which by simple definition means serving an audience over the airwaves). Broadcasting was originally called "wireless telephony," and is the principal technological focus of this book. It also is a philosophical and social concept, one that Charles D. Herrold may have been the first to fully realize. During most of the 20th century, and even today, the influence of broadcasting has been revolutionary and pervasive. But how did this evolution of "wireless" into "broadcasting" come about, and who were the individuals and groups responsible for this metamorphosis?

Birth of Broadcasting

Wireless evolved much the same way that wired electrical communication did. Starting with simple long and short bursts of signals— dots and dashes— in the work of Marconi and others, wireless telegraphy quickly became indispensable to commerce and the safety of life and property at sea. But the idea of using speech, rather than code, took hold among experimenters and amateurs much as the need and desire for the telephone attracted would-be inventors—such as Alexander Graham Bell—to the problems of transmitting speech. Amateurs and experimenters tried to communicate by voice with early spark transmitters, the wireless instrument used to send code. They failed, since these primitive transmitters didn't generate continuous waves. Some—including Charles Herrold—tried using the telegraphic instrument in early experiments but soon gave it up when they found that speech sent by spark transmitter was distorted to the point of unsuitability.

It wasn't until new wave-generating systems were introduced during the first decades of the 20th century that several of the early voice experiments succeeded. Canadian Reginald Fessenden found a way to transmit voice and music, as did Americans Lee de Forest, Charles Herrold, Frank Conrad and others. At first, these were separate and isolated instances as one after another succeeded in transmitting talk and music. Their successes produced the wireless phone, or the radiotelephone. It allowed people to communicate over distances without wires, person to person. The fact that they called it a "phone" indicated that experimenters thought this new invention was an extension of existing technology and would most likely replace the Bell telephone. With few exceptions, these individuals were seeking the best means of person-to-person two-way communication. The system they were trying to perfect was narrowcasting. Almost accidentally, a small number of these experimenters began to consider whether there were advantages to what seemed to be one of early radio's most annoying attributes—that anyone could eavesdrop—and wondered how it might have a possible benefit. The idea that there might be reasons to seriously engage in "broadcasting"—one person sending out messages to many—started to percolate.

Radio Finds an Audience

Until radio became an industry, aided by the investments made by government in the first World War, most private experimenters worked hard alone, seeking the rewards of invention. They poured their energies into trying to find something new that could be patented and thus provide them a financial return. The only listeners they sought at the beginning were investors. But, when they began testing or demonstrating their radiotelephone equipment, their experimental transmissions usually sent out strong, clear signals—from a human voice or a phonograph record—which traveled far beyond the intended receivers. This content was so wonderful and marvelous to hear, whether it was de Forest's operatic recordings or someone simply reading a newspaper, that anyone hearing it eagerly came back for more. These happenstance listeners constituted a ready-made audience, and as their numbers grew their collective whole came to be known as "radioland." Although brought into a somewhat imaginary association by receiving instruments scattered far and wide, this body of listeners was equipped and ready to tune in. It was a disparate group, which included amateurs who happened to be listening for code, radiotelegraph operators handling commercial traffic, ships' operators sending and receiving signals at sea, and others urged to procure their own instruments by friends and neighbors who were wireless enthusiasts like Herrold, de Forest and Conrad. When wireless set listeners picked up occasional singing, gossip, weather reports, and phonograph music coming over the airwaves, it startled and puzzled everyone who heard it for the first time. It got an immediate response. Expecting Morse code in their earphones, and then hearing voices and music, they immediately asked for more. This audience response encouraged the experimenters to continue and it was the fledgling beginning of "broadcasting."

Unappreciated Discoveries

The work of researching and writing radio history is understandably difficult because audio recording was in its infancy and rarely used for interviewing at the beginning. Inventors ran the risk of having their ideas stolen and were cautious about seeking publicity. Secrecy was necessary to protect an inventor's experimental results until his idea was patented, but this concealment often denied him credit, and in some cases left him out of history books altogether. More often than not, the inventor himself did not see the full potential of his invention at the moment of its creation. This is what happened to Lee de Forest in 1912, when he was working with two colleagues in the Federal Telegraph Company laboratory in Palo Alto, testing a radio tube that he had patented in 1906. For this experiment, one of them dropped a handkerchief onto a table and listened to hear its sound. Instead of landing quietly and softly, the linen produced a loud thud in their headpieces. The noise was far louder than expected. It showed that de Forest's triode vacuum tube had amplifying properties never before realized. Its importance was not immediately appreciated. It took a few more years before this hitherto unappreciated "Audion" would become one of radio's most vital elements, yet its power was not recognized by its inventor de Forest until six years after its discovery.[3] History is replete with success stories in the independent laboratory whose importance was neither seen nor acknowledged until years later.[4] When records were never kept or have been lost, there is insufficient evidence to learn what happened. That is why the preservation of the work of Charles Herrold has been so important toward a broader understanding of one small corner of the field of electronic communication — the origin of broadcasting.[5]

Thus radio — as the news and entertainment medium we know today — came about accidentally. It did not happen deliberately or with the full realization by participants of the great communications industry that lay ahead. One of the early students of radio's origins, E.P.J. Shurick, who personally saw how the young listeners made it grow, said in his book, "Its development can be traced back to the hours of experimentation in technical laboratories — in the remote farmhouses — and in the townhouse basements where youth with a far-away look in their eyes thrived in the squawks and squalls of homemade 'wireless' sets."[6] Broadcasting developed because audiences wanted it and experimenters began to provide it. It was fun and entertaining. It was available and free. Only later did it become commercial and profitable.

A New Century and Inquisitive Minds

Scientists, engineers and inventors were described as heroes at the turn of the century in the popular press. Readers were told a new world was coming, fashioned by the discoveries of great men who were building, creating and doing something absolutely never seen before. Evidence of this surge in creativity by the makers of practical things was easy to find. There were countless stories about men and women making breathtaking new discoveries, the implications of which could only be guessed. Writing in 1901 in the *Saturday Evening Post,* Samuel Moffett saw with uncanny accuracy that "if the enthusiasm on the subject of the wireless transmission of electricity were to be believed ... when we know how to tap it, we can carry little instruments in our pockets and make our power felt as if by magic wands in any direction and at any distance."[7]

Whatever the new century promised to be, it was fascinating to follow the work of creative genius in magazines, newspapers, and the cinema. The names and faces of world famous inventors became familiar — Edison, Bell, Ford, Tesla, Einstein, the Wright brothers, and Westinghouse, to name a few. Recalling the thrill of those turn-of-the-century days, journalist Ray Stannard Baker wrote: "I remember going to a much-advertised 'Electrical Lecture,' in the district school house at St. Croix Falls, in Wisconsin, where I grew up to see a contraption of batteries set up, one in the girls' cloak room, the other at the most distant corner of the schoolroom (probably sixty feet away) with wires connecting them, over which we could actually *talk*— even with the door closed. What a miracle! It was our earliest acquaintance with the telephone."[8]

Inspired to Invent

Charles Herrold was an eager follower of these new developments. This new world of science and invention caught his fancy at a young age. As the story of his life reveals, it would be almost an accident of fate as to which direction his inventive mind would take. Son of an intelligent businessman-farmer-inventor and a bright educator-mother, young Herrold was taught the discipline, forbearance and patience of a farmer as he grew up in a Midwestern agricultural community, and then had his inquiring mind set afire as a teenager when his family moved to a far western region unafraid of new ideas, the San Francisco Bay Area.

A voracious consumer of history, religion and science, Herrold allowed his formal schooling to introduce him to ideas of the great minds of the past. His own peripatetic reading soon acquainted him with leading thinkers of both past and present. While Herrold's interests led him to focus upon astronomy and physics as a Stanford University freshman, a professor called his attention to something else. Herrold was startled to learn from his instructor's demonstration that messages could be sent silently through the air and picked up some distance away with a wireless telegraph receiver. It started him thinking — if Marconi's device could transmit dit-da-dits without wires, why not the human voice? Or flowing music? The wireless demonstration inspired his imagination. By a series of deliberate steps, aimed at trying to send the human voice great distances without wires, Herrold finally did something with tools of communication no one had quite done before — aiming for one thing he unintentionally discovered another. While trying to improve wireless telephony, which others finally did better, Herrold's work led to something new — radio broadcasting.

As he would be the first to admit, he did not originate the idea of broadcasting overnight and he did not do it alone. Herrold and his wife and students were running a radio station long before they realized what they were doing. Soon after his first experiment in 1909, Herrold knew he had an audience and in 1910 published a statement to this fact.

Oversights and Lost Years

If this was the gradual and peculiar way broadcasting came about, why isn't it reflected in radio's published history? Questions about who-did-what-for-whom ahead of others remain controversial. Without more evidence, we may never have common agreement. One reason is that early practitioners were careless record-keepers, too busy or too ignorant to archive what they were doing. Some tried to preserve their work but through no fault of their own lost it due to accident, fire, or theft. Others were misled into believing radio's popularity had guaranteed them a place in history as audiences flocked to its programming and they became well known to local audiences. Unfortunately, broadcasting as contrasted to more permanent paper records of print and telegraphic media always has been ephemeral, especially during its earliest days. As far as we know, none of the early stations had equipment to record the content of what they were broadcasting. Credit, therefore, has gone to those few foresighted individuals who seized the day, publicized themselves widely in print, and established claims which may or may not be true.

Father of Broadcasting

The case for honoring Charles Herrold as the first broadcaster was best made by Herrold himself in a 1934 radio interview. He came to the San Jose KQW studios on the 25th anniversary of his radio station and was interviewed on the air about his role as a pioneer radio broadcaster. Some historians believe the series of questions and answers taken up by the interview make for a very good case on behalf of Herrold. Therefore we offer the interview in its entirety, allowing Herrold to explain how broadcasting should be defined, what he considers its peculiar distinctions to be, and after acknowledging what other experimenters claimed to have done, why he felt he was entitled to be called "The Father of Broadcasting." The interview between the emcee Myers and, as scripted, follows:

MYERS: *They call you the Father of Radio Broadcasting, do they not?*

HERROLD: Yes, and I believe that I earned the right to be called the Father of Radio Broadcasting.

MYERS: *Were you the first man to talk over a wireless instrument?*

HERROLD: No! I would not be foolish enough to claim such a thing.

MYERS: *Why I was of the impression that you were the first man to talk via wireless or as we say to day— radiotelephone.*

HERROLD: If you had such an impression, you were mistaken. I have never claimed such a distinction, unless Amos Dolbear can be said to be the first man in America to talk to a receiving station at a distance without connecting wires of a telephone line. He did this at a distance of one mile, ten years before Marconi's time. In Europe such men as Count Arco and Professor Slaby; Reumer; Valdemar Poulsen, the Danish Edison; Simon; Dudell; and Thompson were far ahead of Americans in evolving wave producing devices modulated by voice. In America we had Collins and Francis McCarthy [*sic*] in San Francisco, who talked from Twin Peaks to San Francisco, about three miles, using a spark telephone. Dr. Lee de Forest in this country did considerable development work on experimental wireless telephones before I did my work, at San Jose in 1908.

MYERS: *Well, would that not make any or some one of these men the Father of Radio Broadcasting?*

HERROLD: No, most certainly not.

MYERS: *Why not?*

HERROLD: Because, in the first place, they did not broadcast—they narrowcasted.

MYERS: *Would you mind explaining the difference between a broadcast and what you call a narrowcast?*

HERROLD: Gladly. The word broadcasting is an old word used by the Marconi wireless telegraph operators to designate a message "to all ships and stations." In the very nature of things, such a message was intended for receiving stations widely distributed.

MYERS: *Was it used in connection with the wireless telephone?*

HERROLD: No. For the simple reason that wireless telephony was unknown at that time. Marconi developed no wireless telephone because he used a spark system and such a system could not be used to transmit the voice practically.

MYERS: *Then a broadcast is something intended for anyone who may receive it. What is this "narrowcast" that you mentioned?*

HERROLD: A "narrow cast" is a message sent from one transmitting station to one certain receiving station and intended for none other.

MYERS: *I think that I begin to grasp the idea— the early experimenters in wireless telephony were narrowcasting.*

HERROLD: Yes. Exactly so. When Valdemar Poulsen talked from his laboratory at Lyngby, Denmark, to a test receiving station, that was a narrow cast. Court Arco, Professor Slaby, and many other Europeans did the same thing. When Lee de Forest in this country had a singer from the Metropolitan Opera sing in his laboratory and he himself talked, this was intended for reception by a group of newspapermen located on a ship in the harbor, equipped with receiving instruments.

MYERS: *Is not that hair-splitting, professor?*

HERROLD: Absolutely not. Certainly de Forest had no thought of a broadcast. He was merely developing the wireless telephone for pure communication purposes, with the idea of selling it to the government and the commercial companies. Broadcasting, as we know it, certainly was no part of de Forest's plans, or any of the others.

MYERS: *I see, these early experimenters in wireless telephone had not conceived of the idea of furnishing the public with broadcast music and speech.*

HERROLD: That is correct. There is not the slightest evidence to show that Collins, McCarthy [*sic*], de Forest, Poulsen, or any of these early experimenters had in mind the use of their experimental radiotelephones for entertainment purposes.

MYERS: *When did you first start broadcasting?*

HERROLD: In 1909, Mr. Newby, who for some time has been the field engineer with Bausch Radio, and I built an enormous antenna containing 11,500-feet of wire — this was a carpet aerial — and commenced immediately broadcasting music. This was a daily event up to 1912 when the federal radio law came into effect and shortly afterwards a license was granted for us to use a radio telephone.

MYERS: *Was the license granted to broadcast?*

HERROLD: No. The government granted the license for experimental purposes. The government did not recognize broadcasting stations till their new allocation of the classification "broadcast" and KDKA was the first station to secure a license under the new rulings.

MYERS: *(laughingly) That makes them the pioneer, does it not?*

HERROLD: (chuckling) Well, let's just leave that to the public. They are a pretty good judge and the Court of Public Opinion is usually quite just in its decision. But seriously, certainly thousands of amateurs who made it a religion to listen every day to our dance music and the thousands of [Victor Red] seal records we played, certainly the hundreds of homes who connected a dozen pairs of telephone receivers to their receiving sets and invited the neighbors to listen —certainly they knew what I was doing, since I had nothing to sell at that time.

MYERS: *But Dr. Herrold you were interested in the transmission of voice long before that, weren't you?*

HERROLD: Yes, it all happened when I saw tests performed in a laboratory at Stanford University from newspaper reports of Marconi's first tests of transmitting wireless telephone back in 1895. I started testing along the same lines and it is safe to assume that they were among the first radio tests performed in this country.

MYERS: *Then you were old Doc Stork's right hand man when radio was born, weren't you?*

HERROLD: Yes. It was a wonderful thing to be able to say I was present at the birth of the infant radio industry. Those were the days when that station was full of tanks of alcohol and deadly fumes and hot arcs burning at high temperatures and then there were the microphones water cooled to keep them from burning up. It is a privilege to have been present at the christening in 1912 when we received our first licenses. This infant industry was sickly in those days and it cost me $40,000 to nurse it along and keep it in clothes and another $40,000 to help it over a sick spell. In 1920 I saw the howling, squalling infant radio industry weaned and overnight become a husky, independent youngster. Today what do I see? Listen to the tremendous chain broadcasts as well as those from the independent stations, each serving its own community. Dial about as I do and read the printed programs of the chains, revel in the marvelous symphonies, lay as I do with a single receiver fastened to your ear while you read, grow up with this industry as I have off and on for the past 25 years and see if it wouldn't get into your blood and grip you. Yes, the radio industry is certainly a stalwart bronzed young giant.

MYERS: *But what was the use of broadcasting in the early days if no one had receiving sets?*

HERROLD: Ah, but I took care of that. I established a studio at the Wiley B. Allen Company in San Jose. There were several dozen telephone receivers around the wall of the studio and seats for the convenience of the listeners-in. They came in and listened free to the programs being broadcast. Then I started putting out radio sets.

MYERS: *When was all this, doctor?*

HERROLD: Just prior to 1912.

MYERS: What was the next step?

HERROLD: Well, I established two-way communication by radio between San Jose and the Fairmont Hotel in San Francisco—a heretofore unheard of feat. That was in 1912.

MYERS: *How about those broadcasts you made during the Panama Pacific International Exposition here in San Francisco in 1915?*

HERROLD: Yes, that was an interesting experiment. I broadcast programs from San Jose to the crowds at the World's Fair from six to eight hours a day every day for months. It was the only radio music in the world then being broadcast.

MYERS: *Did you have any artists in the flesh in those days or did you use all phonograph records?*

HERROLD: It may interest you to know that Al and Cal Pearce, then living in San Jose, were the first to sing over KQW. How well I remember it. They sang "On the Trail of the Lonesome Pine." Juanita Tennyson, who since has made quite a name in radio, was the first woman to sing over KQW.

MYERS: *Say, you didn't have Amos 'n' Andy down there, did you?*

HERROLD: (laugh) No, I didn't. But E.A. Portal, who is now in the retail radio business in San Francisco, was associated with me during those early day experiments.

MYERS: *Have you divorced yourself from radio altogether, Doc?*

HERROLD: Not by a long shot, I haven't. But I'm playing an entirely different end now—radio advertising. You see, KQW was the first radio station to do direct advertising and I was the first man to sell a bill of goods in front of a microphone. There's a great future in it. I am now acting as advertising counselor for various stations and writing for radio merchandising purposes. If you don't mind, Mr. Myers, before I close, I would like to pay a tribute to Mr. Fred Hart, present owner of KQW. Since he acquired the station eight years ago, Mr. Hart has done a remarkable work—particularly for the farmers of Northern and Central California. He is their mouthpiece—their guide. He has fought hard and diligently for the rights of the agriculturists of this state and doesn't get half the credit that he deserves. He has built this radio station to an enviable position in the ether firmament. I congratulate him—heartily. Thank you.

MYERS: *On behalf of my boss, I wish to thank you for those nice words, Dr. Herrold. Goodnight.*

To put Herrold into the context of radio history and understand what others were doing at the same time, we need to return to the time when the "Race for the Radiotelephone" began.

2

Race for Radiotelephone

> *The pity of it is that the hard work which went into the art of radio, and which contributed so largely to its present state of development, is not recognized by most of us in this latter day. Many are the heroes of radio who are buried in darkness, and who have had little recognition, if any.*
>
> Hugo Gernsback, "50 Years of Radio" (1938)[1]

To fully appreciate why Charles D. Herrold was the first man in the 20th century to introduce the public to broadcasting and why he became its earliest advocate, we need to understand the times in which he lived and those who were trying to invent similar technology for the same or other purposes after the start of the new century in 1900.[2] They, like Herrold, were trying to find a way to perfect radiotelephony. Researchers and inventors whose work finally led to broadcasting were engaged in their experimentation between 1900 and 1920. Call it the race for the radiotelephone.[3] These were the years when they sought to perfect a two-way wireless telephone and quite by accident began to use it in a new way and produce a new medium of communications—to attract an audience. Before anyone had the proper instrument to do this, various kinds of wireless technologies were put to use, such as the spark, arc, alternator and vacuum tube, which, in turn, resulted in them being tried, improved, discarded or embraced.

During this important transition period, many experimenters tried, most of them failed and only a few managed to succeed. Besides Herrold, who persevered and refused to give up, there were at least three other outstanding and ambitious individuals whose work was significant at this time: Reginald Fessenden, Valdemar Poulsen, and Lee de Forest. It also would be unfair to omit a fourth contender, someone who was not quite as scientific as the others but still uniquely situated to make a contribution, Frank Conrad. They began as scientists and inventors, some later became businessmen and promoters, but overall they were primarily responsible for either the discovery, the invention, or the realization of the broad uses of a talking wireless. And while Charles Herrold ultimately benefited like everyone else from the results of all their efforts and even took them in bold new directions, it was this small group of inventors who really defined the early technology of the radiotelephone. It began as a quest for a wireless replacement for the wired telephone; it ended with the broadcasting of entertainment programming for an audience.

A Pre-Wireless Perspective

Early rumblings of the possibility of what radio might become sounded several decades before Marconi's wireless became part of the vocabulary of the 20th century. Books like Edward Bellamy's *Looking Backward: 1887–2000,* and other political and social satire in the form of editorial cartoons, encouraged public discussion of what might result if a system were invented to send a speech or music of a live orchestra simultaneously to a number of receivers. Some editorial writers thought it would be an intrusion, others believed it would destroy society, as it might keep people out of the concert halls and away from the orators' public soapboxes and isolate them in their homes. Nevertheless, there was discussion about such a system, and in several European countries, such music and news subscription systems actually existed for a time.[4] Of course, those fictional and real systems all used connecting wires. The precedents for communicating over long distances by wire existed right up to and beyond World War I: the telephone, the telegraph and the transatlantic cable.

There were also a handful of pre-wireless inventors who constructed and even patented voice transmission systems using other means—modulated light, ground conductivity or magnetic inductance. One of these individuals, Alexander Graham Bell, tried some of these methods but finally chose another direction to perfect voice communication by wire, leading to his greatest invention, the telephone. Others, like Nathan Stubblefield, went to their graves believing they had been foiled by unknown conspirators or that if they could have found one more financial backer, or the time and money with which to make one more improvement, their system would be the one in use today. While failure was common and often went unreported, the important triumphs of a gifted few became well known. Such achievers included Heinrich Hertz, Oliver Lodge and Guglielmo Marconi, who experimented with the sending of small signals in the form of a spark at one end of the room related to a spark gap generator at the other side of a room. Their work was made possible by the theories and writings of James Clerk Maxwell and others that led to the belief that a wireless system was waiting to be discovered and exploited. Others looking into the possibilities of wireless in the early days of the century included Popoff in Russia, Majorana in Italy, Colin-Jeance in France and Slaby-Arco in Germany.

What was tried didn't always work. Inventors saw problems in using wired systems, modulated light, or inductance methods and eventually turned away from them. The limitations of these wireless transmissions included the fact they were relatively slow, went one direction at a time, and required having operators trained in code and physically connected by wire to a receiver at the other end to interpret them. Experimenters soon turned instead to the wireless telegraph, being widely used

Best known for his radio telephony experiments was Lee de Forest, shown here with his 1906 Audion (courtesy Perham Foundation Electronics Museum).

and popularized by Marconi, as the likely base on which they could launch a new communication system, one capable of carrying voice and music to countless listeners scattered everywhere. However, solving the issues raised by this new electromagnetic method of long-distance communication would change forever the direction electric communication was taking. The actual outcome of the experiments with the new medium, while never anticipated, would ultimately lead to a vast new industry of radio broadcasting.

The Nineteenth Century Imagination

Prior to the introduction by various radiotelephone experimenters of their competing wireless systems, there already had been some discussion in the newspapers about how the technology of sending music into homes might be accomplished. More than talk, there actually were a couple of systems in place that today might be categorized as "subscription music services," 19th century versions of today's TV cable and satellite-delivered audio services. Perhaps influenced by the Bell telephone and the Victrola, everyone thinking or imagining how to build such a system saw that it would be dependent on wires for distribution. The significance of this network of telephone subscribers to this story is that for the first time it introduced to the public the possibility of family entertainment that was closer to what radio would become. It suggested life could be different from what then existed at home in the form of books, magazines, stereopticon cards, and the piano. What those few interconnected systems attempted were certainly ahead of their time, unknowingly awaiting a successful wireless telephone.

In Bellamy's popular 1887 novel *Looking Backward*, the author describes a wired music system of the future. The influence this prediction had on the public cannot be minimized. As an exciting and popular piece of speculative fiction, it placed a system of musical entertainment in every home in the context of a utopian society in the year 2000. Within each home there was a future version of the radio: "They have devised an arrangement for providing everybody with music in their homes, perfect in quality, unlimited in quantity ... you can hear by merely pressing a button."[5] But even before Bellamy's ideas went into print, there was a prophetic cartoon on the front page of the March 1877 issue of the *New York Daily Graphic*. Captioned "Terrors of the Telephone," it depicted an angry-looking orator yelling into a floor-mounted oversized telephone microphone. From the back of the device are hundreds of tiny wires connected to large receivers in a dozen places; London, New York, Dublin, Boston, San Francisco, Peking, and curiously, a lone native American Indian out on the prairie. With the exception of the Indian, all of these receivers are in public halls, none in a living room setting.[6]

That same year a similar idea had been advanced in the form of a song. Written in 1877 by Thomas P. Westendorf, "The Wondrous Telephone" predicted lyrically: "You stay at home and listen to the lecture in the hall or hear the strains of music from a fashionable ball"[7] Then there was Albert Robida, a political cartoonist and lithographer who in 1882–83 did a series of lithographic drawings depicting broadcasting, this time aimed at a home listener rather than an audience in a public hall. At the "transmitting" or originating end, a musician played what appeared to be a combination organ–steam calliope, its sound somehow gathered and connected to many wires. The late George Clark, RCA historian in the 1920s and 1930s, added a note to the bottom of the cartoon calling it a "Radio Broadcasting Station, 1882." In Clark's words, "Note the wires leading up to the pole, and then outward to subscribers."[8] In Robida's 1883 lithograph a home receiving setup was portrayed, with the husband, wife and daughter sitting around a table listening in rapt attention to several telephone loudspeakers. It's described by Robida as "a telephonic installation by which newspaper reports are to be transmitted."[9]

If the systems described in the books and editorial cartoons of the day seemed more like science fiction than fact, consider the actual working systems. In a system patented in 1881 and demonstrated by French inventor Clemen-Agnes Ader, microphones were installed next to the footlights of a stage and the sounds they picked up were sent to listeners far away by wires. According to Ader's patent, "The telephone allows us to convey songs, music and the spoken word to distant places."[10] Apparently, the existence of wired systems was more commonplace than realized: "European capitals had a service of wired broadcasts via the telephone system. Paris naturally had such a system. London telephone subscribers could participate in the two-tier tariff *Electrophone* service at five or ten pounds per year, and eavesdrop on concerts, music halls, theatres or church services. The London system ran from 1899 until radio finally killed it in 1925."[11] And in 1893 "the *Telephon-Hirmondo* in Budapest was transmitting news, weather reports, market quotations, lectures and music over the telephone from 8am to 11pm for a large number of subscribers."[12] This system continued to operate into the 1930s.[13]

Pre-Wireless Radiotelephone

Early on, there were a number of individuals who apparently saw a need for a non-wired voice communication system. Much of this activity, if not all of it, happened prior to the introduction of Marconi's wireless telegraph. Before the successes of Fessenden, Poulsen, de Forest and others, most early experimenters had based their devices on wave-like principles different from those found by Heinrich Hertz. Whether over land or water, most of the early attempts to send voice without wires fell into one of two categories of technology — modulated light or inductance. These were sound-carrying systems that used a bright, focused light which was modulated or made to "flicker," analogous to what happened when one spoke into a carbon button telephone placed in series with a DC voltage. The receiver used a light sensitive element, selenium, in combination with batteries and earphones. The flickering of the received light falling on the selenium created tiny currents of sound similar to what could be heard in a telephone receiver. The range was limited to a few miles, and depended on the atmospheric conditions and the brightness of the light. The most successful of those limited devices was known as the "Photophone." Originally offered to the public by Alexander Graham Bell in 1878, this light telephony system had been improved by 1904 and was demonstrated at the Louisiana Purchase Exposition in St. Louis, but never caught on. Bell called it the "Radiophone," and while it may have attracted attention, it never found practical use.[14]

Bell's Radiophone

While Bell clearly saw and marketed his device as a wireless accessory for his wired telephone, at least one member of the press thought it was an early look at the future. This is how one reporter in 1904 described the utility of Bell's invention, in which, incidentally, he uses the word "radio":

> The radiophone, which forms a part of the exhibit of the Bell Telephone Companies at the Louisiana Purchase Exposition, is the only practicable method of telephoning without the use of wires yet discovered. By its means the blinding rays of a searchlight may be made the path for human speech and other sounds. The rays of light will carry for miles every tone and inflection of the voice, the delicate shading and varying effects of orchestral music, every note and cadence of a song. With the help of the radiophone electric lights may be made to talk or be transformed into musical instruments. The radiophone is the embodiment of much that is wonderful in the transmission of sound, and it suggests the marvelous possibilities hidden in articles of common use.[15]

Other less well-known scientists were also working on variations of modulated light voice transmission using an arc as a light source. Moving closer to what would be called the Poulsen system of wireless arc transmission, H.T. Simon in 1897 discovered that a direct current arc would give out tones and speech by superimposing telephone currents on an arc used for a line-of-sight transmitter. This may have convinced Bell to use an arc for his Photophone. Around this same time, the German inventor Ernst Ruhmer equipped several naval vessels with his version of a light telephone device. Distance limitations and the soon-to-be-invented wireless telephones would rapidly doom all development of this and other line-of-sight devices.

The Stubblefield Mystery

Then there were the controversial demonstrations of Nathan B. Stubblefield, who lived from 1860 until 1928. His two radiotelephone systems, one based on ground conductivity and the other on induction, caused quite a stir in his native Kentucky. Stubblefield had a friend come to his farm to witness the inventor's first non-wired voice transmission over land as early as 1892.[16] In an attempt to free the telephone from its wires, Stubblefield did not use true wireless methods, but rather, two non-radio systems. The first of his systems used the conductive characteristics of moist ground, and featured a carbon telephone transmitter, many batteries in series, and long rods stuck in the wet earth. According to a newspaper account:

> Nathan Stubblefield, a Kentucky truck farmer, claims to have discovered telephoning without wires. At a public exhibition in Murray, Calloway County, Ky., on Jan. 1, he convinced a thousand people of the truth of his claim ... Stubblefield placed his transmitter in the courthouse square and ran two wires from it into the ground. He established five 'listening stations' in various parts of the town, the furthest six blocks from the transmitter. Then Mr. Stubblefield's son took his place at the transmitter and talked, whispered, whistled and played a harmonica. Simultaneously everyone at the receivers heard him with remarkable distinctness.[17]

Since the technology it employed was primitive and limited, the importance of this demonstration was in something else. Its significance was its capability of sending voice and music without wires to more than one receiver, making it available to the public at large and more than a single message to an individual. This demonstration, organized by the Wireless Telephone Company of America, was followed by the sale of 500,000 shares of stock in the Stubblefield inventions. For a while it looked as if Stubblefield might become rich:

> The company also organized an experiment in Central Park, New York City, in June 1902. This event, however, was nearly a total failure, due primarily to the rocky soil in the park which would not conduct electricity. Company executives suggested that Stubblefield surreptitiously run a wire underground to connect the rods. Nathan became immediately suspicious and, upon further investigation, discovered that the company was nothing but a stock fraud. He returned to Murray and urged all his friends who had invested to demand their money back. The company collapsed and the swindlers involved eventually went to prison.[18]

Did news of Stubblefield's work influence Sir William H. Preece, who in 1899 in England used telephones and a parallel-wire induction system to transmit voice three miles?[19] No one knows. But Stubblefield's second system was based on magnetic induction, a technology similar to modern day systems that connect to a hi-fi receiver and allow a listener to walk around a room wearing headphones with no connecting wires. Stubblefield received a patent in May 1908 for his magnetic induction system, which, unlike the Preece system, used a telephone and a battery fed into large inductance coils. The receiving coil was connected to a telephone receiver. After his earlier failure with ground conductivity, Stubblefield refused to show his induction system to potential investors for fear that they would steal it from him. He used the induction system for a while but later gave it up, having unsuccessfully spent four years trying to raise the money needed to develop it. Its range was probably limited to less than half a mile. In the March 1930 issue of the *Kentucky Progress Magazine*, the publication chose to call "Murray Kentucky, the Birthplace of Radio." The article told how a plaque had been placed on March 28, 1930, at Murray State Teachers College to honor Stubblefield, saying he was the "first man to broadcast and receive the human voice without wires. Although he undoubtedly gave the world its greatest invention, the radio, he failed to get the honor due him."[20]

Marconi's Importance

The name Guglielmo Marconi began to attract world attention late in the 19th century. As a young man born in Italy of Italian and British parents, he migrated to England with his wireless invention because the Italian government would not support his work. From sending Hertzian waves across a room as early as 1894 to the highly publicized transmission of the letter "S" from Poldhu, England, to Newfoundland, Canada, in December 1901, Marconi's system made obsolete all non–Hertzian systems of wireless communication. Today some believe Marconi's success was less as a scientist and more as a coordinator; he was first to successfully combine the relevant practical and theoretical wireless ideas and experiments of others into a business. Said historian Hugh Aitken: "What differentiated Marconi from his contemporary rivals was initially neither his scientific knowledge nor the distinctive excellence of his technology. It was his sense of the market, of where a demand for this new technology existed or could be created."[21]

So it was in the context of Marconi's wireless system that a new group of experimenters began to look at better ways of sending voice through the air. After all, the light and induction schemes were limited to a few miles and never would be taken seriously, especially if a voice transmission system with the range of Marconi's wireless telegraph could be found.[22] The future development of radio would be based on a wireless system using Hertzian waves. And between the time of Marconi's wireless and the full realization of broadcasting in the 1920s, systems based on spark, alternator, arc, and the vacuum tube quickly overshadowed all earlier non–Hertzian systems as a carrier of voice. Determining which one was best would consume the first two decades of the 20th century. Scientists and inventors like Poulsen, Fessenden and de Forest explored new ways. Others like Herrold and Conrad joined in. While none of the participants realized it at the time, it would be a race for the radiotelephone.

Another limiting technology that for a time delayed the transition from modulated light systems to a wireless-based radiotelephone was the receiver. For translating the dots and dashes of spark into a signal, the device used in the Marconi system was a variant of Branley's Coherer, a small tube containing iron filings which closed like a switch when receiving the electromagnetic pulses of the Morse code. Each time the filings "cohered," and caused the circuit to close, current from a battery flowed, causing a buzzer to sound or a telephone receiver to click or an inking device to record a coded symbolic component of the message, a dot or dash. A small hammer would "tap" the filings apart and the entire process began again to detect the next dot or dash. In addition to being extremely slow, the mechanical coherer could not receive audio. A coherer did not allow a receiver to "hear" sound, obviously a serious technical impediment to the development of the wireless telephone. From a 1909 operator's handbook one learns that among "the leading wireless systems the coherer has become almost obsolete."[23] New systems of detecting signals like Fessenden's "Liquid Barretter" and Pickard's galena had to be discovered before an operator could "hear" a human voice using a headphone. Radio could not succeed until a new generation of detectors came along that converted radio frequencies into audio frequencies. When they did arrive, it was a big step in advancing the use of the Hertzian-based radiotelephone.

The New Radiotelephone Pioneers

Like the land-based wired telegraph, originally demonstrated by American artist and inventor Samuel Morse in 1844, the development of the Marconi wireless, commonly known as the wireless telegraph, enjoyed certain technical advantages as a communications medium. Even today some amateur radio operators prefer continuous wave systems for low power, long distance communications. The reason is that its signal is easier to detect, can be heard over interference, and has less fading. But with the introduction of the wired telephone by Bell in 1876, it was possible to actually talk with another person without the whole world listening in, and in the process connect one human being with another. Phoning allowed one to easily understand the other person's feelings— excitement, depression, hesitation, avoidance, the range of human emotions not possible with telegraphic code systems. While an ordinary human can speak 150 words per minute, a fast Morse code operator can send only 30 to 40.

Thus in the opening years of the 20th century, the stage was set for a practical radiotelephone based on Marconi's success with the wireless telegraph. But it awaited the right man or woman to do it. In the beginning, some experimenters only wanted to discover and reap the financial rewards from finding a replacement for the wired Bell telephone, just as Marconi had done by sending messages through the air, freed from dependency on the land-based telegraph. Fessenden and de Forest were serious scientists who tried to invent and profit from a practical system, but apparently in the beginning saw no value in the fact that their experiments were attracting small, unintended audiences amongst those having wireless receiving sets. This is exactly what gave Herrold the lead when he recognized its worth and used a type of Poulsen arc as a means of sending programming to audiences regularly. Poulsen's importance was that his arc system was the major transmitting technology for wireless code (not voice) between 1907 and 1916, a technology which was brought from Denmark to the San Francisco Bay Area in 1909 by a Stanford engineering graduate, Cyril F. Elwell. The arc attracted some of the brightest minds of the era to Palo Alto to help in its development.[24] One of them was Lee de Forest, who worked there in 1912 and came to realize the full potential of his previously patented radio tube while experimenting there. In 1919 Westinghouse learned how popular Frank Conrad's programs were becoming with the public and began building receivers and transmitters. By 1920 the race for the radiotelephone no longer involved a few lonely inventors, but a vast number of entrepreneurs who suddenly realized the profit-making potential of what years of research had brought about. Now it was to be called "radio" and most of those who pioneered its development soon would be forgotten.

Reginald Fessenden and His First Broadcast

Reginald Aubrey Fessenden was born in Bolton, Quebec, Canada, in October 1866. As the son of a minister, he was educated in New York and Canada, and "at an early date manifested a particular liking for mathematical and scientific subjects."[25] Between 1887 and 1890 Fessenden worked for Thomas Edison, after which he became a professor of electrical engineering at Purdue University and at Western University of Pennsylvania. Described by colleagues as a hard working, hard driving intellectual, by 1902 Fessenden had 13 wireless patents issued in his name. His inventions covered "improvements in construction of antennas, means of amplifying received signals, [and] wireless telephone."[26] Probably his most important early contribution was the 1903 invention of the Liquid Barretter, used for the "reception of amplitude-modulated wireless signals."[27] In lay terms, Fessenden invented the first receiving device that made hearing the human voice by wireless transmissions possible.

Fessenden may have also been the first person to send and have received a voice transmission using Hertzian waves, accomplishing this as early as 1900. Writing in *Scientific American* in 1907, Fessenden described his work with all three systems: spark, arc, and alternator. About his early spark experiments, he wrote how he "transmitted speech wirelessly for the first time in the summer of 1900 by the method disclosed in US patent 706,747. While the speech transmission could be understood, there was a great deal of extraneous noise in the telephone, and various devices were devised for eliminating this."[28] Next, he turned to an arc with "an improvement on the original Thomson singing arc method, recently discovered by Poulsen and others, but which was used by the National Electric Signaling Company [NESCO] in 1901 and patented in 1902."[29] Fessenden also described his work with General Electric engineer Ernst Alexanderson in developing his alternator for NESCO: "During this test not only speech but phonographic talking records and music were transmitted, all being received with perfect clearness and distinctness, the wireless telephone being in this respect markedly an advance over the regular wire lines."[30]

As an eccentric genius, he was reported to be tough on his staff:

> Fessenden and Alexanderson worked well together, although that was not the case for many others who fell into Fessenden's orbit. His assistants, for example, grumbled about his high-handed ways with them. "Don't try to think. You haven't the brains for it!" was one of the kinder ways he addressed them. Alexanderson recalled that Fessenden was domineering and bombastic with people he thought were beneath him. When something went wrong, he sometimes would fire everyone only to rehire them the next day.[31]

While he continued to work with Alexanderson on the design of a super-alternator for radiotelephone communication, he continued to intimidate his staff:

> As Fessenden's prowess in wireless grew, so did his eccentricities. He experienced growing paranoia that any number of people ... were out to steal his inventions. His Brant Rock, Massachusetts laboratory became a top-secret outpost, where information and apparatus were kept under lock and key at all times. His visions of industrial espionage were not entirely imaginary. A casual visit by de Forest to one of Fessenden's workshops in 1903 resulted in a round of court battles regarding de Forest's theft of the Barretter receiver design.[32]

After three court appearances, he finally received an injunction against de Forest for patent infringement. It cost Fessenden over $100,000 to defend his work in court and the experience increased his paranoia.

The 1906 Broadcast

Fessenden's longest lasting and most public claim was his 1906 Christmas Eve broadcast from Brant Rock, a small New England coastal village north of Cape Cod Bay, Massachusetts. In a letter he wrote in 1932, he reflected on this event:

> This broadcast was advertised and notified three days in advance of Christmas, the word being telegraphed to the ships of the U.S. Navy and the United Fruit Co., which were equipped with our apparatus that we intended broadcasting speech, music and singing on Christmas Eve and New Years Eve. The program on Christmas Eve was as follows: first a short speech by me saying what we were going to do, then some phonograph music, Handel's Largo. Then came a violin solo by me, being a composition by Gounod called "O, Holy Night," and ending up with the words "Adore and be Still" which I sang one verse of, in addition to playing on the violin, though the singing, of course, was not very good. Then came the bible text, "Glory to God in the highest and on earth peace to men of good will," and we finally wound up by wishing them a Merry Christmas and then saying that we proposed to broadcast again New Years Eve.[33]

Many historians categorize the 1906 Brant Rock musical program as a "broadcast," although Fessenden's admitted goal was to simply build a radiotelephone for commercial purposes. He was a musician by avocation, as evidenced by his performances on the 1906–07 Brant Rock transmissions, and he admitted sending phonograph music many times to "rest my voice," but other than Brant Rock, he never made any claim to being a broadcaster. His two most important contributions to actual broadcasting were in the technology, not the art. Using a transmitter of his own design, Fessenden showed with his 1906 Brant Rock broadcasts that clear speech and music could be transmitted.[34] And most important, his earlier invention of the Liquid Barretter detector forever changed the receiver from its earlier mechanical roots. It was "the first device to enable operators to receive signals 'by ear.'"[35] Homemade variants of his device were used widely by experimenters until the crystal and silicon detectors began to appear in 1906.

Reginald Fessenden was truly an original thinker. But his eccentric personality caused his early undoing. By 1910 his backers at NESCO had had enough. The company fired him and removed his equipment. According to a witness, "He needed a bathtub of especial size to accommodate his huge frame, and had one installed at Brant Rock, covering it by a requisition as 'Blueprint Washing Machine.' Fessenden had just returned from a voyage to Europe and had turned in a prodigious expense account, which the backers would not pay. So he was fired. The workers chose sides. The order came to dismantle the plant, and especially to get the records packed in boxes and sent to Pittsburgh. Up came a van with large packing boxes, into which the papers were hastily stowed. Then arose a battle between the ins and outs, and the upshot was that the pro–Fessendenites sat on the box covers all night to prevent them being taken away by the renegades. The matter was settled amiably and the records put back."[36] But after that insult, and with a divided staff and little or no money with which to continue, Fessenden got out of the radiotelephone business.

Valdemar Poulsen, the Danish Edison

Another early and important influence on radiotelephony was the Scandinavian scientist, Valdemar Poulsen, who was known in later years by the complimentary title, "the Danish Edison." From 1907 through 1917 his direct current (DC) arc-based system of transmission was the model on which most inventors based their devices. Poulsen, who had earlier discovered the fundamentals of magnetic tape recording used today, improved on the theories of others to develop a system of arc telephony. Just as Marconi built on the work of Hertz and Maxwell, Poulsen based his arc system on what had been revealed in 1900 by W.B. Duddell's discovery of the singing arc. "The principle of this discovery was that when an arc lamp, fed by a direct current of about two-hundred and fifty volts, is shunted with a suitable capacity, and an inductance, alternating currents of a frequency of 40,000 [cycles] per second were established."[37] Poulsen discovered that when the singing arc was placed into an atmosphere of hydrogen or other gas, the frequency of the oscillations increased to almost 500,000 cycles per second, putting it in the radio frequency range where it could be modulated and detected as audio. He was also the first to introduce the use of "six arc lights in series as generators of an oscillating current of high frequency."[38] For the transmission of voice, most inventors used and attempted to legally improve upon Poulsen's arc technology.

In 1903 Poulsen patented "an improved arc oscillation generator using a hydrocarbon atmosphere and a magnetic field."[39] The modifications of the Poulsen-Duddell discovery were continued by the German commercial company Telefunken. Their arc telephone system in 1906 covered 25 miles: "The arcs used by the Telefunken Company were burned either six in series on 220 volts direct current, twelve in series on 440 volts, or twenty-four in series on 880 volts."[40] Then there was the problem of the microphone. Every Poulsen-based arc radiotelephone system required a microphone capable of handling high current, the most popular of which used a carbon microphone with some form of circulating liquid to keep the element from overheating. In 1906 the Italian Count Majorana used a modification of the Poulsen arc system but added his own special invention, a "hydraulic microphone." Majorana's solution was based on the hydrodynamic principle: "Water is made a conductor by the presence of acid or salt and by continuous change so that even the heat produced by the current is removed from the set."[41] His microphone, based on earlier experiments by Chichister Bell, showed that a column of liquid responded to mechanical energy, and was not a carbon system but a liquid-filled microphone; water to which salt or acid is added was used to change electrical current when exposed to acoustic events.[42]

Poulsen's significant contribution was the first wireless system that made possible clear transmission of voice, and it was the only option for radiotelephone experimentation until the vacuum tube in 1917. But the story of Valdemar Poulsen and his arc had a hidden significance, one that was important to the development of the modern electronics industry in a garage near Stanford University. The genesis of this digression began with a San Francisco radiotelephone experimenter named Francis McCarty. In 1907 McCarty used a spark transmitter to send voice from a boat anchored at the foot of Market Street to other boats plying between San Francisco and Oakland. Describing how it was done, one analyst said:

> This was the system employed by A.F. Collins, consisting of a 1" induction coil, with very nicely adjusted vibrators, so that vibration frequencies or primary interruptions could be obtained up to about 1500 cycles. The oscillating circuit spark gap was composed of two silver discs, spaced from .0005 inch to 3/16" when the microphones were good. There were three to eight telephone type microphones placed in parallel, all in series with a six volt battery in the primary.[43]

The fidelity of this spark coil system was limited and could not possibly be a practical means of transmitting speech or music. Fessenden's earlier experiments with similar technology had already proved that spark transmissions were so overpowered by the noise artifacts of the system that it was next to impossible to hear clear audio. By McCarty's time, spark as a carrier of voice and music was already a dead end technology.

Nevertheless, McCarty's financial backers took into their employ a recent Stanford electrical engineering graduate, Cyril F. Elwell, to help them evaluate and perhaps improve the McCarty system. In 1907 Elwell set up a transmitting station at Palo Alto and constructed McCarty's device based on the details in his patent. While it produced mostly unintelligible speech, Elwell found that when he closed the spark gaps to as narrow as possible, an arc developed and the voice quality improved. He told the backers not to waste their money on the McCarty spark patents. But based on what he had learned from the McCarty failures and having read something about arc systems being used in Europe, Elwell decided to travel to Denmark and negotiate the American rights to the arc transmission system of Poulsen.

> "I telegraphed to Poulsen from Palo Alto in 1909, asking his price for his U.S. patent rights and asked the Henshaw brothers to finance me," Elwell recalls. "They refused, so I decided to do it myself and I did with great help from Dr. Jordan, Dr. Marx, Dr. Hopkins, and numerous other members of the Stanford faculty. That is why ... Stan-

> ford is reaping the crop from the seeds sown by the early Stanford faculty and myself."[44]

After bringing several of the Poulsen transmitters back to Northern California in 1909, he demonstrated them in Palo Alto for a group of Stanford professors, leading to the formation of the Poulsen Wireless Telephone and Telegraph Co.

Even though Elwell used the Poulsen arc for his two-way radiotelephone commercial message business and never to provide news and entertainment for the public, in later years he wrote in his autobiography about the early radiotelephone experiments in Palo Alto, 1909–10: "Little did I realize that we were laying the foundations of broadcasting...."[45] The Poulsen connection to the Bay Area of Northern California is important, not only because it helped create the earliest foundations of Silicon Valley and the modern electronics industry, but because the local presence of the arc in 1909 might have been known to Charles Herrold and therefore influenced the development of his own broadcasting technology.

Lee De Forest: The Underrated Inventor

The single most important individual in the 20-year evolution from point-to-point, two-way wireless telegraphy to the technical perfection and use of the radiotelephone to attract listeners for entertainment by broadcasting was Lee de Forest. There are three major events that defined de Forest as a radiotelephone pioneer in the development of broadcasting: (1) his equipping in 1907 of the Navy Fleet with radio telephony, (2) his publicized broadcasts of opera in New York City between 1907 and 1912, and (3) his transmitting of news and music by radio in New York and San Francisco, 1916–17 and 1920–22.

No wireless and radio inventor is more surrounded by controversy than Lee de Forest. He fought for decades to convince the technical community that he deserved to be known as the "Father of Radio," and he spent millions in court battles trying to validate and re-validate his patents. Still, whether one decides to sanctify him or vilify him, the evidence strongly suggests that more than any single inventor, Lee de Forest was the best known of all the individuals who were experimenting with radio. While he was among the earliest to recognize that wireless could be used for something other than two-way commercial message traffic, it's not easy to say he realized the importance of having a regular radio audience before Herrold. Throughout his early career, his work came close to becoming broadcasting, as he did indeed send entertainment and musical programs to a defined audience, but they were never sustained. De Forest was a peripatetic demonstrator, never settling down long enough to establish a schedule. He seemed always to be searching for investors. Nevertheless, de Forest's endless demonstrations, frequent changes of venue, and challenges to competitors, inside and outside the courtroom, won him such publicity that he is often associated more than anyone else with the development of the radiotelephone. And while he failed time and again to establish a permanent home, failed to broadcast on a regular basis and therefore failed to gain a regular audience, his contribution to the art and science of radio is unprecedented. The evidence strongly suggests that for the technology he devised, Lee de Forest could rightfully claim to be what he struggled his entire life to be called, the "Father of Radio."[46]

Lee de Forest was born in 1873 in the Midwest but really grew up in the South. After attending grammar school, he went on to the Mt. Hermon School for Boys in Massachusetts, preparatory to his entrance into Yale University's Sheffield Scientific School. De Forest completed his higher education and received the degree of Doctor of Philosophy. His 1898 dissertation was titled: "The Reflection of Hertzian Waves at the End of Parallel Wires." Well-educated, Lee de Forest worked as an engineering graduate for several Chicago companies, Western Electric being one of them.[47]

Although de Forest's work slowly moved him from radiotelephone to broadcasting, he is best known for his technical contributions and improvements to the basic invention of all radio and television, the vacuum tube. Thomas Edison's electric lamp earlier had been modified by the Englishman Ambrose Fleming, who added a second element, a plate, and called it the Fleming Valve, using it as a rectifier or detector. By 1906 de Forest had modified Fleming's Valve by adding a grid (which allowed control of the electron flow) and called this device the Audion.[48] And while today it is believed that de Forest did not fully realize what he had invented until years later, and while he battled Edwin Armstrong in court for decades over the regenerative or feedback principle using the Audion, it was really Lee de Forest's work in early arc radiotelephone experimentation and its broadcast-like applications that proved to be the most interesting activities of his career. In the beginning he seemed to have followed the work of Marconi, attempting to develop better communication between ships and shore stations. And like Fessenden and Herrold, de Forest first tried spark and later a Poulsen arc in an attempt to give voice to his wireless.

Person to Person

The reality is that none of these early inventors saw any profit to be made using their equipment to broadcast music and information into homes on a regular schedule. If you seriously wanted to interest financial backers, to sell stock certificates or acquire money of any kind, you had to show these investors you were ready to market a wireless telephone for serious, profitable two-way communication purposes. You needed to convince them your system would be an improvement or replacement for the wired Bell telephone. And further, as de Forest and numerous inventors lamentably discovered, you had to be a promoter as well as an inventor, and that often meant that you found yourself allied with an unsavory, easy money crowd. De Forest himself was accused but acquitted of stock fraud, although his backers went to prison. Controversy notwithstanding, de Forest began early and often to find public uses for his version of a Poulsen-like arc radiotelephone transmitter:

> In 1906 he devoted his entire energy to the problem of wireless telephony. His first invention of importance was the use of the microphone in the earth connection,

> where it has been used in practically all (arc) wireless telephone transmitters ever since.[49]

That Lee de Forest was both a promoter and a music lover led him and his arc radiotelephone into two areas; one was practical, a demonstration for the Navy, the other reflected his penchant for bringing culture to the masses—the use of opera music to demonstrate his wireless telephone for newspaper reporters.[50]

An early recipient of the de Forest arc radiotelephone system was the Navy. He recalled in a 1929 interview:

> In 1909 I was manufacturing wireless telephone sets for the US Navy; each set was tested by means of phonograph records. Much to my surprise, many wireless amateurs and professional operators intercepted and enjoyed these test transmissions. They came to look for these "programs." And quite naturally, the idea of mass communication occurred to me, whereby attractive music and interesting talks might be placed on the air, thus creating a profitable demand for wireless equipment by those desirous of listening in.[51]

De Forest equipped the Navy Fleet's lead ship *Ohio* and others with his arc transmitter and a wind-up phonograph for the fleet's trip around the world between 1907 and 1908. During this well-publicized piece of radio history and while he was on the West Coast aboard the *Ohio*, de Forest played music from the phonograph and communicated with Mare Island during June 1908. Radio operator Herbert J. Meneratti of the U.S.S. *Ohio* documented these events well in correspondence with historian G.H. Clark in 1948: "We gave music regularly to the Mare Island Station. Our record shows that from June 1 to July 5 [1908] we did not miss a day in giving out music to the fleet in the Bay at the time."[52] Meneratti claims that on January 12, 1908, his ship, the U.S.S. *Ohio*, was sending out band tunes to other ships, even responding to requests, a "date he [de Forest] considers the beginning of broadcasting, although we didn't call it that."[534]

Another early claim of "broadcasting" by de Forest was connected to his love of opera. He had long admired this form of music, and while he realized it appealed mostly to the upper classes who could afford the time and money to attend live performances, the evidence suggests that as early as 1907 he believed that in the future even the common man would be exposed to opera using the wireless telephone: "It will soon be possible to distribute grand opera music from transmitters placed on the stage of the Metropolitan Opera House by a Radio Telephone station on the roof to almost any dwelling in Greater New York and vicinity.... The same applies to large cities. Church music, lectures, etc., can be spread abroad by the Radio Telephone."[54] And so between 1907 and 1912 the press was invited to a half dozen of his opera experiments using his arc transmitter. By using lovely voices of well known divas like Mazarin and Farrar, de Forest got coverage in all the major papers each time he staged these promotional events. But they were one-time demonstrations, and afterward he packed up his equipment and went away.[55]

Of course, in later years, in the 1920s and 1930s when broadcasting was an established fact, all these early day inventors, including Herrold and de Forest, reflected back on all their radiotelephone work and all wished their admirers to believe they were broadcasting from the start. But in those early years, their major purpose was to create a business either by finding a dependable wireless replacement for the wired telephone or an acceptable system that they could sell to the government. Nevertheless, there is some evidence that de Forest was on the verge of realizing, long before anyone else, that the radiotelephone could be used for something other than narrowcasting. Around the time of the Navy experiments, de Forest wrote, in an article about his radiotelephone, an early harbinger of what broadcasting might become:

> still another feature of the invention ... the supplying of music and other forms of entertainment to passengers traveling on the passenger vessels. A service of this kind, aided by a large receiver, so that all of the passengers gathered in a large salon could hear the music or operatic air....[56]

While this account is imaginative, it reveals that de Forest still did not see what radio was to become. His proposed use of radio—even if novel and daring—was simply to transmit and amplify music as though it were a public address system, transmitting it through speakers to small groups gathered in halls or salons, rather than to widely scattered hundreds, thousands or millions of individuals listening privately in their homes.

During the radiotelephone years, 1900–1920, nearly all ambitious, profit-seeking inventors had focused their attention on developing competing voice transmission technologies. While spark was quickly rejected as too noisy and the alternator as too costly, it was the many versions of the Poulsen arc that clearly dominated the interest of radiotelephone inventors. Most experimenters, de Forest and Herrold included, had between 1910 and 1916 spent countless dollars perfecting the arc as a carrier of voice and music. It would not be the final technology.

Radio Goes on the Tube

By 1913 de Forest had left his work with the Poulsen arc in Palo Alto and returned to New York. After a time-consuming court case involving stock fraud and the collapse of his company, of which he and a partner were found not guilty in 1914, he wasted no time in seeking another fortune.[57] He took steps to open a new factory at High Bridge in the Bronx and began a series of experimental transmissions in New York from the Columbia Phonograph Laboratories on 38th Street, in which he finally abandoned his version of the arc transmitter and began using his Audion as a transmitter of radio.

Now realizing the remarkable capabilities of his new tube transmitters and receivers, Lee de Forest was more anxious than ever to make money from them. So in 1915 he packed up his equipment and returned to Northern California to put them on public display. Hoping to do radio programs from his own booth at the Panama Pacific Exposition in San Francisco, de Forest felt he would get endless publicity for this new, improved radiotelephone. But something unforeseen happened. When his transmitter failed, the only way de Forest could demonstrate the capability of his new receiver was to pick up the programs coming from Charles Herrold's radiotelephone, which was in San Jose and was on the air every day 50 miles away. This is what he did during the entire world's fair. When it ended, de Forest returned to his home in New York. Had he been influenced in knowing that Herrold was operating a radio station daily in California?[58] We know that after he got his own recalcitrant radio transmitter working again, he did something significant. He began entertaining New Yorkers with news and music in 1916 from his High Bridge facilities using experimental license 2XG.[59] Now he was using his Audion for the important task of carrying voice and music, not using it merely as a receiver, and making it serve as an oscillator for the radiotelephone.[60]

How it worked is described in this simple sentence: "The radio telephone equipment consists of two large Oscillion tubes, used as generators of the high frequency current."[61] One of his early broadcasts received a mixed review: "Columbia phonograph records played from the laboratory of the company at 102 West Thirty-Eighth Street were distinctly heard in the receiving room of the [Hotel] Astor, with the exception of a few interruptions by the powerful naval wireless apparatus at the Brooklyn Navy Yard, when the warning of a storm was heard intermittently with the music."[62] One month later, de Forest told a *New York Sun* reporter that by using a wavelength of 800 meters (372.51 kHz) he "will be setting another record by giving the first public concert by wireless in history." Since there is ample evidence that he had received music from the Herrold station at the San Francisco World's Fair in 1915, it is hard to understand why he made this statement. In later years de Forest would recant this claim and acknowledge what Herrold had accomplished, but strangely, not on this occasion.[63]

A few months after de Forest had moved his tube transmitter to High Bridge, New York, he startled his East Coast radio audiences with what was truly an historic radio event. Four years before Pittsburgh's KDKA aired election returns in 1920—sometimes thought to be first—de Forest was using his New York station to provide election returns on the night of Nov. 7, 1916. By installing a private wire to the editorial offices of the *New York American*, de Forest easily provided election news bulletins every hour on the outcome of the tightly contested Hughes-Wilson presidential election.[64] Advance publicity seems to have given him a fairly large audience: "Seven thousand wireless telephone operators within a radius of 200 miles of New York City received election returns from the *New York American*. They heard not only election returns, but music as well. Between the bulletins, music was sent through the clouds. The crowds heard 'The Star-Spangled Banner,' 'Dixie,' 'Columbia, Gem of the Ocean,' 'America,' 'Maryland,' 'Yankee Doodle' and all the other anthems, songs and hymns that Americans love."[65] Because it happened in New York, it attracted a large listening audience, got a great amount of press attention, and became one of the most important pre–World War I events in radio broadcasting.

When the U.S. entered the European war in 1917, de Forest's station was taken off the air by government order. When he returned to the air in December 1919, it was only briefly because it was shut down again in February 1920. Writing to Herrold many years later, de Forest said the New York radio inspector shut him down "on the technicality that I had voided my license by moving my station downtown without his authorization."[66] Earlier he had detailed the affair in an article in the *New*

York World, saying that the federal inspector, whom he identified as Arthur Batcheller, "peremptorily closed the service after a few weeks, with the definite statement that program broadcasting for entertainment had no place, no legitimate place, in the ether, and should be terminated, and he terminated it."[67] Seeking a better bureaucratic climate, de Forest packed up his New York station and by April 1920 was back in California opening a radio station in San Francisco.[68]

In a letter de Forest wrote to Charles Herrold about how he saw the art and science of broadcasting in 1916, he discussed both his and Herrold's early experiments in the context of the vacuum tube: "Until the 3-electrode tube had been developed sufficiently to serve as a reliable oscillator for radio telephone purposes, and the audion amplifier could be used at the receiver in connection with the detector, those early efforts at radio broadcasting were necessarily unsatisfactory. In 1916, after we had learned how to build 'Oscillion' tubes of 50 to 100 watts power, I began a regular nightly broadcasting service from my station at High Bridge, NY. This service was regularly maintained until the federal government caused a suspension of all nonmilitary radio communications shortly before our nation entered the European War."[69] Were it not for the Great War and the closing down of all nonessential, nondefense uses of radio, de Forest, who was already exciting small audiences with interesting, entertaining and informative broadcasting, might have succeeded with this new service four years ahead of KDKA.

The Public Awakens

Most of the early work by Herrold, Fessenden, Poulsen and de Forest took place out of the public eye. Based on what was happening in the laboratory and reported in specialized journals and hobbyist periodicals, news of what the radiotelephone might mean aroused comparatively little interest in the first decade. While an occasional story did appear in such magazines of general circulation as the *Saturday Evening Post* as early 1901, editors did not begin to give wireless any widespread notice until the sinking of the *Titanic* in 1912. From the day of its sinking until America went to war in 1917, this period of time became important to the future perception of the radiotelephone because they were the first years in which the latest invention news made its way into the daily newspapers. Beginning in 1912, the general public finally began to hear about the inventors and their experiments, and therefore the editorial comments surrounding that new media. Those were also the years in which several unrelated events convinced the youth of the day that any occupation related to wireless was an exciting place to be. Perhaps it began with the publication of exciting reading material aimed at the high school boy. The 1911 book *Tom Swift and His Wireless Message*[70] was all the impetus many boys needed to sell their parents on the idea that a little "higher education" at a wireless school could translate into a living wage. Herrold's College likely benefited from it by enrolling more young wireless enthusiasts. Certainly interest in wireless also was stimulated in 1912 by news of the sinking of the *Titanic*, which came in the form of a Morse code wireless message: "We have struck an iceberg. Badly damaged. Rush aid." To many newspaper readers, the value of wireless had been solidified.

By 1912 the work of the radiotelephone inventor was being reported in the nation's newspapers.[71] No longer confined to the technical and wireless hobby publications, the radiotelephone was being discussed on Main Street. As the newspaper stories indicate, dozens of inventors, having constructed their own radiotelephones, began working on the next steps—promotion and sales. Newspaper reporters during those years seemed to be interested in two things: how these inventors planned to replace the wired telephone and the type of audio content they were using to promote, test and demonstrate it. Often it was the inventor himself shouting, "Hello, can you hear me?" Sometimes it was music from a phonograph. Always, the goals were to both augment the wired telephone for two-way personal conversation and add a voice to the message-handling work of the wireless telegraph business. As the public record clearly shows, with the exception of the early publicity surrounding de Forest and Herrold, the content of broadcasting was rarely discussed until 1916. By then increasing numbers of would-be broadcasters were on the air, each with their own small audience.

In 1917 the prediction of an inventor named Earl Hanson, who was doing radio work in Los Angeles, was published in a popular trade magazine: "Municipal wireless phonograph concerts may also soon be a reality. For these a single centrally located sending station would be necessary, the waves from this having a radius of the entire city."[72] And a 1915 Pittsburgh newspaper story carried the headline "Wireless Talk-fest Planned," a story about a Professor Van Dyke of the Carnegie Institute of Technology who planned and pre-announced a wireless "talk" about general news, politics, etc., aimed at "every amateur wireless operator in the county." Another single event, "the test was for the benefit of amateurs within a radius of ten miles."[73]

Sarnoff's "Music Box"

Whether anyone truly saw the future in radio's crystal ball in those days is debatable, but among the soothsayers, there is a recently debated claim made by a captain of the radio industry. This is the anomaly of David Sarnoff, who when a young Marconi wireless operator, played no more of an important role than a handful of others during the sinking of the *Titanic,* but being adept at self-promotion and exaggeration, he manufactured the belief that he alone was "the sole wireless link" that saved lives.[74] With this kind of bravado and self-promotion, he got a desired transfer within the Marconi organization and by skillful maneuvering eventually worked his way up the management ladder to become head of what became the Radio Corporation of America. By 1920 Sarnoff had presumably found evidence showing that he possessed unusual foresight about radio's future. According to Sarnoff's story, he submitted a memo to RCA head Owen Young in January 1920 entitled "Sales of Radio Music Box for Entertainment Purposes," putting forward ideas which he said were originally expressed in 1915. In other words, five years previous to 1920 Sarnoff claimed to have predicted to company executive E.J. Nally that a "Radio Music Box" could soon be put in every home. This music box, he said, could become a "household utility" as valuable as a piano or phonograph. "The problem of transmitting music has already been solved in principle," Sarnoff is claimed to have said. "There should be no difficulty in receiving music perfectly when transmitted within a radius of 25 to 50 miles." By calling attention to this prescience, Sarnoff hoped that RCA would take seriously his newly submitted urging that the company in 1920 begin making and selling radios at $75 per set. Added Sarnoff, "Aside from the profit to be derived from this proposition the possibilities for propaganda and free advertising of the Radio Corporation are tremendous; for, its name would ultimately be brought into the household and wireless would receive national and universal attention."[75]

Not until recently has the actual date of the Radio Music Box memo been put into question. Originally, researchers were influenced by historian Gleason Archer, author of *History of Radio to 1926*, who accepted the claim that Sarnoff had actually written it on November 9, 1915.[76] Researcher Louise Benjamin first presented evidence suggesting that the oft-cited memo may not have been composed in 1915 but in 1920 when broadcasting was "literally around the corner."[77] In her search for documentation, neither Sarnoff's 1915 memo nor the response by Nally could be found. Recently Benjamin has apparently found documentation suggesting that the original Sarnoff claim might be true after all. Since Sarnoff is known to have been a quintessential self-promoter, the jury is still out on this one.

Controversy notwithstanding, some would say Sarnoff's idea was significant even in 1920. He proposed using available technology to convert broadcasting entertainment into a business proposition. In 1919, the Radio Corporation of America was created when British Marconi interests in the U.S. were purchased by General Electric Company, which used the newly acquired radio patent rights as the foundation of a new company. It elevated two previous Marconi officers to high positions—Edward J. Nally became RCA president, and David Sarnoff, at the age of 28, was made commercial manager. Sarnoff then put more ideas to his boss, sold radios to thousands and with the foresight of an administrative genius, he eventually attained the presidency of RCA.

Radio's Rise Delayed

Since broadcasting to audiences actually was underway prior to America's entering the war in Europe, the question arises, "Why didn't radio capture the public's attention earlier than the 1920s?" The reason radio was unable to fascinate the public sooner was far beyond the control of those doing it. Radiotelephones were taken off the air when the United States entered the Great War on April 6, 1917. It was an instant decision brought on by the wartime emergency affecting all of these experimenters. The government assumed control. All licensed amateurs were ordered off the air. They received a letter from the Department of Commerce and the U.S. Navy District Communication Superintendent ordering them to take down their antennas, disconnect their grounds and halt all transmitting and receiving.

The race for radiotelephone was suddenly suspended unexpectedly and unceremoniously. There was no finish line, no cheering crowds, and no medals for those shut down by the war, an event which completely overshadowed anything remotely connected to entertainment or pleasure. It would not be until the conflict ended that broadcasting by radio would be allowed to resume. By this time the radiotelephone's technology, economics and conditions had changed so much that the position of previous front-runners were no longer the same.

While it's now abundantly clear that the wireless "fone" was on the verge of becoming "radio," the question of who would fill the ranks of radio's leadership in the 1920s was about to be answered. Could Charles Herrold reassert his inventive genius as a practicing broadcaster and advocate? Or would he be overwhelmed by more powerful forces and forced to drop out? Everything he had learned from life, whether from experience, education, or ingenuity, was about to put him to the test.

3
Education of a Gentleman

Everywhere there were signs, if one had eyes to see them, of the growing pains of a new age ... a new world, then just opening to the discoverer and the explorer — I mean the world of science and invention.

Ray Stannard Baker, *American Chronicle*[1]

With the arrival of the 20th century, the area of San Jose, California, which someday would become Silicon Valley's most prominent city, was little more than farms and orchards. By 1900 it was the fruit shipping capital of the state and a thriving town of 21,500. The new century ushered in a widespread use of new inventions, some underway, others on the horizon — the telephone, typewriter, adding machine, electric light, automobile, airplane, motion picture, and the radio or wireless telephone. Growing to become the world's leading industrial power, America was to see its new president, Theodore Roosevelt, attempt to break the "robber barons" using anti-trust laws, and California governor Hiram Johnson free his state from railroad domination with progressive voting rights legislation. As journalist "muckrakers" exposed corruption in business and government, and people read about it in their daily papers, it alerted inventors to be wary, else their intellectual property might be stolen as well.

In this promising new era, Charles Herrold, like many other hopeful young men of his day, grew to maturity in the college of hard knocks but also in a land of opportunity. His story is typical of many inventors. Although he poured talent and energy into developing many new ideas, including a working radiotelephone system, he would learn bitter lessons as unscrupulous partners attempted to take away those inventions. He would struggle long to secure patents for all the accomplishments which were truly his, and wonder to his dying day why a great national radio industry at the height of its glory gave him a cold shoulder when he claimed recognition for what he invented — broadcasting.

Charles Herrold with his parents — Mary Elizabeth Lusk Herrold and William Morris Herrold as they appeared in their mature years, circa 1900, with an earlier photograph of young Charles, taken when he was four years old (Stephen True Collection).

Herrold's Heritage

Hardly a full decade had passed since the Civil War when Charles David Herrold was born November 16, 1875, in Fulton, Illinois. His father was William Morris Herrold, a small town entrepreneur, and his mother was Mary Elizabeth Lusk Herrold, a schoolteacher and musician and William's second wife.[2] In later years Charles Herrold said about his father, "He was an inventor and can be said to have produced practically every important improvement to machinery used in the prune industry," but added, reminiscent of his own experiences, "he was bluffed out of the ownership of the prune dipper."[3]

Charles Herrold's father, William Morris Herrold, was born in Johnstown, Pennsylvania, on February 28, 1837, into a family well satisfied with what they had in that community.[4] In fact, so secure were their lives that William's father had held only one job his entire life, that of a bookkeeper and comptroller for the Cambria Steel Company, then the town's major employer. His tinkering with machinery and gadgets was an avocation, although he probably would have preferred it to be profit-making. Deciding that such a life was not for him, William broke family tradition and left Pennsylvania for Fulton, Illinois, in 1857, becoming the first of his family to take a chance in the newly settled and not quite civilized Midwest. It was the first of several moves by William. This wanderlust would carry him west again, infuse his sons with some of the same initiative, and help develop in them a habit of always seeking something better.

In Illinois, William began working as a bookkeeper. What happened next was partly due to William's own initiative, but unbeknownst to him, largely the result of epoch-making decisions taken by other men on larger issues of the day. This is how his first son George H. Herrold described it:

> A traveling salesman for a New York wholesale house became interested in him, and he was offered a job as manager and owner of a store if he would go to St. Paul and pick out a site for a store. He took a steamboat to St. Paul but while he was there Fort Sumpter [*sic*] was fired on early in 1861. There was so much excitement over this that father had difficulty getting anyone to talk business.[5]

With the issues now dividing America culminating in the outbreak of Civil War, men had to take sides over slavery and the survival of the Union. It put beyond control the career plans of William Herrold. He joined the Union Army, and was commissioned a captain of Company F, 93rd Illinois Volunteer Infantry. According to family legend, he became one of its "most popular commanding officers."[6] When the war ended, Herrold returned to Fulton to start a business and a family. He married a woman he had known socially before the war, Mina Vista Parker. They were married in April 1865, and in 1867 they had one child, George Herbert Herrold. A year later, Mina died of an illness, leaving William with the responsibility of raising one-year-old George and running the family business. By 1871 William had married for the second time. His new wife was Mary Elizabeth Lusk, a woman from Illinois who was barely twenty years old. In 1875 she bore Charles David Herrold and three years later gave William his third child, another son, who was named Roy.

Home Influence

Having been given some training as a teacher, Mary Elizabeth soon realized the local schools were inadequate for someone who seemed as bright and curious as young Charles. So his early schooling in the basics of reading and writing, in music, and in the Bible took place in the family home. In addition to books used by his mother, Charles also began to learn by observation and questioning. It was in Fulton that he first noticed his father working in the building outside his home that was used as a tool shop, constructing what to his young son looked like some of the implements he had seen at neighboring farms. Charles was fascinated with all the mechanical devices in his father's shop; he asked plenty of intelligent questions. Barely six years old, he was already observing an inventor at work and learning his future from his father.

The Herrold family left Illinois in 1883. William had decided to move to a town where he could open a larger store, to establish a farm with livestock and to raise his young family. He believed he had found it in an adjoining state, deciding to move first to Sioux City and a year later to Sloan, both promising agricultural towns in Iowa. While the area was rich in farming opportunities, it was impoverished educationally. According to Charles Herrold's recollection years later, "The only books on scientific subjects in town were two volumes of *Zell's Encyclopedia,* and these books were read cover to cover until they fell apart from sheer use."[7] Having learned as much as his mother was able to teach him by the age of eight, Charles now was ready to enter the public elementary school in Sloan, where he met his first mentor. In that one-room schoolhouse in rural Iowa, he received a sound academic background, and, under an especially gifted teacher, he realized his interests in astronomy and electricity. Years later Herrold told a biographer he "had a teacher at Sloan named J.M. Jaynes who was above average for the times and gave him his elementary school basic education in English and math." Thanks to this teacher, Herrold recalled, he acquired all the necessary technical and scientific skills to build, unaided, "a perfectly working telegraph line, including all the instruments and batteries."[8]

While Herrold's mother, Mary, was largely responsible for his moral, educational and spiritual underpinnings, it was his father who nourished his mechanical and engineering curiosity. Among all of William Herrold's innovations, the one Charles remembered most was the house his father designed and helped construct in Sloan: "People who were used to the ordinary form of construction came from miles around to see the walls put up. My father had his own ideas as to how a prairie home could be kept warm in the long, cold winter."[9] The Herrold home used a double-walled, double floored, double-ceiling construction, and placed between the two layers was creosoted tanbark. It was an inexpensive yet practical engineering solution for insulating a house to keep it cool in the summer and warm in the winter. Charles remembered how the Native Americans living there in Iowa would gather outside to stare at the Herrold house, it looked so different from their own.[10]

Fateful Event

As with other farmers throughout the Midwest, weather greatly influenced how the young Herrold family endured. The town of Sloan was on the prairie and while a great place for farming, its winters were brutal. Most people survived each winter to plant and grow in the spring and summer. However, others grew increasingly unhappy with such severe conditions. In the last quarter of the 19th century the major defining moment in the life of the Herrold family was the "Great Iowa Blizzard of 1888." Charles remembered it well:

> It had been a mild winter and the morning of the February day that was to be so eventful for me, and so nearly my last day on earth, was balmy as spring. The sky was a lovely blue; not a breath stirred the few leaves still clinging to the trees. My mother, therefore, was greatly surprised when she saw me about to leave the house for school wearing my heaviest winter clothing. I had even put on Arctics over my shoes, and carried my heavy double-woven muffler, a yard wide and three yards long, over my arm. "Why in the world are you all bundled up in that fashion on this warm morning," mother asked. I said rather reluctantly, knowing how little she thought of my Indian friends, "because Chief Running Rabbit told me yesterday that a big storm was coming and I'd better be ready for it."[11]

When young Herrold got to school his classmates began to laugh. They thought he looked ridiculous in a muffler and such warm clothing. But he marched straight into the schoolhouse to see the principal, Mr. Jaynes, a man with no experience of Iowa weather, having moved there recently. He was from the East, and had been only a short time in the state. Though surprised at Herrold's winterized attire and obvious concern about the likelihood of a big storm coming, the principal nevertheless listened to the boy's story:[12]

> I told him the Indians had moved their camp to Bend, because of the coming storm "Thank you son," he said. "We'll keep a weather eye out for that storm of yours," but I knew by his quizzical smile that he did not take it seriously. But a few hours later the sky began changing rapidly, and Jaynes, who was just as scared as the students, turned to Charles for advice: "There's a lot of rope in the basement," I reminded him. "If it came to leaving the schoolhouse, I'm sure my father would use it to tie the children together in groups, with a couple of the big boys in each bunch for guides. I'll go for help, Mr. Jaynes. If I don't make it, well, better wait about three hours, then start out with the kids. And be sure (I remembered my Indian lore) you notice where the winds come from and keep it always on the same shoulder, or you'll travel around in circles and get lost."[13]

Thirteen-year-old Charles fought his way through the great storm, and the kids were returned safely to their homes. Not only had he had learned survival skills from his Native American friends, but also leadership from his father.

The Move to California

Most folks could endure the storms with their icy winds and bone-chilling cold. Plenty of hardy Midwesterners learned how to put up with one cold winter after another in the heartland of America. But the blizzard of 1888 was different. Nothing in memory had matched this storm. William had known for a long time the weather was better in California and had heard about folks who had gone out there and found good land, jobs, and opportunity. As Mary had not been well, a vacation trip to California would tell them if the stories were true. Knowing the conditions of Iowa, William decided to try California. He decided to pull up stakes and move his wife and three children, his business and his investments west.[14] Having realized a better than expected profit from selling their Iowa land, including the Herrold store in town, everything was packed for their move to California. But none of them were aware it would take a year to reach their final destination. After a temporary detour of one year in the little city of Stockton, California, the Herrold family explored farther and learned that rural San Jose, located 50 miles south of San Francisco, was a good farming area. So they headed there.

San Francisco was called "The City" because it was the major metropolis on the West Coast, a center of banking, commerce, art and culture. San Jose, compared to its neighbor up the peninsula, was a small agricultural community. San Jose's main attractions were wide open, fertile fields and expansive orchards spread across a valley burgeoning with prunes and peaches in season. In writing about the leading men of this community, which was Santa Clara County, local historian Eugene T. Sawyer noted in 1922:

> William Morris Herrold owned a fine ranch of eighty-three and one half acres, highly improved with peaches and apricots, which he planted at Riverbank, as well as having developed some of the finest ranches in Santa Clara County. Mr. Herrold was of unusual inventive mind, although he had been denied a technical education, and he gave to the world several practical, useful inventions, including the automatic prune dipper, used in every prune section of the country, and the "jumbo" wagon, so con-

> structed as to be able to turn in a very small space, making it especially useful in orchards.[15]

William personally constructed a large Victorian house within walking distance of downtown San Jose and the family settled in.

Comfortably settled into the family's new home by 1890, 15-year-old Charles predictably plunged into science, set up a laboratory in the basement and began to reinvent his life. He had started San Jose High School a year earlier, where as reported to the family by his teachers, he was an excellent student who often tutored his classmates in math and science. Charles easily fulfilled his school assignments and found plenty of time outside of his formal studies for personal passions. He composed songs and experimented with counterpoint. Like his father, he spent much time in the basement workshop conducting experiments, building cameras and microscopes, and learning about optics and lenses, all of which eventually led him into the construction of telescopes for studying the heavens. He had also begun to read books divulging ideas of the great electrical minds of the day: Faraday, Maxwell, Hertz, Volta, Edison, Tesla and others. Studying their work piqued his interest in science, but instead of choosing wireless for his career, he picked astronomy. The University of California's mountaintop Lick Observatory, located within sight of his home, was having a tremendous influence. Herrold visited and corresponded with some of these Lick scientists, who encouraged him in his interest. As a high school student at the turn of the century, his aim in life was to become an astronomer; that is, until new circumstances and events unexpectedly occurred to change his mind.

The Stanford Influence

Curious and well-rounded, filled with knowledge, brimming with interest in all things scientific, young Herrold began as an astronomy major at Stanford University in 1895, commuting the twenty miles between Palo Alto and San Jose. There were only two students in that degree program and Charles received plenty of personal attention. Older brother George Herbert Herrold remembered young Charles's passion for astronomy, recalling what happened after he began college:

> Charles was a student at Stanford. He conceived the idea of making a replica of the telescope at Lick [Observatory on Mt. Hamilton, California]. Working nights and Sundays at a machine shop he turned or made a completely equatorially mounted telescope to fit a two-inch lens, which he purchased. This so pleased father that he had a carpenter build a revolving dome on top of the barn. Charles set up his telescope in this dome. It was equatorially mounted, operated by a can of sand hanging over a pulley. If the telescope did not follow a star as it moved through the heavens, he would put a few more grains of sand in the can to hurry it up or take some out, as the case required.[16]

Herrold kept a diary of his observations to accompany the photos taken with his homemade camera and telescope.[17] But in spite of an apparent future observing the skies, the direction of young Herrold's life was to be decided by a combination of timing and luck. Since he was only one of two students majoring in astronomy,

he was forced to quickly choose a new field of study when his instructor, Prof. W.J. Hussey, left the West Coast for Chicago in 1896. Herrold changed his major to physics.[18]

The Coming of Wireless

Charles had spent only one year in the astronomy program at Stanford. Entering the physics and electricity department now meant that he would study for a Bach-

Top: **Charles Herrold on the roof of his San Jose home observatory in the early 1890s. He and his father built this addition to the family garage (Stephen True Collection).** ***Right:*** **Charles Herrold poses with his homemade telescope. Since he began mapping the stars while in high school, this interest led to the astronomy degree program at Stanford University in 1895 (Stephen True Collection).**

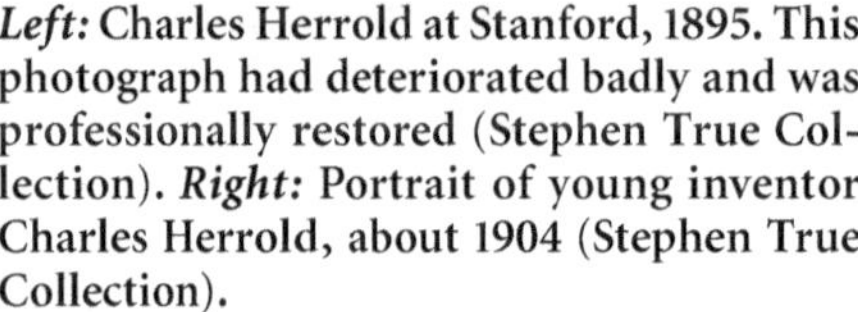

Left: **Charles Herrold at Stanford, 1895. This photograph had deteriorated badly and was professionally restored (Stephen True Collection).** ***Right:*** **Portrait of young inventor Charles Herrold, about 1904 (Stephen True Collection).**

elor of Science in Electrical Engineering (B.S.E.E.). It was at this time in the mid–1890s that he learned Guglielmo Marconi and Oliver Lodge had performed and validated the pre-wireless electrical work of Hertz and Maxwell. There were reports about a device that might someday replace the wired telegraph. Both Herrold's studies and his home experiments began to reflect the times. According to Herrold, he was inspired by an account of Marconi's successful wireless experiment of 1895:

> In that article appeared the name of that great German, Hertz, who experimentally proved the existence of electromagnetic waves, mathematically discovered by Clerk Maxwell, the great English mathematical physicist. I re-read that classical experiment of Hertz and that very afternoon, I took a Rhumkorff coil, a Branley Tube, and an aerial wire and transmitted and received wireless telegraph signals one mile. This was my first introduction to Hertzian waves and I worked with them for over ten years, in the hopes that someday I might be able to be the one to do with the human voice and music what Marconi did with the wireless telegraph.[19]

This story Herrold told many times, the first time publicly to the Commonwealth Club of San Francisco in 1928: "I performed some experiments in my laboratory in San Jose, repeating the Marconi English Channel experiments on the very morning they were reported in the papers...." Herrold said he also was interested in wireless telegraph experiments prior to 1900.[20]

What Charles Herrold knew and did in the late 1890s was overshadowed by what wireless was starting to mean at the end of the 19th century. From the outset, it was apparent that wireless was highly useful to maritime shipping and naval vessels everywhere, as it could easily link up ships at sea, or ships and shore, but on land it was a different story. The telegraph had long been used for cross-country messages, and between train stations and cities. The telephone allowed business people and others who could afford it the opportunity to actually converse in their own voices, better for some types of communication than the coded telegraph. And the transatlantic telegraph cable already connected continents. Nobody yet knew what new uses there would be for the wireless telegraph besides oceanic commerce.

Reviewing what most influenced him at Stanford University, Herrold said in later years that his interest in the potential of wireless was kept alive by one of his professors who, like himself, had taken a special interest in wireless. This instructor assembled an apparatus and showed how Marconi's invention worked in a laboratory as part of their education in electricity. The engineering program at Stanford had taught Herrold much about electricity and allowed him to learn from and experiment with many of the brightest academics on the West Coast. While this classroom education was useful and stimulating, he yearned for more. It apparently was the beginning of his thinking about a career as an inventor, as he soon began to design and make some of the electrical devices that would improve wireless. He began to hope that he might combine his university skills and an inventive mind to harness electricity. He was an admirer of Edison, Marconi, Tesla, Poulsen, and others. Though he intended to finish the final year and get his engineering degree, another decision was made for him when his health began to fail. A serious unnamed illness forced Charles to stay home and miss classes long enough to pause and reflect. Before he could begin his fourth year of studies, he was ordered by his doctor to drop out and recuperate. He never returned to graduate.[21]

The Call of Invention

With Stanford behind him and his health back to normal, Charles was eager to invent. In 1899, according to recollections he later approved in a paper for publication, he moved to San Francisco to begin his career as an inventor:

> During the period he was able to keep active, Mr. Herrold produced over fifty different electrical devices in dentistry and surgery, and he perfected an electrical deep-sea diving illumin for use by salvage companies and in pearl fisheries, and he attained reputation as a pioneer in some remarkable developments in electrical machinery for pipe organs.[22]

Now in San Francisco, living where he saw ships coming and going every day, Herrold was spending his leisure time on the waters of the surrounding bay, the adjoining Sacramento and Stockton deltas, and the wharves and marinas of the Pacific Ocean, where as a boating enthusiast, he made friends with many of the commercial divers. They had a unique problem that might be solved by an electrical inventor like Herrold. Limited by an ability to see more than a few feet in deep and muddy water, Herrold's 1900 innovation was the addition of a specially fitted watertight lamp and reflector assembly attached to the diver's helmet, and the electricity for the device was carried from the surface using wires inside air hoses. With it, divers could see farther and better. His final invention in San Francisco remains unexplained, it seemingly being an electrical device of an undetermined nature. Studying its front

Inventor Herrold at his desk in San Francisco, where he sketched out new ideas and tested them later, circa 1903 (Stephen True Collection).

panel in a photograph, one sees what appears to be a combination of switches needed to send the flow of electrical current to several preselected locations, with the indicator lamp telling the operator when it is on. Perhaps it was designed to send electricity to motors in a factory. Whatever its intended use, the purpose of this Herrold invention remains a mystery.

Six years after moving there, Herrold's San Francisco plans were abruptly cancelled by what was probably the most damaging earthquake to hit the North American continent in historical times. On April 18, 1906, the earth shook San Francisco to its very foundation, did great damage to is streets and buildings, and caused a fire that ultimately destroyed most of the city, including all of the possessions of the up-and-coming inventor. He lost many drawings, and a large number of completed inventions and early prototypes. Most devastating of all to Herrold personally was that his apartment was destroyed. He lost his furniture, his grand piano, even his clothing.[23] He was suddenly a man without a job, without a home. Along with the population of the entire Bay Area, Charles Herrold found life forever changed by the effects of those few minutes of the natural violence. As he left the burning city, he photographed some of what he encountered along the way.

Left, top, and right: This unidentified device is labeled "Chas. D. Herrold Manufacturer San Francisco." Young Herrold created and sold a number of new devices, mostly electrical, between the late 1890s and 1906. Front and rear views are shown (Stephen True Collection). ***Left, bottom:*** Charles Herrold, San Francisco entrepreneur, confident of success as an inventor, looked forward to opportunities of the new 20th century, circa 1903 (Stephen True Collection).

A Young Teacher

Disaster notwithstanding, Charles was determined not to return home, where he would most likely become dependent upon his parents. He needed to prove that he could "make it" on his own. Many new inventing opportunities still awaited him. It was at this time that he also found he could use his considerable mechanical and electrical skills to do what his mother had always done best, teach others. Herrold summed up why he left San Francisco in a biographical sketch years later, the decision largely influenced by the 1906 earthquake, as follows:

HERROLD HOME AT SAN JOSE WRECKED BY EARTHQUAKE

G. H. Herrold, division engineer of the Great Western road, of this city, received the following from his father, W. M. Herrold, following the earthquake disaster. Mr. Herrold, Sr., lives in San Jose, and his beautiful resi-

dence, a picture of which is shown above, was badly wrecked. Of his experience on the fated morning of April 18, he wrote: "We are unhurt but the house is terribly wrecked by an earthquake at 5:15 this morning. The chimney came down and with it all the ceiling of our bed room. It crushed our bedstead down at the foot with brick and plaster. We were not hurt any. It took me some time to dig our clothes out of the debris. I could not get the door of our room open so climbed up into the garret and came down and forced it in from the outside. Up town the store buildings are said to be terribly wrecked and a big fire is raging. I am cooking breakfast out in the back yard."

Top: **Charles Herrold with his students at Heald College of Mining and Engineering in Stockton, California, 1907 (Stephen True Collection).** ***Bottom:*** **Herrold and several students demonstrating the marvels of electricity, Stockton, California, circa 1907. (Stephen True Collection).**

> After the great disaster to the Bay City, he removed to Stockton, took up the teaching of engineering, and became the head of the technical department of Heald's College, where he remained for three years. Much important work was accomplished during this time, including the designing and constructing by student labor of a high-speed turbine and electric generator, and he also laid the foundation of subsequent developments in underwater wireless, the firing of mines by wireless impulses, and radio telephony.[24]

Joining Heald's College in Stockton, California, on the Sacramento Delta enabled Herrold for the first time to support his interest in inventing with the steady pay-

Opposite, top: **The 1906 Great San Francisco Earthquake destroyed Herrold's home and lab. He took a series of photographs of the destruction (Stephen True Collection).** ***Opposite, bottom:*** **The news of the April 18, 1906, San Francisco earthquake reached the Midwest based on a letter William Morris Herrold of San Jose wrote his son George living in St. Paul, Minnesota: "Herrold Home at San Jose Wrecked by Earthquake" (Stephen True Collection).**

check of a teaching position. Like academics today, he used students to help with his experiments, and the students in turn benefited by learning from their teacher.

But it was not his students or classes that Herrold remembered most about his tenure in Stockton. According to his own writings and those of others, there were three events that most defined his time there: the development of a system of using underwater mines (wireless signals to fire explosives), a prophetic revelation about broadcasting — and another natural disaster, this time a flood.

Sending Signals

In the summer of 1908 Herrold set out to conduct a number of experiments on water which dealt with explosive mines. He chartered the oceangoing sloop *Dorothy* and performed the first of several successful experiments— the firing of mines at a distance.[25] These early investigations of wireless, much of it the sending of signals, closely paralleled his ongoing experimentation with wireless telegraph devices:

> The little sloop, *Dorothy*, on the San Joaquin River was the scene of many interesting experiments. A key would be pressed and a small mine would be fired by electromagnetic waves. These waves were sent through the earth, without raised antenna. [Herrold] was trying to develop earth telephony by waves of radiant energy so as to get rid of the bugbear of fading and static.[26]

Although he did not then realize it, standard (AM) radio signals have always traveled best in the daylight hours because of the buried underground radials that are part of the antenna system — ground conduction. It is at night, when the waves bounce off the Heaviside-Kenelley Layer, that fading and static occurs.[27]

It was after moving to Stockton in 1906 that Herrold began to think about broadcasting. He wrote that while aboard his boat, he was inspired toward further experimentation from reading a best selling novel of the final years of the 19th century. What caught his imagination was a science fiction book called *Looking Backward — 2000–1887,* written in 1887 by Edward Bellamy, in which the author predicted that there would be a device similar to the radio in every home. Of course, since it was written before Marconi's wireless experiments, Bellamy utilized the technology available to him in 1877, the wired telephone.[28] Herrold later told early biographer Fred Wells that "he received his inspiration that led to his first 'broadcasts' of music and speech by reading *Looking Backward*."[29] So it may have been that the imagination of a novelist provided the inspiration Charles Herrold needed to begin to put together the pieces and ideas that guided his experimentation leading to radio. It was in Stockton while teaching at Heald's College that Herrold found a purpose and a goal that defined him from that time on. Was it timing? Coincidence? The only thing that is known for sure is that Charles read as much material as he could get on wireless. Early in the decade he apparently concluded that wireless could be used for applications beyond just the sending of messages between two stations. He remembered thinking at the time, "If I can only find a system of wireless telephony that will produce clear speech and music and broadcast to the whole world, using the earth as a conductor, what a boon it will be to humanity."[30]

Lessons of a Flood

The final Stockton event that influenced Charles greatly was the occurrence of another natural disaster, large enough to be dubbed locally as the "great" flood of 1907, which he described in a letter to his mother. Charles told how he was living in a dormitory residence of the college, one apparently shared with staff, administrators and students, when he sensed the conditions were present for an impending disaster:

> I awakened and went to the back to get a drink, and lo and behold the water, which is always very cold and pure, was murky and warm. I said 'flood.' I walked out to the channel and the water was way up.... I kept watching it during the morning and bothered Mr. Gardiner by advising him to get the stuff out of the basement... .We worked like beavers but the boys only got a part of the stuff, which consisted of chairs, tables, household furniture, bedding, desks, books, maps, fixtures, when the whole gang deserted me to go home and look ... after boys who lived in town.[31]

That night Herrold continued to lead the school staff in moving everything they could out of the way of impending flood water. His efforts undoubtedly protected lives and saved property.

The Stockton flood of 1907 should have been a wake-up call for the residents of the town and it frustrated Charles, who reasoned that the town's annual flooding could be easily solved by proper planning. Writing to his mother, he recalled how he advised a local business leader:

> I could go out with a mere handful of men, ... build a breakwater four feet high ... and stop any ordinary flood by the mere expenditure of a few thousands. You could have a dredger that would keep your channels clear and you would not have this thing to repeat every year. You people sit on your gluteal muscles and talk about sending committees to Congress....[32]

The letter ends abruptly there; the rest of the pages are lost forever.

During his three years in Stockton, Charles envisioned himself as a man having a dual mission, one being that of a teacher and the other a wireless experimenter. While Heald's College was a general technical and commercial institution with degree programs in mining and business, it seemed to Herrold that there was a growing interest in wireless. Since Marconi's work began to attract attention, being reported widely in the press, an increasing number of young men seemed to be looking for an education that would lead to a career in wireless and electricity. Soon after 1900, dozens of companies and hundreds of stations had been set up to serve the new wireless communications industry, plus every shipping company which could afford it seemed to be equipping its vessels with the new invention. During his now-frequent demonstrations and talks about wireless and electricity, the young engineering professor must have noticed that the lecture hall always filled to capacity. Herrold's students at Heald's were well aware of the romance of the shipboard wireless operator, known as "sparks," and many read of how an operator saved the day by summoning help from a nearby ship during a big storm. No doubt about it, the interest of young men in wireless was going to be a winning combination. Charles Herrold knew he could be a part of it if he acted quickly.

Herrold College Begins

Late in 1908 Herrold decided it was time to resign his position at Heald's College, and to follow up on an idea which had occurred to him some time ago. He felt the time had come to start a wireless school of his own in San Jose. So he returned to his family fully convinced that establishing a college there would lead to a good future. In Stockton he had learned how a college had been organized and carried out its particular educational mission. It led him to believe he could start a specialized training school of his own, built around and devoted to this growing interest in wireless. Thus he opened his own trade and technical school on January 1, 1909. He called it the Herrold College of Wireless and Engineering. He discovered an entire floor vacant in a newly completed bank building in the center of downtown, and with some financial help from his father, rented it quickly and began to set up classrooms and laboratories. His school was dedicated to training young men to serve the rapidly growing wireless industry. First, there were several rooms set up with keys, sounders and earphones. There, students would learn to send and receive both Morse and Continental (International) codes, a basic requirement in any wireless facility. Classrooms also would be used for lectures in mathematics, physics, and other scientific subjects. This was a well-equipped school where young men would actually build spark transmitters and crystal receivers. They had to make many of the electrical devices they needed, because a handful of companies held patents on them. So in addition to learning code and understanding how wireless equipment was assembled, students were encouraged to find improvements, that is, better ways of solving a wireless problem.

The Herrold College was immediately popular with the young men, who were avid followers of the progress of modern day inventors like Edison, Tesla, the Wright brothers, even the fictional "Tom Swift." These youths seemed as excited as their mentor about the new wireless hobby. San Jose historian Clyde Arbuckle said he became aware of Herrold's teaching and radio work soon after he opened his college: "I think he was a good teacher. He was pretty well up on wireless and radio. We hadn't got around to using radio as a household word yet. He knew his subject and he knew how to put it over."[33] Those students who soon nicknamed him "Doc" and "Prof" knew that an education at the college could be the key to an exciting and well paying future as wireless operators.

For Herrold, starting the school was also a practical decision since the money earned from training students helped to pay for his true passion — inventing. Unknown to most of Herrold's students, their professor was spending more and more of his creative time trying to give a voice to the wireless telegraph. As the late broadcast historian Eric Barnouw noted in his comprehensive radio history book, there was a connection between Herrold's inventing and his work as a teacher:

> In San Jose, Cal., "Professor" Charles D. Herrold or "Doc" Herrold, a genius without formal qualifications, started in 1909 a College of Engineering in which radio became the main attraction. He began transmitting from the Garden City Bank building in San Jose in that same year, and promptly took up voice experiments. Wireless students assisted, and of course learned from the activity.[34]

Charles Herrold, standing, is seen teaching wireless students in his Garden City Bank classroom, before World War I (courtesy Perham Foundation Electronics Museum).

The college was the stage upon which Herrold launched his career as a wireless telephone inventor and broadcaster.

The Inventor Takes a Wife

Herrold College, being located in the heart of downtown San Jose, had little trouble attracting students. Originally on the fourth floor of the Garden City Bank building, it signed up students from secondary schools as well as from the nearby teachers' college, thanks to its wireless transmissions being heard far and wide, especially by those living in Santa Clara Valley. Little did Herrold know that one of these listeners would be a young, attractive woman attending the neighboring college, whom he would instruct at his own school, marry, and employ in the operation itself. Before this happened in 1913, however, Herrold was busy conducting classes in wireless code and carrying out experiments which would lead to broadcasting. By 1910 his programs of music were being heard throughout Santa Clara Valley. He was, in fact, operating a college radio station, although the term for it in his day was a "radio telephone" or "wireless telephone." Perhaps he felt financially secure with the success of his college and the fact that his radiotelephone had begun to interest financial

Top, left: Charles Herrold's first wife Sybil, age about 16, when she was a student at San Jose Normal School, now San Jose State University, circa 1912 (Stephen True Collection). ***Top right:*** Charles and Sybil, circa 1913, around the date of their marriage (Stephen True Collection). ***Below:*** Students drew on this blackboard in a Herrold College classroom. It was a prank, making light of their mentor's announced marriage in 1913 (Stephen True Collection).

investors as well as listeners. All we know is that 37-year-old Herrold met an attractive teenage girl and fell in love. She was Sybil May Paull, a lovely 16-year-old student who was studying at nearby State Normal School.[35] Although he was 21 years older than she, Herrold had much to offer. The success of his college seemed assured. His inventive skills had earned him an electrical engineering position with the National Wireless Telephone and Telegraph Company in San Jose. Herrold could promise his bride-to-be a secure economic future. There are no surviving letters explaining why an attractive young girl became interested in a man much older than herself and a teacher.

Recalling what her husband was like 50 years later, Herrold's former wife had nothing but praise for his mind, character, and social behavior.[36] Their marriage was summed up by a local historian with the flair and courtesies of a social register:

> At San Jose, on October 20, 1913, Mr. Herrold was married to Miss Sybil May Paull, the daughter of William and Maud Eva Paull, formerly of England. Her parents came to the United States and Montana, and for many years her father was chief of the Butte City Fire Department, where he was highly respected for his personal worth. Two children have blessed this union: Robert Roy Herrold and Donald Sanford Herrold. Mr. Herrold is genial, kindly, tactful and generous, and with his gifted wife, whose public spirit is in harmony with his, he takes a keen interest in all that pertains to the development of the West, and especially of San Jose and Santa Clara County.[37]

Their first son, Robert, was born a year after the marriage, Donald two years later. In the beginning, Sybil was confined at home with her young family. Before too long, however, she would be able to go to her husband's college and become his valuable assistant, both as teacher and broadcaster.

With Family and Boys

Recalling his childhood, son Robert easily remembered when his mother came over to the building and taught at the college:

> My first memories are of when my mother was teaching the code to students. On shipboard they were the radio operators. And I have a memory of coming into the room and in this L-shaped table students were sitting around learning the code. She was running the phonograph. She would wind it up and run it. And they would listen to the code on it and transcribe it.[38]

Robert also remembered life with his father: "I remember him playing the piano. He would play the piano quite often and I would come in and listen." But sometimes Herrold needed to get away. He found it necessary to balance his business life, his family life, and his role as mentor to the students at the college by taking frequent camping trips, which his son remembered very well:

> I used to go to the cabin with him. And I remember those quite vividly because we had a lot of fun. And he had some of the students [along with him], and he would

Left: **Herrold and an unidentified student experiment with wireless devices aboard a small boat around 1911 (Stephen True Collection).** ***Above:*** **Charles Herrold often experimented with wireless devices. Many tests were conducted near Herrold's cabin in the Santa Cruz Mountains, circa 1913 (Stephen True Collection).**

> give them an outing that way and a rest. They had quite a rigorous routine during the week studying and whatever they were doing.[39]

So if the young Mrs. Herrold ever hoped that her husband was going to spend leisure time with his young family, she was soon disappointed. Weekends were reserved for camping with his students in the nearby Santa Cruz mountains. Charles built several cabins near the Santa Clara side of the mountain at Montevina, just south of the wealthy enclave of Los Gatos. Even though son Robert accompanied his dad to the cabin a couple of times, Sybil went only once. According to Robert, she realized she was not cut out for the outdoor life. More often than not, these camping trips were taken for something more important than recreation. The mountains were a place where Herrold could carry out wireless experiments, free from electrical interference and up high above the valley where the transmitting and receiving was better.[40]

Those who knew Herrold personally spoke highly of the man. None represent the views of relatives, friends and acquaintances better than his grandson Stephen, whose interest in the lives of his grandparents led him to become the Herrold family historian. He remembers vividly what his grandmother used to say about Herrold: "There wasn't any topic that you could talk about that he didn't know about. He was very educated [even though] he didn't graduate from Stanford, but ... he had a terrific ability for the knowledge he had."[41]

Herrold's experiments led to an accomplishment far beyond wireless technology itself. His efforts to get wireless to talk resulted in Herrold becoming the first to recognize the value of serving ordinary listeners, the public at large. By striving to attract and enlarge this radio audience in San Jose, California, which he encouraged by serving them regularly with news and entertainment, Herrold was doing something unusual for his time and place. No one outside of California seemed to know about it. But he was, in fact, becoming America's first broadcaster.

4
Shaping of an Inventor

Inventors are a strange breed: they differ both from scientists and from artists, yet partake of the qualities of each. They tend in general not to be especially well educated, sometimes not even in the field of their own work... Some inventors mine a single rich vein of invention... Other inventors will be all over the court.
Joseph Epstein, *The New Yorker* (1998)[1]

While it was a frequently tortured path and he wasn't always sure where it was going, Herrold took his first steps toward a career in radio in 1907. It began during his tenure on the faculty of Heald's College of Mining and Engineering in Stockton. There he was known to his colleagues as someone perpetually enthusiastic about some new invention. He shared his knowledge with anyone who would listen, recounting the successes and failures of such electrical luminaries as Nikola Tesla and Thomas Edison. Between thinking about how to create a practical wireless telephone and imagining the uses for such a device, he began doing what any good professor would do, he started studying the subject intensely. He read, he researched, he dialogued with students and other teachers. He told them that in order to develop his wireless telephone, he had to improve upon all the existing technology.

At Heald's College he enlisted his students in practical projects, like the construction of a "500,000 volt static transformer, a mercury turbine interrupter producing 4000 breaks per second and a 400 cell battery."[2] In later years he told about his work in a series of letters to Lee de Forest:

> I have experimented on many types of sparks; among others a high speed mercury interrupter attached to a spark coil.... I experimented with practically all the existing sparks and arc, with the exception of the Alexanderson high frequency generators, which very obviously were outside the reach of my pocket book.[3]

In 1908 Herrold moved to San Jose to carry out what he had been thinking. Shortly before he opened the door to his wireless school on New Year's Day 1909 and got it ready for students, he realized that he couldn't do it alone. He needed help with teaching as well as experimentation. So he chose young Ray Newby, 16, a crackerjack wireless operator, to be his assistant. Once classes got under way, Herrold had no trouble involving Newby in some serious inventing during their off hours, using the school wireless facility as a base of operations. Newby met Herrold in the spring of 1908. A local boy with a great wit and wry sense of humor, Newby's youthful demeanor complemented the normally serious and relentlessly formal Charles Herrold. Newby was full of enthusiasm about the wireless hobby, and he was already a skilled Morse operator. So Herrold had offered him a part-time instructor position just before the college opened. Asked years later in an interview whether he could remember those days with the professor, Newby answered:

The Garden City Bank Building in San Jose where Herrold rented space on the third floor. On January 1, 1909, he opened his trade-technical school, The Herrold College of Wireless and Engineering (courtesy Perham Foundation Electronics Museum).

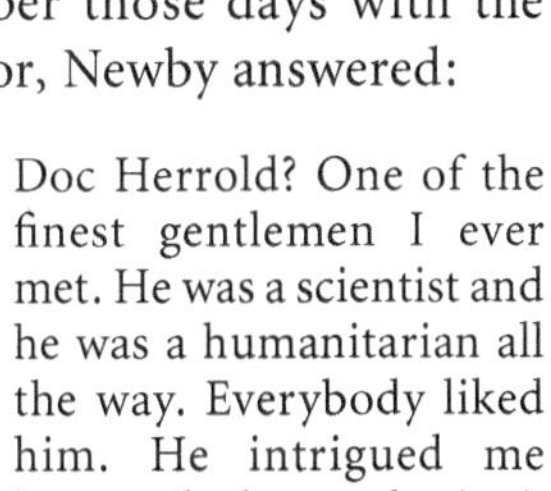

> Doc Herrold? One of the finest gentlemen I ever met. He was a scientist and he was a humanitarian all the way. Everybody liked him. He intrigued me because he knew physics in such a way as to tie in with what knowledge I had of the ABC's of wireless or electronics and we just hit it off right from the start.[4]

Newby developed an immediate respect for Herrold as a mentor, recalling working with him as though it were yesterday. In the same interview, he said: "I think he realized I could handle the testing, the practical end.... We made a good team, I know that." Newby became Herrold's first and most important wireless telephone collaborator.

The Spark of Invention[5]

How did Charles Herrold describe the wireless work that he and Newby attempted to improve upon? In later years, Herrold told readers what they had been

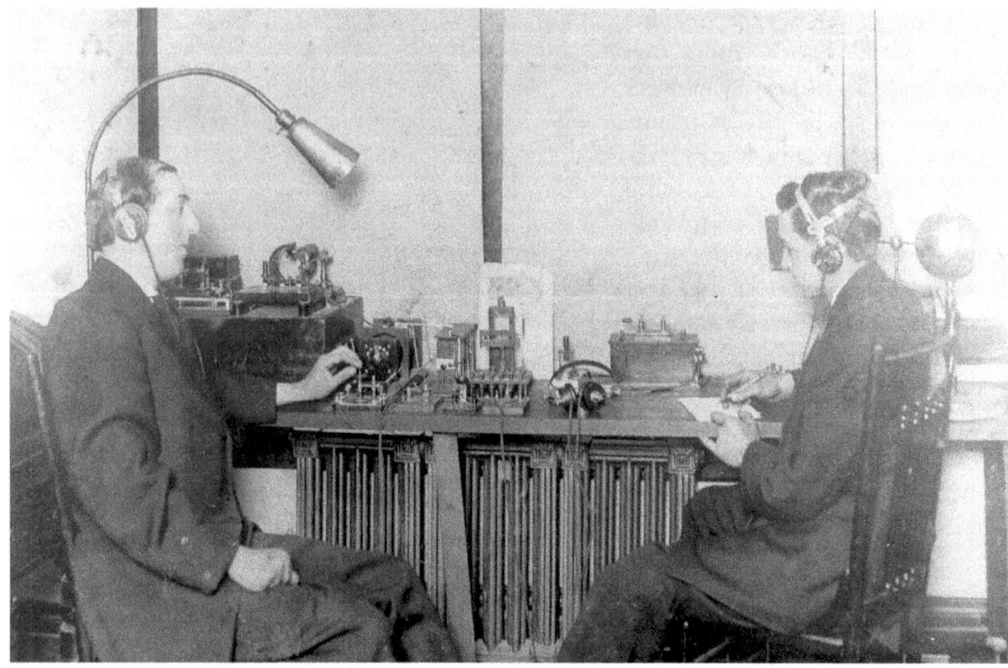

Ray Newby (right) remembered using this "spark" transmitter with Herrold (left) when he first became his assistant in 1909 (Stephen True Collection).

attempting to do. In particular, he explained how and why he decided to use a spark.[6] He knew that most attempts by a variety of experimenters to transmit the human voice had failed. He was familiar with all the local experiments, including what Herrold thought might have been the first attempt on the West Coast to communicate publicly by wireless telephone. That was the attempt made in San Francisco by Francis McCarty, a cash boy at Hales Store who had hooked up a primitive microphone to an ordinary spark wireless transmitter.[7] Herrold's description of what occurred would have been understandable to the specialist of the time, but it's a bit obscure today:

> Accidentally stumbling upon the old inductivity system and the old system of Collins employing spark coils, and the Dolbear arrangement, he [McCarty] succeeded in communicating one way between Twin Peaks and the center of San Francisco. All attempts to get further than 3 miles failed. This was the distance originally covered by Collins. So the old McCarty Telephone was a failure except to the promoters. A split in the McCarty family sent [the brother] Ignatius in one direction on a wild goose chase, the father on independent attempts to extend the original tests of Francis (who was killed in an accident), and Jack, who used a high frequency alternator known at the time as the "Pea Nut Whistle."[8]

Knowing what others were trying to do before 1909 as radiotelephone experimenters, Herrold and his young assistant worked to invent a better spark-based radiotelephone system, using every combination they could think of. Newby remembered an early version:

> I had a cadmium spark gap [made of] a soft metal. It deteriorates pretty easy with a spark, but that don't matter. I had a micrometer gap with this spark gap ... you can put close together, so close that it would spark without the vibrator—providing I could interrupt the current in the primary. There's two windings on an induction step-up coil. So the six volts in the primary, interrupted by the microphone vibrating [and] turning on and off the current according to the frequency of your voice and ... the micrometer gap—you could hardly see a spark when I'd say 'Hello' through the mike. But a spark would occur there.[9]

Although they tried that method for a time and found it to be startling and somewhat effective, it was "too experimental and too ragged and rough," Newby recalled. Before giving up on the spark, the two made sure that no single part of the system had been overlooked. Every combination of antenna, microphone, and coils was tried and discarded.

For example, it began to dawn on Herrold early in 1909 that antenna height and mass might differentiate his radiotelephone from the others by increasing its effective range. If the main drawback of the Collins-McCarty induction coil was its three-mile sending limit, Herrold was able, by constructing what he called an "umbrella antenna" between the tops of buildings in downtown San Jose, to dramatically increase the range. He believed the effectiveness of his 1909 large antenna to be such an important advancement that it was publicized in a 1910 magazine article, which carried a headline claiming: "Ray Newby, a clever young operator of San Jose Cal., worked up to 90 miles in broad sunlight."[10]

Newby explained what they did, saying:

> I merely connected the ground to one side of the gap and this big umbrella antenna to the other side of this little spark gap and when I'd talk in there you could see the little spark if you'd look real close. If the lights were out you could really see it. Every time you'd talk you'd see a little bit of a very small spark. And that was a reproduction of the frequency of my voice so that you could understand it.[11]

Newby recalled that they modified a commercially available microphone purchased from a mail order catalog:

> The microphone came from Sweden, and I could rattle out pretty darn good voice. You could understand it readily. But music was, of course, rattily because for music you have to have several octaves or differences of pitch to get color in the voice. Even to recognize one person talking from another, you must hear the harmonics of the voice.[12]

Whether experimenting with voice, music or code, it became apparent before 1910 that in all their wireless applications, the "spark" method was a technological dead end. Given the preponderance of evidence available as early as 1908 against the spark, it is puzzling why Herrold didn't immediately begin to use what many at that time believed to be superior—the Poulsen arc transmitter. Herrold offered this explanation in a 1919 magazine article:

> About this time (1908) the technical magazines published reports of the improved systems of Valdemar Poulsen, and shortly afterwards the American Company took over the patent rights and commenced development after the truly American fash-

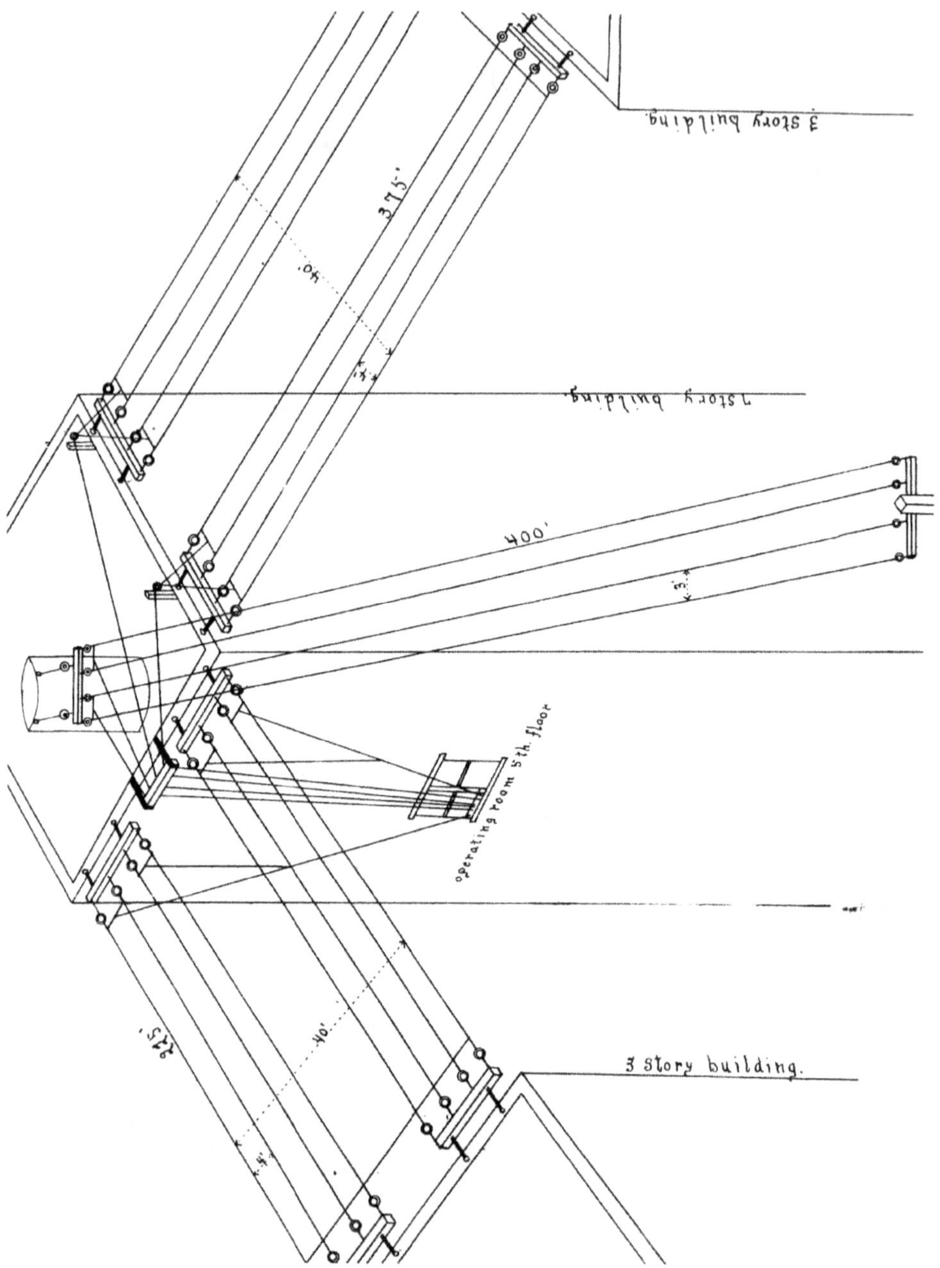

This is a drawing by Herrold of his 1909 "umbrella antenna," installed on the roof of the San Jose Herrold College, Garden City Bank Building, circa 1909 (Stephen True Collection).

> ion of overlooking no details.... The greatest secrecy was maintained over the improvements being made on the laboratory sets furnished from Copenhagen, so those of us who of the original experiments would profit intellectually were obliged to content ourselves with the comparatively meager reports.[13]

While early information on arc systems was difficult to find, at least in the popular press, Herrold knew there were arc experiments and transmissions being conducted in and around Stanford University in 1909.[14] That was the year the Poulsen Wireless Telephone and Telegraph Company was started in Palo Alto. Its founder, president and chief engineer was Cyril F. Elwell, who, encouraged by Stanford professors, went to Denmark and acquired rights to use the Poulsen arc from the inventor himself. By 1912 this was a highly successful wireless operation, later to be acquired by the Federal Telegraph Company, to provide coded wireless telegraphic service to commercial customers worldwide in competition with Marconi.[15] Top university scientists were advising or assisting Elwell on improving the arc for long-distance code, as well as lab researchers like Lee de Forest, Charles V. Logwood, and Herbert Van Etten.

Working on a similar system about 25 miles away in San Jose, Herrold must have become completely familiar with the Poulsen operation without revealing publicly what he was doing in his own laboratory. In other words, the San Josean needed a "continuous wave" and the Poulsen transmitter was proving to be one way to do it. But to use that transmitting device or any adaptation of it, Herrold had to be wary, else his apparatus might infringe on Poulsen's patent rights.[16] While Herrold without doubt began using an arc early in his broadcast experiments starting in 1909, no blueprints or sketches of it exist today. Details of how it worked were kept deliberately vague during the time Herrold was testing and developing. Only when Herrold began to apply for his own patents in 1913 do we begin to learn how his arc operated and see how it looked from drawings and photographs. Herrold differentiated his system from Poulsen's by calling it an "oscillating arc." Fearful of litigation, Herrold waited till he was certain of acquiring his own patents before talking to the press. Beginning in 1912, however, he began to show off his station's equipment and capabilities. In the long run all this secrecy made no difference, because radio eventually would be operating on entirely different principles. But it was the idea of broadcasting which originated in those years that became Herrold's most significant byproduct. It is important to recognize that Herrold used his radiotelephone in San Jose for the purpose of entertaining an audience with "voice and music," whereas the Federal Telegraph Company of Palo Alto employed its Poulsen arc exclusively to send and receive long-distance messages in code.[17] While eventually these technologies became obsolete, the idea of broadcasting soon caught on and grew. That was the important difference.

Building the Arc

Asked years later how Herrold went about developing a transmitter based on an arc, Ray Newby recalled what seemed to have inspired Herrold's thinking:

> It all started from the old street lamp. I think most everybody has heard of the rattle of the old arc lights starting. There was millions of 'em in San Jose at that time. They had 'em up on the tower at Market and Santa Clara Streets. Those arcs had to be trimmed very often and adjusted and new carbons put in because they deteriorated and burnt away. Herrold took that arc and he said, "If I can increase the frequency of that singing tone that's in this arc light, the street arc lamp, I have a chance

> of having a carrier wave that will support voice or music maybe." And that's exactly what he did.[18]

Newby explained the basic technical principle of all arc systems: "He [Herrold] took a direct current arc and shunted a capacity and inductance around it and got it to oscillate at a pitch that was not audible by the ear."[19]

According to Newby:

> To handle more power, [he] put the arcs in series, and he took six arc lights and put them in series, one after another like you hook up dry batteries. But these arc lights were [placed in liquid-filled containers]. In order to increase the frequency to an inaudible sound, he had to burn them under distilled water. He had a magnetic lift that would pull all six arcs apart and they were automatically adjusted like the street lamps. To travel, they'd get a new hold on the carbon and when they'd burn too far away and had to go round and be reset, then they'd break and lift again. That same principle of the street arc light was used in here but instead of having only one, he used six and they were burning under distilled water. He found that distilled water contaminated and gave problems. There's a lot of technicalities involved in this deal. He even used alcohol in there. I was afraid he'd blow the roof, burning arc lights underneath alcohol. He says, "It's safe as long as the alcohol doesn't evaporate." I didn't believe it but he proved it. He had 'em actually burning under alcohol, six arc lights under alcohol, about three inches underneath the level of alcohol.[20]

A Technical Explanation

According to wireless historian Thorn Mayes, a retired General Electric engineer who in later years studied how the Herrold system worked, an oscillating arc is able to serve as a radio transmitter if it is set up properly. In his analysis of Herrold's "arc phone" which Mayes published in a book, he concluded that Charles Herrold had developed a highly improved version of what others were using. Mayes said in his 1989 book that Herrold was using

A Herrold arc device, circa 1912. This version featured six arcs and became the basis for Herrold's technology, the arc transmitter (courtesy Perham Foundation Electronics Museum).

> an iron core choke coil in series with six arcs. The choke limits the inrush current at the first striking of the arcs and it also acts as a radio frequency choke to prevent high frequency current from flowing back into the power supply. Thus it chokes in two directions. The oscillating circuit consists of the coil and the variable capacitance. The radio frequency current is inductively coupled to the antenna and the antenna is resonated by a loading coil. Speech modulation of the antenna current is done by a carbon microphone connected in series with the ground lead.[21]

It's believed today that Herrold's arc system was probably capable of generating less than 15 watts of power. The arc transmitters required direct current (DC) power. They could get it from either the San Jose trolley's overhead wires or the elevator in the college building: "The power was taken from the street car line, 500 volts DC and that makes a beautiful arc light. He stole the juice there for a while. But then later he hooked to the elevator circuit, 500 volts DC."[22] Because the 500 volt DC supply found in Herrold's bank building was too much for a single arc, six arcs were wired in series in order that each could operate at around 100 volts.

Said Newby:

> The microphone would get too hot to hold in the hand. Later, he water-cooled each and every of six buttons in the microphone with a little tube of water running through a cooler with a little pump and a motor and he used a water-cooled microphone. I think that's the first I ever heard of it. The one that was the most successful on the arc transmitter was the six-button microphone.[23]

Herrold's Second Wireless Telephone.
Arc Transmitter.
July 1909.

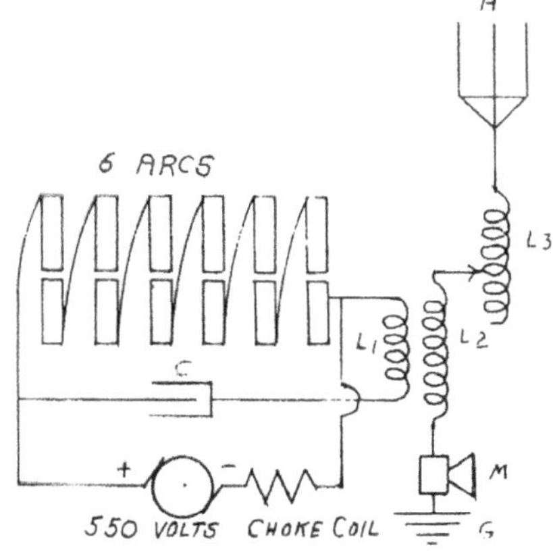

Fig. 3

A — Aerial.
C — Condenser.
G — Ground.
L_1 — Primary Coil.
L_2 — Secondary Coil.
L_3 — Loading Coil.

This is a labeled schematic drawing by Thorn Mayes of Herrold's 1909 arc-based wireless telephone transmitter. One of the simplest of technologies, it consists of a water-cooled microphone, a direct current power source, and several coils for tuning. There is an antenna and ground (courtesy Perham Foundation Electronics Museum).

Nearly all radiotelephone inventors, de Forest included, used some form of an arc powered by 200–500 volts DC, in series with inductors in the form of transformers with primary and secondary coils. A water-cooled microphone was typically in the ground circuit of the secondary of the antenna coupling coils. To understand all the components necessary to operate a Herrold radiotelephone, the reader should consult the various illustrations reproduced in this book which show the patents and actual devices. It is a system representative of what practically every inventor was attempting to do during the first two decades of radiotelephone development. Having invented, tested and proved his technology, Herrold began filing applications to patent the various versions of the pieces that made up his system of radiotelephony between 1913 and 1917.

The Herrold "Arc" Patents

Charles Herrold's radio station which operated in San Jose between 1909 and 1917 was only possible because he was able to develop an effective arc transmitting system. The principles of its operation are generally understandable to radio engineers by showing them his patents, drawing and photographs. As seen below, Herrold's patented system consisted of several important parts, including variations of single and multiple arcs burning under liquid. Also, the Herrold broadcasting station needed magnetic lifting devices, a water-cooled carbon button microphone, and an antenna coil to couple the arc to the antenna. The following U.S. Patent Office "arc" applications and patents by C.D. Herrold are reproduced elsewhere:

1. Oscillator for Wireless Transmission, filed on April 21, 1913, and patented May 12, 1914 (not shown)
2. Magnetic Lift for Electrodes in Electric Oscillators, filed May 7, 1913, patented Dec. 8, 1914 (p. 79)
3. Telephone Transmitter, filed by Herrold and E.A.B. Portal, Jan. 14, 1914, patented Dec. 21, 1915 (p. 84)
4. Conical Helix, filed June 2, 1913, patented July 6, 1915 (p. 83)
5. Oscillator, filed Oct. 20, 1915, patented April 17, 1917 (p. 80)

Actual photographs of Herrold's radiotelephone work and apparatus are shown as follows:

1. Photo, Oscillator with 6 arcs (p. 70)
2. Photo, several arcs in metal cans for submersion under alcohol, three sizes/versions (p. 76)
3. Photo, water-cooled microphone and its individual parts (p. 76)
4. Photo, original notarized drawings for Herrold "Telephone Transmitter" microphone, 1913 (p. 78)

Since the term "radio" was still not widely used, Herrold and his assistants began to call their new transmitting system the "arc fone." In seeking to perfect the instrument, he felt it could serve three distinct purposes: One was to serve as a dependable wireless replacement for the wired Bell telephone. The second was to produce a system of such superior quality it would sell to the U.S. Navy, the major customer of wireless equipment at the time. The third was, in Herrold's words, to make his college known, because "broadcasting for the people of San Jose ... was an obsession with us and certainly, the entire Pacific Coast looked upon the radio broadcasts from San Jose as an established institution."[24] But building an arc fone technically good enough to meet Herrold's three unique uses proved to be an arduous task. If Charles Herrold were going take advantage of his arc fone technology, he would need assistance from a number of people working closely with him in his lab. Later, when one of his helpers found out something that "Prof" was secretly working on, the discovery led to a bitter misunderstanding and produced a schism which never quite healed, as Herrold wrote:

> I was very "close-mouthed" in those days and my students knew little of my private experiments. At one time one of my student operators, E.A. Portal accidentally stumbled onto an item on which I was working, and rather than enter into a controversy with him, I took him in as an equal partner and we secured a joint patent, on a scheme for hooking a series of multiple carbon "buttons" onto the diaphragm.[25]

The Main Team

Although Ray Newby was Herrold's friend and original assistant during the early days of their spark and arc telephone collaboration, by 1913 Newby had acquired a job as a ship's wireless operator and was spending more time at sea. With Newby gone, Herrold put three new individuals on the arc fone "team" to assemble and operate the Herrold radiotelephone system at various locations around the Bay Area. No longer solely confined to the Herrold College building in San Jose, stations were put together and tested in San Francisco and Oakland by Frank Schmidt, Ken Sanders and Emil Portal. Middle-aged Frank Schmidt was the senior member of the trio. He possessed the kind of practical skills needed by Herrold in assembling and maintaining various kinds of apparatus.

Ken Sanders was a San Jose boy, who, having heard the early experimental transmissions of voice and music by Newby and Herrold prior to 1912, made the decision that hundreds of young men made during those years. Listening to the Herrold station night after night on his own receiving set, Sanders decided this was for him. He would seek a career in wireless. Young Sanders enrolled in Herrold College, became one of its outstanding students, and was selected by Herrold for extra-curricular projects. Between camping trips designed to learn about the behavior of radio waves in a mountainous setting and operating the arc fone at San Francisco's Fairmont Hotel, Sanders became an integral and trusted member of the Herrold team. The same could not have been said about Emil Portal. Though also a student at the Herrold College, Portal was highly ambitious and thought of going into the wireless business on his own. At the time Portal had his own radiotelephone at home, was highly regarded for his own talent and abilities, and was a valuable addition to the staff. However, assisting Herrold in the development of the water-cooled microphone, Portal came to believe that this particular idea originated with him and that he deserved full credit. It became impossible to convince Portal otherwise. So Charles reluctantly added his name to the patent. In the 1920s Portal started his own radio business and

Left: Ken Sanders and Emil Portal listen to a Herrold broadcast on a crystal detector and loose coupler tuner, 1912–13 (Stephen True Collection). **Right:** Herrold students listen to broadcasts from the radiotelephone laboratory, circa 1913 (Stephen True Collection).

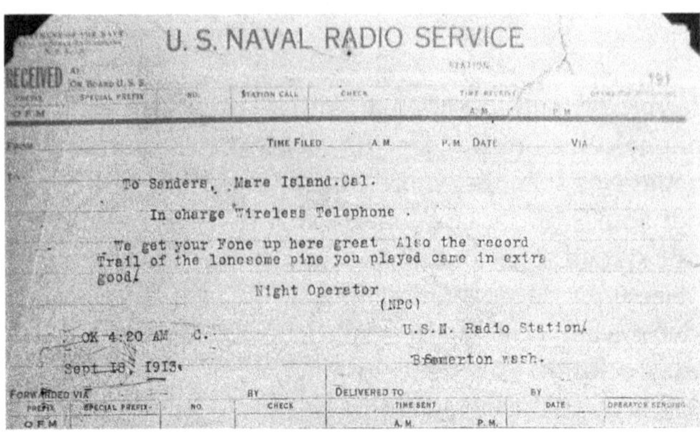
U. S. NAVAL RADIO SERVICE

RECEIVED

TIME FILED A.M. P.M. DATE VIA

To Sanders, Mare Island.Cal.

In charge Wireless Telephone .

We get your Fone up here great Also the record Trail of the lonesome pine you played came in extra good.

Night Operator
(NPC)

OK 4:20 AM C.

U.S.N. Radio Station.

Sept 18, 1913.

Bremerton Wash.

FORWARDED VIA BY DELIVERED TO BY

PREFIX SPECIAL PREFIX NO. CHECK TIME SENT A.M. P.M. DATE OPERATOR SENDING

OFM

A telegram dated September 18, 1913, from a Bremerton, Washington, wireless operator to Herrold student Ken Sanders, acknowledging hearing a phonograph record played from the Herrold College station. Such offers of proof were solicited by Herrold to promote the sales of his wireless phone technology (Stephen True Collection).

offered several stories to the press telling how he was the first to broadcast. He never mentioned Herrold in those interviews.[26]

Seeking Investors

By 1912 Herrold was ready to make money from his inventions. He began preparing drawings and technical descriptions to send off for early patents and assembled a small team to build new equipment. But to begin manufacturing his arc radiotelephone system on a large scale, he needed investors. With money, he could compete nationally for private and government contracts. Confident that his arc fone was the best and aware of widespread publicity being given other radiotelephone experimenters, he decided to use all possible means to introduce his system to the public. Herrold became a salesman. He brought local businessmen into his lab to sell them his technology, and soon succeeded in interesting the National Wireless Telephone and Telegraph Company, which decided to try it out. When offered the position of chief engineer, Herrold felt this would allow him the chance to prove the practicality of his inventions and give him a financial backer when the time came to sell them. Welcoming a chance to demonstrate his inventions, he began to assemble and prepare several radiotelephones for testing, while the company looked for buyers. Believing success was at hand, Herrold began to cultivate the local press.[27] After inviting a local weekly newspaper reporter to visit his station in the summer of 1912, he got a headline in the *San Jose Herald* which said, "Concert by Wireless Telephone a Success." During the two-hour long broadcast, music was played on a phonograph and listeners phoned in to say they heard it "for many miles around." Herrold's program operator, E.A. Portal, took requests and spun the songs on a phonograph provided by the Wiley B. Allen Music company. The *Herald* reported:

> Immediately after the first record was played numerous amateurs from various points in the valley notified Mr. Portal that they had heard the music distinctly. Mr. Portal gave the names of records he had on hand and asked those with whom he was communicating to signify their choice, saying that he would play any record they desired. One asked for "My Old Kentucky Home," which was furnished.[28]

Herrold also began giving talks around town. Some were reported in local newspapers. One of them reported: "Trinity Men's Club Hears About Wireless," and its story told how "Prof. C.D. Herrold, head of local school, discusses the new telephony." In this talk, Herrold said that the radiotelephone in the Garden City bank building was only one of several he already had in operation. He revealed that he already had a number of experimental stations, including one in the Santa Cruz Mountains, on which

> his students not only converse with his wireless telephone station in the Fairmount[29] Hotel in San Francisco but are able to recognize voices and enjoy phonograph music without an "aerial." The Herrold station in the Garden City Bank Building is in constant communication by wireless telephone with the Fairmont station and several times daily talks with ships at sea.[30]

The story goes on to say: "CD Herrold, a wireless inventor of this city, claims to have held a conversation between this city and Point Arguello, Wednesday night. Although the distance is 300 miles, Herrold says the conversation was clear and distinct."[31]

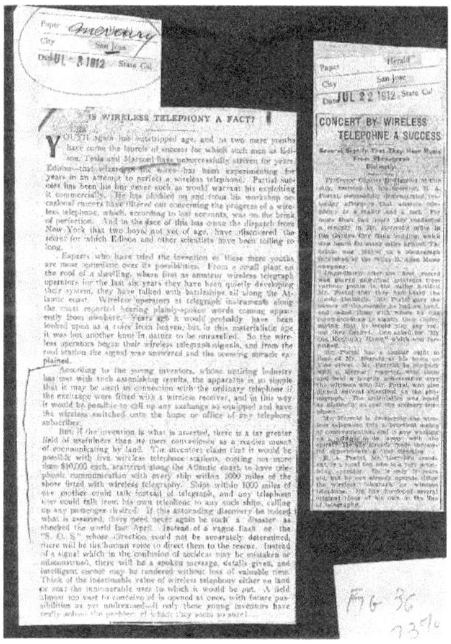

Herrold's broadcasting was covered from time to time by the local press, such as this clipping from the *San Jose Mercury* on July 8, 1912. Two weeks later the *San Jose Herald* told how these broadcasts included telephone requests for records from listeners on July 22, 1912.

Herrold was demonstrating that he had a broadcasting machine that could reach far and wide. Now working with the National Wireless Telephone and Telegraph Company to demonstrate the proficiency of his invention, Herrold provided transmitters for the U.S. Navy, whose successful operations at Mare Island, California, and Bremerton, Washington, made the news.[32] However, not all wireless operators thought this was a good thing. For example, G.H. Baxter, using code at the Marconi wireless station at Balinese, California, complained to his superiors and the local radio inspector in 1913 that

> the arc from the San Jose wireless telephone cut his signals down considerably.... "SJN" stayed out for a minute or so, and then broke me right in the middle of the message. Mr. Portal was using the [wireless] telephone and wanted Mr. Sanders (LQ) to come up there.... His talk was entirely unnecessary....[33]

It was the beginning of conflict between commercial wireless operators, the radiotelephone and the early amateur experimenters over use of the airwaves. It would continue until the federal government stepped in to regulate frequency allocations in the 1920s.

Enter the National

When Herrold sought financial backing in 1912, he was looking for a company eager to profit from his radiotelephone. Almost at the same time the National Wireless Telephone and Telegraph Company of San Francisco (NWT&T) was looking for

Top: Herrold arcs in containers, circa 1912. The arcs burned in liquid, usually alcohol (courtesy Perham Foundation Electronics Museum). ***Bottom:*** One of several Herrold water-cooled carbon microphones with a button design. Carbon continued to be used in telephone handsets into the 1960s (Stephen True Collection).

new technologies to rally around.[34] As each was looking for moneymaking opportunities, agreement was not hard to reach. They saw Herrold's work as an addition to their current wireless holdings, the McCarty and Janke patents.[35] They contracted with Herrold and paid him $100 a month to develop and demonstrate a wireless telephone that could be patented and sold. Everyone assumed there would be profits all around. Years later, NWT&T's former vice president, George M. Davis, was asked to explain the brief relationship between Herrold and his company. He wrote:

> Dr. Charles Herrold was employed as chief engineer of the National Wireless Telephone and Telegraph Company at a time when I was Vice President of said company. He was employed by us from early in 1912 till late in 1913 during which time he was engaged in developing radio telephone sets at his own laboratory in the Garden City Bank Building in San Jose. He had an established radio station which to my best knowledge and belief had been in operation for three years and it was his achievements in this field of development that led to our employment of him. Prior to his employment by us we had practically confined our operations to tests between our station at the Fairmount Hotel [*sic*] and the Williams building. His first act being to open communication between the Fairmount Hotel station and his own radio telephone station in San Jose.[36]

Managers or owners of the company besides Davis whom we will get to know include J.B. Young of the Board of Directors and shareholders Alfred H. Cohen, Frank Golden, T.H. Yarnell, L. Seidenberg, and William M. Herrold (the inventor's father).

To celebrate the new relationship, the NWT&T sent out a press release under the headline "San Jose California and San Francisco Linked by Radio Telephone." The story detailed the company's goals and described the activities on that first historic day:

> Two transmitters and their water-cooled microphones were in place, one in the test station on the roof of the Fairmount [*sic*] Hotel in San Francisco and the other in the Herrold Laboratory in the Garden City Bank Building in San Jose, California. At the Fairmount station was Alfred H. Cohen, a heavy stockholder in the company who expected to purchase the inventions of Chas. D. Herrold. There was also Mr. Geo. M. Davis, vice president of the company, financing the tests. There was also present Mr. Henry Victor Anzini, ship radio operator and in charge of the station on the Fairmount Hotel. Mr. Frank G. Schmidt was mechanician. At the San Jose laboratory was Mr. Emile Andrewboski Portal, Mr. Kenneth Sanders (both expert telegraph operators of the Continental Morse system). Charles D. Herrold who had designed and constructed the system was also present. Test broadcasts had been sent out during the morning and locally received and everything was in readiness for the supreme test, the linking of the two cities by radiotelephone.[37]

It was the summer of 1912 and it must have been an exciting time as commercial and amateur listeners heard the inauguration of this major Northern California radio event:

> Mr. Frank G. Schmidt, mechanician of the Herrold Laboratories had been sent before noon to his station at the Fairmount station and he and Victor Anzini were on their tiptoes. There was a hush of expectancy as the time of the official test drew near. Schmidt was at the oscillator and Anzini handled the receiving set and the water-cooled microphone. At the San Jose laboratory there was a fever of excitement. All

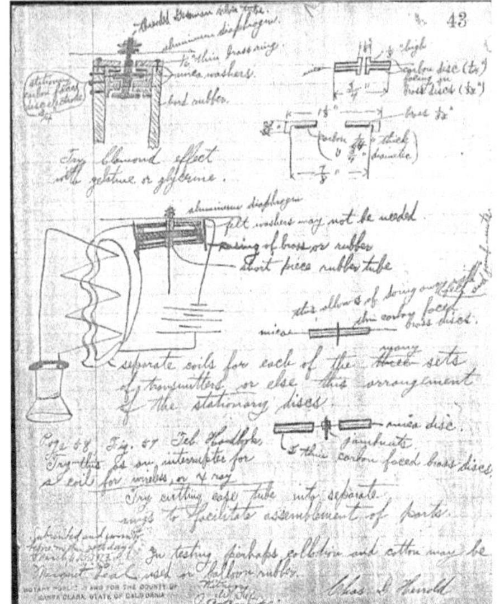

Herrold's original hand notes and drawings, dated March 1913, which led to the invention and patent of another important piece of the Herrold arc voice technology, a water-cooled microphone (Stephen True Collection).

> visitors were barred. The room was empty except for Messrs. Herrold, Portal and Sanders. At ten minutes to two, men took their stations, Portal at the oscillator #1, Sanders at oscillator #2 so that in case #1 should fail, #2 could instantly be thrown in. In an instant the radiation meter of The #1 oscillator showed full radiation. Doc Herrold said: "Portal, she's charging the antenna — there! Change that condenser just a trace — there!"[38]

You can sense the excitement that the public relations writer must have felt, being the witness to that historic first.

Work with the Navy

Charles Herrold had impressed Cohen and Davis of the NWT&T during those first months. Before the end of 1912, the Herrold system had been successfully demonstrated for the U.S. Navy. The event was reported in *Modern Electrics*, which told its wireless enthusiasts,

> It is possible to talk by wireless telephone from Mare Island to Point Loma, California, a distance of 450 miles. The Navy department has accepted the installations of the National Wireless Telegraph and Telephone Company, and the system will be put in operation immediately at Mare Island and Goat Island, the Farallone Islands, Table Bluff, Point Arguello and on two of the American Cruisers."[39]

Herrold's arc fone accomplishments were also documented by a series of telegrams and other progress reports between Herrold, his assistants and the NWT&T brass. The telegrams were used by Schmidt, Sanders and Portal to request that supplies and replacement parts be sent from the San Jose headquarters to the hotel and naval base. They offered Western Union confirmation that the transmissions were clear, effective and reached the distances claimed.[40] Herrold himself wrote a report under the title: "National Wireless Telephone and Telegraph Company report on instruments and accessories in situ at government and demonstration stations."[41] In those formal reports he described in great technical detail his growing network of stations, for example:

> Mare Island: Janke-Herrold radiotelephone set, six-spark oscillation generator in glass lined, water jacketed barrel. Provided with automatic system in which each set of moveable tubular carbon electrodes is separately lifted by a solenoid and separately adjusted by hand screw and jamb-nut.[42]

C. D. HERROLD.

MAGNETIC LIFT FOR ELECTRODES IN ELECTRIC OSCILLATORS.

APPLICATION FILED MAY 7, 1913.

1,120,306. Patented Dec. 8, 1914.

2 SHEETS—SHEET 1.

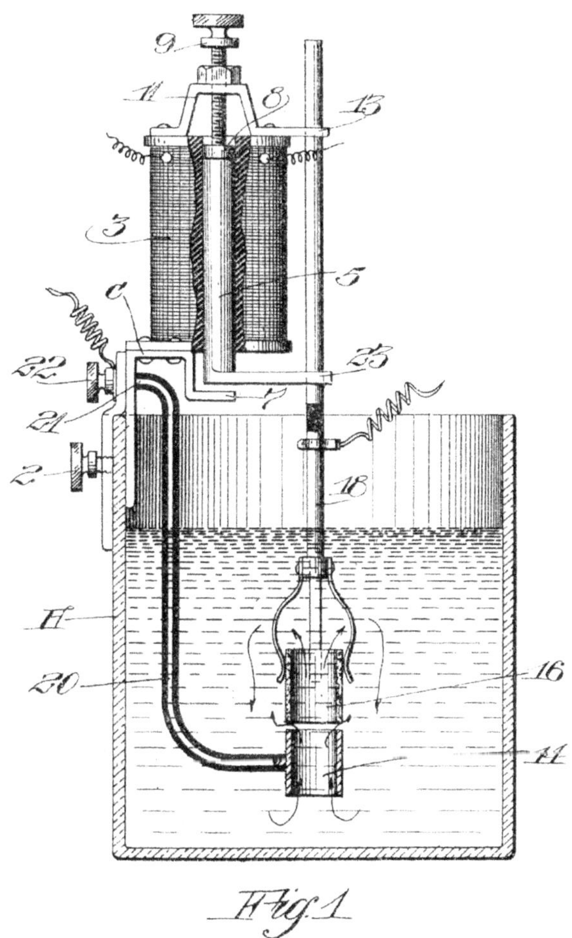

WITNESSES:

Thos Castberg

R. S. Berry

INVENTOR

Charles D. Herrold.

BY G. H. Strong.

His ATTORNEY

One of several arc patents, granted December 8, 1914 (Clark Papers, Smithsonian Institution).

C. D. HERROLD.
OSCILLATOR.
APPLICATION FILED OCT. 20, 1915.

1,222,761. Patented Apr. 17, 1917.
2 SHEETS—SHEET 1.

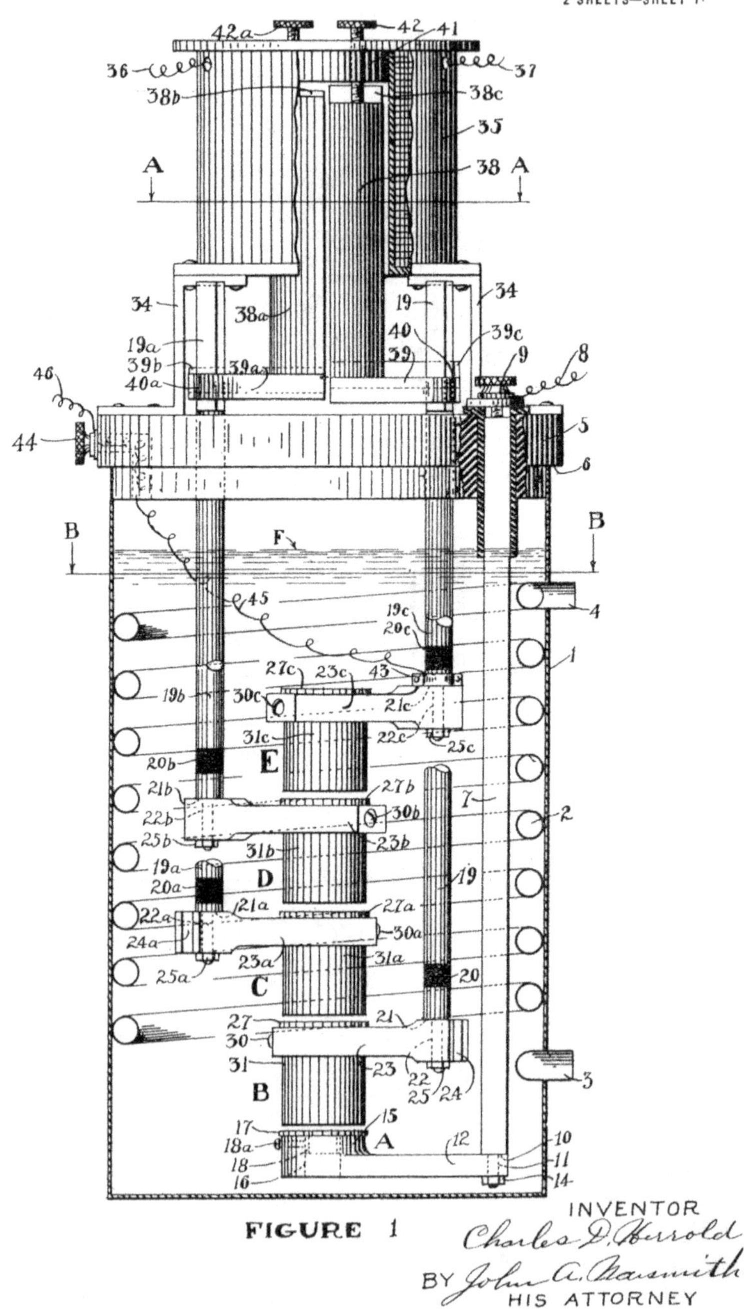

One of several arc patents, granted April 17, 1917 (Clark Papers, Smithsonian Institution).

Herrold at Berkeley

It is difficult during this time to separate Herrold the inventor from Herrold the businessman from Herrold the professor. Whether in his role as chief engineer for the NWT&T or as director of his college radio station, throughout the year Herrold was on the air daily, testing equipment, asking for listener response and trying to improve the quality of his voice and music.[43] On the Berkeley campus of the University of California, which was 50 miles away, students reported listening in on Herrold's "telephone talk through the air from San Jose to Point Arguello, a distance of 300 miles. Prof. Charles Herrold, who accomplished this communication, claims that it is the longest distance the wireless telephone as yet has successfully spanned."[44] Although this was not broadcasting, it attracted an audience anyway because Berkeley students were curious to learn how Herrold was trying to improve two-way wireless telephone communication.[45] According to a story in the *Electrical Experimenter*:

> Professor Herrold is leading a corps of students in the development of wireless telephony, which is counted upon to have highly practical value. Communication between vessels on the Pacific and the shore may be carried further through the ordinary telephone service, so that a person on board ship may presently be able to call up a home telephone through an exchange equipped with both wire and wireless instruments. From the roof of the bank building in San Jose, where he made the record length of talk through the air, talk with Honolulu is a nightly event.[46]

But would the "arc fone" ever be good enough to replace the wired system for land-based conversations, or adequate enough to supplement the wireless telegraph for ship to shore communication? It was in that context that Herrold asked engineer James Hestwood to evaluate the arc fone and communicate the results to the NWT&T. Hestwood's report read:

> I was requested by Professor Chas. D. Herrold to make a statement to your company in regards to some measurements I recently made on your wireless telephone outfit at the San Jose station. I measured the wavelength of the San Jose station and found it to be 763 meters very sharp and pure, with no harmonics. I find that the voice during the last month has been coming in clearly from the San Jose station and comparatively free of arc noises. This I consider very remarkable from the fact that we are located only one and one half miles from the above-mentioned station. So sharp is the wave that only 3/100 (.03) of one inch on my wave meter slide suffices to cut out the sounds.[47]

During 1913, Cohen, Davis and the NWT&T attorneys worked with Charles Herrold in order that all the pieces he had designed and assembled for the "arc fone" would be protected by government patent. This is where the inventor's life began to get complicated. True, Herrold had now proved that his was a viable and dependable system. On this point there was little disagreement. By that time there were hundreds, if not thousands, of San Francisco Bay Area amateur and commercial wireless operators who could hear not only the San Jose station but also Herrold's NWT&T stations testing from the Fairmont Hotel and Mare Island.[48] But the novelty of the transmissions was now giving way to business and legal realities. No longer was this just a fun device to entertain the rapidly growing audiences of students and local amateurs. Herrold had to make a serious attempt to legally protect his radiotelephone system.

Which Arc to Use? Conflict Begins

Charles Herrold was a well-known and respected professor and broadcaster in San Jose and Santa Clara County at the time he joined the National Wireless Telephone and Telegraph Company in 1912. He was running a successful college and radio station, and appeared to be starting a promising business career with his new inventions. But behind the scenes, signs of rancor and misunderstanding were beginning to develop between him and his investors. It was one thing to build the "arc fone" and put it on the air. Defining it and differentiating it from the arc systems of Poulsen and others for the NWT&T's patent lawyers was quite another matter. And it was not just a single patent that covered the entire NWT&T system. Every unique piece would have to be looked at in minute detail. Every coil, every condenser, every arc, every microphone. How did an inventor prove to the government that this piece or that was really his? How did he differentiate his system from other wireless technology patents, of which there were many? And by disclosing to NWT&T how to manufacture and operate the Herrold "fone," what prevented them from challenging his patents and casting him aside? As questions like these arose, what began as a mutually beneficial relationship soon turned into a tenuous and strained relationship between Herrold and the NWT&T Board and certain of its stockholders. In the end, Herrold resigned and took the company into court, claiming he was owed back wages.[49]

While Herrold had been given the title of chief engineer, he was still an independent contractor and the sole owner of his "oscillating" arc fone. In order to document what he was doing and negate some of misunderstandings so common between inventors and their backers, Herrold began keeping meticulous records. He wrote letters, generated reports, and submitted notarized statements on every tiny observation and change in the arc fone. He traveled to Oakland to see a competing system by the Golden brothers. In his assessment of their work, Herrold wrote that they were "using the fundamental principle of the NWT&T's system, namely, an oscillating spark in liquid. The instrument, as installed, is an ingenious mechanical method of control of the oscillating system, and, as such, has merit. I would recommend a further investigation and a demonstration."[50]

In 1913 an application was made for a patent on the first and most important piece of Herrold's transmitter. But Alfred H. Cohen, the major NWT&T stockholder and the man who would emerge as Herrold's nemesis, was beginning to insist that other board members look closely at Herrold's science. He controlled the money and he asked numerous technical questions. Over time Herrold came to suspect that Cohen was not sincerely seeking information but looking for a way to take over the system and squeeze the inventor out. Whether or not Cohen's motives were ulterior, Herrold was forced to answer Cohen's charges, defend his technology and explain in detail how it differed from other systems tried by the company prior to Herrold's employment as its technical expert. Responding to questions, Herrold wrote:

> Why is it that the San Luis Obispo station comes in at our mountain station louder than PH [the Marconi station] with much less energy and further away? I refer him [Cohen] to Nikola Tesla on stationary waves, Hertz on the same, and Marconi and Fleming on "directivity." I have not the time to go into the directive effect of the bent L antenna, but have traced the curves of the three types some time ago and have them on file here.[51]

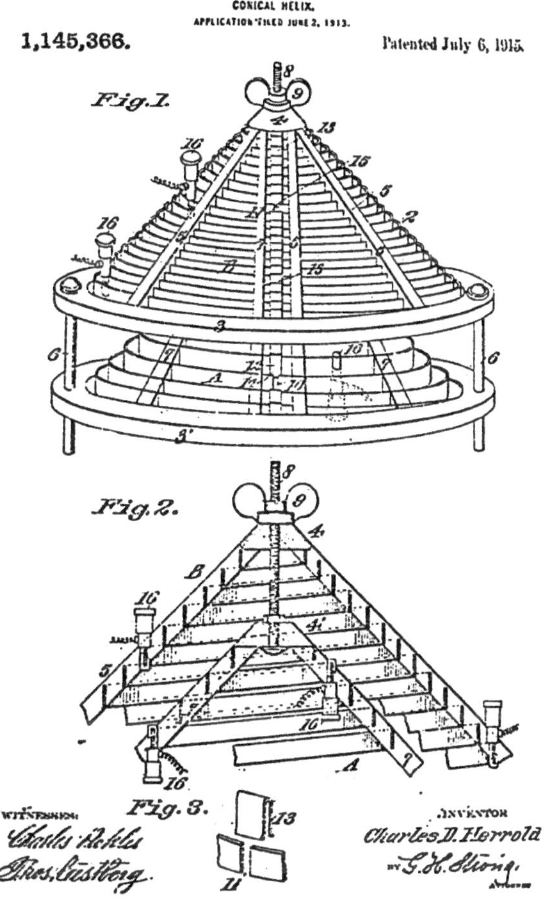

Patent for conical helix antenna, granted July 6, 1915 (Clark Papers, Smithsonian Institution).

Herrold attached to that same letter several pages of mathematical computations, titled "Calculations of lengths of principal waves emitted from a coupled system with gradually increasing coupling coefficients, with damping decrements placed opposite."[52] While Herrold was not a fully trained engineer like de Forest and Fessenden, and while many believed him to have been more of a technician than a qualified scientist, he seemed to have mastered sufficient theory and knowledge to stand up to any interrogator. Clearly Herrold was losing patience with Cohen:

> I shall probably forget the seniority of the author [Cohen] and in somewhat ruthless fashion practice a little vivisection on its text and meaning, introducing errata at all points where necessary. If he, in criticizing the work done at this station, was influenced by a learned analysis of the wireless telephone, then why did he give me pages of references to the wireless telegraph to support his contention on the fone?[53]

Now satisfied that he had properly responded to the concerns of Cohen, Herrold began to gather together a series of notarized statements to offer in defense of his work. He believed that there was a possibility that the NWT&T might not treat him fairly, and if a major disagreement developed, he would have summaries of his work in a quasi-legal format. He described his oscillator as a "wireless telephone system employing oscillating spark or arc,"[54] and he devoted several dozen pages to

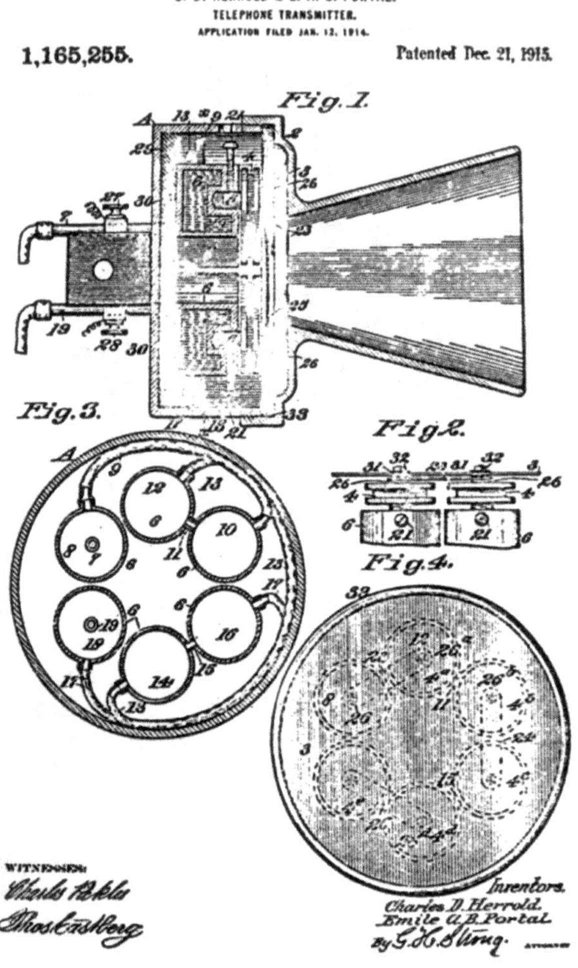

Patent for water-cooled microphone, granted December 21, 1915 (Clark Papers, Smithsonian Institution).

every tiny part of his arc fone: magnetic lifts, conical antenna coils, a condenser using air as a dielectric, a system of double grounds, automatic arc switching, tubular carbon elements, and more. He began to further fortify his claims of having invented an original arc transmitter, saying, "I designed my first set near the end of June 1912."[55] He even asked NWT&T director J.B. Young to generate a notarized statement in his behalf, which contended that Herrold was "the first man to actually put in operation at any of the stations of the National Wireless Telephone and Telegraph Co., a wireless set."[56] There was dissension within the NWT&T. Cohen, the majority stockholder, for reasons unknown became increasingly hostile to Herrold, while Young, less powerful but one of the directors, remained sympathetic to him.

Going to Court

Getting patents took time. With the help of lawyers, Herrold now began submitting applications to the U.S. Patent Office for the wireless telephone he had invented in 1912. Although Herrold believed he had designed and put into operation a unique and original "wireless fone," there is no evidence he applied for any patents before the spring of 1913.[57] The process was extremely slow. From start to finish, it took more than four years. His most important patents were issued between 1914 and 1917. Out of dozens applied for, five patents were actually obtained. Only one patent was issued jointly.[58] The other four went to Herrold alone. It was obvious that neither the company's radio engineering head nor its major shareholder trusted the other. As the records now show:

> There were to be made voluminous reports to the company so that in the event of anything happening to Herrold the work could go on without delay. Cohen attempted to hold up the company by going into the patent office several days before Herrold with a broad claim on a device which had been in use on company instruments for at least four months. Herrold offered to give this patent to the company if Cohen would eliminate the broad claim.[59]

Claims, counterclaims, patent rights and competing personalities within the company caused the relationship between Herrold and NWT&T to go from bad to worse. It ended in court.[60]

By the time winter arrived in 1913, Herrold was feeling completely out in the cold. He saw no future in a company dominated by Alfred Cohen, who was continually questioning everything the chief engineer was trying to do. Constantly frustrated by this man and the clique who supported him, Herrold decided to resign. In quitting NWT&T, Herrold also initiated a suit for damages, demanding back wages for work already performed. Herrold had more than one grievance with NWT&T. Not only did Herrold feel that he was laboring long hours without adequate pay, but he was irritated by the constant taunting of the company's major stockholder, Alfred Cohen. Their relationship broke apart over the so-called "Golden matter." Wireless developer Frank Golden had been dealing with NWT&T over a wireless telephone system for a long time. The Golden brothers of Oakland had originally approached the NWT&T in 1912 and had a system they thought the company should adopt. That is, until Herrold came along. As one of Herrold's first duties as chief engineer, he was asked to evaluate the Golden system. He found it less than satisfactory and his recommendation to the company was "that you make a settlement with the Goldens, getting from them such an agreement that will absolutely and for all time remove them from the field as competitors of the National Wireless Telephone and Telegraph Company."[61] Herrold went on to explain how the Golden transmitter suffered because of "weak radiation" and "poor enunciation," and that he had tried its system and discarded it. This report advocated settlement but was not accepted by the NWT&T Board. After their split, the company still had to associate itself with Herrold to protect a shared interest. They filed an application together on April 1914 seeking patent protection for the original "Oscillating Sparks in Liquid" and it was granted to them jointly one year later.

Herrold had become increasingly uncomfortable trying to work in a company which made him so subordinate and whose final decisions always seemed to put capital above science. He had served as chief engineer of the company for not quite two years when he severed his relationship.[62] But clearly, he was not pleased with the fact that adversarial relationships had developed:

> It has been a theory of mine that internal friction in any organization as in any machine is so much lost power, and it is my heartiest wish that the old sores in the side of the "National" be healed and the most cordial relations maintained ... the success of "National Fone" is above the interests of any one man.[63]

Bitter Parting

On October 28, 1913, an extraordinary conversation occurred at a San Jose restaurant among company directors Davis and Ruegg, a San Jose judge named Hayden, and two Herrolds, father and son. At issue was whether Frank Golden and others were going to go ahead with a planned four million dollar investment after an unfavorable report on their plans made by Herrold.[64] Golden had money to invest in new wireless technology, but he got upset when Herrold evaluated the technology they proposed to use and found it inferior. William Herrold took notes at the meeting:

> Frank Golden's ultimatum was that he would not furnish any more money unless Herrold was eliminated as Chief Engineer. Davis, Hayden and Ruegg all said Herrold was perfectly satisfactory to them and that they wanted to keep him. But the question is how are we going to raise the money? Charles said that for the good of the company and to relieve the situation I will resign as Engineer of the company if you will give up my contract as demonstrator.[65] Mr. Davis said emphatically I will never consent to that. Each one of the members of the board present expressed satisfaction with the work done by Chas. D. Herrold. Someone remarked that if he resigned now he could be taken back later.[66]

The relationship ended anyway. Owing to a combination of misunderstandings, personal squabbles and claims for compensation not received, Herrold left the NWT&T by the end of 1913, filing his suit in December of that year. He was replaced as chief engineer by William Hanscomb. In early January 1914, Hanscomb notified the Directors of NWT&T that he would write to the U.S. Radio Inspector to have the company name removed from Herrold's San Jose station license: "Please be advised that the application for a license for the San Jose station of the National Wireless Telephone and Telegraph Company, filed about December 4, 1912, is to be canceled as the station is no longer the property of the company but has been turned over to Mr. Charles D. Herrold, formerly chief engineer of the company, but no longer connected with it."[67] Hanscomb acted swiftly to end Herrold's influence with the NWT&T. He wrote to Herrold assistant Frank Schmidt, asking him to go to Point Arguello to dismantle the arc station there and return it to the company. Replied Schmidt, "Arguello is hard to ship from there. We must go to Lompoc to get team to haul set to freight depot and if we must make two trips it will cost 10.00 per trip for it is an out of way place. To do hauling it takes four horse team to haul through the sand hills."[68] The Mare Island station was also dismantled under orders of the new chief.

A Day in Court

Built in 1866, the Santa Clara County Superior Court building still stands tall and resplendent in downtown San Jose, its Greek columns reminding visitors that law has carried weight for a long time. Charles and his father must have walked all the way from home on that day in December 1913. It was five blocks from the Herrold family home to the court, where a complaint in the form of a civil suit for money owed was filed. For the next year and a half it would be known as *Herrold v. NWT&T*, or case number 21282.[69] Plaintiff Charles Herrold was suing the corporation—NWT&T—and its major stockholders, who in addition to Cohen included T.H. Yarnell, L. Seidenberg and W.M. Herrold. Yes, it technically put Herrold the son on the side opposite Herrold the father. Bizarre, to be sure, but in an earlier attempt to shore up the company in which his son was then employed, the senior Herrold is said to have purchased 80,000 shares of NWT&T stock, which made him the third largest shareholder. This unusual situation was further complicated by what would prove to be an expensive and acrimonious trial, but one that Charles hoped would be a vindication for all his hard work on the arc fone. The NWT&T saw it strictly as a business contract issue, but more disinterested observers could see it otherwise. This trial was not about science or the invention of the radiotelephone as much as it was about a disagreement among strong personalities. And although Herrold would call many witnesses and argue emotionally about his time spent in the laboratory on behalf of the NWT&T, in the mind of the court, the case was going to turn on a simple contract between an inventor and a company.

Since Herrold's complaint was composed of two parts and the dispute was over money, a modern-day reader needs to realize the sums involved were substantial for their day.[70] First, under his contract with NWT&T, he asserted, the company owed him back wages for one month plus interest, which amounted to $120. Second, he said, the company owed him $5,484.50 for all the services and materials he had provided NWT&T in improving the radiotelephone. Of that total, he claimed, $5,000 represented the extra labor he spent on the arc fone. Altogether Herrold demanded $5,604.50, plus all the court costs, to settle his grievances. In response, the company claimed it only owed Herrold $429.50, which they had offered to Herrold but he refused to accept, saying it was not enough. NWT&T based its defense on the terms of the original contract, signed June 22, 1912, which stated it had agreed "[1] to pay Herrold $100 per month to operate and demonstrate his wireless; [2] to protect the secrecy of his wireless equipment, keeping the system safe under 'lock and key'; [3] to put all patents in Herrold's name, making them his property; and [4] to pay for his patenting inventions, allowing the company the option to buy the rights from Herrold at a price set by an independent arbitrator."[71] This court case would narrowly focus only on the extra money that Herrold believed was due him.

In February 1913 the NWT&T filed a motion for a change of venue from San Jose to San Francisco. The company claimed that all their witnesses, major stockholders, papers and business offices were in San Francisco. Herrold answered, claiming that he performed all work for them in his San Jose laboratories and that it would be impossible to transport the "arc fone" to San Francisco as an exhibit in a trial. He also claimed that his father, William Herrold, had 80,000 shares of NWT&T stock and that there were more stockholders residing in Santa Clara County than elsewhere. He also claimed that William Herrold would pay for the litigation because the plaintiff was without funds and therefore could not afford the change of venue anyway. Charles further claimed that all his witnesses resided in Santa Clara County, and he listed in his answer forty-five names, among them Sanders, Schmidt, and Portal. The NWT&T countered Herrold's claim concerning his father's ownership of stock, saying that according to the company books he really owned only 8,500 shares and was not a major stockholder and the claim "that Herrold is the owner of 80,000 shares of said capital stock was made solely for the purpose of making it appear that he is a large stockholder in said corporation ... that W.M. Herrold was not in good faith made a defendant in this action but was made such for the sole purpose of having this action tried in the Superior Court of said Santa Clara County."[72] Nevertheless, the NWT&T change of venue request was denied and the trial remained in San Jose.

Witnesses Called

There was one major witness who would not be available for trial. Victor Anzini was an 18-year-old Marconi operator who operated the NWT&T's Fairmont Hotel station at the time of Herrold's employment with the company. As Anzini was about to leave for Australia and the plaintiff needed his testimony, he gave depositions for attorneys on both sides during February 1914. Anzini was typical of the wireless operators of the day. At the age of fifteen he attended Herrold College and a Marconi school for wireless operators. After serving on the steamship *Ventura* at the young age of sixteen, he was employed by the NWT&T to run the Fairmont station. From late in 1912 to early in 1913, Anzini worked closely with his former professor in an attempt to improve the "arc fone" for the NWT&T. He recounted in his deposition that while at the Fairmont, he received daily messages from Herrold in San Jose: "The telephone, about one month after I worked at the Fairmont, was improved at the San Jose end. Part of the improvement was due to a new aerial and also to the development of a new oscillator by Mr. Herrold. As to the improvement of the oscillator the increase was noted fairly, and I would say it was considerably increased as to constancy and distinctness."[73]

Other witnesses for the plaintiff continued testimony that Herrold was making small, incremental improvements to the device.[74] Other technical people testified for the company. The trial was noted in the local newspaper, which reported:

> William W. Hanscomb, who is now the chief engineer of the National Wireless Telephone and Telegraph company, having succeeded Charles D. Herrold, testified yesterday afternoon ... that most of the improvements made by Herrold were ultimately abandoned by the company. A night session of the court was held so Mr. Hanscomb would be able to get back to San Francisco in time for work this morning. Hanscomb was put on the stand by L. Seidenberg, attorney for the company, and was cross-examined by E.M. Rea, attorney for the plaintiff.[75]

Although witnesses on both sides presented plenty of technical evidence, it was clear from the beginning that the only real issue was the compensation due Herrold. And while the company looked upon their contracted relationship as a simple one, Herrold saw his agreement with NWT&T in the much larger context of the invention of a successful system of wireless telephone. He foresaw radio's future development as a great industry, in explaining why he was so interested:

> I am enthusiastic over the phone as there is a great field open before us. You will find that after the demonstrating period of the phone is past we will go into the field to build an impregnable monopoly. You have a phone that can be depended upon to do some things that no other phone will do: (1) perfect simplicity of control; (2) perfectly undamped electric wave trains; freedom from sizzling and frying common to ordinary wireless phones. The poor wireless has been in the hands of unscrupulous promoters, so let us see to it that we keep this great phone on the proper basis.[76]

It was clear that Herrold had read more into the importance of his invention and his relationship with NWT&T than did the company. Herrold claimed he continued to make improvements during the contracted period, and communicated those improvements in writing. Considering the fact he hoped to profit from his inventions, Charles Herrold's paper trail seems to have numerous strengths and weaknesses during his inventing years. Perhaps the gaps exist through inadvertence. Herrold said in later years that he lost valuable records and photographs in a fire and that other documents loaned to a wireless researcher doing a book were never returned.

A Losing Fight

Charles Herrold believed he could win this case because he was known to be an honest man. His reputation was beyond reproach. He had won the respect and gratitude of nearly everyone who knew him throughout the greater San Jose area, especially associates in his work and the students he taught in college. But appealing to people's better nature and common humanity as the basis for a settlement, which was Herrold's final plea, had little or no weight in a court of law and certainly none in the competitive arena of the marketplace. Nevertheless, Herrold the dreamer and dedicated scientist tried to reach an equitable settlement based on fairness and logic, despite the fact such terms did not appear in the original contract. Herrold's final appeal was to the company's better nature, which he expressed as follows:

> I am happy to serve you in any way that is possible. I have been averaging 14 hours per day including Sundays for 7 weeks, and for ten days averaged 16 hours per day. I have given my whole time and attention to your work. I am going to let my school go, so as to give all my time to engineering work connected with the NWT&T. I would appreciate it very much if you would sign over to me at this time a modest little block of stock, say 15,000 shares or more, if it should suit your generosity. You should know that rent $35, power $3, two boys, one of them practically all day, besides all running expenses and personal expenses come out of the $100.00 that I receive from this company for demonstrating the phone.[77]

The company replied that the "board has no power to dispose of stock in payment of labor."[78] To Herrold's chagrin, the company used his letter against him. It was suggested that Herrold's real motive was simply to gain for himself a "block of stock." The appeal injured his reputation rather than enhanced it. Charles Herrold was seen to be naive in matters of business and the law.

Judge Gosbey considered the evidence and issued his final opinion on June 7,

1915. Siding with the company on purely contractual issues, he ordered NWT&T to pay the amount they originally agreed that they owed to Herrold, which was $429.50. The determining legal basis for the judge's decision on Herrold's suit for compensation owed may have been in Herrold's own words: "I have no complaint to make at all regarding salary: I am merely counting on the future of this company, and trusting that in return for tangible results and faithful service I will be generously rewarded."[79] Herrold had hoped and trusted but he didn't get it in writing. The judge stated that Herrold did not formally request additional compensation and that he was only entitled to the contracted amount. Although Herrold asserted, "I am working day and night through the month without stop except to eat and sleep," the terms of the contract with NWT&T allowed him only $100.00 per month, no matter the extra hours and sacrifice. Judge Gosbey had no choice but to conclude:

> It is the opinion of the Court, from the correspondence had between the parties, the evidence produced at the trial, the demands of plaintiff, the answers by the defendant, and the actions of the plaintiff during the entire time of his employment by the defendant, that he is not entitled to any compensation for his services as engineer of said company.[80]

The case was dismissed. Herrold had lost more than money and what he had believed to be the greater moral argument. It was a disappointing ending to his relationship with NWT&T.[81]

Lessons Learned

Undoubtedly there was in Herrold a certain naiveté, which left him not fully grasping everything he needed to know about both the technology and the business of wireless. As an inventor, Herrold was a man who in many ways would have benefited from exposure to the rigors of a first rate graduate school. The two decades between 1900 and 1920 were peopled by formally educated men like Reginald Fessenden and Lee de Forest, and graduate engineers like Valdemar Poulsen and Cyril F. Elwell, serious inventors who followed scientific method, wrote down their experiments and communicated their results with other scholars using scholarly publications. Charles Herrold was an engineering dropout who in later years allowed himself the titles "doctor" and "B.S.E.E."[82] The evidence suggests that unlike his more successful peers, Herrold was remiss in failing to follow and apply the traditional tenets of science and invention as well as basic lessons from the field of business. It's incomprehensible why Herrold as "independent contractor" allowed a private company to have free use of his technology without adequate compensation at the outset. Perhaps he hoped future profits would eventually accrue by interesting the company in the sale and development of his technology. Instead of leasing his proved and unique technology to the company, however, he took a monthly salary as a paid "demonstrator" and agreed to be the company's "chief engineer" in showing them how it worked. This meant he agreed to tell them all they needed to know to copy, manufacture and operate the Herrold radiotelephone while he was still in the process of seeking patent protection. If an explorer on the frontiers of knowledge announced that he has found something of value, he would be well advised to have the shield of law as well as the sword of truth if he hopes to profit from it. Of these, Herrold the teacher, inventor and entrepreneur had only one. In a Hobbsean world, having a sword is not enough.[83] To survive, a man also must have a Locke-type shield of a social contract.[84]

5
Evolution of a Broadcaster

> *The first radio in my family was a crystal set that my Uncle Ivan gave me for my birthday. It consisted of … a numbered wood tuning dial and a tiny piece of quartz crystal.… You whirled the dial which turned the condenser and music came into your ears.… It was my set but my mother and dad would occasionally slip on the earphones and listen to the new wonder.*
>
> Jerry Flamm, *Good Life in Hard Times*[1]

When radio became a popular pastime in America, a single word was already in use to describe the new medium. That word was "radio." It originally came from radiotelephone, which was aimed principally at transmitting voice. But a more descriptive word, broadcasting, came alongside it to clarify the fact this was not strictly communication from person to person. It was understood to mean that you were reaching a great, wide audience, scattered in all directions. According to a common dictionary definition, a farmer was broadcasting when he sowed seeds in every direction. Thus the term was familiar in 1922 when Hugo Gernsback, the editor of a national radio magazine, decided to explain its new meaning and authoritatively wrote, "By modern broadcasting is understood a radio intelligence that is sent out at a certain pre-determined schedule or program."[2]

When, many years later, RCA writer-archivist George H. Clark considered the question of how to define broadcasting, he decided that a broadcaster had to have scheduled, pre-announced, publicly advertised programs directed to a "citizen audience." The problem with this definition is that it left out everybody before 1920 who didn't have radio receivers.[3] Since the United States had about 125,000 amateur wireless listeners before World War I, that definition made it impossible to conceive of any radio listeners in the early days. The manufacturing and sale of radios on a large scale didn't occur till the mid–1920s. And while Clark was but a single individual, his definition was adopted by Gleason L. Archer, whose 1938 *History of Radio to 1926* dominated radio history scholarship for several decades. His opinion was challenged years later by deeper and more inclusive research by Erik Barnouw, plainly evident

Famous photograph of Charles Herrold's San Jose radio station as it looked in 1912–13. Control room operators Ken Sanders and Emil Portal are using a water-cooled microphone and windup phonograph to broadcast to West Coast listeners. Charles Herrold supervises, standing under the doorway with a slide rule, while technician Frank Schmidt monitors equipment (courtesy Perham Foundation Electronics Museum).

in his several landmark histories, and the equally authoritative work of broadcast historian Christopher Sterling. If amateurs, experimenters or hobbyists could not be counted as "audience," as Clark said, how does one classify the average citizen for whom Charles Herrold loaned or built a radio for the purpose of listening? This is what he did in 1913, telling readers of the *San Jose Times Star*, for example, "If any boy of your home possesses a wireless telegraph outfit, ask any of them to permit you to listen any night between 9 and 9:30 o'clock and you can hear my station experimenting with the wireless telephone."[4]

While Charles Herrold began experimenting to perfect a radiotelephone in 1909 and was making test transmissions every day, it took him nearly three years to be fully prepared for regular broadcasting. What led him to finally commence regular programming from his college were several factors: first, it really couldn't happen until he had perfected an "arc phone" having a steady, pure signal capable of carrying voice and music without interruption; and second, during the very early years of his experimentation when testing with phonograph recordings, he learned to his surprise there was considerable interest in "voice and music" from his listeners. Discovering that he had an audience of young boys and that they could be encouraged to come to his wireless school, Herrold began transmitting at times when they could tune in. What led him finally to go on a regular schedule in 1912 to serve the general public had its inspiration two years earlier.[5]

A seemingly innocent statement in a wireless parts advertisement, coming as it did in 1910, ranks as one of the rarest and earliest pieces of evidence that Herrold learned from point-to-point communication that broadcasting to an audience was worthwhile. We know when this happened because Herrold published a notarized statement saying, "We have been giving wireless phonograph concerts to amateur men in the Santa Clara Valley." This announcement, appearing in an early 1910 New York publication of the Electro-Importing Company, qualifies it as the earliest and most prophetic statement in the national public record descriptive of what broadcasting was to become.[6] It was entertainment. It was aimed at an audience. It was transmitted regularly. Not Fessenden, not de Forest, not anyone else engaged in wireless telephony was saying about their transmissions and listeners anything close to resembling what Herrold was saying. Of course, Herrold's 1910 "concerts" were aimed mostly at young boys listening for the code on their wireless receivers and they could hardly be considered a citizen audience. But it encouraged Herrold to think about seeking a larger, more general audience. By 1912, he was deliberately trying to widen and enlarge his listenership, advocating that neighbors ask amateurs to let them listen on their crystal sets. Thus Herrold not only was a practitioner, but also an exponent of broadcasting during the pre-war years, 1912–1917, the highlight being his "music concerts" to the public at the San Francisco World's Fair in 1915.

The Evolution of Broadcasting

Published reports and interviews with former students indicate that beginning in 1909 there were experimental musical and voice transmissions coming from the Herrold College every day. One of the students was Simpson Reinhard, who remembered starting classes that year and participating in some of Herrold's earliest broadcasting. He recalled:

> I first became associated with Prof. Herrold in 1909. The reason I remember that is because I attended Heald's College at Second and San Fernando streets in the mornings and would go to the Garden City Bank Bldg., "Herrold's Ham Factory," we called it, in the afternoon. He taught wireless and … had the boys construct both transmitting and receiving sets.… Prof. Herrold tried to get over the air [with] both wireless and voice.… It was Bill Erich who first suggested that I try playing my violin over the air. I cannot remember the exact date but know it was either in late 1909 or early 1910.…[7]

We learn from the Electro Importing Catalogue that the Herrold radiotelephone in San Jose was providing "wireless concerts for amateur men" in 1910 and had a schedule by 1912, according to laboratory assistant Ray Newby, who says their station was broadcasting to more than a handful of listeners. "It was a religion for 'Prof'

Herrold to have his equipment ready every Wednesday night at nine o'clock. He would have his records ready, all laid out, and what he wanted to say. And the public or listeners, it became a habit for them to wait for it," Newby said.[8] What we're being told by Newby and confirmed by other witnesses of that time is that Herrold had the first regularly scheduled radio broadcasts of entertainment programming for an audience.[9] Said Newby, "We even had a San Jose music store that supplied us records, of course free of charge, and I think we played them all. We would take the *Mercury*, the *Mercury-Herald* in San Jose, and we would read headlines and discuss them a little bit, just something to yak about and make it interesting at the same time, to develop an audience, I would say."[10]

The major significance of Herrold's accomplishment is that he, before anyone else, began the transmission of regularly scheduled programs of entertainment and information for an audience. All the evidence points to the fact that San Jose had the world's first regularly scheduled broadcasting station in 1912.

Herrold Attracts an Audience

What happened to bring about broadcasting between 1909 and 1912 was evolutionary. No one, not even Herrold, simply woke up one morning and said: "Let's broadcast to the public." It happened gradually, so slowly that even a major San Jose newspaper failed to see its significance until educated by a demonstration at Herrold College itself. The press, like most of the public, continued to see the radiotelephone as a replacement for the wired telephone. Stories published in the *San Jose Mercury-Herald* show why most people didn't see the future of the wireless telephone in the way that Charles Herrold did. Three months after the *Titanic* sank, the main purpose of the wireless phone was still considered merely for two-way communication, as evidenced by this July 8, 1912, editorial:

> It would be possible with five wireless telephone stations, costing not more than $10,000 each, scattered along the Atlantic coast, to have telephone communication with every ship within 1000 miles of the shore. If this astounding discovery be indeed what is asserted, there need never again be such a disaster as shocked the world last April.[11]

Obviously, it was the sinking of the *Titanic*, with its great loss of life, that influenced the thinking and set the practical agenda for the new invention.

Few people outside of California knew or heard what was happening "on the air" in San Jose, but the innovation with which Herrold was using his radio waves in 1912 was taking radiotelephone away from person to person communication toward a regular broadcasting station. As though to enlighten those who had read the *San Jose Mercury-Herald*'s story praising point-to-point communication ten days earlier, Charles Herrold in the July 22 edition told readers how he was using his wireless telephone in an entirely different way.[12] Herrold and assistant Emil Portal demonstrated to a reporter how the San Jose station was engaged in "broadcasting." The reporter wrote:

> For more than two hours they conducted a concert in Mr. Herrold's office in the Garden City Bank building, which was heard for many miles around. The music was played on a phonograph furnished by the Wiley B. Allen Music company. Reports from amateurs around the valley came in to Portal, who solicited their requests for records.[13]

What Herrold began doing on the air in 1910 continued to attract widespread interest from listeners in 1912. Whether accidentally or on purpose, this operation at Herrold College was like our modern-day radio stations, seeking and catering to an audience. While Herrold's original motive, as described in the earlier editorial, was to invent a successful system of two-way radiotelephony and thereby profit from its manufacture, he finally came to value something else — the benefits of publicity and advertising which came from broadcasting to an audience regularly. While at the start he used music and talk as a way to test his system, he soon realized it was attracting students to his school. Years later, Herrold acknowledged that his idea of transmitting entertainment on a schedule gradually evolved from his daily testing. He learned from his experimentation that he had developed a loyal audience which wanted him to continue. He said, "Broadcasting was an obsession with us and certainly, the entire Pacific Coast looked upon the radio broadcasts from San Jose as an established institution."[14]

Herrold and his assistant Frank Schmidt operate a small wireless phone device about 1912. Schmidt was the "mechanician" who fabricated working prototype devices from the inventor's drawings in preparation for patenting (courtesy Perham Foundation Electronics Museum).

What Newby Remembered

Closer to the action than station listeners was Herrold's assistant, Ray Newby. Appearing as a guest on the 1950s CBS television show *What's My Line*, Newby signed in as the "world's first disc jockey." Later he described a typical 1912 broadcast:

> In general we would just ad lib and play a record like you would today, more or less. We would read the newspaper headlines and carry on with whatever came into the mind that you would think would be important. We had the old Caruso records. Many a time we'd sing with the records at the old bank building. We had musical instruments come in, such as a harp. We had a lady play a harp one time and she was a little disturbed by the proximity of the microphone. She was afraid of the thing.[15]

This is student Emil Portal on the air with one of the Herrold portable arc devices. An arc like this was assembled by young Robert Stull on the campus of the University of California at Berkeley in 1916 (courtesy Perham Foundation Electronics Museum).

Since the Herrold station was transmitting daily and scheduling programs at least weekly, the question naturally arises, "Who did Newby understand his early audience to be?"

> The listeners were all amateurs who had crystal detectors listening to ships or codes or whatever they could learn and read and find and they were startled to find music coming in on their ears. Oh, they'd call us right up and say put on such and such a record, or play it over and over, certain ones they liked better. And we had callers coming in from around San Jose, even as far as San Francisco. We had listeners within, I'd say, at that time, even in the earliest arc days ... as far away as 900 miles but under very favorable conditions. We had listeners all over the Bay Area.[16]

Broadcasts Confirmed by Others

Further evidence of what the Herrold broadcasts were like is contained in the personal correspondence, patents, newspaper clippings, notarized affidavits and photographs known as the Herrold Papers.[17] When an academic journal expressed interest in the Herrold station and research finally was undertaken to evaluate his "first station" claim for a scholarly paper, everyone connected with the original operation was sought for audio and videotaped information.[18] Interviews by the authors were spread over a period of 34 years, 1958–1992.[19] Among those located were dozens who participated in, witnessed, or listened to the broadcasts. Audience member Joseph Cappa wrote to author Greb in 1959: "By the time I had my crystal set [circa 1912,] 'Prof" put on regular broadcasts on Monday, Wednesday and Friday, 7 P.M. to

10 P.M. schedule."[20] The Vice President of the National Wireless Telephone & Telegraph Company, George Davis, who had Herrold under contract for technical services between 1912 and 1913, and who also was a defendant in a lawsuit instigated by Herrold, nevertheless said: "Chas. D. Herrold was the first to maintain a broadcasting station on a daily schedule."[21] Robert Stull wrote ten years later about the 1912 broadcasts that "continuous daily concerts were given to interest and educate the public."[22] Reinforcing Stull's belief that daily concerts were the equivalent of "broadcasting" is the fact that as late as 1922, popular radio literature used the term "radio concert" rather than "broadcasting" to describe what some few stations did on the air.[23]

In 1915, Stull, a former Herrold student and a University of California at Berkeley electrical engineering major, borrowed equipment from the San Jose station, and demonstrated the radiotelephone by setting it up in the Mechanics Building on the campus. In collaboration with several other electrical engineering students he wrote a paper on it shortly before World War I.[24] Young Stull knew first-hand about broadcasting in San Jose, before and after the war, because he had been with Herrold from the start and later became a business associate of Herrold. Stull said the theory of modulating voice on a radio telephone was unknown "when I did my thesis," adding that "we described our experiences, the construction, the circuitry, the antennae, how the modulation was done, and a few of the technical parts...."[25] Stull earned his electrical engineering degree in 1917. After the war, he became the manager of Herrold Laboratories and radio parts business in 1920, and recalled how Herrold first started broadcasting from the Herrold College between 1910 and 1912: "Ray Newby and I operated the Herrold station on a regular weekly time schedule and if I'm not mistaken, gave the first commercials. Because we plugged the man who allowed us to use his phonograph records for the broadcasts I was probably the first man to make a commercial over the air."[26] Wrote another former student, Terry Hansen: "I remember that voice and music was clear and distinct and that daily broadcasts were made with the transmitter."[27] And from longtime Herrold assistant and former student Emil Portal: "Although there were few receiving stations in 1912, he gave weekly programs of phonograph music from his broadcasting station topping the bank building."[28] Former San Jose City Historian Clyde Arbuckle was there and told author Adams: "Well, he was broadcasting in 1909. That was the year that I started to grammar school. But he was absolutely broadcasting, and he was publicizing his programs in the *San Jose Mercury*."[29]

The Little Hams Program

What clearly defined Herrold as a broadcaster was the use of his station to send out regularly scheduled programs, specifically aimed at entertaining a known public audience. The two events having the most significance were the 1914–1917 weekly *Little Hams Program*, and the 1915 daily broadcasts to the public receiving stations at the Panama Pacific International Exhibition in San Francisco. According to Newby, Herrold believed that after a week of hard work spent on invention and study, both the students and the audience were entitled to some fun: "Every Wednesday night at nine o'clock he would be on because he knew he had fifty or more listeners with crystal detectors to report to him. They'd call up on the phone and ask for records. They'd request or call in or ask what records we had and also we'd yakity yak and sing. I used to sing on it myself. (chuckle) And news. We'd give out news from the *Mercury-Herald*."[30] Eventually, Newby and the students were joined by Herrold's young wife Sybil, who recalled:

> I really believe that I was the first woman to ever broadcast a program. We used to get cards from the little hams asking us to play after we started playing the records for their little programs on Wednesday nights. And I went to Sherman-Clay (a San Jose music store) and arranged to borrow records from them at no cost but just for the sake of advertising these records to these young operators with their little galena sets. And we would play the up-to-date young people's records and they would run down the next day and be sure to buy the one they heard on the radio the night before.[31]

Sybil took requests from listeners, and apparently there were contests and what today is called a promotion. She explained this to author Greb in 1959:

> I would call out and say this was their [the little hams] Wednesday night program. We would ask them if they would come in and sign up their name and where they had their receiving set and we would give a prize away each week, a little piece of

Sybil Herrold holding her baby Robert before the microphone to entertain listeners in 1914. Sybil was "on the air" Wednesday nights between 1914 and 1916, taking requests for records, playing them for an audience of amateur operators she later termed her "little hams." This one-frame image comes from a short 35mm motion picture made at the Herrold station in 1914 (Stephen True Collection).

Charles with his son Robert when the child was not quite five years old (Stephen True Collection).

> galena or a pair of headphones. It would be some part they could add to their receiving set. The little boys would come in from all over the Valley to register for these prizes. That was 1914 or 1915.[32]

The evidence available today indicates that such a novel use of the infant radiotelephone in 1914 was absolutely something that no one had even thought about, a new use for a relatively new medium.

In the 1950s Sybil talked about the "little hams broadcasts" with her grandson, Stephen, who commented:

> I did spend a lot of time talking to my grandmother about Charles Herrold. She always referred to him as Charley. Most everybody else referred to him as Doc. She was quite fascinated with her early life with him in that she had a lot of contact with the radio station particularly in the days when my dad was young, and my grandmother always told me that she was the first female disc jockey, she thought, in the world at least. She would run the station for certain periods of time. What she would do—and I don't know how much of this was her invention to do—she would go to downtown San Jose and borrow the old round wax Victrola discs from Sherman Clay in San Jose. She would take them back and play them over the radio. Sherman Clay loved it because the next day they would sell out of whatever she would play over the radio.[33]

Sherman Clay & Company, the music store at 190–192 South First Street, was easily accessible to Sybil. It was hardly a block away from Herrold's station, upstairs in the Garden City Bank building, located at South First and San Fernando streets. Long time San Jose resident and New Almaden Historic Museum operator Connie Perham remembered talking with Sybil in the 1940s about her days as a radio personality:

> She worked very hard and she was really the first announcer and all in the early wireless. She'd go down one door below in the music house and get the names of the records and she'd play — they'd play them — advertise them.[34]

The Panama-Pacific Exposition of 1915

While the Wednesday night programs were true "local radio," with an audience mostly of young experimenters, it was at another event that the Herrold broadcasting apparatus was placed into service to entertain what probably was their largest public, non-experimenter audience ever. The 1915 Panama-Pacific International Exposition (PPIE), held in San Francisco, was designed to celebrate the opening of the Panama Canal and the rebuilding of the city after the 1906 earthquake. Billed as a "World's Fair," the PPIE featured the very latest technology. Newspapers from all over the country in 1914 began identifying some of the big names in wireless who were expected at the event:

> William Marconi, [*sic*] the wireless inventor, announced today that he had decided to participate in the Italian section of the Panama Pacific International Exhibition [*sic*] at San Francisco. He said he hoped to be able to communicate from the exposition by radiotelephony with all of the states and Canada.[35]

The reporter not only got Guglielmo Marconi's name wrong, but he also failed to understand that the Italian wireless inventor was never much interested in "voice" transmissions. There is no evidence Marconi did anything closely approximating what the story predicted during the course of the 1915 World's Fair.

The true radiotelephone pioneer making plans for the San Francisco World's Fair was Lee de Forest. He had been working off and on at nearby in Palo Alto, was invited by AT&T to participate in its exhibit in the fair's Liberal Arts building, and was eager to show off a major advance he had made in long distance wired telephony. Here was an opportunity to demonstrate the "de Forest Audion amplifier licensed to the American Telephone and Telegraph Company as a telephone relay that made the transcontinental service possible."[36] It had been rumored that a smaller part of the telephone exhibit would be devoted to a demonstration of how de Forest had been able to make his three-element tube, the Audion, oscillate at the radio frequencies necessary for the transmission of voice and music. But when the time came to demonstrate it, this particular de Forest transmitter didn't work. By this quirk of fate, Charles Herrold was given the opportunity to demonstrate what he had been doing for a number of years— to broadcast from his San Jose station to a public audience specially alerted to hear it. Since "de Forest at that time did not have a workable transmitter" to use in San Francisco, Herrold was asked to expand his "concerts" to provide it.[37]

In a radio interview years later Herrold described how in 1915 he participated as a broadcaster at the Panama-Pacific International Exposition:

> At the personal suggestion of Lieutenant Ellery Stone, U.S. Radio Inspector, I carried on a special daily schedule of radiocast music from 6 to 8 hours per day for the World's Fair at San Francisco, California, in 1915. This was received at the radio inspector's booth, also at that of Dr. Lee de Forest, in the Liberal Arts building. The antenna ran up onto the Tower of Jewels. I have the statement of many people who heard this music on the new Ultra-Audion receiving sets of de Forest. There were no other radiotelephones in operation on the Pacific Coast, and it is certain that at this time there was no other broadcasting in the world outside of that from the Herrold Laboratories in San Jose.[38]

The only station announcement made in those days was: "This is the wireless telephone on the Garden City Bank building in San Jose, California."[39] Broadcasts sent out by the San Jose radiotelephone and carried to San Francisco fairgoers were heard at the foot of the Tower of Jewels by Herrold and wife Sybil. She recalled, "I was at the fair with him when he received the programs that our station was putting on here in San Jose. He was anxious to see what the reception was like there. We'd been sending out these things but this was the one time when we got to hear it ourselves."[40]

It must have made quite an impression on Sybil, as she often told the story in later years to her friends and family. Grandson Stephen True recalled:

> What I remember her saying was that people wouldn't believe it, it was so eerie. People wouldn't believe that it was wireless because they'd never heard voice coming over the air before. Not that they hadn't heard phonograph records, but that was a different story, that was right there on the table. And she said people would look in the back of the booth and look under the table because they thought for sure that it was coming from there — somewhere. Or that there were wires coming that they just couldn't see and they had to convince them that it was coming from fifty miles away in San Jose.[41]

In addition to the Tower of Jewels receiving stations, there were several in the Liberal Arts building at the de Forest display. In a 1929 interview, Herrold remembered:

> Dr. Lee de Forest exhibited a radio booth at the exposition but his transmitter was able to operate for only a few minutes at a time and he finally abandoned it and the music received in his booth was furnished during the exposition by the San Jose radio station. These daily broadcasts, the first regular presentation of music and entertainment, brought a flood of letters from amateurs, both young and old.[42]

Many witnesses came forward in later years with their recollections of the fair, including an unidentified person who said:

> During my frequent visits to the Exposition, I became aware that he, Dr. Herrold, was doing what seemed to me phenomenal work in the development of radio or wireless of the character we quite generally called phone transmission. I listened a number of times at the Exposition grounds to what were broadcasts from San Jose, and was dumbfounded to note the clarity and purity of speech and music fully equal to the best then obtainable from the so-called phonograph.[43]

Added Ray Newby:

> We had been broadcasting a long time before the fair started and when the fair opened Dr. Lee de Forest of radio tube fame had his receivers and equipment there. And we had a schedule so that he could listen to the music from San Jose, fifty miles away. It was a daily deal there. That was quite a "first" at that time, 1915. All he could do was receive. And they used the Herrold transmitter to hear fifty miles away at the booth and the public could come in and listen.[44]

Someday the PPIE transmissions of 1915 may be listed in the history books as the first daily broadcasting schedule absolutely designed to entertain a non-technical, non-amateur public audience. Unquestionably, the PPIE broadcasts were for a general public audience. This event was beyond doubt Charles Herrold's most important contribution to the art of broadcasting, one that could have influenced others in a way that is still not entirely understood. What is known is that for the remainder of his life, Herrold continued to single out this yearlong daily event as his most significant contribution to broadcasting for a real public audience:

> If there was any other broadcasting station in the world at that time and if there was any other inventor who had perfected a reliable radio telephone capable of transmitting undistorted music and speech day after day in actual broadcasting, I certainly never heard of such.[45]

The questions might be asked, "If this actually happened, why did it not make the headlines, why was it not publicized? Why did the introduction of 'radio' at the 1915 Fair not get the attention accorded to television at the 1939 World's Fair in New York?" We offer these possible answers. First, even though Herrold was doing it, a few other experimenters were actually using the radiotelephone as a device to entertain and inform, as we would expect it today. It was a local novelty not known nationwide. Second, when television was introduced publicly in 1939, radio as a medium of entertainment was well known.[46] Finally, because a large corporation like RCA decided to introduce TV at the 1939 World's Fair, it was very well advertised and publicized, films were made of Sarnoff's official dedication, and the corporation's formidable public relations department made certain that news of it reached the newspapers and a national audience. It is known that electronic television, as invented by Farnsworth, Zworykin and others, had been around for a decade prior to 1939, yet the public was led to believe RCA introduced it first at the fair. Despite the fact that mechanical TV had been on the air since the late 1920s, the pioneer telecasts received minimal newspaper coverage. Since these early TV audiences were small—like those which had listened to Herrold—few members of the public knew in 1939 that television existed prior to that time.

Herrold Promotes Broadcasting

Apart from Herrold's achievement of broadcasting by radio to the World's Fair in 1915, there is some evidence that, however accidentally, between 1912 and 1917, the San Jose professor was continuously trying to solve a major broadcasting puzzle: How do you create an audience? Herrold believed that the publicity surrounding the Panama-Pacific International Exposition was one way to gain listeners. He knew that if he were on the air regularly, more and more young men and even commercial operators would tune in. Wrote former Herrold student Robert Stull: "A Marconi operator stated that he had danced to our 'wireless' music from San Jose on the deck of a trans-Pacific liner, using a long extension cord on his fones."[47] In a 1940 letter to Lee de Forest, Herrold wrote about where his audience came from:

> My audience was not always made up of amateur wireless telegraph operators. During the period of 1909 to 1917 I trained over 1200 students in the theory and practice of wireless telegraph and telephone. The interesting part is that these students built apparatus and installed sets with which people could listen to the telephone

> music. It was a beginning, and my students were building my audience, and incidentally they were publicizing my school.[48]

Early Herrold biographer and confidante Fred F. Wells described what it was like in those early days when the wireless concerts were introduced to the wives and girlfriends of local experimenters: "Dr. Herrold and his colleague, Mr. Newby, were able to entertain with dance music those having receiving sets. In those days each dancing couple had to use a 20 foot extension cord (for headsets) and the delicate crystal detector was padded with cotton batting so as not to jar out its adjustment."[49] Can you visualize a roomful of couples, obviously dancing very slowly and carefully, each trying to avoid the other's connecting wires? Can you imagine this form of courtship? If this early harbinger of audience use and acceptance is even close to being true, it was no wonder that Charles Herrold was motivated to establish a broadcast station and be on the air every day.

The evidence clearly indicates that between 1912 and 1917 what Herrold was doing met the later criteria of what qualified as "broadcasting." Most historians today would agree that broadcastings is "a radio communication service of transmissions intended to be received directly by the general public."[50] In the text of one story published in 1914 it seems apparent that Herrold was trying to appeal to the non-technical public, the non-wireless parents, friends and neighbors of the local young experimenters. He encouraged them to listen through the boys' wireless sets for his nightly concerts: "Phonograph concerts over the wireless telephone are not all uncommon. You can hear the phonograph as distinctly as if it were placed in the next room to you."[51] As Herrold began seeking a general audience for his programs after 1912, he came up with a novel way that year for them to listen in.[52] Biographer Wells wrote about this innovative attempt to reach beyond the amateur and experimenter-listener:

> A receiving studio, the first in the world was opened in the Wiley B. Allen music store in San Jose where the public could hear the daily concerts. Since loud speakers were unknown, the studio was equipped with many telephone receivers. An immense amount of effort was put forth in trying to arouse public interest. Even as it was a large number of people listened in on home receivers of simple construction.[53]

The Wiley B. Allen Company store at 117 South First Street was only a short distance away from Herrold's studios in the Garden City Bank building and was managed at the time by individuals named Austin and Walgren. As described by Herrold in his own records, this 1912 receiving studio "consisted of two master receiving sets and two dozen pairs of earphones hanging around the walls, with chairs arranged for the comfort of the guests."[54] The eyewitness accounts suggest that at a time when the use of radio for entertainment was practically unknown, Charles Herrold was already beginning to understand that an audience could be and must be developed for the new service. In one Herrold obituary (1948) a writer for the *Oakland Tribune* recalled: "He and his students built hundreds of radio receivers and scattered them up and down the Santa Clara Valley to encourage radio listening."[55] Early wireless school colleague Ray Newby believed Herrold also did it partly in an effort to attract business to his college. Recalling regular programming as an early form of radio advertising, Newby said:

> Herrold used to build these little receiving sets for the kids and get 'em interested to come and learn code and then come to the school. That was part of his advertising. That's where he made his money. That's the only way he made his money, was his school. He charged for his tuition.[56]

In a 1959 interview with one of the authors, Herrold's wife Sybil described how he attempted to get radios into the homes of both friends and family:

> He would go out into the barns and their garages and help them with their crude little sets and when he got through they would be able to receive the small programs we had at the time. He fixed it so I could have a receiving set at home and when he broadcast I could receive the music there. It got to be such an interest that school teachers used to come to our home and bring their classes to hear the radio broadcasts. And the children used to think I was playing records and I had a hard time making them believe that I was not playing records in my living room but it was coming from the Garden City Bank building.[57]

Herrold's son Robert apparently got his own radio: "I remember I had one as a young boy, he fixed me up with a little set that I had by my bed and I would sit by it and listen with the earphones and you would get different stations."[58] Charles apparently knew what he was doing and why: "I installed a receiving set with 24 telephone receivers in a local music store so that their customers could hear the wireless telephone music."[59]

Finally, men who were his students in the early days told the authors years later why Herrold might have been so personally interested in his audience. Ron Gordon remembered Herrold the person:

> He liked to just help; he was a personable person. And he would go out and visit people in their homes and barns and places where they had their crystal sets and help 'em hook their crystal sets up properly with the antenna and the ground and the whole bit and got a lot of pleasure out of that part of it.[60]

And from another student at the Herrold college, Edward Altenbach:

> Doc was very encouraging to young people and he didn't talk down to kids at all. He encouraged 'em to go ahead and anyway he could help them out, he did. He was a very warm person.[61]

And if the audience was mostly composed of boys and young men, what did they want to hear? Were they similar to present day listeners? Quite a lot, as evidenced by this Ray Newby description of a broadcast: "People would call up and ask to play certain songs. They'd call back and we'd answer the phone, take the message and if we had the record we'd play it for 'em.[62]

Christmas Concert of 1916

It happened at the end of 1916, a time when the public seemed ready to embrace the concept of entertainment coming over the air, that Charles Herrold decided to promote his San Jose radio station with something special. Even though nascent public interest in broadcasting still was being poorly served by radio manufacturers, Herrold must have estimated that he had enough listeners in his signal area to start giving them something special. The situation in 1916 was that all the various inventors of the pieces that would make up radio transmitters and receivers, including de Forest's three-element vacuum tube, had up to this time seemed unable to put their pieces together and so a complete system was legally impossible. Then the U.S. went to war. As a result of our entry, the holders of various radiotelephone patents were forced to pool their inventions in order to make the best radio equipment possible for the Army and Navy. But it took until after the war for the patents to finally be sorted out and cross-licensed through the 1919–1922 patent pool agreements associated with the formation of the Radio Corporation.[63] Nevertheless, you can tell from some of the newspaper stories in 1916 that the public was beginning to embrace radio and increasing numbers seemed interested in hearing it. As mentioned earlier, Lee de Forest was starting to do important broadcasting from his station at High Bridge, New York.[64]

While not widely known, Charles Herrold was also finding ways and means of attracting listeners to his West Coast broadcasting. What he tried to air in 1916 to publicize his station and how it was reported by a local newspaper is a good example. It began with Herrold seeking publicity for a special holiday program he planned to give on his the radiotelephone, which got a favorable report in the local paper. First, readers were told the broadcast would take place on December 22, 1916:

> An extremely novel form of musical entertainment is planned for Christmas morning at 11 o'clock. The place will be anywhere that wireless waves can reach. Ships at sea as well as commercial and government stations within a radius of 1000 miles will be listening to catch the first strains of the opening numbers of the program. Professor Charles Herrold, the well-known radio and electrical engineer, assisted by Emil Portal, well known in wireless circles, will have charge of the concert. A modern talking machine will be placed in front of the transmitter through which flows a stream of cold water to protect against the powerful currents used. This system of wireless voice transmission has been subjected to the severest tests during the past three years and represents the highest development of the art.[65]

News of the concert's apparent success was reported on December 26:

> Edward Bellamy's prophecy in "*Looking Backward*" that some day people would turn on a button and listen to music from a central plant came true yesterday in San Jose when the wireless operators of the city and beyond within a radius of 1000 miles listened to a program of Christmas music in their homes. It was made possible by connecting their own wireless apparatuses with the central apparatus of the Herrold-Portal aerial system of telephony.[66]

The reporter had an odd way of describing it, or at least what he wrote could be confusing. While it was true that radio waves from Herrold's station brought music to listeners, there was no real connection between the "central plant" and homes. That was the point. Later in the article, a listener marveled at what he had heard: "It was as clear and sweet and beautiful as if it had been played and sung in the next room. The sounds came in distinctly. There was no disturbing noise and we listened to the whole program, which lasted about 20 minutes, without the slightest difficulty."[67] Since the station's signal was said to have been picked up 1,000 miles away, Herrold may have had verification. Sometimes Herrold's broadcasts would be acknowledged by wireless operators on ships at sea.

And what about the public? What about those in radio's early-day audience who would wonder themselves what it all means? The *San Jose Mercury-Herald* provided its editorial opinion on the morning of the Christmas broadcast. The newspaper compared what was to be aired — a "concert" — to other media forms of the day: film, records and the player piano. The editorial said it could be thoughtful. It could be impressive. But it called for caution. The entire 1916 editorial is an early indicator of what an attentive critic thought radio would become, and how the audience might come to view this revolutionary use of the radiotelephone:

> So now we can have a whole concert repertory shot through the air — a Christmas hymn, a Sousa march, an affable "Perfect Day," intermission and all complete — and science careens on to bankrupt space and link up those it divides. For this morning radio and electrical engineers in this city will transmit from records a musical selection that all with proper receivers within 1000 miles radius will hear — they say — and so the message of Christmas morn and a variety of other things will go out from San Jose, to Salt Lake City on the east and the storm-tossed sailor on the west.
>
> What will it all lead to? Here we have Paderewski drawing divinity from a piano; an impress is taken and unrolled on mechanical pianos, and so the master's touch is duplicated ad infinitum. Melba sings once, and the song is heard a million times by machinery. Bernhardt acts, and her gestures are thrown on the screens of all the world. And soon one transmission will entertain the Esquimaux, the Maori and the Basutos at one and the same time with complete symphonic concert.
>
> Here is the making of a revolution in human nature that needs to be watched and studied. It means that in the general process of centralization where mankind finds efficiency in government, industry and trade, something very similar is taking place in the realm of art. It is no longer necessary for artists to be present in the flesh when the busy, bustling public have half an hour to spare for musical or dramatic relaxation. For at a trifling cost the scientists will reproduce their skill with his machines, and the fruits of their labor are distributed, to order, with more or less precision.
>
> But one cannot afford to ignore the dangers that arise from this organized distribution of art. For art refuses to be governed by the ordinary laws that pertain to efficiency. The greatest achievements of science could never make the Jew dance in the bramble-bush or rid the town of rats. In its mechanical reproduction it loses all that subtlety and magnetism that the artist himself can give; it loses that mysterious force that touches the very soul of those who listen. It is all the difference between a Rembrandt and a copy of a Rembrandt, between the thunder of Jove and the thunder of the "flies." In other words, it is an imitation which, however faithful, cannot shed all the inherent defects of an imitation.
>
> And if we hear none but reproductions and imitations, whether by wire, needle or air, we may raise our standard of taste somewhat if these be good, but we shall inevitably dull our keenness of our appreciation of art through the lack of human magnetism and soul.
>
> The soloist then will do wonders yet undreamed of; will make the world so small that he will long for other worlds to conquer; but the singer and player of ancient history will always be abreast of modern times and will defy the efforts of science and machinery to place him in harness.[68]

Undoubtedly buoyed by the success and good press he received from the Christmas day concert, Herrold planned another attention-getting event. It was to happen a week later, New Years Eve, December 31, 1916. Probably owing to the success of the earlier Christmas concert, the local paper planned to cover this event as well:

> In front of the transmitter of the radio phone will be placed a pistol which will be fired at 12 o'clock. At the same time a brilliant electro-chemical flash will be ignited on the roof of the Garden City Bank which will be visible a long way, probably as far as the curvature of the earth will allow. As a preliminary, Messrs. Herrold and Portal will check their time from Arlington and Mare Island. The full strength of current will be used in the wireless telephone test and the pistol shot should be plainly heard to the full limit of distance by all stations in tune with the waves sent out from the San Jose station.[69]

The reality was something less. As described by both those present and those listening at home, the shot knocked Herrold's transmitter off the air: "When the pistol was fired the reverberation caused the multiple carbon microphones to blow up. The operator was showered with so much soot he looked like a minstrel show comedian. The listeners reported later that the only thing they heard was something that sounded like the striking of a match."[70] The stunt was a failure.

Before the April 1917 United States entry into the widening European war, both Herrold and de Forest were just beginning to see larger public interest in their broadcasts; those same editorial writers who had five years earlier discussed the radiotelephone as a replacement for the Bell wired phone were beginning to speculate on the entertainment possibilities of the new device. Although the technology admittedly was imperfect and in transition, it seemed to have a future. Herrold was still using his arc transmitter and de Forest had just begun to use his vacuum tube Oscillion system. Both men boasted of having audiences. But just when de Forest and Herrold were receiving the greatest public notice of their broadcasting careers, most of the public's thoughts were directed toward the news from Europe.

War Closes Broadcasting Stations

In the same newspaper that three months earlier had lauded the Herrold broadcasts and their promising future, a story was published of how the war forced him and others like him off the air:

> Under heavy war penalty for delay or disobedience, all persons owning or operating wireless plants, no matter of what size, have been ordered by the government to dismantle them and remove every wire immediately. In compliance with this order the large antenna of the Herrold school of wireless telegraphy, on top of the Garden City Bank Building, has been taken down and stored. This plant, which had a long range and was considered one of the most up to date on the coast, has been offered by Mr. Charles D. Herrold to the government, but before the formal tender reached the government officials, the order to dismantle was received and immediately complied with. Mr. Herrold stated yesterday that this order was probably the first step in government ownership of all wireless communication in this country.[71]

And while he and others were prohibited from going on the air to transmit, receive or entertain, Herrold realized a greater patriotic mission. Too old to serve in the Army or Navy, he formally dedicated his wireless school to the war effort. And while he tirelessly taught the wireless code to potential military radio operators, this period in history in which America is at war was a major transition time for Herrold and other wireless communications professionals.

It was no surprise that by the early months of 1917, due to passenger vessels being sunk by submarine warfare, paranoia over the threat of Germany was widespread and growing. Some became concerned that foreign spies could be lurking everywhere, even in Mexico. News reports implied that they were taking over the wireless right next to our border. From San Diego:

> That there are three wireless stations being operated by German officers along the Lower California coast, and that a number of German officers in civilian clothes are making their headquarters at Tijuana, Mexico, a few miles south of this city, was the substance of a report made tonight to the press by Don Stewart, city treasurer and senior officer of the naval militia. Stewart based his report on the statements of two young men who apparently discovered the stations.[72]

Apparently an investigation was made, but what it uncovered is not clear. What was clear was that any and all Germans were definitely perceived and portrayed as the enemy, both in casual conversation and in the dozens of stories in the daily papers.

An Order from the Commander-in-Chief

President Woodrow Wilson listed the specifics of the United States' involvement and put into motion a series of emergency measures having a direct effect on wireless and communications. One of them shut down what was considered to be the unnecessary use of transmitting and receiving equipment by amateurs and experimenters. On April 7, 1917, all licensed amateurs were sent a letter from the Department of Commerce and the U.S. Navy District Communication Superintendent that said:

> To all Radio Experimenters, Sirs: By virtue of the authority given the President of the United States by an Act of Congress, approved August 13, 1912, entitled, "An Act to Regulate Radio Communication," and of all other authority vested in him, and in pursuance of an order issued by the President of the United States, I hereby direct the immediate closing of all stations for radio communications, both transmitting and receiving, owned or operated by you. In order to fully carry this order into effect, I direct that the antennae and all aerial wires be immediately lowered to the ground, and that all radio apparatus both for transmitting and receiving be disconnected from both the antennae and ground circuits and that it otherwise be rendered inoperative both for transmitting and receiving and radio messages or signals, and so remain until this order is revoked. Immediate compliance with this order is insisted upon and will be strictly enforced. Please report on the enclosed blank your compliance with this order; a failure to return such blanks will lead to a rigid investigation.[73]

Never again in the 20th century would such a ban on both transmitting and receiving radio signals be implemented in the United States. It was a blanket order that included everyone. It immediately closed down Herrold's broadcasting to an audience and experimenting as station 6XF. Even more onerous, emboldened by the shut down and asserting that amateurs should have no place in the future of radio communication, the Padgett Bill, known as HR 2773, was introduced on April 9, 1917. It proposed that all American radio systems of communication in the future be turned over and controlled by the U.S. Navy. And while that bill did not immediately become law, the issue would be raised again to portend an uncertain future for wireless and radio.

Herrold College Serves the War

The war also changed the composition of the students and staff operating the Herrold College. Those who were able-bodied and already trained in wireless immediately went to war. Volunteering in advance of the draft was Ken Sanders, who had been with Herrold since 1912. A news account said:

> C.K. Sanders, 784 South Seventh Street, has passed his examination at San Francisco for first class electrician in the naval coast defense reserve. Sanders has had wide experience as a radio operator and will take up his duties at Honolulu some time next week. He will be a first-class radio operator at the island station until peace is declared, and may at length be placed in complete charge of the base. Mr. Sanders has worked and experimented with Emile [*sic*] Portal and Professor Charles D. Herrold, long an authority on the science of electricity, and the inventor of several new radio methods.[74]

Other Herrold students, especially those already trained in wireless operation, either volunteered immediately or waited for the draft. Even young and able-bodied students only partly trained in wireless wanted to serve. Many left before completing their wireless training programs. This patriotic act on the part of those young men enrolled in the Herrold College suddenly meant that Herrold would no longer have enough students paying tuition to keep his wireless and engineering school in full operation unless he could recruit a vast number of new students. Because of the exigencies of war, his full attention would have to be on the rapid training of code operators. While Herrold could continue as an educator, one practical result of the Great War was the end of the Herrold College as a center for the research and development of radio technology.

Charles Herrold, now 41 years of age, did not need to worry about being drafted into the armed services himself in 1917. Middle-aged, he was too old to volunteer or be conscripted. He did, however, discover rather quickly that he could serve the war effort in an important and unique way, by training men going into uniform in the code and the operation of wireless equipment. The Great War was the first major conflict to make use of wireless communication, and Herrold wanted to be involved:

> Immediately after our entry into the Great War and the closing of my broadcasting station, I opened a war radio school at 467 South First Street in San Jose. Here I

> trained men for Signal Corps and Navy. This was not an official school, but more or less recognized by Departmental Chiefs since I trained some 200 men and placed in service about 130 men.[75]

While Charles Herrold had a service to offer and he gave it without charge to the government, it is likely that the importance of Herrold's partial donation was minimized by the Mare Island Naval facility 50 miles to the north. It was the main official wireless training facility on the West Coast.

A decade later Herrold recalled his wartime activities in a letter to a friend:

> My War School was conducted in a glassed in enclosure 15 × 60 feet and operated from 8 in the morning till 10 at night. My first wife (Sybil) was a crack code instructor up to 15 words per minute (Continental Morse) and I brought them up to a speed of 25 words per minute. For higher speeds and as a matter of convenience I had one perforated ribbon Wheatstone Automatic Transmitter and three Omnigraphs like those used in the U.S. Radio Inspector's office. I use hand signals to build the training of my students and was very successful in rendering intensive training. I estimated that I sent an average of 45,000 signals per day personally and lifted an average of 21 tons per diem with my signal finger. I estimated that I made a conservative saving to the government of $65,000 dollars and made my living at the same time, since the students paid their own tuition.[76]

Since there was no time or money for inventing and since non-military transmission was outlawed, Herrold devoted all his time and effort to a rigorous training schedule. His son Robert remembered Sybil Herrold's role in the War School, as a teacher of code. Students would transcribe code as they listened to it on phonograph records.[77]

The year 1917 also brought a disease that killed millions worldwide. Its personal threat was reflected in Herrold's description in a letter he wrote:

> One of the most interesting sights was my war class working during the height of the Flu Epidemic, with Ozema Masks of perforated zinc filled with sponges saturated with Dobel's Solution. At ten o'clock at night I set a number of formaldehyde candles going and at 6 in the morning opened the two ends of the enclosure and set an electric suction fan going and by 8 o'clock had cleared out the air. I did not lose a single student nor did one of them even have a mild attack. My wife contracted it and was quarantined with a double dose of pneumonia and for five days I worked 14 hours with a spot on my lung which the City Physician said would kill me if I did not go to bed. I could not stop. I had 20 students that were nearing a completion of their training and 10 that were on deferred classification and liable to be called any minute and it was absolutely necessary that they attain the necessary speed so that they could take the special code test for Signal Corps or Naval Reserve. Sometime I will tell you how I fought death for five days and then went home and collapsed at night and spent hours clearing out my lungs of fluid and getting myself together so as to start my early morning class. One morning I found the boys in front ready to stampede. I heard one of the boys say before I got close to them, "I tell you he is going to die, he's got the flu." Then I argued them to a finish and got them back into the enclosure and started the automatic transmitters and charged their masks. Death hovered close to me those days, for I was breathing on about half lung space and a raging temperature.[78]

Herrold recovered and the students completed their preparation to be wartime wireless operators.

The Fate of Herrold's Broadcasting?

Before the war, the federal government was slow to recognize, categorize and license stations like that of Herrold. While neither condoning nor rejecting the broadcasting of entertainment programming to an audience of more than one, the agency in charge of licensing stations, the U.S. Commerce Department, began to issue a special category of radio license. Known as an "experimental radiotelephone license" and given a special "X" designation, some now very well known radio pioneers were granted this kind of approval to broadcast.[79] According to licensing records, Frank Conrad got 8XK in 1916, began playing music in 1919 and by 1920 Westinghouse had transformed it into KDKA. In 1919 Lee de Forest used 2XG at High Bridge, New York, and one year later 6XC to broadcast a daily schedule in San Francisco.[80] The University of Wisconsin was on in 1917 and again in 1919 with 9XM, which in two years became WHA. Charles Herrold acquired experimental licenses 6XE and 6XF for his early operations. One of these was issued as early as 1916, according to government records. Responding to an author's query to the Federal Communications Commission in 1959, the agency said,

> The only old records available are those found in the old Department of Commerce listing "Radio Stations in the United States." Mr. Herrold appears in the edition dated July 1, 1916, and that shows the issue of 6XF in his name. Unfortunately, the above publications did not indicate the date of the issue of licenses or the license term. The original applications and records referring to these old licenses have long since been destroyed.[81]

When the war ended on November 11, 1918, the question on the minds of early-day broadcasters was how soon they could return to the air. As Herrold joined a happy nation in celebrating its victory, he was faced with sobering thoughts about the future. Despite the fact he was an experienced educator and broadcaster, trying to get reestablished in the postwar world for Herrold was not going to be easy. The war had been a major setback for Herrold, both financially and personally. Between 1917 and 1918, he had to vacate his classrooms and studios in the Garden City Bank building, remove everything, and silence his radio station for the duration of the war. He had to dismantle the huge "carpet" antenna system from the highest buildings in downtown San Jose. His "arc telephone" had become outdated by newer technology. He had invested and lost a fortune in what was now absolutely gone — the Herrold College of Wireless and Engineering and the "arc phone" technology which had enabled him to carry on his broadcasting. Would Charles Herrold be able to return to broadcasting? This is exactly what challenged the inventive mind of Charles Herrold at the end of World War I.

6
First Station Survives

> *It would be a commonplace remark to say that when wireless telephoning became practical, about the year 1914, no one dreamed that its use would ever be general or popular. Even two years ago few enthusiasts would have dared to assert that they would live to see hundreds of thousands of persons interested in radio-telephony. The rapidity with which the thing has spread has possibly not been equaled in all the centuries of human progress....*
>
> *American Review of Reviews*, 1923[1]

With the end of the war, Charles Herrold could not completely return to his old way of life. Too much had changed. The technology of radio and the prospects of educating students in it were no longer the same. The war had handcuffed Herrold and given an advantage to others, particularly those who got government contracts. The very research and development Herrold needed to do was denied him from the spring of 1917 until restrictions were lifted. Only his wireless training program continued. But this lasted only as long as the war did. When the war ended, thousands of Army and Navy radiomen came back into the civilian economy and wireless school enrollments began to dry up. Herrold had to come up with some new ideas. If enrollments declined too much, he would have to cut expenses and find other ways of making money. However, if civilian students returned in peacetime, perhaps things wouldn't be so bad after all. Urged by those who missed the programs and music, Herrold decided to put his radio station back on the air. It made good practical sense. Broadcasting ought to encourage young boys to enroll in his school again. Thus Herrold worked out a threefold plan to solve his financial problems: first, resume his radio concerts to recapture his old listening audience; second, open a retail store for the public to buy radio receivers and supplies; and third, use radio broadcasting to publicize this new retail business as well as classes at his school.

Wartime advancements in vacuum tube radio had made it virtually impossible for Herrold to go back on the airwaves using his old radiotelephone. His arc phone system not only was obsolete and his patents useless, but he was prohibited under

"Logo" for KQW showing the twin towers of the station's antenna that loom above the San Jose First Baptist Church, to which Herrold granted his license in 1925 (Gordon Greb Collection).

the new Department of Commerce rules to resume broadcasting on the longer wave frequencies he had used previously. His prewar arc radiotelephone would be difficult, if not impossible, to operate on the new radio frequency set by the government, which was 360 meters. Herrold either had to construct his own tube transmitter or find the money to purchase one of the powerful but expensive new Western Electric transmitters. He was faced with a financial dilemma. What could he do?

Reaching for Revenue

From the day he was forced to go off the air, Herrold was fortunate in receiving help from two former students. First to come to his aid was Ray Newby, who had become a ship's radio operator, and Robert Stull, who had earned an electrical engineering degree from the University of California–Berkeley. Newby acted quickly in 1917 on learning that the federal government had forced Herrold to take down his antenna on the Garden City Bank building. As soon as he found out that Herrold's station was off the air and that the professor was vacating rooms he had used for research and broadcasting, Newby came up with an offer. Newby's timing couldn't have been better, because Herrold needed somewhere to reopen his wireless school without delay. Herrold couldn't believe his luck when Newby made available to him an empty, one-story facility at 467 South First Street, which had been the business location of Newby's father. Furthermore, for the time being he gave it to Herrold rent free. Newby recalled:

> I rented the building in San Jose [from T.S. Montgomery & Sons] in the old Taylor block on South First Street. And Herrold took up a quarter of the front section and set up his transmitter and small school and carried on there. Later I sold the business and Herrold moved over to my office side and stayed there after I left town.[2]

During the war, Herrold kept his college going at this new location, only a few blocks down the street from the Garden City Bank building. Quickly reopening his school, Herrold soon had no trouble enrolling new students, now much older young men, who were interested in learning wireless for military service. Herrold put his radiotelephone equipment in storage to await the war's end and concentrated on his teaching. Out of friendship for his old mentor, Newby didn't charge rent until Herrold returned to his financial feet.

Soon after the armistice was declared, Herrold was called upon by former wireless student Robert Stull, now an electrical engineer looking for postwar opportunities in radio. Stull wondered what Herrold was planning to do. Keenly interested in Herrold's talent for inventing and sensing there might be new opportunities in radio with the war's end, Stull agreed to go into business with him. Stull was the son of a prominent local businessman and had financial resources of his own as well as a lot of youthful energy. After rearranging the interior of the new building, Stull and Herrold had ready a retail store at the front, and inside, a wireless classroom and another room for a radio station and laboratory. Joseph D. Cappa, who became a student at Herrold's College of Wireless on South First Street in the fall of 1919 and had been a regular listener before wartime restrictions closed the station in 1917, remembered what the place looked like: "His school was two rooms partitioned from the garage. The front room had a long table at which the students received code instruction and theory. The second room had a work table and lathe equipment. I built a receiver using four Audiotron tubes in his shop...." Until Newby moved out and gave the Herrold laboratories more space, the back room was also where they located the transmitter.[3]

Ray Newby, five years after he had been Herrold's 16-year-old lab assistant, was a handsome uniformed ship's radio operator, circa 1915 (Stephen True Collection).

Relicensed Herrold Returns

This rush back to radio was the result not only of the government lifting restrictions on amateurs in 1919, but also because of an executive order issued by President Wilson. He decreed that all government-seized stations were to be returned to their owners by March 1, 1920, and the ban lifted on private operation.[4] This meant Herrold could use his radio station again. According to those associated with him at the time — Stull, Cappa, and Newby — Herrold was eager to do just that.[5] Cappa often went with some of his high school friends and the professor to his cabin in the Santa Cruz Mountains on weekends, and recollected that in the fall of 1919, "We students were chafing at the bit for the restrictions to be lifted and for 'prof' to get back on the air. 'Prof' discussed it with me one time and he was anxious to get on the air."

He was held up, though, because the old arc transmitter could not operate on the new frequency. While civilian radio experimenters were allowed back on the air, they were given a new classification by the government and ordered to operate on a new wavelength, 360 meters.

Herrold recalled, "I had to divide time with all the stations within a radius of 100 miles, and I had to build a new composite tube radiotelephone that was copied from the others because my high powered arc system would not operate below 600 meters."[6] According to government licensing files, Herrold beat many of his competitors in the speed with which he was authorized to return to the air. Records show he was approved to use his old 6XF license on March 9, 1920.[7] Some contemporaries remembered him being on the air as early as 1919, presumably trying out voice and music with his old arc transmitter.[8] Others were certain Herrold was using his newer vacuum tube equipment early in 1920. Recalling everything he was doing at school, work and home at the time, Cappa said, "I definitely feel that he was on the air before May 1920." He added, "There is no doubt in my mind about the summer of 1920—Prof was on the air with a good readable station, very likely a tube transmitter."[9]

Open for Business

The letterhead on the business stationery showed that the Herrold College of Engineering was located at 467 South First Street in San Jose, declaring "Chas. D. Herrold, E.E., R.E. as engineer and Robert J. Stull, E.E. as manager." But at the entrance to the building itself the nature of their business was identified quite differently. The front window proclaimed the enterprise to be:

HERROLD LABORATORIES
RADIO
ELECTRICAL ENGINEERS
COLLEGE <> ENGINEERING <> RADIO

When Herrold's wartime teaching ended, there was no way of knowing whether new students from the civilian economy would come to the school and restore tuition as a source of income. Thus Herrold and Stull had to figure out how to make interest in wireless and radio profitable in some other way in case students didn't show up. One way Herrold decided to branch out was to go into manufacturing and selling radio receivers of his own design, which became known as "Spider Webs" to readers of Herrold's advertisements in radio publications.[10] In addition to going after mail order sales, Herrold opened a radio retail store in the front section of his downtown San Jose location to handle other radio products. So Herrold, who already had a reputation as a radio broadcaster, began displaying receivers, parts and supplies made by a variety of manufacturers in his store front and promoting, selling, and servicing radio sets to customers who walked in.[11] In the rear room of this large ground floor building, Herrold returned his station to the air to help advertise his new business. According to Stull, he replaced his old "arc" phone with a homemade tube transmitter, and resumed transmissions using one of the experimental licenses

Herrold's most novel, inventive step in the early 1920s was this Mobile Radio Sound System. With an outside Magnavox horn connected to an inside car radio, Herrold could "broadcast" radio concerts wherever he drove his automobile. Frank Schmidt, wearing headphones, is the only other person identified among this group gathered outside Herrold's place of business at 467 South First Street, San Jose (Stephen True Collection).

assigned to him by the government. Documents in Washington, D.C., show he was officially authorized to resume experimental transmissions on March 9, 1920, with the reissuance of his old "land station" radio license 6XF by the Radio Service of the Bureau of Navigation. A few months later, on September 24, 1920, the government returned to Herrold his old "portable" transmitter license, 6XE.

When Herrold got back on the air, he was being heard again for miles around. It seemed as though the old pre-war days were back—teenage boys began showing up at the station to see what was going on and some of them signed up to study the fundamentals of radio. When students weren't learning code in class, they would hang around helping to broadcast or learning how to do it. When signing on, Herrold or his student announcers would give the station's call letters but thereafter identify themselves by saying something like this: "We're talking to you from Herrold Radio Laboratories in San Jose, where 'Doc' Herrold has the parts and services you need." By 1923 there were two radio parts and services retailers listed in the *San Jose City Directory*, Herrold Laboratories and City Electrical Company.[12] Most stations in the early 1920s made sure they not only identified themselves by their call letters but also by their lines of business.[13] For Herrold, this meant letting listeners know about his school and retail store.[14]

Herrold and a colleague inside Herrold's downtown retail radio store. Many stores like this sprang up around the country in the 1920s. One of the most successful in business today is Radio Shack (Stephen True Collection).

By the time the Department of Commerce got around to giving Herrold his commercial license on December 9, 1921, naming the San Jose station KQW, other so-called "commercial" licenses had been issued ahead of him. All stations broadcasting "news, lectures, entertainment, etc." were put on a single frequency, 360 meters (today approximately 833 kHz on an AM radio) when the Commerce Department created the new broadcasting category in the 1920s. Broadcasters like Herrold who already were doing "concerts" with experimental licenses simply moved their transmissions, as soon as they could, to the newly authorized frequency and stuck to their schedules. Longtime experimenters applied for the new licenses but saw no reason to hurry. Receiving "limited commercial" licenses by the Department of Commerce, they figured, may have given most stations new call letters, but this didn't change the order in which they began broadcasting. A station with a number like Herrold's had been on the air with their "experimental" licenses long before anyone else. In fact, some early radio pioneers who began doing "concerts" with "experimental" licenses were still being authorized to use them for broadcasting into the 1930s.[15]

Although it seemed unimportant at the time, the order of being licensed by the Commerce Department eventually became a sticking point for stations seeking a place in history. Stations like KDKA, Pittsburgh, and WWJ, Detroit, each claimed it was "first" or "oldest," based on being licensed first by the Commerce Department — a controversy which goes on between them till this day. Actually, it can be argued

Small vacuum tube radio transmitters like the one pictured here on a Herrold School laboratory table put his station back on the air at the end of the war. Using licenses 6XE and 6XF, which he had renewed since 1917, Herrold soon had students engaged in "talk radio" when this photograph was taken in February 1921 (dated by wall calendar) (Gordon Greb Collection).

that plenty of people in America first heard radio programs long before any licenses were required. Herrold is only one of a number of experimenters who were broadcasting before commercial licensing came along in the 1920s. Because there were early experimenters and amateurs doing "talk radio" well before licensing, finding out who they were, what they did, and when they did it should settle the question of their true rank order.

The chronology of Herrold's radio work in this post-war period, according to those who were present at the time, went like this: By the early months of 1920, Herrold had discarded his old oscillating arc transmitter and replaced it with a primitive but new, low-wattage vacuum tube transmitter. He and Stull had built it themselves. Stull said he was there when Herrold acquired vacuum tubes and assisted him in putting them together to create a small-wattage transmitter to resume transmissions after the war.[16] He was licensed to do this as an experimenter before the war and he lost no time in seeking license reissuance from the government after the armistice was signed. Government records show that Herrold got his first personal postwar license to broadcast weeks before KDKA's chief founder and engineer, Frank Conrad.[17] Other evidence that Herrold was engaged in early postwar broadcasting can be seen in a photograph taken at the new Herrold station in February 1921, the date made certain by a calendar on the wall.[18] It shows his San Jose radio station equipment spread out on a long table, displaying everything that was needed to trans-

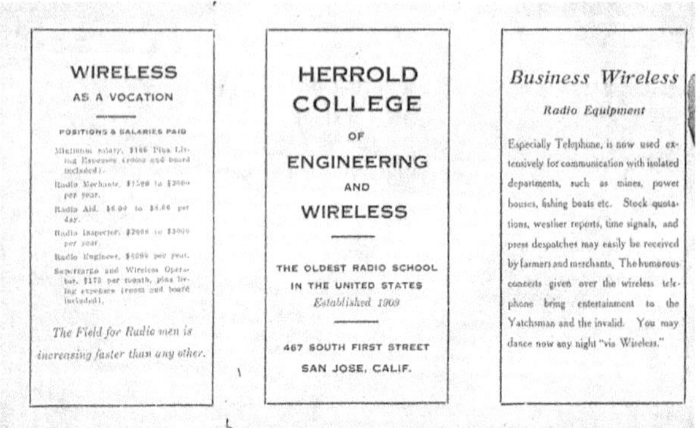

Herrold did this kind of postwar advertising to attract students to his wireless college after the conflict was over in Europe, circa 1921 (courtesy Perham Foundation Electronics Museum).

mit voice and music. The wall above the table is covered with the memorabilia of students. Not only does this show that classes were taking place in the Herrold laboratory in 1920, but proof has turned up in the form of a receipt saved by Leonard J. Fairfield, one of the students. It showed that he had paid his tuition "in the amount of $20, covering period 3/14/21 to 4/14/21, signed by Robert J. Stull, Herrold Laboratories."[19]

Assembled from what spare parts he could borrow and equipment he could afford, Herrold's little 1920s radio apparatus could easily be termed a "haywire" outfit, for it certainly was not impressive to look at. The station (6XF) nevertheless put Herrold back on the air "immediately after the war."[20] By comparison to those with more funds to invest — Westinghouse, Detroit *News*, and the American Telephone and Telegraph Company, for example — Herrold was like David going up against Goliath. He was a small investor, a poor struggling private entrepreneur without the resources of affluent experimenters, and someone who had to do the best he could with a homemade set-up that wasn't big and powerful. Nevertheless, he put his little vacuum tube station into operation and got back on the air.

As the postwar decade of the 1920s began, wireless and CW operators began interfering with each other because regulations restricted where they could operate.[21] The editor of the *Bay Counties Radio Club Newsletter* published the comments of one of its readers on this subject in October 1921. The writer, Sgt. Tavers, 6XW, who was in charge of the radiotelephone station at the Presidio of San Francisco, predicted that difficulties "are going to face the amateur within the next year and these will multiply with the increase of stations and the intermingling of spark and CW — especially where voice modulation is used with CW." [22] Then the editor saluted what he called the "Famous Herrold Radio Laboratories" in an article in the same publication in October 1921. By referring to him as "the real CW man," the editor clearly identified Herrold as one who was preeminently a voice and music broadcaster. CW was understood to stand for "continuous wave," the electro-magnetic wave commonly used in long-distance radiotelephony.[23]

> Mr. C.D. Herrold, 6XF, is the real CW man about town. He has graduated from the five watt class and has a 1000V M.G. and two fifty watt tubes underway. Many important experiments have been conducted in his laboratories, and we all expect to hear some noise when he puts the fifties in the sockets. Recently he was heard over 400 miles at sea, power used 1.2 Amps. The Prof. also has a classy line of radio stuff on sale. When in San Jose, drop in and see him.[24]

As America's first broadcaster, Herrold easily knew how to use new, modern facilities. Here he checks the meters of KQW's new 500 watt Western Electric transmitter in 1925 (courtesy Perham Foundation Electronics Museum).

On Dec. 9, 1921, when Herrold got the call letters KQW from the U.S. Department of Commerce, he was licensed to broadcast for one year from his place of business at 467 South First Street, San Jose. He was authorized to use 50 watts of power, on unlimited time, at 360 meters. Not long afterward, Herrold observed the holiday season by scheduling special Yuletide talks and music. On checking his records for a former sponsor, Herrold noted that one of the program participants was J. Hart Desteel of the Union Oil Company of California, acknowledging that the "date of your Christmas speech from KQW at 467 S. 1st St., in San Jose was Christmas, 1921."[25]

San Joseans who had been prewar fans of Herrold's station were glad to learn he was broadcasting again on Wednesday nights. According to *Radio* magazine, KQW was scheduled to broadcast brief periods of concert music on Wednesdays from 8:15 to 9:00 P.M. and Sundays from 5:00 to 6:00 P.M. in April 1922.[26] But nine months later in December 1922 *Radio* magazine shows that the length of KQW's Wednesday evening program has been increased to one full hour, 8:00 to 9:00 P.M., and that daily programs lasting one hour were being scheduled, Monday through Saturday, 1:00 to 2:00 P.M. This wasn't much time on the air, but it was the result of there being too many stations trying to share the same frequency. Herrold and others in his region had to engage in time-sharing because they were all placed on the same channel.

In Northern California, 10 stations in Oakland, San Jose, and San Francisco had to use the same spot on the dial (360 meters). Each station's broadcast lasted only an hour or two, Monday through Saturday, closing down on Sunday unless they carried religious services. Also continuing to operate on Sunday was the Army's Presidio station on 420 meters. However, stations which could prove they were geographically separated by a distance of 50 miles or more could broadcast simultaneously, as it was presumed these broadcasts would not interfere with one another. Thus it was possible for San Francisco's KDN in the Fairmont Hotel to broadcast daily except Sunday at the same time as KQW in San Jose, 1:00 to 2:00 P.M.[27] In the New York area, KDKA had no such problem in 1922. The Second Radio District gave the Pittsburgh station all the airtime it needed, according to *Radio* (April 1922). KDKA had a lengthy daily schedule, 11 am. to 6 P.M., except Sunday, and late evening, and had no time sharing obligations with others in the region such as WNO, Jersey City, N.J; WDT and WDY, New York City; WGY and Union College stations, Schenectady, N.Y.[28]

Creating Local Radio

Herrold's early 1920s studio set-up can be seen in an old photograph. It provided announcers with one hand-held microphone on a long cord, which could be passed around to at least three people, each equipped with headphones to hear what was being broadcast. The lone microphone also could be placed in front of a Victrola phonograph player to pick up music, which, besides an operator's impromptu news and chitchat, was the main programming at the start. Thus Herrold, Stull, and Newby and a handful of young wireless enthusiasts who enrolled in his school took regular turns at the microphone; Herrold had equipped himself with a small tube transmitter to tell listeners that he had returned to regular broadcasting. Undoubtedly excited at Herrold's station being back on the air, dozens of wireless enthusiasts in the San Francisco Bay Area began hearing, "Hello, out there! Do you hear me? If you do, call me up. This is 'Doc' Herrold at the Herrold Radio Laboratories in San Jose! How's it coming in? How do we sound?"[29] With help from his boys, Herrold strung a wire from his studio transmitter to a tall one-pole antenna on the rooftop of the one-story building, short of the wide-ranging capacity of the old prewar carpet antenna, but good enough to radiate an audible signal for miles around. Years later Stull remembered they had great success with their small, homemade, low wattage operation:

> I can remember building a tube transmitter so that we could talk — these were receiving tubes I'm talking about. We used receiving tubes for building a voice transmitter. And on one voice that Mr. Newby made — he was still an operator on board the ships— he heard us by voice on this tiny tube, which rated probably five watts, perhaps. He heard us as far away as Honolulu.[30]

Someone else who remembered being there was one of Herrold's students, young Joe Cappa. He remembered listening with his brother to Herrold's station as an amateur before the war and "went to the Charles Herrold wireless college when he was out on South First Street directly after the war ... about late 1919 or early 1920." He recalled that all of Prof. Herrold's arc equipment worked on 600 volts of direct current and the only people using direct current in those days, as far as Cappa knew, were the streetcar companies. So when Herrold's station needed plenty of electricity for his transmissions, at a time when he could hardly afford to pay for it, one of the student operators would hook a wire onto the streetcar power line with a long bamboo pole, pull it in, and go on the air. As Cappa remembered it:

> The streetcar company never could figure out why they ran one street car a night out South First Street that used 9 kilowatts of power almost constantly for two or three hours while "Prof" was broadcasting. Eventually they got wise to us and they put a meter in and gave the "Prof" the juice legitimately.[31]

Growing Pains

Herrold's station, generally operated by young students, was hardly different from most others in the early 1920s. Everyone was an amateur learning a new trade. If owners couldn't find an operating contraption, they had to buy it new for staffers to use for the first time. Consequently radio was plagued with technical difficulties. Besides squeaks and squawks, fading away of signals, or absolute "dead air," a listener might hear a frustrated voice say, "One moment, please." Then airwaves would go silent and an unseen hand would tinker with a bad microphone or attempt to reestablish a connection. When radio became popular throughout America in the late 1920s, no reputable station failed to have a phonograph record handy to fill time with organ, concert, or march music when things went wrong. When that happened, you heard, "We bring you now a short interlude of music." This uncertainty in radio lasted well into the 1930s.[32] Anyone using profanity over a live microphone lost his or her job. While almost half the new stations were owned by radio dealers or manufacturers in 1922, the vast majority—289 out of 570—couldn't distinguish a radio tube from an Edison light bulb.[33] Radio was making broadcasters out of people you knew on Main Street, such as the local poultry, grain or meat dealer; auto supply, music or jewelry store owner; or the hardware, bicycle or laundry man. Wealthier newspapers, banks and telephone companies could afford to hire good help, but rarely the lowly endowed YMCA or fraternal organization that was trying to broadcast. It was a listening menagerie.

Its Marvels Hailed

Ten years after Herrold established a radio hookup between San Jose to its famous metropolitan neighbor to the north, San Francisco Mayor James Rolph congratulated all the radio pioneers who helped make this possible, saying, "To those whose genius and industry have made possible this feat in which I have been honored with a part, I extend my hearty congratulations." He spoke from the Fairmont Hotel atop Nob Hill, the very place to which Herrold had made a radio communications link from San Jose in 1912, to an audience of the Parent-Teachers' Association at Jefferson School in San Jose. Now, 12 years later, Herrold's dream was being realized. It took more than a decade for the layman to see the potentials of broadcasting, as Mayor Rolph said:

> I wonder if it strikes you as it does me — this short speech of mine by radiotelephone from the Fairmont Hotel in San Francisco to an audience seated 50 miles away in San Jose. I wonder if you are thrilled by the marvel of this achievement, wherein a speaker addresses a group he cannot see, with whom not even a strand of telephone wire connects him, and yet to whom his words are as audible and understandable as if he actually stood before them in the flesh.[34]

The mayor went on to recall the thrill of hearing the U.S. President's voice coming into the radio across the country last Armistice Day. On that day, Nov. 11, 1921, the mayor said that about 13,000 people in Exposition Hall and an even larger number outside heard that nothing today is impossible. Next, he said, people will be seated "listening to the voice of a European ruler, the sounds of the battle drums in the jungles of Africa, the strains of martial music from an East Indian durbar — all transmitted by radio telephone and amplifiers across oceans and continents just as if space did not exist. " Thirteen years later in 1934, Rolph, as governor of California, would continue to praise the marvels of radio and would congratulate Herrold himself on the 25th anniversary (1909–1934) of his pioneer station, KQW.[35]

Concerns of Radio Clubs

While newcomers were totally fascinated being in radioland, some old "hams" were complaining about this so-called progress. Typical were comments by H.J. McCoy of Berkeley, California, which appeared in the February 1922 issue of *Radio*. He complained that "there are too many radio phone concerts. It's getting to be that so that you cannot tune one completely out from the other, and when it's amplified — but who can dance to two different fox-trots at the same time?"[36] Radio enthusiasts were forming clubs all over the country to protect and advance their hobby. Early in 1922 there were so many radio enthusiasts in the San Jose area that they decided to form a Radio Club. They were nearly all acquaintances or former students of the Herrold College. Its first president was Harry Engwicht, one of Herrold's own students, who eventually would become an engineering professor at San Jose State College. After earning advanced degrees at Stanford University, Engwicht carried on the Herrold tradition by creating a radio club among his own students at his college. Like old Prof, he had them running an amateur radio station in the engineering building. Professor Engwicht was one of the first persons contacted by author Greb when he began researching Herrold's claim in 1958. Engwicht recalled studying under Herrold and authenticated from personal knowledge facts that would establish Herrold as America's first broadcaster. In the 1920s, the San Jose Radio Amateurs met regularly in the home of Frank Quement and heard talks on the subject of radio by various experts, including "Doc" Herrold himself.[37]

Lightning to the People

Radio became popular in the 1920s because people who tried it enjoyed it and told others, not merely because they had nothing better to do. For Herrold there was no time for publicity until he updated his operation with a tube-transmitter and got enough cash to buy what was needed to use his new call letters of KQW. By the spring of 1922, public interest in radio was heating up. Professor Herrold was in his finest element. His voice began to be heard not only over the airwaves but also in lecture halls, hotels and meeting places of civic groups and fraternal organizations. Invited as the local radio expert to address the San Jose Lions Club in March 1922, Herrold told his fellow business and professional associates that radio had answered one of the questions posed by the Bible. When Job was asked "if he couldn't send lightning to the people to tell them we are here," Herrold said radio had answered the question in the affirmative. To their amazement, he did more than discuss radio as a miracle. He explained it scientifically when he proceeded to show them how easily a signal could be picked up by doing exactly that for everyone seated in the banquet room of the Montgomery Hotel. With help from his assistant, Newby, who ran the controls, and amplified the sound through loud speakers, "the audience heard a musical concert and lecture from the Herrold laboratories in South First Street." Although licensed as KQW, Herrold still was using his own name to identify his station. Others in the San Francisco area were doing the same. Herrold said his San Jose station would soon carry programs featuring the local Elks orchestra and the San Jose high school glee club. The *San Jose Mercury-Herald* summed up the meeting by saying Herrold's talk "sparkled with illuminating facts concerning the tremendous strides in the radio world."[38]

Visible by Splendid Illumination

To tell people about the advantages of listening to radio in the home and hoping to sell them radio receiving sets, Herrold took his equipment to many public gatherings and events occurring around Santa Clara County. He wanted curious onlookers to see and experience what radio was all about. Notable among these efforts were Herrold's "Radio Concert Programs" which one could not avoid noticing if you lived anywhere near them. On the two-day weekend of April 1–2, 1922 he set up an outdoor booth at the Saratoga Blossom Festival which few could ignore. The receiving apparatus was made "visible by splendid illumination." Herrold also made certain that anyone seeing it could not avoid hearing it. Using a multi-tube receiving set coupled to a powerful amplifier and huge 12-foot horn, he "blasted"—a term used in the newspaper report—music all over Santa Clara Valley during the two-day event. Aided by two of his students, who operated the apparatus, Herrold not only picked up radio broadcasts from his own station but also from San Francisco, Oakland, and Los Altos and amplified them over the widest possible area of the festival grounds. Altogether an estimated 20,000 people heard his music. They heard it coming from the Herrold Radio Station in San Jose, 10 to 11 A.M. on Saturday and 1:30 P.M. to 2:30

At public events like the Saratoga Blossom Festival (seen here), Herrold introduced sounds coming from radio. Huge loudspeakers re-broadcast concert music from his own station, KQW, as well as others in the area (Stephen True Collection).

SARATOGA BLOSSOM FESTIVAL

RADIO CONCERT

PROGRAM

Saturday and Sunday, April 1st and 2nd, 1922
At the Radio Field

SOMETHING NEW EVERY MINUTE

Given under auspices of Blossom Festival Committee, in conjunction with regular program. Under personal direction of Dr. Chas. D Herrold, E. E., R. E., of the Herrold Laboratories, San Jose, Calif., and Mr. Ray G. Herold, Saratoga.
Special Blossom Festival music has been prepared for this occasion.

SATURDAY

Morning Program—Musical Concert:
10:00 to 11:00 - - Herrold Radio Laboratories
11:00 to 12:00 - - Fairmont Hotel San Francisco

Afternoon Program—Musical Concert:
1:00 to 2:00 - - Fairmont Hotel, San Francisco
2:00 to 2:30 Rock Ridge Radio Station, Oakland, Calif.
4:00 to 4:30 Rock Ridge Radio Station, Oakland, Calif.
4:30 to 5:30 - - Fairmont Hotel, San Francisco

Evening Program:
8:00 to 11:00 - Grand Open Air "Carnival Dance" in the Streets at Saratoga

Special Radio Orchestra Music will be given for this occasion direct from Atlantic-Pacific Radio Broadcasting Station, Rock Ridge, Oakland, Calif.

SUNDAY

Morning Program:
10:00 to 11:00 - Concert, Fairmont Hotel, San Francisco
11:00 to 12:15 Trinity Program, Sermon, Sacred Concert Rock Ridge Radio Station.

Afternoon Program—Musical:
1:30 to 2:30 - - Herrold Laboratories, San Jose
4:00 to 5:00 - E. Portal, Los Altos Radio Station
5:00 to 6:00 - - Herrold Laboratories, San Jose

Evening Program: - - Presidio, San Francisco
Special "Farewell Concert" from the mountain top.

NOTE: The receiving apparatus for this concert will be visible by splendid illumination

RECEIVING SETS AND PARTS STANDARD RADIO INSTRUMENTS
HERROLD LABORATORIES
Complete Radio Equipment
467 SOUTH FIRST ST. SAN JOSE, CAL.

If you attended the Saratoga Blossom Festival in April 1922, you knew what radio stations were coming over Herrold's loudspeakers because he gave everyone a free "Radio Concert Program" (Stephen True Collection).

P.M. on Sunday and at other hours from stations in San Francisco, Oakland, Berkeley, and Los Altos. At 10 o'clock in the morning Herrold began radio concerts, which lasted all day and halfway into the night.[39]

A few months later, Herrold moved his elaborate radio exhibit and sound system to the Fourth Annual Industrial Exposition for a nine-day appearance, May 27 to June 4, in San Jose. He planned an even grander exhibit to demonstrate radio's capabilities. When the huge exhibition tent was being erected to enclose 35,000 square feet of floor space, sheltering displays of autos, tractors, and manufactured products, Herrold was on hand as the tent poles were raised to make sure his "squirrel cage antenna" went up with them. It was an aerial system used by the British Navy, connecting an 800-foot wire to large Magnavox speakers facing the crowds outside, over which Herrold announced he would send out musical programs from 14 different California radio stations. For the duration of the exposition, listeners got radio music from 10

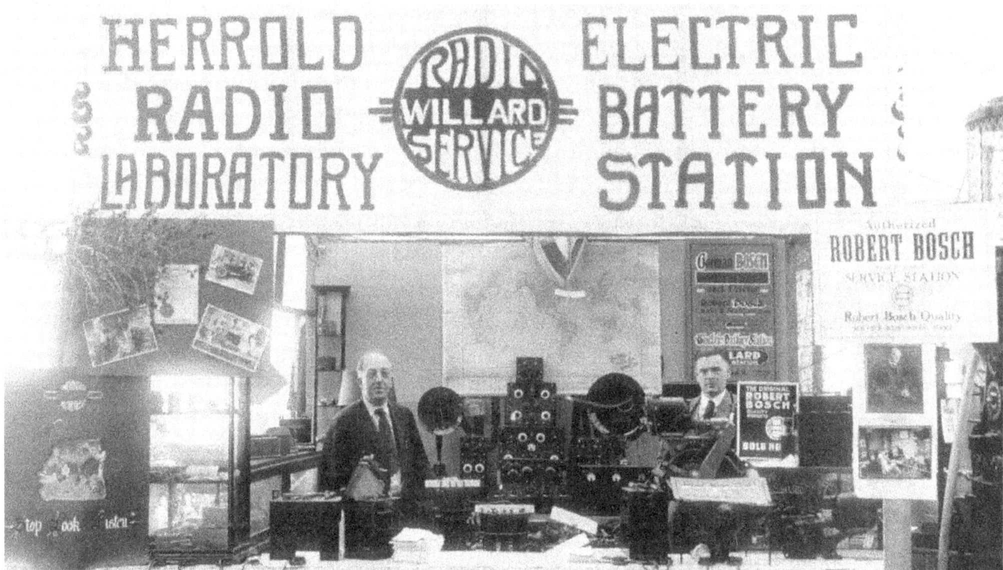

Herrold rarely missed a chance to sell radio to people at country fairs and outdoor exhibits. When they asked about radio, he soon converted them into listeners. He is at the left, waiting for customers at his Herrold Radio Laboratory booth, circa 1922 (Stephen True Collection).

o'clock in the morning till 9 o'clock at night. When regional concerts picked up by Herrold's San Jose station ceased in the evening, fairgoers continued hearing music from stations located out of state. One of these was owned and operated by a newspaper in the state of Washington, the *Seattle Post-Intelligencer*. With student assistants running the sound system, Professor Herrold was free to provide lectures on wireless telephony and appear personally at a "question booth" to clear up doubts about radio from amateurs and others. While Herrold was glad to provide entertainment and merchandising, he said his aim was to forward radio as an industry and a profession because his principal interest was research and development.[40]

Of significance to observant visitors at the Industrial Exposition booth was a subtle presentation of Herrold's own history. At the rear of the exhibit a sign identified an odd and mysterious looking piece of equipment as the "original Herrold arc fone transmitter from 1912." Even at the onset of licensed broadcasting, Charles Herrold was attempting to enlighten those who visited his booth about his own role as the first broadcaster.

KQW, the Municipal Station?

A startling new idea came to Herrold in the spring of 1922. What exactly Herrold had in mind when he promoted the concept of a city-owned radio station among business and professional leaders of San Jose will never be known. It may have been that he had in mind that the city would take over his own station KQW. Largely through his influence, the idea of establishing a municipal station for the city of San

Jose was brought to the attention of the San Jose Commercial Club on April 28. It was proposed to the Board of Directors by the club's president, H.F. Parsons, the district engineer of the Standard Oil Company. Based on the advice of Herrold and A.L. Anderson, former chief engineer of the Federal Telegraph Company of Palo Alto, Parsons urged the Commercial Club to encourage the development of a city station in order to make San Jose known everywhere as "one of the nation's great broadcasting centers." In the letter, he said, "Gentlemen, a municipally-owned and controlled radio broadcasting station properly operated on a daily schedule will do more real advertising for this community than all the newspapers, magazines and motion picture films ... that money could buy." With board approval, an application for a license was sought and Herrold announced that while it was pending, he would use his own station to "commence broadcasting in the name of this municipality until the regular station was constructed."[41]

On Herrold's recommendation, Ray Newby was asked to play a prominent role in the station's development, but since Newby was leaving the next morning for Mexico, the project had to wait until he returned. Meantime, Herrold said he would tour the valley in a radio-equipped automobile to find the perfect place to locate the new station, identifying with his testing apparatus "blind spots" and "live spots." Within three months the proposal came up before the city council and members were told such a station would be a high-class operation, "free from any bias of politics or religion, or the direct advertising of individuals or firms." When the city council approved, *Radio* magazine gave the news the headline, "Municipal Station for San Jose, Calif." on the same page it carried another story about a "New York Municipal Station" being planned. The only difference between the two proposals was that San Jose's proponents were told to raise their money "by private subscription," whereas in New York City the council appropriated $50,000 in public funds. San Jose never got its city-owned radio station, but New York got a world famous, non-commercial station known as WNYC, whose operations continued throughout the 20th century and beyond.[42]

While Herrold's station customarily provided "concert music" as its most regular feature, audiences occasionally heard other innovative programs, depending upon whether entertainers visiting town needed publicity, the staff exercised its imagination, or there was talent among local people who volunteered to go before the mike. The following story from San Jose *Mercury-Herald* is a sample:

> Monometer Boys to Be on KQW Tonight
>
> Tollinger and Wolfe, the Monometer Twins, will be heard in a return engagement over KQW tonight, beginning a program of musical and vocal numbers at 8 o'clock.
>
> The Twins are billed as superpower radio musical comedians, both of them full of pep and possessing delightful personalities as they sit before the "mike." Like a pair of friendly pals, they seem to enjoy every minute as much as their audiences. "Radiocast singers could well take pointers from them for they have reduced their work to a science, there being no sense of restraint," is the way Dr. Herrold, local pioneer director, speaks of them.[43]

Herrold Finds a Savior

Despite all of his efforts, station KQW still was not turning a profit in 1925 and Herrold was facing a rather desperate financial situation. Having spent every penny of his inheritance, he was practically broke and could no longer afford to keep the station going out of his own pocket. Since no one wanted to buy his station, what was he to do? When similar calamities happened to other radio station owners, they simply closed the doors, walked away and forgot about it. It is noteworthy that Herrold did not quit. Knowing he was a pioneer broadcaster, he could not let his station languish and die. He was so resolved to keep it on the air that he was willing to give away his precious KQW license without any compensation whatsoever, provided that the recipient would promise to keep the pioneer station on the air. One of the community leaders Herrold had approached in San Jose in the spring of 1925 seemed keenly interested. He was Pastor William Keeny Towner of the First Baptist Church of San Jose. The historic moment is recorded in church records:

> Dr. Towner came into the Church Office all excited; for in mulling over the potentialities of radio, he had the vision of the church using their very own station to broadcast the Gospel. The possibilities loomed to him, as being unlimited in their ability to reach the people with the Good News of salvation. He then took the idea and his enthusiasm to the congregation who immediately voted it into reality. With that voting, First Baptist Church of San Jose was thrust into a new, completely unplowed, but extremely fertile area of radio Bible preaching.[44]

Herrold reached an agreement with Pastor Towner to turn over the license of the station to the First Baptist Church of San Jose, but he insisted the new owners accept certain simple and rudimentary conditions. Before allowing control of the station to pass over to someone else, Herrold made a simple request — that the new owners regularly credit him for his accomplishment on the air. It was agreed that every time the station signed on each day an announcement would be made, "This is KQW, pioneer broadcasting station of the world, founded by Dr. Charles D. Herrold in San Jose in 1909."[45] In addition, it was understood that Herrold would be retained as the station's director, using his reputation and connections in the community to build good will, give talks to local social and business associations and help solicit contributions and advertising to keep the station alive financially.

There was one nearly fatal glitch. KQW almost lost its license before the transfer of ownership had occurred. Change of ownership could not occur immediately because processing of the required Department of Commerce paperwork in Washington took time. Whether it was simple negligence by someone who did not file proper forms on time or something of a more serious nature, the problem was one that Herrold blamed on the station's new, inexperienced owners. The difficulty happened sometime in the middle of 1925 when the programming and relicensing responsibility passed from Herrold to the church. It is unclear as to what exactly occurred because Herrold was vague about it afterward. He simply said,

> There was a slip somewhere on the part of Towner or the Exchange Club and KQW actually lost its wavelength allocation for a short time and was reinstated through the efforts of Colonel Dillon out of respect for what I had contributed to the art.[46]

Since the Commerce Department shows both names were on the license renewal when it was issued at midsummer 1925, and the threat of canceling the license had occurred the previous spring, when KQW was still in Herrold's name, it is difficult to see why church management was to blame. However, Herrold had earlier tried to work out a deal with the Exchange Club of San Jose to run his station, instead of the Baptist Church, and a lapse could have occurred during a period of time when he believed one or the other had assumed responsibility.

Finally on July 10, 1925, the First Baptist Church of San Jose took the first step in acquiring Herrold's license. The U.S. Commerce Department added the church's name on KQW's license together with that of Herrold, providing for joint ownership for another three months. While the name "Charles D. Herrold" also appeared in parenthesis on the face of license, it was there for the last time and was gone completely several months later when renewed by the church. From now on, the benefits and costs of operating KQW became the responsibility of the church. What was more important, the government allowed the new owners to increase the station's transmission power from 50 to 500 watts and to operate at 1320 kilocycles. To do this KQW needed to replace its old transmitter. Funds had to be raised and new program schedules worked out. In the transition period, Herrold was given the responsibility of sales and promotion while others took care of providing the station with a new transmitter and studio. Harry Saine, who had worked for the telephone company, was hired to install the station's new 500-watt Western Electric transmitter and serve as chief engineer.[47]

New Powerful Transmitter

First Baptist parishioners were set to work, under the guidance and enthusiasm of Pastor Towner, to raise the money necessary to enable KQW to carry the church's gospel message high and wide.[48] As soon as it got the license, the Baptist congregation inaugurated its campaign to raise $20,000, the amount needed to purchase and install the new transmitter, as well as to erect a new high antenna and more modern studios on church property, located near downtown San Jose. However, once the money was raised, the construction was not an easy job. The task, as Towner and other planners saw it, involved putting up twin transmission towers side by side outside the church's front and back doors, each rising to a height of 150 feet, and stringing antenna wire between them. Before this could be done, part of the front porch had to be removed. Church member Guy Lantz undertook the job of doing this, as well as putting up the towers. As each tower stood on four steel legs, Lantz saw to it that they were given solid foundations. He sunk ten-foot holes for each leg and poured four tons of concrete around each. And when the work was done, church leaders learned they had forgotten to get a city building permit and had to clear up that matter before new church programming on KQW broadcasting could begin. Perhaps this oversight indicated to church leaders that they were in dire need of a new station manager.

KQW Sales Power

Although Pastor Towner could ask parishioners to help finance the purchase of new equipment, studios and transmitter in order to give the church a more powerful voice in the community, he soon realized they could not be expected to pay for the station's day-to-day operating expenses. Parishioners simply could not be expected to carry such a burden and Towner knew KQW had to find a way of obtaining regular revenue. This is where Herrold came in. In the course of making public appearances before civic, business and social clubs around town and explaining radio to local audiences, Herrold was someone people in San Jose had come to know and were glad to listen to. He was well acquainted with civic and social leaders, and was dignified and respected. He was welcome in most places of the business community. If there was a new role for him to assume, Herrold was in a position to be KQW's perfect salesman.

By 1925 radio stations from coast to coast had adopted a new programming concept which would be a revolutionary development in American radio. They began to advertise the names of those who sponsored particular programs. There were no blatant sales messages at first, only the naming of sponsors in the titles of their programs such as the *Eveready Hour*, the *Kodak Chorus*, and the *Cliquot Club Eskimos.*[49] Herrold agreed to see what he could do to attract revenue to the station if KQW owners would relieve him of the daily burdens of radio engineering, administration, and programming. Based on what he had learned previously, Herrold knew the great publicity and advertising power given anyone mentioned on radio. For example, when the Wiley B. Allen Music Store loaned him records for the Wednesday night programs, it sold musical instruments, sheet music, and phonograph instruments when listeners found out KQW's music came from there. Success stories like that, he said, would interest the local business community. In fact, if allowed to do so, he figured he could persuade a good many San Jose merchants to try radio advertising. Thus in 1925 Herrold turned salesman. Remembering that Commerce Secretary Herbert Hoover had wanted to discourage advertising on radio, he decided to contact the Commerce Department in Washington to find out whether this attitude had changed. Herrold asked whether there were any laws or rules against it, and recalled the "unofficial answer" in a 1930 booklet he authored, "Sales Power of the Radio in Advertising." The federal government replied through a local radio inspector's office "that there was no law to prevent us from selling merchandise in front of a microphone but they hoped someone would stop us." It would be easy for one to conclude from this experience that Herrold's inquiry may have helped, along with similar requests from others, to suggest a development which some hoped to avoid — the cluttering of the airwaves with radio advertising.[50]

In San Jose, Herrold developed what he called "direct selling methods" for his clients. He realized small merchants had to get immediate results if they were to afford continued radio advertising. So Herrold began giving them daily sales messages in the *Shopper's Guide* program for the Central Market of San Jose. Listeners were told of special offerings, sales and bargains in each of shopping center's 14 departments in separate, one-minute messages. While the term "spot announce-

Having sold broadcasting to sponsors, Herrold goes before the KQW microphone in 1925 to prove to local merchants that radio advertising gets results (courtesy Perham Foundation Electronics Museum).

ments" had not yet been invented, this was exactly what KQW was doing. "At the end of eight months," said Herrold, "I still had the fourteen departments of the market using these announcements and, although I had no contracts with any of them, there were no defections." Every day Herrold visited each of the departments at this central location to gather material for his broadcast message. During this time, Lociscero's Market once sold and delivered 300 broilers in two hours. Springer's Candy Store had its largest one-day sales to customers in the history of the store. It was using a 100-word spot announcement every day for a period of 16 weeks. In summary, Herrold saw "no limit to the possibilities of radio advertising."

> During the year 1925 and well into the next year, I found it possible to sell restaurant or cafeteria service; clothing, either tailored or ready made; beauty parlor products or service; machinery or mechanical service; fruit ranches and farms as well as general real estate and selling service; dental, medical, and, in fact, any form of service applied to the care of the human body as well as animals and pets; hotels and resorts; every branch of the building trades, either merchandise or services; ideas, intellectual service or "brain brokerage"; legal service or education; entertainment or recreation.[51]

To prove the pulling power of his programs, Herrold experimented with a give-away offer. Having gotten an incense manufacturer to agree to supply a free sample to everyone who wrote in, Herrold said an "avalanche of letters and post cards resulted." Four thousand samples were requested and delivered through drug stores and novelty dealers in the KQW listening area after the offer was made.[52]

KQW: King's Quickening Word

While Herrold's old station had always featured musical concerts, the First Baptist Church joined a growing list of church-owned stations programming radio for a religious audience, emphasizing hymns, songs, and services traditional to their church, waiting for the new studios and new transmitter. KQW prepared to celebrate

Because phonograph reproduction was inferior to radio in 1925, Herrold knew his audience would enjoy "live" music. So he would play piano himself to entertain listeners to KQW (courtesy Perham Foundation Electronics Museum).

in a big way when the day arrived to operate from its new facilities located right there on church property. But another problem arose when someone pointed out that the church risked being taxed as a commercial enterprise by having the KQW's towers on its land. To avoid tax liability, the church management thought of deeding the relatively small space taken up by the feet of the towers to a couple of church members. But in the long run, it rejected this gimmick and the station had to pay taxes the same as any other legitimate business.[53] Finally, the day approached for the official dedication, the announcements to potential listeners were made, and the special dedicatory programming, which always included church service broadcasts every Sunday, began on Sunday, December 6, 1925. Church historian Bob Hill described what people heard on KQW:

> During the time of our agreement ... radio broadcasts were made (everything was "live" then) at 7 o'clock in the morning, six days a week. This, of course, first got Pastor Dawson, then Pastor Sands out of bed in time to get rid of their "just woke up" voices; and so also with Dilys Roberts who sang and sometimes played the piano, too, at all those early morning broadcasts. And then the Sunday Morning Sunday school Hour was also broadcast "live" from the main auditorium.[54]

With the official transfer complete, new meaning was given to the station's identity as the letters K-Q-W were now interpreted by the church owners to mean "King's Quickening Word."

A Good Man Is Hard to Find

During the six months elapsing between summer and winter of 1925, while KQW awaited its new quarters and transmitter, the First Baptist Church's main interest was in developing new programs of church services, sermons, and religious music to reach a vastly larger audience. However desirable it was to spread the gospel by radio, it was not producing appreciable income. What money KQW was earning from commercially sponsored programs just wasn't enough to pay the monthly bills, despite the efforts of Herrold and everyone else. So Pastor Towner and his church associates decided they needed a new manager to help put the station on a sound financial footing. In searching for ways to meet their expenses and carry out their plans for expansion, Towner found a man with good business ideas among the church parishioners. He was Fred J. Hart, a smart, peppy, and gregarious go-getter who was an editor and publisher of a series of agricultural publications for a California farm organization. He had moved to San Jose from the Salinas Valley for the health of his daughter. In him, the new station owners felt they had a man who knew exactly what to do. The pastor made a proposal, which Hart recalled years later in a radio interview.

> Dr. Towner said, "Well, Fred, you're a member of the church. Why don't you do something for the church?" So I said, "Well, what do you want me to do?" He said, "I want you to run KQW." And I said, "Well, I never ran one." He said, "We're paying you five thousand a year." I said, "Where do you get five thousand? You can't even pay for the station." And he said, "Well, maybe you'll make it." And I said, "No, I'll tell you what I'll do. I'll run it for nothing for one year, provided you give me one hour of time every night between 7 and 8 ... seven days, because I want to put on a complete radio newspaper for agriculture, with news items, editorials, funny page, everything. Every night and editorials." So he said, "Okay." So we set out to do it.[55]

A deal was struck. Hart agreed to take over the station's management, effective January 15, 1926, provided the church owners gave him a free hand to run KQW as the voice of California agriculture. As farm families constituted 30 percent of the population, according to what was learned by the 1920 U.S. Census, Hart came to believe the station could survive and prosper by serving the agricultural interests of California, since it could give the station a potentially large audience. The station's transmitter and studios had been moved to the property of the First Baptist church at Second and San Antonio streets. They legally still belonged to the church, but the day-to-day operations would be run by Hart and the Farm Bureau organization. The Baptist Church as station owner was being taxed $2,400 annually because the radio towers rested on church property, which caused the tax collector to assess the whole property. Hart knew he had to do something to relieve the church of that burden. Since the earlier tax avoidance scheme had not worked, he reasoned, "We had to build another tower in another location."[56] In promising to manage KQW, to build its audience and to help pay off the station's debts, Hart agreed that the station would continue carrying Sunday church services free of charge for 20 years. To help in this task, Ira L. Smith was brought up from the nearby coastal town of Santa Cruz to work on business and administration. Smith proved himself to be an able assistant to Hart and eventually he became KQW's operational manager.[57]

Napoleon of KQW

While Herrold didn't realize it at the time, the church's decision to put Fred Hart in charge of KQW would ultimately cost him his job. Hart was described in the local press as "a very large, strong, impressive-looking man." This is how Hart looked to R.L. Burgess, a *San Jose Evening News* reporter who wrote a series of articles about him in the spring of 1926.[58] According to the newspaper account, KQW's manager gave one the impression of being an English prizefighter with "lots of energy and reserve force." When he took charge, Hart told everyone he envisioned San Jose becoming the farm center of the Pacific Coast by serving up special farm programs to a potentially huge audience of growers and ranchers every night on KQW, 6:30 to 8:00 o'clock. By giving them entertainment as well as market reports and agricultural advice, Hart said he wanted radios in farm houses tuned to KQW from all over California, Oregon, Washington, Idaho, Montana, Utah, Arizona, New Mexico, British Columbia, and Alaska. On the other hand, shortly after KQW began doing its newspaper-of-the-air programming for farmers in this early evening period, the station was besieged with complaints. According to Hart and his assistant Smith, a sizable body of irate listeners rose up to protest, arguing they were entitled to a half-hour for distant listening. In a 1962 interview, the men recalled:

SMITH: That half-hour [7:30 to 8:00 P.M.], by some previous custom, had been religiously observed as a DX period. In other words, a distance-fishing period. Then you could tell your neighbor, "Last night on my crystal set I listened to the 'Hoot Oils' at Portland" or "I heard Keokuk, Iowa."

Q. You mean, traditionally local stations went off the air?

SMITH: Local stations, all over the Bay Area and us, supposedly, we went off the air to permit this particular group to do their fishing.

HART: [But KQW was broadcasting] 7 to 8 at night. That's the time a farmer would listen best. But here's what I did. I had my news section first, and then I followed it with my few little jokes, and then we had some market reports.... That got us to 30, and then we had a 15-minute editorial. I don't remember what we did on the last 15 minutes. We had a full hour, and what I had in mind was to broadcast a full newspaper every night except Sunday.[59]

Because KQW was located 50 miles south of San Francisco, Hart reasoned he was not subject to any Bay Area agreement to stay off the air during the traditional DX period. So the farm programs went on. Critics began calling KQW's burly station chief "Haywire Hart," and worse still, the "Napoleon of KQW." Hart found himself in a mess of trouble. In addition to interfering with distant listening, KQW was putting out such a broad and powerful signal it overwhelmed every station in the vicinity. Recalling what this situation was like in San Jose in the late 1920s, Warren F. Hodges, an amateur radio buff, said, "KQW so dominated the airwaves you could hear it in your bed springs." At his parents' home at 14th and Julian streets, he heard its powerful signal on a crystal set when he was ten years old, learned code and became a licensed amateur radio operator (W6DHX) at age 14 in 1932.[60]

By early spring of 1926, Hart had angered a lot of listeners. They resented losing their DX time. They complained bitterly, which caused the *San Jose News* to investigate the "donnybrook" and to print the pros and cons in a half dozen articles.[61] Although the initial blast against KQW originated with Thomas Lorenzo Kennon, a self-described radio expert who castigated KQW for preempting the DX time, it was later revealed that he was a disgruntled candidate for the job of managing KQW, and having lost out to Hart, he naturally became bitter. However, after making headlines in the press, Kennon's attack prompted others to make their opposition known and similar complaints were registered by other DX enthusiasts. The feelings against Hart were best summed up by N.L. Sherward of 374 South Second Street, who wrote, "Hundreds of boys under the range of KQW have invested their last nickel and denied themselves other wholesome privileges to buy parts to build their own sets." Now because all they heard was "the shouting of this soap box orator of KQW," he predicted that "this Napoleon of KQW will in time find his Waterloo."

Hart was irritating a group of outspoken listeners by giving the community farm programs when some people in its radio audience wanted to hear something else. The KQW transmitter radiated such a wide and strong signal it drowned out nearly all competition. When asked years later why KQW seemed so strong, the station's former executives said:

> SMITH: You see, in the early days the principal radio receiver was a crystal set. It was just as broad as a barn. The broadcasting stations in those days didn't have the narrow beam that they have now, you see. [With] our ground waves and our antenna waves—we just blanketed everything within blocks of the station....
>
> HART: The other thing that made it bad is—you may not remember—the old Atwater Kent with three dials. They were wonderful. They got everything. But they got it all at once.... When we [KQW] went on the air, I had a captive audience. They had to listen to me, or go to bed.[62]

Citing complaints by other letter writers, Burgess wrote a *News* column that said, "I know how a man feels, who, having tuned to KGO or KPO in San Francisco or KFI in Los Angeles, suddenly gets KQW all over the dial with nothing but the one-man band and harmonicas and dope on chickens and asparagus to listen to." In response, Hart argued that if San Jose fans used their little crystal sets only "to hear a little jazz and do a little DX fishing," they were making themselves subordinate to San Francisco and Oakland. That was thinking small. While it would take time to adjust to what KQW was doing, he said everyone should realize it was "a big new thing" and would put San Jose on the map. Hart said many Pacific Coast farm leaders appreciated what KQW was doing, citing support from the Grange, Prune and Apricot Growers, Farmers' Educational and Co-operative Union, Challenge Cream and Butter

Association, and the California Dairy Council. To make his point, Hart analyzed the specific criticism of his main opponent. "Mr. Kennon says that the farmers here are all fruit men and that they're not interested in how to raise ducks and chickens. It all depends upon what you mean by 'here.' If you mean by that merely Santa Clara County, then there is very little hope of San Jose becoming an important center. What KQW means by 'here' is British Columbia, for one thing. We mean the entire Pacific Coast." Many years later the donnybrook seemed to have been completely forgotten. It happened in 1934 when, KQW celebrated its 25th anniversary and, according to the *San Francisco Chronicle*, its broadcast "was picked up and rebroadcast by the DX Club of New Jersey."[63]

Problems Not Over

If Herrold had hoped that by giving the responsibilities of KQW over to others he would be relieved of his own personal financial worries, it was not to be. All the time and effort which he had invested in developing radio broadcasting in San Jose finally had taken an unhappy toll. His continual and frequent absences from home had cost him his marriage. When 37-year-old Charles swept the teenaged Sybil off her feet, the young girl had been initially impressed by how bright and energetic he appeared to be. But as the years went by, Herrold was seldom at home. These absences proved costly. At first she understood why her husband was preoccupied with wireless work. He had his school, where he both ran the business and served as headmaster. As the owner of a private school, Herrold needed a constant supply of new students, which made him a businessman in addition to being an educator who advised, taught and examined them once they were enrolled. And to ensure that the quality of education was maintained, he taught many of the classes himself. Added to those responsibilities, he desperately needed to find time to experiment, for he wanted to be the primary developer of the wireless telephone. Most of this experimenting had to take place at night, after the last student left for the day. For many years Sybil had tried to understand these needs, becoming a part-time broadcaster herself. But by the early 1920s the couple had little in common. Herrold's work took all his time. So in 1924 Charles and Sybil were officially divorced. After their marriage ended, Sybil took away both of his boys, Robert and Donald, and did something which puzzled both youngsters. When she remarried, Sybil not only acquired a new name for herself, becoming Mrs. Henry True, but she also changed the last names of both of Herrold's boys. The youngsters were told, "Your name is no longer Herrold. From now on it's True."

A few years later Herrold sought happiness in another marriage. He was attracted to a young woman who had been assisting him in sales and promotion at the station. She accepted his proposal and there was a "radio wedding" over KQW of Charles D. Herrold to Belle Coleman, which was broadcast on January 21, 1926. Although the wedding took place at the First Baptist Church itself and was widely publicized at the time, little is known of what happened to the marriage afterward. In trying to trace some important papers for a researcher in 1930, Herrold recalled, "These were

Charles Herrold married a woman named Belle Coleman on the air January 21, 1926, which KQW promoted as a "radio wedding." This may have been a publicity stunt, as little exists in the Herrold papers except this image and a script of the event (Stephen True Collection).

at the home of my second wife's sister in Richmond." Many years later, when Herrold passed away, his death certificate named only Sybil as his divorced wife and no other spouse was mentioned.[64]

Herrold's Downfall Begins

By the time the fall season of 1926 had arrived, the role Herrold had assumed at KQW was becoming untenable. KQW's financial problems were forcing the church into court and they were desperate to save money. This crisis was going to cost Herrold his job because the station was losing too much money to keep him on. It's not entirely clear when Herrold learned he had to leave KQW, but unhappily, it was the day before Herrold's 51st birthday, November 15, 1926, that a local newspaper printed the headline: "Move to Oust Herrold, 'Father of Radio,' As Director of Local KQW."[65] By a strange twist of circumstances, Herrold had become vulnerable. The First Baptist Church had acquired full control of Herrold's KQW license on or about Nov. 25, 1925, by signing a one-year contract retaining Herrold's services, agreeing to pay him $250 per month. The understanding was that if he made good during his year of service, it would be renewed. Dr. Towner said the church "had to take him" to secure Herrold's license. With the license, the station was authorized to commence broadcasting seven days a week.[66] When the Commerce Department approved KQW's renewal application the previous summer, the license showed both names as owners. While Herrold always said he turned over the license to the church at midyear, it didn't actually happen until many months later. Herrold is quoted in the press saying he gave the station away, but he had an agreement, too, with the Exchange Club, which had to be satisfied.[67] It wasn't satisfied until the Baptist church took over the local Exchange Club's contract with Herrold. According to the *San Jose Evening News*, "Herrold and the Exchange Club and officials of the First Baptist Church got together and Herrold turned his license over to the church, he being given a contract as director of the station and the club being given a contract calling for two hours a month which it could use at its discretion — which two hours it has never used."[68]

Why Herrold Was Let Go

KQW got too expensive for the First Baptist Church to run and too many members were adamant that they cut costs. Herrold's contract obligated the church to pay him $3,000 annually. By contrast, when Hart was hired to run the station, his contract required no salary at all, because his compensation was free airtime given to the California Farm Bureau organization, whose publications gave Hart an income of $6,000 per year. Herrold's contract came up first, on Nov. 25, 1926, and the farm group's renewal was two months away. Hart's was a one-year lease of the station by the California Farm Bureau, which would come up for reconsideration on January 15, 1927. As reported in the press, "Hart receives not a penny from station or church, being managing director of 31 farm publications, for which he receives a salary of $6,000 per year."[69] Hart said, "I like Herrold very much, personally but I can't support him. We've been supporting him for a year. It's just a straight business matter. Let somebody else support him for awhile."[70]

THE EVENING NEWS, SAN JOSE, CALIFORNIA, MONDAY, NOVEMBER 15, 1926

Move to Oust Herrold, "Father of Radio," As Director of Local KQW

Dr. Charles D. Herrold and his assistants operating the original "Radio KQW," the first radio broadcasting station in the world. The license which Dr. Herrold owned for this station was taken over by the First Baptist Church for its present station.

That Dr. Charles D. Herrold, the world's first radio broadcaster and one of the earliest pioneers in the art of wireless, is to be discharged as director of Radio KQW at the expiration of his contract, November 25, 1926, became known to The News on reliable sources today.

MADE FIRST BROADCAST

San Jose Evening News, November 16, 1926 (Stephen True Collection).

In responding to the church's petition that there be a fair and equitable adjustment of its $20,000 mortgage and some relief from its other obligations, Superior Court Judge J.R. Welch issued two types of opinions, one which was advisory and permitted some discretion and the other obligatory and had to be carried out. First, the judge recommended to the station owners that: (1) they rid the community, as far as possible, of the interference that KQW was causing thousands of private radios; (2) they take KQW out of business and use it entirely for religious purposes; and (3) they observe, as other stations observe, the DX period for one-half hour each night. Second, he issued enforceable orders that the church: (1) pay the station's indebtedness of $2,817 on or before January 1, 1928; (2) pay the remainder of church debt, totaling $5,646 within three years; and (3) place radio pledges totaling $10,000 due in 1927 in the hands of a bill collector and use the money to pay off the station's indebtedness.

By not renewing Herrold's contract, KQW saved $3,000 in annual salary. Yet despite this personal calamity, Herrold made it known that he was leaving San Jose without bitterness or animosity. "I kept the license alive for sentimental reasons," he said. "I let the Baptist church have it because I was anxious to see KQW an operating station, taking its place among the great broadcasting stations of the coast. I regarded it as a monument to my father, William Morris Herrold, who helped me during our pioneer days of experiment. No matter what happens to me or Hart, I desire more than anything to see KQW 'carry on'; to see it placed on a basis which insure[s] popular support."[71] And in "Herrold Makes Last Broadcast," the *Mercury-Herald* published his final words: "Don't knock KQW. Boost it. I am making this personal appeal to each and every one of my friends— if you want to do the greatest thing for me — put your whole support back of KQW ... Goodbye, my friends of radioland."[72]

7
Broadcasting for Everybody

Radio-phone broadcasting has changed.... A year or more ago, radio appealed to the boy and young man in search of some intricate, mysterious, time-consuming hobby.... But our present radio-phone concerts have brought a new element into radio. What with talks by prominent men, weather forecasts, crop and market reports for farmers, bed-time stories for children, shipping news, fashion talks, health chats, musical selections and other features which can now be received every day and evening right in the home, radio has become a means to an end. That end is the entertainment and educational value of the radio-phone broadcasting service. And the public is becoming more and more interested in that end....

Austin C. Lescarboura, Managing Editor,
Scientific American (April 10, 1922)[1]

Where did the idea of "radioland" come from and why was it finally realized at the end of World War I? It is easy enough to say the time was ripe for it to happen, but the underlying reasons why it happened when it did are much more complex than that.[2] The fact that America was thrust into the European war was perhaps one of the most important influences on radio's accelerated development. If victory were to be assured, the country had to organize its military, economic and productive power. The United States government needed to advance all forms of new technology, radio being one them. To set the country on a course toward victory, American businesses were told to cooperate, and all relevant radio patent holders were brought together to develop and improve communications technology. Thus the way was paved immediately after the war for some public and private leaders to continue cooperating. It became easier in the postwar period to reach agreements influencing radio's future.

For many large American corporations, the war years of 1917–1918 were extremely profitable. In those particular areas of production that were useful to the Army Signal Corps and U.S. Office of Naval Communications, this meant those in

San Francisco Bay Area radio stations typically looked like this in the 1930s. Many had offices and studios downtown, which made radio a part of the community (courtesy Perham Foundation Electronics Museum).

charge were given a green light to further develop wireless telegraphy and wireless telephony. The government directly or indirectly was paying for research and development. All disputes over patents and other claims were moot. The government insisted that all legal contenders put their litigation in abeyance and the arguing parties were told to share their inventive genius in order to help win the war. One of those who issued such orders was a future U.S. president — Under Secretary of the Navy Franklin D. Roosevelt.[3] The result was that the war accelerated research and development of wireless communication at an amazing speed.

What began during the war carried over into arrangements between government and business afterward. Encouraged by some in Washington, D.C., who did not want vital communications under foreign control, General Electric, the American Telephone and Telegraph Company and later Westinghouse were encouraged immediately after the war to come together to resolve their interests and to find a way of protecting wireless telephony for the United States. Thus came into being what was known as the "patents pool," the creation of the Radio Corporation of America and other compacts which allowed American business to take the leadership in radio's development. These post-war historic and complex business and manufacturing arrangements had enormous influence on the future of electronics and radio, but they were not always advantageous for the individual amateur, experimenter or inventor. During the conflict and immediately thereafter, radio became so important it was taken from the hands of hundreds of individuals and given over to what amounted to a government- and industry-sanctioned monopoly.

Every business involved in the war effort profited not only by receiving handsome contracts with the government, but also advanced its own technology and capacity to manufacture new kinds of radio apparatus. There is no question that wartime work by its parent company is what helped the early development of radio station

KDKA, said to be the oldest station in the United States because it came on the air in 1920.[4] The station unabashedly credited its head start to the "Westinghouse experience with the vacuum tube while working on World War I radio contracts for the United States and British governments."[5] At the end of the war, the government decreed that all radio facilities taken over during the war were to be returned to private hands. When this happened, AT&T, Westinghouse, General Electric, and the American Marconi Company were ahead of everybody else.

One individual who was particularly harmed by this development of corporate radio during the war was Charles Herrold, who with the coming of peace discovered that his arc radiotelephone technology had been made completely obsolete by the sudden advances. Years of hard work and large investments of money had been lost. He was no longer relevant as an inventor, patent-holder, or wireless school educator. And while the evidence shows that he was the first person in the early part of the 20th century to actually operate a radio station on a regular schedule, this record of achievement had not made him rich or famous. While the lives of people everywhere were about to be enriched and changed in the new decade of the 1920s with the production and marketing of this new form of mass communication, no one could be more astonished at the suddenness of its happening and the enthusiasm for its development than the first explorer of radioland itself—Charles Herrold.

Wireless Knowledge Grew

During the war, the Army and Navy needed highly skilled and well-trained men to send and receive Morse code. Hundreds of radiomen were produced from 1917 to 1918. To help serve the needs of the military, Herrold College of Wireless and Engineering was one of a number of schools which offered its services to the government. For example, Harvard and the University of Wisconsin had begun offering new wireless training courses for military purposes shortly after America entered the conflict. In San Jose, Herrold was forced by government edict to close down his radio station, but he kept a wireless school in operation. Thus new recruits flocked to the Herrold College, enabling the San Jose school to prepare hundreds of young men for radio communications service. Between 1909 and 1917, Herrold calculated that he taught about 1,200 students. If the Army and Navy had paid Herrold to turn out wireless school graduates during the war, he estimated his income based on the number who entered the military would have been at least $65,000.[6] But as it turned out, Herrold's college contributed to the war effort without a government contract, and he had to make do with student-paid tuition. In 1919 the President of the American Radio Relay League, Hiram Percy Maxim, said that before America's entry into the war, the country had 8,562 persons scattered about the land licensed to use transmitting equipment and 125,000 able to receive what was being sent out. But during the war, the number trained for the military amounted to about 100,000 wireless operators and "they would be back home, looking for ways to apply their special knowledge."[7]

Before the war, thousands of American radio amateurs were interested in wireless. Many of them had been using code, listening for "spark," or accidentally picking up stations offering voice and music. They constituted the audience for concerts transmitted by Herrold, de Forest, and the few other experimental broadcasters. While no one took any surveys, it was estimated that 125,000 amateurs had receiving sets and were regularly putting them to use. Every prewar community had an audience of amateurs equipped and ready for radiotelephony. When the war ended, these amateurs were eager to resume their activity. Added to their number were thousands of military veterans, mostly wireless men of the navy, who also were eager to set up and use radio equipment when the ban was lifted. That occurred on October 1, 1919 — less than a year after the war ended — when permission was given amateurs to resume wireless sending and receiving. This returned a vast number of radio enthusiasts to their wireless apparatus and also laid the groundwork for the development of a boom in commercial radio. Within a year, 6,000 had applied for and received amateur licenses.

Armstrong Receiver

What also helped popularize radio at the same time was an improved way of tuning in radio signals. It was the regenerative receiver, developed by Edwin H. Armstrong. He had originally conceived of it while serving as a student lab assistant at Columbia University in 1913, and principles he discovered served as the basis for amplitude modulation (AM) radio. Able to continue his radio research as a wartime officer in the Signal Corps, Major Armstrong improved the concept and produced the superheterodyne circuit. By war's end he had given the radio industry a highly sensitive and selective radio receiver, capable of picking up signals over a wide range of frequencies. Although Armstrong had to spend two decades defending his work against Lee de Forest, who finally won the patent rights in a controversial 1934 Supreme Court decision, Armstrong is believed by most historians and scientists to have been the true creator of the regenerative receiver.[8] As they enabled listeners to fine tune stations without the need of earphones, these new receivers were welcomed into family homes everywhere, and before the end of the 1920s were in widespread use.[9] Radio had become a new form of mass communication.

Discovering Radioland

Radio's most exciting development began in 1920s and before the decade was over, its popularity had spread worldwide. As early as 1922 radio listening was no longer the exclusive province of the hobbyist, the amateur and the experimenter. One household out of 500 in the United States owned a receiver. Free entertainment, which you easily could pick out of the air, prompted a rush to buy or build receiving sets everywhere.[10] People heard their friends and neighbors talking in amazement about the distant stations they had heard coming from far away on their radio receivers the night before. The country became aware of a new phenomenon. No longer was "wireless phoning" a complicated mystery limited to the do-it-yourself set builder. New technology now made it available to everyone. Although early radio resembled latter day non-commercial broadcasting because it was largely free of overt advertising, what people heard in the early 1920s was rich in its variety of programming. It was an astonishing economic, behavioral and cultural revolution.

Some historians have described the rush to radio as one of the most extraordinary booms in the history of the American people, because radio stations sprang up everywhere and audiences sprang up with them. It was a boom of a new industry. People were astonished by radio broadcasting, which like magic brought news and entertainment into their homes no matter where they lived. Talk, music and entertainment came through the air, it was free to everyone and it could be picked up simply by procuring an easy-to-operate receiving set. As shown below by a letter Merle Stearns of the Perham Foundation of San Jose got in 1922 from his sister "Birdie" in New Jersey, radio seemed to her to be something of a miracle. She said that radio showed "how very simple and easy it is to believe that God in Heaven hears the unuttered thoughts of our hearts. If puny man can catch sound vibrations miles away, over the heads of thousands of people who can't hear them, what can not our wonderful God and Heavenly Father do?"[11] This audience started building in the 1920s and surged into the next decade.

Radio ... is a marvelous thing

2113 S. Alden St.
May 12, 1922

Dear Merle,

I heard "something new under the sun"—at least to me—this week. I "listened in" on a radio concert. Really it is a marvelous thing. I don't care how common it becomes. The very idea of putting a wire apparatus up on the roof over your house, attaching it to nothing at all, but just setting it like a trap to catch all sorts of messags that the air is full of. I wonder if you have seen one.

It is quite a fad here to set up home made ones. The one I "listened in" on was home made. Of course, I'm no electrician or mechanic, and couldn't make head nor tail of it, but I am sure you could make one, though of course you have to have the electric power to reproduce the sound after you have caught it. The wire apparatus is put up on the roof and is attached to a sort of machine placed or really built on a table, usually in the dining room or living room. Then there are two ear pieces that one person can use, or two persons, one each. And you start the thing going like an electric battery, and turn the spindle until you get it keyed to the pitch of the instrument sending the message.

When you get to the right spot you will hear the music. We listened to a concert given in Gimbel's Store, at least three miles away. Gimbel's name is given first, then a man's voice says Mr. So and So will sing, and we heard the piano playing and then the man singing. It was very soft and sweet and far-away, but perfectly clear and distinct. And when I realized that there was absolutely no connection between the instrument I was listening to, and the place where the music was, other than the air that is all round us,—really it is a wonderful thing.

It made me think of prayer, and how very simple and easy it is to believe that God in Heaven hears the unuttered thoughts of our hearts. If puny man can catch sound vibrations miles away, over the heads of thousands of people who can't hear them, what can not our wonderful God and Heavenly Father do? These machines can

> also if keyed high enough catch messages of all kinds from Camden and New York.
>
> Well, dear, I must run now. Lots of love to you both,
>
> Your loving sister,
> Birdie

(Merle Sterns saved this letter because of his lifelong interest in radio. He continues doing so as a member of the Perham Foundation in San Jose, California, which preserves radio history and memorabilia, most notably, surviving Herrold technology.)

As radio historian Gleason L. Archer described this rush to radio: "From all over the United States orders for equipment for prospective radio broadcasting stations came pouring into the manufacturers of such apparatus. The unexplainable part of it is that no one at that time, except the manufacturers, had any reasonable prospect of monetary gain. No one knew how radio could earn any money for the owner of a station unless such owner chanced to be a dealer in radio supplies."[12] But there was a sure profit to be made by manufacturing and selling receiving sets. So a flock of enterprising Americans didn't hesitate. The trick was not to wait too long but jump in and get in on the ground floor. All across America, a rash of new broadcasting stations began airing news, music and variety programs. Although many were very short-lived, there were always newcomers to take their place. In the last quarter of 1921, 21 new stations were licensed. By the first half of 1922 the count had risen to 264. The number of receivers sold to listeners jumped as well. In March 1921 there were 50,000 and by May 1922, this figure had increased to 750,000. In Europe a similar pattern of development was taking place. In Paris, the French were broadcasting from the Eiffel Tower by February 1922; in London, the forerunner of the British Broadcasting Corporation had started airing programs in November 1922; and in Germany, broadcasting commenced in October 1923. Europe was experiencing the same rapid growth of radio as that in America, as "over a million radio [receiving] licenses were operative in Britain in 1925 and half a million in Germany."[13]

National Craze

As to which stations were the first to begin radio broadcasting after the war, an obvious advantage went to those who could get their hands on the necessary equipment. As Paul Schubert, a contemporary observer, wrote, "In the quality of reproduction the radio was from the beginning of the vacuum tube era, equal if not superior to the line-telephone and the phonograph, which had set the standard."[14] By mid–1921 the ease of using voice radio was recognized by the U.S. Department of Commerce as superior to radio telegraphy and ordered that commencing on April 15, 1921, the transmission of its weather and crop information would be done using radiotelephony.[15] From 1921 to 1928, the craze for radio among the general public would boost the size of its listening audience from a few thousand to more than ten million. Schubert wrote:

> The thing grew with amazing rapidity. From the moment it was released by the clearing of the patent situation in July 1921, it started to appear simultaneously in all parts

of the country. That summer and fall the masts and antennae of broadcasting stations were going up from coast to coast. In September 1921, the first three broadcasters to follow "KDKA" went "on the air." There was another in October, one more in November, and then in December there were twenty-three.[16]

Business Engaged in by Owners of Broadcasting Stations in 1922

Source: *Radio Broadcast* (April 1922)

Business	*Number*	*Percent*
Radio and Electronic Manufacturers and Dealers	231	41%
Newspapers and Publications	70	12
Educational Institutions	65	11
Department Stores	30	5
Auto and Battery Companies, Cycle Dealers	17	3
Music and Musical Institutions and Jewelry	12	2
Churches and YMCAs	10	2
Hardware Stores	8	1
Banks and Brokers	5	1
Stock Yards, Poultry, and Grain	4	1
Clubs and Societies	4	1
Mine Supplies, Marble, Oil Companies	4	1
Railroad and Power Companies	4	1
Telephone and Telegraph Companies	4	1
Parks and Amusements	3	1
State Bureaus	3	1
Theaters	2	-
Laundries	2	-
Unknown	86	15
TOTAL	570	100%

While a few technical magazines had been serving amateurs and experimenters with news about wireless for more than a decade, periodicals of general circulation like *The Literary Digest* suddenly awakened to the fact that radio had caught the public's fancy. In 1922 it made the new radio fad one of its regular departments. By July of that year its radio editor was reporting, "It is estimated in the last three months at least 1,250 new corporations have been organized to manufacture radio apparatus.... Shoemakers, jewelers, hair-dressers, cloak and suit manufacturers are stampeding into the radio business...."[17]

Who's Who of the Airwaves

New owners of radio stations believed the chief benefit in broadcasting was creating name recognition in the community. It was hoped free programming for listeners would bring good publicity because the idea of advertising anything for sale on the air in the early 1920s was still in its infancy. Stations identified themselves by the names of their owners—the *Examiner* (newspaper), Earl C. Anthony (automobile dealer), Hales (department store), Westinghouse (manufacturer), the community church, school, college, and so forth. As Schubert observed in the late 1920s:

> In the beginning of commercial broadcasting, many of its proponents labored under a fundamental misconception. They believed that the publicity accruing to a single broadcaster would make a station financially profitable or at least self-sustaining if operated in his interest alone.... This is precisely the cycle that radio-broadcasting went through, for rather strangely, not one per cent of the original broadcasters entered the game as "publishers".... The immediate result was that it failed in its purpose.... It came to be realized, then, that the broadcasting station must be, in truth, a publishing house—that the broadcaster must ... sell "time on the air."[18]

Those who thought of putting advertising on the air in the early days did not have an easy time of it. As the promise of the medium began to be realized in the mid–1920s, editors like Bruce Bliven of the *Century* magazine editorialized against radio advertising, saying it would be "wholly undesirable" and "should be prohibited by legislation if necessary."[19] When Secretary of Commerce Hoover gathered interested parties together in 1922 for the first Washington Radio Conference, it was generally agreed "that it was against public interest to broadcast pure advertising matter."[20] In the beginning no one really knew how to make radio broadcasting profitable. While the history of competing patent claims is long and complicated, its solution resulted in a number of contractual arrangements between a small number of corporations which deemed them beneficial. Under these rather peculiar and complex arrangements, Westinghouse and General Electric were permitted to manufacture radio receivers, RCA to sell them and Western Electric to make transmitters. The American Telephone and Telegraph Company was given the exclusive right to put programs or messages on the air as "toll calls" and to engage in "chain" broadcasting. The latter was when the telephone company arranged a hookup of a number of stations to carry a single program to many cities, also called "toll" broadcasting. Two things happened in the early 1920s to change all this: many smaller stations began to accept advertising despite its general disfavor, and AT&T decided that its main business was in being the telephone company. In 1926 it decided to get out of broadcasting except for leasing its lines as needed.[21]

When some enterprising broadcasters in the early 1920s believed they could make money by selling a portion of airtime for sales announcements, the idea of doing so was squelched by the head of the Department of Commerce. The man who looked with disfavor on radio advertising was Commerce Secretary Herbert Hoover (who later became U.S. President), who probably had a greater influence on how radio developed in America than any other federal official. Since Hoover spoke out firmly against the idea of advertising on radio when the concept was first advanced to him, it would take several more years before spot announcements or sponsored programs were heard regularly over the radio. Originally, it wasn't advertising, but the moneymaking possibilities of selling the hardware to the public—thousands of receiving sets—that convinced a number of business-minded persons that radio could be made profitable after the war. This idea intrigued more than one third of those who first began applying for licenses. As shown in a survey of 570 stations actively broadcasting in 1922 by the trade publication *Radio Broadcast*, more than 40 percent of the owners were engaged in manufacturing or retailing radio appliances. Twenty-three percent of the owners were newspapers, other publishers, and educational institutions.[22]

Radio for Everybody

What Charles Herrold felt he needed to do in the postwar years was to become a practical businessman. By opening a new retail store in the same building as his radio station in downtown San Jose, Herrold had the chance to educate the public about radio, to help them hook up receivers, string antenna and ground lines, and let them listen to musical concerts. To be a radio listener in those days, the average man or woman needed someone to explain how the newfangled gadget worked. If you had someone like Herrold to help you assemble and tune your receiving apparatus, you were well on your way to enjoying radio at home every day. Or if you had sufficient technical knowledge yourself, you could easily put together a radio receiver. If you could afford one, you bought a tube set and listened to broadcasts with either a personal headset or a large megaphone-type horn, a long antenna wire and another for a ground. Before plug-in type receivers were available circa 1928, all early tube models needed a battery connection of some kind to enable it to operate. Herrold served every kind of radio listener.

While crystal sets were fun and easy to use, radio couldn't become a widespread attraction for the average American family until loudspeakers were available to replace earphones. Radio's popularity depended upon everyone at home being able to gather around the set to listen in. The horn loudspeaker, once it was introduced, would almost completely replace headsets by 1925.

Herrold never lost his enthusiasm for broadcasting in the 1920s; that is beyond dispute.[23] In 1922 he set up public address systems at fairs and exhibitions to amplify and rebroadcast programs coming from many of the stations in the San Francisco Bay Area. Crowds attending these public gatherings could hear KQW and other stations nearly all the time they were at these outdoor affairs. They learned what was "on the airwaves" at that particular moment from schedules he printed and handed out. Throughout the day and into the evening people heard music from the Fairmont Hotel in San Francisco, the Presidio in San Francisco, Rock Ridge Radio station in Oakland, and Colin B. Kennedy station in Los Altos, which was being run by his former student, Emil A. Portal. In the San Francisco Bay Area, no more than one station could broadcast at a time, and none could stay on the air longer than an hour or so.[24] In fact, San Francisco, Oakland and San Jose stations all agreed to remain off the air for a half-hour period in the early evening (7:30–8:00 P.M.) to permit radio fans, amateurs and the general public to listen to distant stations, a hobby which became known as "DXing."[25] There were 17 stations licensed to the San Francisco area in 1922 and of that number 13 actually were on the air entertaining audiences on the same channel (360 meters) and needing to share time according to a schedule.[26] When people heard a faraway station and wrote to the station to report what they heard, they expected the station to send them DX cards in return, which some radio fans eagerly collected and showed their friends. Response of this kind helped a station to "determine its area coverage from the postmarks on listener requests for DX cards...."[27] Bay Area listeners were thrilled if they could pick up Denver (KOA), Salt Lake City (KSL) or Los Angeles (KFI).

Claims and Comparisons

Charles Herrold always claimed that he established America's first radio station and therefore was the first broadcaster. Because others have made the same claim, each deserves a fair hearing. The major contenders for broadcasting honors besides Herrold are Frank Conrad (KDKA), Earle Terry (WHA), and Lee de Forest (New York, Detroit and San Francisco stations).

If licensing were the only criteria for choosing the earliest broadcaster, Herrold might claim it for having obtained "FN" in 1912. Governments began issuing licenses that year. Thus his would be the earliest. Radiotelephone experimenters like Fessenden, de Forest and Herrold had gone on the air without needing any licenses prior to 1912. Since the reason for the first licenses was not to authorize broadcasting but for other purposes, licensing generally has not been accepted as a sound basis for choosing among candidates. Nevertheless, the history of licensing often shows whose work led some early experimenters accidentally or on purpose into broadcasting.

In the 1921 issue of its annual publication, the Radio Service Office of the Bureau of Navigation of the U.S. Department of Commerce lists three of the four major contenders. Each of the three was authorized to resume operations using experimental licenses after the war, and each obtained regular commercial broadcast licenses when they were issued later by the Commerce Department. Although the name of Lee de Forest was not on the 1921 list, it is included below because he was licensed and experimenting both before the war and afterward. With de Forest added to the list, there are four experimenters whose work led to early day broadcasting stations, as follows:[28]

(1) 6XE/6XF—Charles D. Herrold, San Jose, California, founder of KQW/KCBS

(2) 8XK—Frank Conrad, Pittsburgh, Pennsylvania, establisher of KDKA

(3) 9XM—Earle Terry, University of Wisconsin, Madison, Wisconsin, creator of WHA

(4) 2XG, 8MK, 6XC—Lee de Forest, New York, Detroit and San Francisco: builder of WWJ

The de Forest company put the *Detroit News* station WWJ on the air, but de Forest himself never established a permanent radio station.[29] The historic metamorphoses of experimental radiotelephones into popular broadcasting did not happen easily.

The Conrad Experiments

What Herrold had been doing on the air in California since 1909 was fairly well known on the West Coast but hardly anywhere else. When the idea of playing phonograph records occurred to Frank Conrad 3,000 miles away in 1919, the evidence shows he had no knowledge of what was happening in California. He believed entertaining audiences by radio was something new. The fact that his transmissions began to attract nightly audiences was intriguing. A local newspaper thought so, too, and publicized the fact that Conrad and 8XK had been transmitting musical programs from Conrad's home in Wilkinsburg, Pennsylvania, since October 17, 1919. This caught the attention of his employer, the Westinghouse Corporation. Since the company happened to manufacture radio receivers, Westinghouse saw a chance to increase sales to the general public and decided to establish its own broadcasting station. Thus the Conrad experiments were instrumental in putting KDKA in Pittsburgh on the air on November 2, 1920, and because of it received a commercial license ahead of everyone else, the station claims it is entitled to be recognized as America's oldest broadcasting station.[30]

KDKA and Commercial Licensing

There is no question that Frank Conrad, as a Westinghouse engineer, deserves credit for helping obtain the first commercial broadcasting license for his company soon after they became available. Word of their availability was made by the U.S. Department of Commerce on October 27, 1920. Thanks to newspaper publicity given Conrad's early radio experiments, Westinghouse Vice President H.P. Davis awakened to the possibilities of radio broadcasting and decided to take his company into it. When Davis learned that Conrad was entertaining listeners from his amateur station at home, he realized what a radio station could do to promote sales, applied for a license, and got permission to operate with the call letters 8ZZ, which was used for airing the station's election night coverage on November 2, 1920. A few days later Westinghouse acquired the call letters KDKA.

Conrad's background has been recounted by biographer David Kraeuter, who wrote:

> Born in Pittsburgh on May 4, 1874, by age 16 Frank Conrad had quit school to work as a bench hand with the Westinghouse Electric and Manufacturing Company, his life-long employer. Between 1898 and 1942 (the year after his death) Conrad received over 200 American, English and German patents on mechanical and electrical devices such as grenades, refrigerators, carburetors, radio transmitters and receivers, televisions, clocks, arc lamps, gear shifts, air conditioners, insulators, vacuum tubes, and electric meters. His experimentation with radio transmitting in 1919 and earlier helped Westinghouse found pioneer radio station KDKA. In the 1920s Conrad also did pioneering work which helped establish worldwide communications via short wave.[31]

A self-educated electrical engineer who never went to college, Conrad was awarded an honorary doctor of science degree from the University of Pittsburgh in 1928 in recognition of his achievements.

How KDKA Began

Unlike Herrold, who had been forbidden to engage in any form of radiotelephony during the war, Conrad, as a Westinghouse employee, was given a unique opportunity. He was assigned the call letters 3WE by the third naval district and allowed to carry on his experimental work. The Army Signal Corps needed the vacuum tube radiotelephone improved and the U.S. Navy wanted airplane transmitter problems solved. Often Conrad accomplished this by using his voice and a phonograph as an audio source.[32] One wonders whether listener response to his wartime experiments influenced what he did after the war. After the armistice, Conrad continued to experiment, and by the middle of 1920, his Saturday night phonograph concerts had attracted a small audience in East Pittsburgh, Pennsylvania, in the area known as Wilkensburg. Said Conrad in 1940:

> People within radio distance had bootleg receivers, and soon they began picking up transmissions. Then they began to telephone and say, "We have some friends in this evening. They do not believe us when we tell them that we can pick up music out of the air. Won't you please play some selections for them?"[33]

Westinghouse executive S.M. Kintner said that Conrad started putting his music on the air regularly in 1920 — Wednesday and Saturday nights— because of the number of requests he was receiving. The publicity given his programs led Pittsburgh department stores to begin advertising radio receiving sets "suitable for listening to Mr. Conrad's concerts."[34]

According to Leroy Williams, special patent counsel to Westinghouse:

> As a result of the publicity that Conrad got with his sending out radiotelephone signals, Joseph Horne and Co., a department store of Pittsburgh advertised in September, 1920, that they would sell receiving sets that would pick up Conrad's music. H.P. Davis, Westinghouse president, saw this ad and saw the possibilities of radio broadcasting. He thought it was time for the company to take over the work of Conrad.[35]

Soon these Pittsburgh concerts were attracting attention across the country. In the September 1920 issue of *QST*, which was a major national amateur magazine, Conrad's 8XK was written up in great detail.[36] The cover story explained with pictures and text how Conrad's low power transmitter worked. Readers saw a photograph of a microphone aimed at the horn of a wind-up phonograph, the kind of setup which KDKA would use months later in that same year. And unlike de Forest's experience in 1916, when he broadcast returns of the Wilson-Hughes presidential election not knowing whether he would have much of an audience, there was widespread publicity given to the Pittsburgh station's planned election night broadcast. Thanks to successful patent agreements and their effect on the supply of legal radio parts, many more receivers were now available to the general public. In fact, increased sales of Westinghouse-manufactured receivers was what the company hoped to achieve from this highly publicized broadcast. It was eager to sell its Westinghouse/RCA tuner-receiver, originally developed in Conrad's research laboratory during the war, manufactured for the military, and now available as a simple home receiver.[37]

Who Gets Credit for KDKA?

But it was not simply an overnight transition from Conrad's garage experiments to KDKA as a broadcast station. According to Conrad, the whole idea began as a plan for a two-way service, originating with S.M. Kintner of Westinghouse, who had

> planned a city service or rather cities service, placing stations at Pittsburgh, Newark, and Cleveland, for code communication, with radiotelephone working as a sideline. These point to point stations were installed. It was for code operation in these stations, incidentally, that the ... receivers were designed. I went to H.P. Davis, big boss of Westinghouse and said, "Why have this just a point to point affair? Why not let the station talk to everyone, not just to each other?" This was June or July of 1920.[38]

Davis liked the idea of KDKA seeking a public audience so much he soon had a group of Westinghouse stations all doing the same thing: The Pittsburgh station "went on the air, for the first time, on Election Day, 1920. Permission to use the station for broadcasting on that night was granted, the call being 8ZZ. A few days after the election, permission to add broadcasting to KDKA's license was granted.... [We] used the calls 8ZZ and KDKA more or less interchangeably during the night."[39] Frank Conrad described the famous November 2, 1920, election eve broadcast in a 1937 letter to RCA historian George Clark:

> The broadcast was carried out in cooperation with the *Pittsburgh Post* and the publicity was entirely confined to the *Pittsburgh Post* circulation. The broadcast was primarily to announce the election returns and the first returns were received about 8 P.M.; however, some preliminary matters, such as talks and music were transmitted from about 6:30 P.M. The content of the broadcast, other than the news bulletins of the election, consisted of short talks explaining how the broadcast was carried out and interspersed with musical selections. These selections were almost entirely phonograph reproductions. My recollection is that the weather was clear on that day. We had carried out enough preliminary tests to assure ourselves that the service would be reasonably reliable; however, to guard against any general breakdown, such as power or lines, arrangements were made so that (my) private station in the garage (8XK) could be used in place of the station at East Pittsburgh — line facilities being arranged for from the *Pittsburgh Post* building to (my) home. Certain information on the results were known soon after the broadcast started by telephone calls from receiving stations, which previously had been instructed to report on the success of receiving the returns. The broadcast in general was handled by the personnel of our publicity department and the radio engineering department. It would be somewhat difficult to give a complete list of the names of the people taking part in the program. However, so far as the listening audience was concerned, it is probable that only one name appeared, that of L.H. Rosenberg, who did the announcing.[40]

Why Conrad Succeeded

After its November 2, 1920, broadcast, KDKA returned to the airwaves on a weekly schedule and established its daily operation much later. Although Herrold had been entertaining audiences with his San Jose station with regularity many years before, Conrad's activity occurred at the right time and place. The publicity given to Conrad's amateur record-playing appeared exactly at a time when key radio manufacturers could see its significance. It attracted the attention of an important Westinghouse executive, who saw in the newspaper story that people enjoyed listening to radio. Because of this, Conrad was told to acquire a license for the company and get the station ready to go on the air to broadcast election returns. Conrad had the support and organization of a manufacturing company executive who realized there might be profit to be made selling radios. However, Conrad was not the only person at Westinghouse who claimed to be the station's founder. Davis and Kintner each claimed it was their idea in interviews and news stories years later. KDKA finally was content to give the laurels to Conrad.[41]

It is KDKA's record of continuous broadcasting since November 2, 1920, that makes its claim of being the country's "oldest station" legitimate, but it is overstating the case to say that KDKA was "the first."[42] By judiciously restricting its territorial claim to the United States, KDKA has also left open the question of what was happening elsewhere in the world in the 1920s. While there is no evidence Europeans led in radio development, they were not far behind.[43]

WHA, University Pioneer

The claim of being the oldest also has been made by the University of Wisconsin's radio station, WHA, at Madison. This pioneer station began giving farmers' market reports "verbally" over the air as early as 1917.[44] The man who began the service was Professor Earle Terry, who had been using a wireless telegraph in his classroom since 1902. He recognized the value of using university facilities to provide reports on agriculture, advice and news to a widely scattered rural audience by means of a communication system which could reach them quickly and easily. According to one historical account:

> Terry and a group of his physics students had been running a dot-and-dash code station 9XM. They decided that they would build a telephonic broadcasting station, using the new vacuum tubes.... The tubes, which were the heart of the station, were not for sale. Nobody had yet developed a way of making them commercially. What could they do? Make their own. That is exactly what they did.... By 1917, after many months of hard work — marked by long nights in the laboratory — 9XM finally managed to get understandable broadcasts of talk and music into the air.[45]

According to one of Terry's students, C.M. Jansky, Jr., "First we built a continuous wave radiotelegraph transmitter. Then we experimented with circuits for modulating the output of the transmitter for radiotelephony."[46] Although Terry utilized his own radio vacuum tubes to transmit voice before the World War I, his pioneering radio work has been largely unrecognized outside of Wisconsin. When other experimenters were shut down across the country in 1917, Terry was allowed to keep 9XM on the air to serve the needs of the military and the U.S. Naval Training Station at the Great Lakes. A 1987 article titled "World's Oldest Radio Station" recalled:

> By the time the war ended and other stations were again allowed to broadcast, 9XM had developed techniques of transmission to a high degree and had established regular program services.[47]

Soon after the war, the Wisconsin station was equipped to transmit farm reports with a more powerful voice. According to Jansky, "On January 3, 1919, there began the daily radiotelephone broadcasts of weather reports which, according to the records of the United States Weather Bureau, was the first regular service of this kind."[48] And as Werner J. Severin in a paper on WHA wrote, "In December 1920 the first broadcasting set of any power for continuous wave (voice) transmission was completed. It had four large vacuum tubes rated at 400 to 500 watts.... The four kilowatt plant had a day range of 300 miles in voice and 500 miles in code. The vacuum tubes used for voice transmission, made by Prof. Terry and his assistants, were not available commercially at the time. Their design was the result of Professor Terry's five years of research into this phase of radio....[49] Since the University of Wisconsin had voice transmissions in 1917, continued them during the war, and put them on a scheduled basis in 1919, a plaque at the station's entrance at Vilas Hall proclaims 9XM-WHA to be "The Oldest Station in the Nation."[50]

WWJ's Oldest Station Claim

WWJ, Detroit, Michigan, founded on August 20, 1920, by the *Detroit News*, also claims to be "the oldest" station in America. After the first World War when publisher William E. Scripps learned that Marconi's wireless had been transformed into a medium that could carry voice and music, he decided his newspaper was going to be the first to own and operate a "radiotelephone."[51] On August 31, 1920, the day of Michigan's primary election, the newspaper told its readers they could get the latest election news that night directly from the paper's editorial offices by tuning to 8MK. The public was told in a newspaper headline that arrangements had been made for a "News radiophone to give vote results."[52] Although the 8MK call letters belonged to Radio News and Music, a sales subsidiary of the De Forest Company, the station itself with its new tube-operated transmitter was owned by the Scripps organization. The publisher had bought the "radiophone" from de Forest and ordered it installed on the second floor of his newspaper plant, close to editorial rooms. The night before the election, its radio engineers conducted their first successful test of 8MK's capabilities when shortly after 8 o'clock *News* employee Frank Edwards opened the microphone to say, "This is 8MK calling." Then a local record store manager selected some popular Irish tunes to play on an Edison phonograph and directed its music through a megaphone into the transmitter. When Edwards asked his listeners, "How do you get it?" people phoned to tell them the new station had an audience. It was estimated that 8MK was being heard in at least 30 Detroit homes, perhaps even more.[53] From the start, 8MK began attracting listeners with daily programs of news and weather, live and recorded music, and occasional talks and entertainment. An amateur license was used until October 12, 1921, when the government finally gave the station a full commercial license, WBL, which was changed to WWJ on March 3, 1922.[54] It continued operating as a radio and television station with these call letters throughout the 20th century.[55]

De Forest's 1920 Radiophone

Whenever Lee de Forest was knocked down, he got up. The trouble was that he moved around too much. He never stayed put. If he had fought to remain in place and struggled harder to keep a station where it had begun, there would be little controversy over which station was oldest in America today. His California endeavor is a good example. After arbitrarily being forced to close down his New York radio station in February 1920 by the local radio inspector, who objected to his relocating it within the city without permission, de Forest packed up the equipment and headed for San Francisco. He contacted his old associate from Palo Alto days, C.V. Logwood, whose 1916 experimental station 2ZK had operated in New Rochelle until shut down by the war. Logwood signed on as the San Francisco station's full-time operator and helped set up a thousand-watt de Forest transmitter in the basement of the California Theater, Fourth and Market streets. With the call letters 6XC, the station located its microphone, studio, and equipment in the city's largest motion picture house, one of three owned by Famous Players–Lasky Corporation.

Many years later Lee de Forest wrote to Herrold, "I promptly moved the High Bridge transmitter to San Francisco and installed it in the wings of the California Theater, running my antenna up to the roof of the bank tower next door."[56] The term "promptly" was apt because de Forest had returned to the air in April 1920, barely two months after departing New York. He reminded Herrold that his "station was maintained in daily operation, broadcasting the orchestra music of the Weber Orchestra in the theater." This meant that de Forest or someone in his company had to perform a one-time high wire act, because in order to provide listeners with live music from the theater's 30-piece orchestra, he had to suspend a large Magnavox horn in the galleries to gather sounds for the microphone. Soon the station was scheduling half-hour concerts of orchestra, organ, or phonograph music on weekdays at 4, 7:15 and 9 P.M. At 9 o'clock on Wednesday evenings, individual performers gave harp, piano or vocal solos. On Sundays full-hour concerts were offered by the orchestra, 11 A.M. till 12 noon. The station also had de Forest radio receivers placed throughout the area, in hospitals, hotels, clubs, and uncounted private homes.[57]

The significance of this 1920 San Francisco operation has been pointed out by John F. Schneider in his San Francisco State University master's thesis, "Early Stations in San Francisco" (available online), which said:

> This station was notable for many reasons. In addition to the fact that it was established by De Forest, 6XC began operations over six months prior to KDKA in Pittsburgh and it broadcast regularly scheduled programs composed entirely of music, in a time when all of the few "radio concerts" on the air consisted entirely of phonograph records. In addition, while most broadcast transmitters of the time operated at between five and fifty watts, de Forest had installed a thousand-watt transmitter, though it seldom operated above half of its capacity.[58]

Daily programs from 6XC continued throughout 1921. Then the transmitter was moved across the bay into the Oakland hills, near Berkeley. It was thought the new site would give the station better coverage. Relocating was the idea of de Forest's newly appointed western sales representative, the Atlantic-Pacific Radio Corporation. This was an easy decision to make because they picked for its location the hillside view home of the company's president, Henry M. Shaw. Re-licensed as KZY, the de Forest station became known as "The Rock Ridge Station" and the most widely listened to operation in the San Francisco area. Writing to Herrold years later about the Oakland move, de Forest's memory proved correct when he said, "it was maintained in operation for perhaps a year." Herrold knew this was true as he himself had picked up de Forest's Rock Ridge music during 1922 and used it to entertain crowds attending fairs and exhibitions.[59]

But as the year neared its end and the station continued to lose money, facing certain closure, one last effort was made to get the City of Oakland to take it over as a "municipal station." When this effort failed, de Forest's California radio effort was finished. It had lasted nearly three years. De Forest had made quite a run. Beginning with his arc telephone experiments for the Navy and his transmissions of opera music, and ending with his radio stations at High Bridge in 1916 and San Francisco in the early 1920s, the evidence strongly suggests that Lee de Forest, more than anyone, perhaps with the exception of Charles D. Herrold in San Jose, saw a potential for voice transmission beyond just a wireless replacement for two-way communication.

As radio grew in public interest, the good will and publicity, which accrued to station owners, inspired a lot of people to consider doing it. On seeing its popularity, newspaper and magazine editors began to jump at the chance to cover Radio (spelling it with a capital "R"), especially since publishers realized they could sell advertising space to radio manufacturers and retailers. Not only was the new marvel given front page treatment by print media, but some editors began setting up special "radio pages" to carry all the latest news about radio, how-to-do it columns on improving reception, and schedules of upcoming programs.

The California Experience

One of the first national periodicals to recognize the public's interest in radio was the *Literary Digest*, which had a full page on the subject each week for its readers in 1922. Writing about what they had learned traveling across the country in their "dashboard special," Mr. and Mrs. J.C. Davenport wrote in "Radio as You Ride" that they discovered the area around San Francisco had the most stations to listen to. While every state except Wyoming had at least one radio station in 1922, the proliferation of stations in Northern California was easily apparent as the pair operated their portable receiver. By September there were 510 stations coast to coast. Northern California had the most. On a statewide basis, California led with 66 stations, while New York had only 28.[60] But as Sterling and Kittross recounted in their history of that period: "More than 600 stations went on the air that year, but many went off again in a few months, weeks, or even days."[61]

Charles Herrold was on the air in Oakland, California, in the late 1920s and early 1930s as a freelance announcer, program producer and time salesman (Stephen True Collection).

The risky business of leaping into radio is perhaps best illustrated by examining the rise and fall of early San Francisco Bay Area radio stations.[62] Data collected by the Federal Radio Commission reveals that the survival rate was hardly fifty percent for stations licensed the first five years of the 1920s. Of 17 stations listed as programming in the San Francisco region on June 30, 1922, only seven were still operating one year later. The dropouts included four stations which had been granted licenses but didn't even manage a wobbly start. Among those left stranded on the launch pad was KQI, an educational station authorized for the University of California at Berkeley but which for reasons unknown closed shop after only one month of operation. The total number of stations around San Francisco, Oakland and San Jose reached eight in 1923 (including one new station) and sixteen by 1926, and stabilized at that number till the end of the decade. With the 1929 stock market crash and the start of the Great Depression, many businesses went into bankruptcy and radio was no exception. The number operating in the Bay Area dropped to 12 by 1942.

Studying the San Francisco Bay Area as an example, one could easily see the attrition rate was horrendous. From 1922 to 1942, more than 30 stations had been authorized by the government to broadcast in the San Francisco region, but by 1942 only a dozen remained. These stations truly deserve to be called pioneers, dealing as they did with the ups and downs of depression, war, and the vagaries of other media competition. Although today they may have different call letters, new owners and relocated transmitter and studio sites, each can trace its ancestry back to the early 1920s, which were radio's boom years. Of the 17 stations originally licensed to operate by 1922, five were still on the air in the San Francisco area at the end of the 20th century[63]:

- KQW (now KCBS), licensed in 1921; founded in 1909 by Charles D. Herrold, San Jose
- KPO (now KNBR), started in 1922 by Hales Department Store, San Francisco
- KLX (later KNEW), begun in 1922 by the Tribune Publishing Company, Oakland
- KLS (later KWBR), licensed in 1922 to Warner Brothers Radio Supplies Co., Oakland
- KRE (now KVTO), established in 1922 by the Maxwell Electric Co., Berkeley

Besides these five from 1922, which became firmly established in the broadcast spectrum, another small group got on the air a few years later but also kept going despite all the odds. Out of 12 new stations that went on the air between 1924 and 1927, these seven can be added to the list of stations which survived[64]:

- KGO, 1924, licensed in Oakland to the General Electric Company
- KFRC, 1924, owned & operated by Radioart Studios at the Whitcomb Hotel
- KJBS, 1925 (KFAX), founded in San Francisco by Julius Brunton & Sons Company
- KGTT, 1925 (KGGC) (KSAN), begun in San Francisco by Glade Tidings Tabernacle
- KTAB, 1926 (KSFO), started in Oakland by Associated Broadcasters
- KFWM, 1926 (KROW) (KABL), set up in Oakland by Oakland Educational Society
- KYA, 1927, originated in San Francisco by Pacific Broadcasting Corporation

When the Herrold station, KCBS, celebrated its 50th anniversary in 1959, all 12 of these Bay Area broadcasting pioneers were there to join in the festivities.

A Matter of Survival

In recognizing that a dozen stations survived the early days of radio in Northern California, the question arises, "Why did two-thirds fail?" Although it certainly helped for a station to have a strong financial backer, such as a newspaper or a large corporation, it was no guarantee of success. When the Oakland *Tribune* produced its offspring KLX in 1922, the station succeeded from one decade to another as it approached the next century. Noting that owner and publisher Joseph Knowland placed his station on the top floor of the *Tribune* Tower in downtown Oakland, its location was convenient for keeping an eye on its operation and helping it to succeed. But the San Francisco *Examiner's* venture into radio was an utter failure. Although given great fanfare in 1922 when William Randolph Hearst located his station, KUO, atop the *Examiner*'s San Francisco building, saluting its opening with an inaugural speech by the city's mayor, the station was off the air five years later. Its ambitious programming had started out with live hotel music, stock market reports and regular newscasts. But by the time the station folded, it was reduced to a simple schedule of marine reports for boat captains at Fisherman's Wharf. Although Hearst had ample resources, he lacked the interest to keep his station going. If one thought that having a bank would provide a solid foundation for a station's success, it was not the case of the Mercantile Trust Company of San Francisco. This financial institution placed KFDB near the summit of Telegraph Hill with the intention of attracting farm business from the agricultural west. But when the station was plagued by equipment failures and found its signal too weak to reach a sizable audience, the bank lost interest in its radio operation and removed it from the air by the end of 1923.

Certainly small operations carried a greater risk, particularly if they depended upon one man. Many examples of this existed all over the country, but in San Francisco one of them was the Meyberg station atop Nob Hill. As its site was on the highest of San Francisco's hills, the Fairmont Hotel was originally regarded as an ideal location in the city for radio transmission, until a better understanding of radio wave behavior was known. A radiotelephone had been tried there as far back as 1910. Herrold's company was there for two years, 1912–13. Much later the thought of broadcasting from one of the highest hills in San Francisco led Sheldon Peterson, an enthusiastic manager for the Leo J. Meyberg Company, a wholesale electrical firm, to persuade Mr. Meyberg to establish a station on the Nob Hill (6XG in 1921 became KDN in 1922), for the purpose of publicizing his business. When the proprietor agreed, Peterson hired a man to play phonograph music from a radio shack on the roof of the hotel. But being the brainchild of this lone manager and having no one else quite as enthusiastic, the station ceased operating when Peterson died in 1923. As the elder Meyberg had neither the time, energy or interest to continue, the Meyberg station went off the air.

Radio Needs a Regulator

One reason radio stations kept coming and going on the airwaves was that the federal government had confined citizen use of the airwaves to a single, narrow frequency. The majority of the then-useable air space was reserved for big wireless companies which were considered to be in the more serious business of point-to-point communication, carrying commercial messages nationwide and overseas. They not only wished that citizen experimenters could be swept aside and kept out of their way, but they got government authorities to agree with them. Amateur radio operators found themselves restricted by new Department of Commerce regulations, which kept them silent when broadcasting stations wished to schedule their programming on weather, news and music. The publication *Radio* took notice of this in February 1922:

> To the boy who chafes under the restraint of being obliged to stop sending during the radio concert broadcasting hours we suggest that he utilize this opportunity to interest his parents in his radio set. Ask dad to listen to the press reports and the grand opera stars.... Show mother how to tune in for the afternoon or evening concerts so that she can provide novel entertainment for her guests ... avoid an unpleasant call from the local traffic officer, who under the new "Pacific Plan" will be backed

up by the radio inspector in his demand that you stay off the air when you are liable to interfere with concert reception.[65]

Those who tried broadcasting on the same channel at the same time caused chaos. Signals interfered with one another. In fact, there was an electronic traffic jam caused by too many stations wanting to broadcast. If some tried to illegally overwhelm the opposition by boosting power, the opposition could do the same. Listeners often were unhappy when they couldn't hear the weak signals of a wanted broadcaster, drowned out by a stronger competitor. The need for time, power, and frequency space soon brought complaints to Washington, D.C. This led to lobbying, politicking, and arguing, and at first nothing was resolved. The single dial position allocated to private licensees found the airwaves so jammed up with noise and chaos that broadcasters begged for a solution. A traffic cop was needed to separate and unsnarl a crowded road where many lanes were needed but only one was provided. Commerce Secretary Herbert Hoover tried to perform the role of fair-minded arbiter, to untangle the mess by various innovative directives, but more and more his actions were stretching the Radio Act of 1912. He began calling everyone interested in broadcasting to conferences in Washington in hopes of getting Congress to pass proper legislation. It was mostly government officials and citizen group representatives who attended the first gathering. Broadcasters would come in greater numbers later.[66] At the third National Radio Conference in 1924, Hoover cautioned against allowing radio to become a government monopoly and recommended that a self-regulated private system be created instead. This sat well with nearly everyone till they heard what a young broadcasting executive at RCA got up to announce and then wondered, "Was he proposing private monopoly?"

What young commercial manager David Sarnoff announced was, in truth, a giant step forward in American broadcasting. He told broadcasters that RCA planned to link a series of powerful 50,000-watt radio stations into a chain operation. While it might make smaller regional hookups uneasy, it promised to become an entertainment boon for listeners nationally. This proposal would lead to the creation on November 15, 1926, of the first and most powerful network in the country, the National Broadcasting Company. One million dollars was paid by RCA to acquire AT&T's flagship station, WEAF in New York, and the corporation made that site the center of NBC operations. Within a few months, the forerunner of the Columbia Broadcasting System came into being. In January 1927, CBS was off to a shaky start, and eventually became a formidable rival to NBC after being purchased by William S. Paley for $300,000 in 1928.[67]

1927 and a New Law

Broadcasters and other entrepreneurs who looked to government to help solve their problems finally got their way. With passage of the Radio Act of 1927, Congress finally enacted a new comprehensive law, and removed licensing authority from Hoover's Department of Commerce. Power to regulate radio was now given to a newly created Federal Radio Commission (FRC). But it took the powerful impact of a court ruling to force Congress to even do this. A judge had earlier questioned the licensing powers of the Commerce Department by declaring that the 1912 radio law under which Hoover had been exercising his authority did not actually give him the power to regulate the complex problems facing broadcast radio in the mid–1920s. The ruling held that Hoover had no authority under the 1912 law to withhold licenses from anyone (*U.S. v. Zenith Radio Corp.*, 1926).[68] Congress could vacillate no longer. By enacting the Radio Act of 1927, it gave authority to a new five-member Federal Radio Commission to establish order amidst anarchy. This had a long-lasting result, according to radio historian Phillip T. Rosen, who saw the new government regulations producing a calming effect. He concluded that "chaos and confusion gave way to a national system characterized by government supervision based on a commission form of regulation and syndicated network programming supported by advertising. As this occurred the political, administrative, and economic foundations characteristic of the current American system became recognizably established."[69]

On the other hand, not all critics were happy about the results. For one thing, nonprofit broadcasters were at a disadvantage trying to secure or hold on to valuable frequency assignments in competition with better financed business operations. Commercial networks, major stations and their associations were in a much stronger position to pressure the FRC to get what they wanted. Nonprofit stations found themselves having to surrender good channels to commercial operators out of economic necessity. As Robert W. McChesney discovered in researching the period, "Educational broadcasters repeatedly protested to the U.S. Office of Education and the FRC that they were 'being driven off the air at a rate that threatened their complete extinction.'" Most educational stations, representing two-fifths of the broadcasters in 1925, simply were unable to remain on the air.[70]

Herrold Salutes KDKA

If what Herrold accomplished entitles him to be called the first broadcaster, then the pioneering work of others must be given their proper places in history, too. Honors are due Frank Conrad (KDKA), Earle Terry (WHA), and Lee de Forest (New York, Detroit and San Francisco stations) for their unique accomplishments. Although Herrold fought for his place in broadcasting history over a period of a lifetime, he knew and respected the legitimate claims of others. What were Herrold's competitors doing and what, if anything, were their contributions to broadcasting? Asked by a newspaper reporter in 1925 to sort out the difference between being "first" broadcaster and being the "oldest," Herrold never hesitated in reaching a conclusion. The founder of KQW agreed to share broadcasting honors with station KDKA, saying the evidence showed that the Pittsburgh station had every right to call itself "the oldest," provided that his own San Jose station was recognized as being "the first." This concession was made to a reporter for the *San Jose Evening News* on August 18, 1925. It was an impressive two-part series written by G.H. McMurray which dealt with the pioneering work of Herrold and carried headlines such as "First Broadcasting in History of World Was Done in This City" and "Work of Prof. Herrold Laid Radio Foundation."[71] Unfortunately, the wire services failed to pick up McMurray's interviews with Herrold, because if his statements had been printed in the eastern press, they certainly would have surprised the staff at KDKA and executives at Westinghouse when he said:

> KDKA of Pittsburgh is practically right in its claim of being the oldest "pioneer" broadcasting station of the world because it was the first commercial broadcasting station of the world to broadcast uninterruptedly from the beginning of this era, though San Jose and Herrold can claim the honor of having staged the first true daily broadcasting programs here.

While claims of being the "oldest" station have been made from time to time on behalf of Herrold, it was not the principal prize he wanted for his accomplishment. Only for a short time was he interested in longevity as a legitimate claim. When Eugene T. Sawyer published a *History of Santa Clara County* in 1921, Herrold claimed then — and only then — that he was running the oldest operating radiotelephone in the world. However, there was a good reason for this assumption. When this account was published radio's history was only beginning to be written. When Herrold learned about the pioneering work of KDKA of Pittsburgh, Pennsylvania, it caused him to change his mind. He amended the record and his place in it. Herrold concluded that he was operating the first station in America but not the oldest. It is rather amazing that Herrold found his proper niche in history so early and correctly sorted out what even today it has taken years for others to see. Herrold rightfully felt he could share honors with others. Perhaps if KDKA had known it earlier, it would have done the same, making it unnecessary to call Herrold's' work — and that of others— the "lost years of broadcasting."[72]

8
Fight for Recognition Begins

Radio is no longer in its infancy. It is now a highly developed science with almost unimaginable future possibilities. Anything which permits sound, uttered by the human voice in California, to be heard as far away as London, England, not faintly but amplified many times in intensity, is not just another fad.

"San Jose Station, One of First,"
San Francisco Chronicle (1924)[1]

While costly at the time, because he was forced to look for new employment, Charles Herrold was not bitter about leaving KQW in 1926, believing as he did that his departure would give his pioneer station a chance for survival. Now it would be up to that dynamic go-getter Fred J. Hart to find the ways and means of paying the station's indebtedness and put it on a sound financial footing. In future years Hart and Herrold would develop a strong mutual respect for each other. For the moment, though, it was a turning point in Herrold's life. He had to decide what to do. Now 51 years old, Herrold had little to show for all his years of work, having lost his inheritance, personal savings, business investments, wireless school, radio station, marriage and job. Thanks to the fact he had friends, former students and acquaintances scattered around the San Francisco Bay Area, and was still highly regarded and liked by many members of the First Baptist Church, Herrold's financial and career needs soon became widely known. He was not unemployed for long.[2]

On the morning of December 1, 1926, the *Mercury-Herald* told its readers, "Herrold to Join Oakland Station."[3] The announcement was made in a talk given the previous evening at the San Jose First Methodist Church by W.S. Tupper, manager of station KTAB. He revealed that Herrold was joining his Oakland station in an engineering capacity. Because it had "TAB" in its call letters, the acronym told listeners the Tenth Avenue Baptist church owned the station. By noting that this job offer was from a Baptist-owned station, one might suppose that Herrold was simply the beneficiary of Christian charity. If that consideration had played any role in providing Herrold with employment, it certainly must not have been a major factor, because

Tupper praised Herrold for his competency and was genuinely glad to get him. He told his audience, "Herrold has a complete knowledge of both the financial and mechanical end of radio and in obtaining him we are adding to our staff one of the best radio experts of the state." That day the *San Jose Evening News* summed up what KQW's troubled times had brought about: "So San Jose gets a Salinas man and a continuation of farm programs in exchange for a distinguished genius of its own, whose great dream had been that the pioneer radio station he founded should spread the best of the abundant musical and literary artistry of this section of the world."[4] It regarded Herrold's leaving as an unfortunate loss for the community of San Jose.

Herrold is still formal and dignified despite the turbulence and disappointments of the previous decade. Formal portrait, circa 1930 (Stephen True Collection).

The Sponsored Broadcaster

After he first arrived in the early months of 1927, Herrold lived near the heart of the city of Oakland at 415 N. 5th Street. But needing a permanent residence, Herrold chose the trendy and upscale Piedmont area, which happened to put him among some of the richest and most well-to-do people of the East Bay. He moved his residence to No. 10 Abbott Drive, probably because it was a short commute to the main business district and gave Herrold complete privacy, being more or less hidden away in the hills. While it was not hard to send mail to Herrold at his Piedmont address, the lofty hideaway made it difficult for any first-time visitor to find him there. Because of the odd layout of the streets which ran up and down the hills in a design made by nature as much as by man, it was an impossible maze for strangers. As KQW Manager C.L. McCarthy remarked years later, it was a place "rather hard to find as it is up in the hills in back of Piedmont."[5] However, Herrold and other people in his neighborhood had a beautiful western view of the bay and surrounding cities. From this panoramic site one could take in the distant city of San Francisco, no more than 15 or 20 miles away; the entrance to the bay from the Pacific Ocean at the Golden Gate (before the bridge was built); three islands known as Alcatraz, Yerba Buena, and Angel; as well as the downtown skyline of Oakland, which was closest at hand.[6]

On arriving at KTAB, Herrold was determined to put the ups and downs of his San Jose experience to good use. But it wasn't long until he saw the disadvantage of

In Oakland, Charles Herrold earned his living as a popular radio storyteller, foreign language program producer, and breakfast show entertainer. He was heard over stations KFWM, KROW and KTAB (Stephen True Collection).

staying in engineering. After serving briefly in the station's technical department, Herrold soon became convinced he could better serve the station by contributing his other San Jose experience, selling radio advertising. It took no time at all for the Oakland station to agree that Herrold was the ideal person to contact local merchants, let them know he had pioneered broadcasting and sell them on sponsoring programs. Radio audiences were growing everywhere and were expressing their enthusiasm not only with fan mail but also in buying what radio advertised. It was now common for stations to finance their operations quite profitably by selling "time on the air" and Herrold realized that for him, too, that was the logical way to go. If newspapers and magazines could earn a substantial income from local merchants and businesses, why not radio?

The Merchandising Counselor

Once again Herrold saw the opportunity to promote radio and he took it. This time, however, he decided to try his hand at getting sponsors for programs and becoming a radio personality himself. When the credentials of a man experienced in broadcasting were presented to likely prospects, Herrold discovered that prominent businessmen and leaders of the community listened to him attentively when he explained how they could use radio advertising to advance their own businesses. On November 8, 1928, for example, Herrold, who was described as "a Pacific Coast expert on broadcasting," was a luncheon speaker in San Francisco before the Commonwealth Club of California, on the subject: " Yellow Dog Advertising over the Air."[7]

Now a radio advertising salesman and producer of programs he scripted and announced on the air himself, Herrold succeeded in acquiring sponsors for shows which aired over such Oakland stations as KFWM, KROW and KTAB. By early spring in 1930 Herrold was employed as "an advertising consultant by KFWM and the Post Enquirer, in Oakland, California."[8] According to a publicity story issued at the time, he made his headquarters at the East Oakland studios of KFWM and he could be heard conducting his own radio show, the "Top-o-the-Morning" program, every day at 8:00 A.M."[9] By summer of that year, Herrold was identifying himself as "Merchandising Counselor with Radio Station KROW (earlier known as KFWM)," located at 1520 Eighth Avenue, Oakland, with studios and transmitter in Richmond.[10] By

August 30, 1930, KROW proudly announced that Herrold, who for the past five years had been in the broadcast advertising business for himself, had become manager of its merchandising and copy department.[11]

KQW, a Farm Voice and More

While Herrold was in Oakland honing new skills in commercial radio, Fred Hart, too, was working hard in San Jose to reduce the indebtedness of KQW. By January 15, 1927, Hart had little trouble in persuading the Baptists to renew the station's contract with the California Farm Bureau. With his usual confidence and optimism, always part of Hart's repertoire, he talked the Baptist owners into leasing the station to him for one more year, promising that money would be flowing in and the bills paid. With the power of his positive thinking, KQW began to build its audience and attract new advertisers. Since Hart's farm publications had a subscription list of more than 250,000, by getting them to become KQW listeners, Hart succeeded in building an increasingly steady and loyal audience. Hart was bold enough to promise business leaders that advertising on his station would get them results and it did. The first major advertiser to try was the Sperry Flour Company, which began sponsoring programs as early as 1925. Gradually others joined the list. By 1930 KQW could name 44 major advertisers using its airwaves, including companies like the Southern Pacific, Union Oil, Standard Oil, State Farm Insurance, John Deere Plow, Ford Tractor, Buick, Montgomery Ward, Navalet flowers, and Hart's Department Store.[12]

Seeing that good times had finally arrived, Hart's KQW management had reason to celebrate. Among the new program ideas which Hart had put into practice from the very start was celebrating the station's birthday every January 15, which in Hart's mind was the date KQW became a "commercial" operation under the aegis of his farm organization. Thus began a tradition which lasted every year that Hart was there — anniversary broadcasts on January 15, marking one, two, three or four years of KQW serving the farm community. But as the 1920s drew to close, it dawned on Hart that he had more to offer than he had recognized. In fact, he was running a pioneer station, not five years old but nearly 20 years old. Realizing that the station's first broadcasting had actually begun in 1909, Hart was eager to get more hard data about KQW's real beginnings. Now he needed Herrold.

When KQW observed its next birthday on January 15, 1930, by airing a special program from 7 P.M. till 12 midnight, it had a lot to celebrate. The station had expanded from a single studio in San Jose in 1925 to three studios where programs could be originated — the main studio in San Jose and two others: one in San Francisco and another Sacramento. There also were plans underway to put a fourth studio on the campus of the University of California at Berkeley by September of the year. To connect these studios, KQW leased over 200 miles of telephone lines maintained by AT&T. Hart also put plans in motion to increase the station's power to 5,000 watts by January 15, 1931. All this progress was the result of Hart's adept leadership in building station support atop the pillars of three major groups — government, business, and the public.

Because the station deliberately aimed to serve the needs and interests of farmers, Hart easily got cooperation from government. He convinced the California State Agriculture Department to let him locate KQW studios at its state farm headquarters in Sacramento, the state capital, and he arranged with government farm specialists to send out the latest farm news and educational programs to listeners every day except Saturday and Sunday. A Federal-State Market News Service was set up combining reports sent by the U.S. Department of Agriculture over a leased wire with information collected from the licensed farm bureau short wave radio stations in Los Angeles, El Centro, Fresno, Salinas, Sebastopol, Sacramento, and San Francisco. Thanks to money donated by the Dollar Steamship Company of San Francisco, which enabled KQW to establish new studios there, and thanks to the generosity of the Union Oil Company, which paid the telephone line charges, KQW was able to serve rural and agricultural interests from the financial center of the Pacific Coast. In return for substantial contributions made to KQW by the California Almond Growers Association, one of the new facilities was named "The Blue Diamond Studio." Weather reports from the U.S. Weather Bureau offices in San Francisco were broadcast daily at 12:30 P.M. and 7:30 P.M., as well as frost warnings in season.[13]

KQW Secures Its Origins

By the summer of 1930, Fred Hart realized that KQW had been publicizing itself as a pioneer station for a number of years, but it had few, if any, documents in its files to substantiate this assertion. It seemed to Hart that boasting about KQW being the first station was all right so long as Herrold lived in San Jose. The inventor could speak for himself and was easily available for interviews, talks, and to show off his old water-cooled microphone, photographs of the 1912 San Jose studios, radio licenses, logs, and documents. But now that Herrold had moved 50 miles north, KQW was left to explain its past on its own. Hart believed the station needed to establish its own file of documents and thus put itself into a position to prove its past whenever necessary. After writing to Herrold in Oakland and getting the station's founder to agree to help, Hart turned over the task of assembling the evidence to his Assistant Manager, Ira L. Smith. His job was to contact Herrold and follow up every lead the old-timer suggested. Hart wanted to gather every document Herrold could find and have them put in a safe place. Thus began KQW's first serious effort at preserving its history and thanks to the initiative, persistence, and dedication of everyone concerned, a systematic assembling of the evidence was begun.

In response to Hart's initial request in early July, Herrold said he would gather "together the parts of the old original station with large pictures and affidavits ... which can be put in a little niche at KQW and form a sort of little museum of 'Antiquities.'" While glad to get Herrold's promise to donate photographs and other artifacts, Smith had to tactfully suggest that Herrold do more. Gathering simple souvenirs of the old station was not enough. So Smith wrote Herrold again:

> I have been itching to get my sleeves rolled up on this job for a long time, both as a just duty to you and because I think it would be a mighty good thing for old KQW.

> "Doc," will you sit down and write me the whole story from beginning to end? Leave out the romance, poetry, and adjectives because this will be a cold-blooded statement of facts. Give me dates, places and names—principally names, because I intend to get an affidavit from every last soul who could have had anything to do with the old station. If any of your co-workers are still alive let me know who and where they can be located.[14]

Correspondence that began that summer on the subject of collecting evidence continued till the end of the year. Data were needed to establish the fact that broadcasting began in San Jose in 1909, years before anywhere else — old documents, photographs, artifacts, testimonials, letters from old listeners, remembrances of co-workers, and newspaper, magazine, and other printed records of the early operation. In addition to assembling this, Smith inquired widely of everyone who could assist Herrold in amassing evidence. He wrote to the Bureau of Navigation of the U.S. Navy, got licensing records from the Director of Radio at the U.S. Department of Commerce and sought the whereabouts of old timers who had once worked with Herrold or had heard the station on the air. Ira Smith, who himself had personal knowledge of Herrold's earliest broadcasts, wrote him that there "used to be a bunch of us fellows in Santa Cruz who listened to your old 'carbon-burner' back in the early days. I think I can locate quite a few of these hams...." From now on, not only would KQW broadcast regularly that it was "the pioneer station," but Hart would see to it that all future advertising, promotion and publicity would credit Herrold for what he had done.[15] Herrold's fight to gain recognition had begun.

What caused Hart to start promoting KQW's historical past in 1930 was undoubtedly stimulated by assertions of broadcasting primacy coming from powerful radio interests to the east — Westinghouse's KDKA in Pittsburgh, Pennsylvania. With the same skill and foresight with which it launched the station in the 1920s, Westinghouse put the full weight of its organization behind KDKA's claim of being the pioneer radio station. Almost from the day it began broadcasting, KDKA maintained it was America's "first" radio station and that H.P. Davis, a Westinghouse's vice president, claimed to be "The Father of Radio Broadcasting" because he helped Frank Conrad put the station on the air. This led to a long lasting controversy. One eastern station opposed to this claim was WWJ, the *Detroit News* radio station in Michigan, which claimed to have made the first licensed broadcast on August 20, 1920, months earlier than KDKA. Another was WHA, the University of Wisconsin station that began its wireless service to farmers as far back as 1916 and began experimenting with radiotelephony the following year.

From the outset, KDKA fought to secure the prize for itself by widespread and persistent promotion. Using the resources of Westinghouse as skillfully and intelligently as a candidate running for public office, KDKA management astutely celebrated its birthdays. This meant the Pittsburgh station not only was wise enough to publicize its claim consistently but also to spread the claim far and wide year after year. One of its major coups took place on April 21, 1928, when Davis got an invitation to address the Graduate School of Business Administration at Harvard University. He chose as his topic "The History of Broadcasting in the United States."[16] What better opportunity to secure prestigious approval and national recognition of KDKA's

Isle of Dreams Broadcasting Corp.

Jesse H. Jay Directing Manager

January 16, 1933

Mr. Ray Newby,
1617 Lombard Street
San Francisco, Calif.

Dear Sir:

I read an article in the Broadcast Reporter regarding the work of Dr. Herrold in connection with your San Jose - San Francisco radio telephone circuit. I would like to see credit placed where it belongs. I have often wondered why no mention has ever been made of these successful broadcasts fifteen years ahead of their time.

I was a wireless operator running on the SS CITY OF SYDNEY out of San Francisco from 1911 to 1913 and often heard the transmissions of both the San Francisco and the San Jose stations. The greatest distance I received good speech was abeam San Pedro and could hear the voice but unintelligible due to extremely weak signals as far south as San Diego.

My receiving equipment consisted of a carberundum detector and a crude double slide tuner known as the type D built by the United Wireless Telegraph Company. I wonder how far your station would have been received had we the present day sensitive receivers........As to quality. The signals were as clear cut and smooth as the present day transmitters. Laying at the dock in San Francisco I many times heard your tests as follows: "Hello San Jose, Hello San Jose, Hello San Jose etc" followed by a phonograph record more enjoyed with the head phones than with a standard Victrola of the time.

I think I can find a diary among my effects telling the exact dates of your transmissions, all of them enjoyed very much. I hope I can be of help in establishing your station as the first broadcasting station in the World.

Yours truly,
Leslie F. Sherwood
Engineer, WIOD.

All of my radiophone work in connection with transmission, has been under the supervision of Prof. C. D. Herrold. Ray Newby.

UNITED AMERICAN BOSCH CORP.
1262 - 1272 POST STREET,
SAN FRANCISCO, CALIF.

January 16, 1933, letter to Ray Newby from a former ship's radio operator attesting to hearing the Herrold station broadcasts, 1911–1913 (Gordon Greb Collection).

claim than an occasion like this at Harvard? While Davis began his talk by admitting there had been "some successful results" prior to World War I "in adapting telephonic principles to radio communication," he discounted the work of Fessenden and de Forest, saying, "No real service, however, was attempted or introduced of a character similar to that now known as radio broadcasting." As the East Coast seemed unaware of radio experimentation on the West Coast, Herrold's pre-war broadcasting got no mention at all. Consequently, broadcasting's history, as recounted by Davis, naturally began with KDKA and once he got to the subject of the Pittsburgh station, it became the sum total of the radio history he was to talk about. So effective was this address that over the years KDKA has reprinted it repeatedly in newspaper and magazine advertising.

KDKA's Tenth Birthday

With the start of a new decade—the 1930s—KDKA made a major effort to celebrate its tenth anniversary on Sunday, November 2, 1930. In a one hour and 45 minute birthday program, which was beamed on its regular transmitter to domestic listeners and on shortwave to audiences around the world, the station commemorated its historic election night broadcast ten years earlier. It laid claim not only to being the first station but also the first to put church services on the radio, to transmit a talk by Herbert Hoover, and to carry a speech by William Jennings Bryan. The next evening, Monday, November 3, KDKA continued its tenth anniversary celebration with a large banquet program at a downtown hotel featuring local, state and national personages under the sponsorship of the Pittsburgh Chamber of Commerce, and airing it to a world listening audience over shortwave station W8XK. In attendance at the festivities were radio's favorite comedians, Amos 'n' Andy, and other radio stars of the period. Prominent dignitaries arose to salute KDKA, such as the Chairman of the Federal Radio Commission, the special counsel to the Republican National Committee, and the National Broadcasting Company's president, who served as toastmaster. When word reached California that KDKA was celebrating itself as the "Pioneer Station of the World," little KQW knew it had a fight on its hands. With this news came the realization that the little San Jose station faced a powerful opponent in contesting the claims by KDKA. One paragraph in the news item told how powerful the Pittsburgh station hoped to be:

> Only last year, September 5, 1929, ground was broken for a new transmitter at Saxonburg, 30 miles from Pittsburgh. The new station which has not as yet been placed in service embodies the most advanced innovations and equipment ever conceived for broadcasting. It has a power of 400,000 watts, eight times as powerful as the power now being used in the broadcasts of the present transmitter.[17]

But while it is unlikely that the "400,000 watt transmitter" was ever placed in service, the publicity given to the tenth anniversary celebration of KDKA's 1920 origins made it clear to little KQW in San Jose that the California Farm Bureau's 500-watter was up against a formidable foe. The San Jose station faced a hugely successful corporation in Westinghouse, which was giving its pioneer radio station KDKA everything necessary to win. A contest between East and West over which location had the "first station" could easily develop into a battle between David and Goliath, provided KQW was willing to enter into a contest and insist that its own historic origins be recognized. If KQW was to fight Goliath, could it depend on Charles David Herrold? What was his slingshot?

Herrold Wants Recognition

Since a growing number of American homes had radios in 1930 — not quite 50 percent at the time — and broadcasters were making handsome profits, Herrold could not help but reflect on what he was missing. Why wasn't he sharing monetarily from the phenomenal growth of the radio industry? And if not profiting financially, why didn't more people know what he had done? While it was encouraging to now be earning a living by selling radio time and to be touted in KQW's promotional literature, Herrold was reluctant to give up the widespread recognition he believed he deserved. As radio became increasingly popular, Herrold decided to fight for his place in radio's history as the founder of America's first regular broadcasting station. Having the backing of Fred Hart and Ira L. Smith at KQW was fine, but Herrold realized he needed more help.

In late 1931 he welcomed an enthusiastic newcomer to his campaign, Fred F. Wells, a former radio broadcaster and past state commander of the Disabled American Veterans, who lived nearby in Berkeley.[18] On becoming acquainted with Herrold and hearing the inventor's story, Wells became incensed to learn that broadcasting had been born in San Jose and few people outside of Northern California knew about it. Herrold told biographer Wells: "I spent over $40,000 in development, and over $80,000 in maintaining this system. When my father passed away, his last words to me were, 'Carry on — you are on the right track —carry on to the last dollar.'"[19] Wells offered to champion Herrold's cause. As one who knew that war veterans sometimes go unrecognized for their heroism on the battlefield, and that it was often necessary to fight for one's rights, Wells told Herrold he deserved not only to be called "the father of broadcasting" but that he should be making money from it.

Wells felt his contacts in California government and business might prove useful. At Wells' urging, it wasn't difficult for Herrold to be convinced he needed to get his story more widely known and to realize that teaming up with a man sympathetic to his cause made perfect sense. Furthermore, Wells offered to collaborate in writing Herrold's story in an article or a book for publication. Agreeing that working together offered them both a chance for rewards and settling on a program of action, Herrold and Wells did more than make an informal verbal arrangement — they signed a typewritten partnership agreement. With Peter A. Quinn, Jr., as witness, they signed their agreement on December 17, 1931. The contract called for them to work together for two years. During this time, the commercial exploitation of Herrold's pioneering radio work was to be accomplished by means of arranging for "stage presentations" as well as "lecture engagements, advertising ventures, writings, radio plays, book sales, and other activities...."[20] Wells was to be manager and Herrold, the performer. They furthermore agreed that monies earned "shall be shared by them on a fifty-fifty basis."[21]

Although these ambitious plans were never fully carried out as Fred Wells' health was deteriorating, their partnership did accomplish one thing—they began to put down on paper what Herrold had done. Together they produced a typewritten manuscript on how Herrold started his radio station in San Jose in 1909. The pages of this work were preserved long after both men were gone. Fred Wells died suddenly of a heart attack in Berkeley in 1932. What Wells wrote was brief and incomplete, but it ended up in the hands of San Jose city historian Clyde Arbuckle, who showed it from time to time to those inquiring about KQW's origins, including both authors of this book. It also was a valuable source to Arbuckle when he described Herrold's work in 1986 in his own book, the *History of San Jose*.

Herrold's Appeal to World Opinion

One spring day in 1932, Herrold picked up a copy of his afternoon newspaper, the *Oakland Tribune*. Although he saw bold black headlines when he unfolded the pages, Herrold spent only moments reading the stories—one about the kidnapping of Charles Lindbergh's baby, another about Ford automobile plant strikers being shot to death by Detroit police, and still another concerning the Nazi party's Hitler suddenly rising to power in a recent German election. But Herrold quickly turned the pages, looking for something else inside. While perhaps to the average reader the front page's headlines would be considered attention-grabbers, none of those stories were startling enough to stop Herrold from what he was looking for. He quickly narrowed his search to back pages of Joe Knowland's conservative daily, trying to find something he knew ought to be there on the editorial page. Once he found that section, his eyes dropped down below the political cartoon to find the column which published letters to the editor, which the *Oakland Tribune* called the "Forum." For a number of days, readers had been discussing, pro and con, who could rightfully be called the first radio broadcaster and how such a person should be honored. Since Herrold himself had appeared several times in the pages of the local press, interviewed, written up and hailed by reporters of the *Tribune* as broadcasting's founding father, he assumed newspaper subscribers would remember having read these accounts and acknowledge him in the "Forum." But today, once again, nobody did. When one contributor argued Guglielmo Marconi deserved the prize and laid out a good case for honoring the Italian-born millionaire, Herrold realized that once again he was being overlooked, and he was determined to enter the fray with all the persuasiveness and evidence he could muster. Herrold resolved to take this opportunity to carry his case to the people with the strongest possible argument he could make. He sat down at his typewriter and composed a letter to the editor which called attention to his own accomplishments. It was published in the paper's "Forum" section on March 11, 1932.[22]

Dear Forum:

I have been reading with interest the many expressions of opinion as to the proper awarding of honors to the First Broadcaster. We are all agreed that to Guglielmo Marconi goes the honor of having first commercialized Wireless Telegraphy. I have clipped all of these letters from your columns. There seems to be a disposition on the part of your debaters to be perfectly fair — I will not criticize — let them stand — they are honest expressions of opinion.

In that great Court of Public Opinion, just as in our Courts of Law, judges and juries do everything in their power to get at the truth, and to prevent "Conclusions" on the part of witnesses. However we may feel that we have accomplished some outstanding act, it is not given to us to force the awarding of honors to us. The evidence must be presented in a dignified and orderly manner — then we must withdraw and await the final verdict.

So, with this forward [*sic*], may I present in the Court of Public Opinion the case of Charles David Herrold, alleged Father of Broadcast Radio? Let him be called to the witness stand and testify in his behalf, and let it be the "Whole Truth and Nothing but the Truth."

I read a news item early in the year 1895 reporting the first experiments of the boy Marconi, in Italy. In that article appeared the name of that great German, Hertz, who experimentally proved the existence of electro-magnetic waves, mathematically discovered by Clerk Maxwell, the great English mathematical physicist. I re-read that classical experiment of Hertz and that very afternoon, I took a Rhumkorff coil, a Branley Tube, and an aerial wire and transmitted and received Wireless Telegraph signals one mile. This was my first introduction to Herzian waves and I worked with them for over 10 years, in the hopes that someday I might be the one to do with the human voice and music what Marconi did with Wireless Telegraph signals. In Stockton, California I worked on this problem and in the summer of 1908 chartered the ocean-going sloop, Dorothy and performed many experiments, among others, the firing of mines at a distance.

Then I opened the Herrold Laboratories in San Jose, California and in January 1909, Mr. Ray Newby and I, with an aerial covering several acres and containing over 11,500 feet of wire, broadcast voice and music to widely distributed listeners. This was continued till 1912, when I developed instruments capable of transmitting continuously clear voice and undistorted music great distances. On the afternoon of June 20th, 1912, I opened inter-communication by Radio Telephone between the Garden City Bank Building in San Jose and the Fairmont Hotel, in San Francisco. This communication was continued uninterrupted for over 8 months.

In the fall of 1913, having built several Radio Telephone sets for civilian tests for the government, a set was installed at Mare Island Radio Station and another at Point Arguello. In September, 1913 my operator Kenneth Sanders at Mare Island communicated by voice with my other operator and laboratory assistant, Emile A. Portal, a distance of perhaps 300 miles. On September 18th, 1913 at 4:20 A.M. my operator Sanders broke all records for transmission of voice and music by radio communicating with the Bremerton Navy Yards near the Canadian Border, about 900 miles. A minute later a private message was handed to me written on a U.S. Naval Radio Service Blank at Mare Island. It read as follows: "To operator in charge of Radio Telephone at Mare Island. We get your voice up here great; also record "Trail of the Lonesome Pine" you played came in extra good. Signed — Night operator, NPC, Naval Radio Station, Bremerton, Wn — 4:20 A.M., Sept. 18th, 1913."

A few minutes later the operator at NAA, Naval Radio Station, at Arlington, Virginia, over on the Atlantic Coast, 3200 miles away reported that he was listening to our voice and music.

During the Panama-Pacific International Exposition at San Francisco, California in 1915 I furnished all the music for all the receiving sets in the Liberal Arts Building, from 6 to 8 hours per day from my Broadcasting Station in San Jose, California. Now if there was any other Broadcasting Station in the world at that time and if there was any other inventor who had perfected a reliable radio telephone capable of transmitting undistorted music and clear speech day after day in actual broadcasting, I certainly never heard of such. I read every scrap of scientific literature on the subject and read claims on over 3000 U.S. and Foreign Patents so as to be thoroughly familiar with every inch of progress made by every known experimenter in the world. Even KDKA, which calls itself the Pioneer Station and who merely had the #1 license under the new Government classification, does not claim to have been on the air before 1921 [*sic*].

Now the very vital question will now be put to the witness—Why did you not immediately profit by all this development? The answer is a very simple one—The Herrold System of Radio Telephony would not work on wavelengths under 600 and the allocation of 360 meters by the Government was fatal. Over two decades of work and expenditure of over $80,000 and a lot of patents went on the scrap pile. My Broadcasting Station, KQW passed into the hands of those who could install the most modern High Powered Western Electric Equipment. This was a blessing in disguise, because this station became the mouthpiece of the California Farmer, a fitting memorial, and the witness is still able to smile.

And so we rest our case, a case which will be carried eventually to the highest Court—the Court of Public Opinion of the whole world.

Chas. D. Herrold
10 Abbott Drive
Oakland, Calif.

KQW Celebrates, Interviews Herrold

Shortly after he took charge in 1926, General Manager Fred Hart began telling everyone who would listen about KQW's accomplishments. Hart had built the kind of audience support which insured the survivability of the station, and so on January 15, 1934, he decided to hold the greatest and grandest birthday party anyone had ever heard on radio. It would celebrate the 25th anniversary of KQW's founding.[23] In an era when most stations signed off at night and stayed silent till early the next morning, Hart planned to keep KQW on the air around the clock for this special event, starting after the clock struck 12 midnight, marking the beginning of the great day and continuing for 24 hours till the clock struck midnight again. While the station's birthday would be saluted each hour, KQW planned to have all the excitement build up to a climax at 7 o'clock that evening, when a master of ceremonies would introduce an all-star program.

To make sure everyone in Northern California tuned in this special broadcast, Hart arranged with ten Bay Area stations to be represented by having their top radio artists appear on the KQW program. To further insure that the San Jose station got proper recognition, Hart persuaded well known figures to send congratulatory messages, including California's Governor Rolph, San Francisco's Mayor Rossi, the U.S. Attorney H.H. McPike, and San Francisco shipping tycoon J. Harold Dollar. Besides ballyhooing the station on the air, Hart also made sure KQW's big party got lots of press coverage. The San Francisco *Chronicle* considered that there were so many well-known local radio artists appearing on the show as to warrant them being listed, as follows:

> The Doric quartet and Emil Polak of NBC; Adhesive Pontoon at KFRC and CBS; Hugh Barrett Dobbs and "Wee Willie" Hancock; Jean Warfield of KTAB; Art Fadden of KJBS; Bob Allen of KYA; Lou Tobin and Jean Scott; the Olympians of KGGC; Fred Skinner of KLX; Cumberland Hillbillies of KROW; and representatives of KRE and KLS [24]

The highlight of the broadcast naturally led to the man who created KQW, Charles David Herrold, who was featured on the program as the birthday party's guest of honor. After being introduced to the audience, the emcee began to politely interrogate Herrold on how he happened to begin his radio work in San Jose in 1909 and to please explain why he should be considered the Father of Broadcasting (see Chapter 1 for the full interview).

New Owner and Power

It was that same year, 1934, that KQW of San Jose was sold to San Franciscans. Both the station and the Pacific Agricultural Foundation were acquired by Julius Brunton & Sons, who had been active broadcasters as owners and operators of KJBS in San Francisco since 1925. The Bruntons were said to have gotten into radio when one of the sons, Ralph R. Brunton, "came back from World War I with a yen to branch out with his father and two brothers from their prosaic storage battery business."[25] They were running KJBS from studios located on Pine Street and soon moved new KQW studios into the same building, giving them studios both in San Francisco as well as San Jose. Although KQW had a transmitting power of only 500 watts when they bought it, the timing of the purchase was convenient in more ways than one, because in 1934 the FCC had just approved a power increase for KQW. This enabled the Bruntons to trade transmitters. They took the KJBS transmitter down to San Jose, upping KQW's output to 1,000 watts, and gave their other station, KJBS, the smaller Western Electric 500-watter. They wasted no time in applying for even more power for KQW, seeking approval from the FCC to go to 5,000 watts, but they had to wait till 1939 before they got it. That is when KQW's transmitter was moved from downtown San Jose to the marshlands of Alviso, on the outskirts of the city, which engineering studies showed would more favorably radiate the station's signal at its 740 position on the dial.[26]

Brunton also moved quickly in 1934 to put C.L. McCarthy in charge of KQW as its new manager, bringing him over from his customer relations job at KPO, the NBC station in San Francisco. McCarthy was remembered years later as a radio executive with a strong and commanding personality. As recalled by San Jose radio station executive Ruth Poindexter Fish of KLOK, McCarthy was admired even by people whom he had fired. Such a person was her husband, Ed Barker, one of the founders of station KLOK, who had once worked for McCarthy. Barker thought McCarthy to be a "great radio man" even though at one time they parted company. Fish once said in an interview:

> McCarthy fired Ed at Christmas. It seems he thought Ed had been goofing off. Later, when Ed Barker put KLOK on the air, McCarthy was our great advisor. He told us

> not to accept commercial religious programming and many other things. He was called "Hell on Wheels" but marvelous. Vangie Barker worked for him. Every-one I ever knew in those days thought McCarthy was the great one, and so did I.[27]

McCarthy became another dynamic leader at KQW and, in the tradition of other managers before him, became a strong supporter and advocate of the station's claim as America's foremost pioneer broadcaster.

East Ignores Herrold

Evidence that the Radio Corporation of America deliberately ignored an opportunity to acquaint itself with Herrold's early day broadcasting can be found in papers collected by George H. Clark at the Smithsonian Institution in Washington, D.C.[28] The files contain proof of an incident which dramatically illustrates the difficulties KQW faced in opposing KDKA for the title of being the world's first broadcasting station. Records there show the cavalier rejection of Herrold's work by RCA in New York in an exchange of telegrams which took place on May 7 and 8, 1935. Eastern insistence that radio could not have originated earlier than 1920 becomes evident by studying what happened. It began with a wire sent to RCA by Howard Neikirk in San Francisco from the Mark Hopkins Hotel in that city telling New York about the California claim. Acting on the belief that there was a "proposed NBC broadcast" on radio's origins being planned, he requested that RCA please establish the "authenticity" of the claim on the West Coast that the "first successful experimental transmission of voice and music by radio was accomplished June 20, 1912 at the Fairmont Hotel, San Francisco." In the event this assertion turned out to be true, Neikirk advised RCA, "please wire collect the historical significance in development of radio in said statements."

Considering the fact that a further investigation of this claim would have revealed that Herrold had conducted daily "concerts" between San Jose and San Francisco for eight months between 1912 and 1913, it is curious that RCA dismissed this notice of West Coast broadcasting out of hand. In replying to Neikirk, an RCA representative by the name of Mr. Colling flatly stated that the Fairmont transmissions were "experimental" like those by Fessenden and de Forest and consequently, not "first" broadcasting, according to the "meaning of the word." The assumption was made once again that nobody could possibly have been "broadcasting" prior to KDKA being commercially licensed in 1920. As the Pittsburgh station was an NBC network affiliate, which made it part of the Radio Corporation of America family, RCA obviously chose to ignore Herrold's claim completely. It did nothing to investigate the evidence which could have been submitted by a potential challenger. Again, radio history was written and controlled by eastern interests.[29]

What is truly ironic about this rejection is that transmissions from a radiotelephone in San Francisco actually had been heard in 1913 by the future president of RCA — David Sarnoff. It happened just before Christmas— one and one-half years after the sinking of the *Titanic*— when Sarnoff took three of his Marconi engineers to hear the regeneration receiver that Edwin Howard Armstrong, a student and radio genius, had perfected in the laboratory of his Columbia University professor, Michael Pupin. It was the best radio receiver these engineers had ever heard, picking up signals from great distances away and with amazing clarity and strength. According to radio historian Tom Lewis, at 9 o'clock that night in the winter of 1913, they heard dots and dashes of telegraph signals coming from two distant Marconi transmitters, one in Canada and the other in Ireland. Then at 9:30 P.M. they heard something entirely different—"a small continuous wave station in San Francisco." Was it the National Wireless Telephone and Telegraph Company's Herrold station in the Fairmont Hotel, or another radiotelephone? We don't know. A more detailed description by Armstrong, Sarnoff or a Marconi engineer would have told us.[30]

Radio and Education

While the recognition he sought continued to elude him, Charles Herrold remained active in broadcasting around the San Francisco Bay Area as long as he could. Now nearly 60 years of age, he may have been thankful that in 1935 the Roosevelt administration had enacted the Social Security law, for which he would be eligible.[31] Knowing that a pension under its provisions was five years away, he still needed to work. No longer quick of step and lacking a salesman's energy, Herrold had to find ways to continue earning a living in the late 1930s. One of those ways was to return to his roots as an educator. He saw in old age that again he could earn a living by advising and teaching others. While not a linguist, he sympathized with recent immigrants who could not speak English. Old "Prof" saw how radio could be used to educate and serve the special needs of minorities, if they could hear radio programs in their own languages, customs, and culture. When asked by the Portuguese community to help them acquire a radio voice, Herrold was glad to lend a hand. Knowing San Jose, San Francisco and Oakland were communities of mixed ethnic, racial and religious origins, where neighborliness and commonality tended to smooth over latent prejudices, Herrold never hesitated to help. Thus with Herrold's assistance, Arthur V. Avila and Celeste Dantos organized the Latin American Broadcasting Company for the purpose of providing Portuguese language programs over Oakland stations. Herrold instructed them in how to write and produce radio programs which served an estimated three hundred thousand persons of Portuguese ethnicity living in cities throughout Northern California.[32]

During this same period, Herrold was approached by the Oakland Public School System to provide advice and assistance on audio-visual education. They needed his expertise in acquiring and using public address systems, motion pictures, and sound for teaching children. For a number of years in the early 1930s, radio was an integral part of instruction in Oakland and in other schools throughout California, as pupils were often assembled each week to listen to classical music broadcast over the radio. One program designed especially for the classroom audience was "The Standard Broadcast," a program for children sponsored by the Standard Oil Company of California.[33] As one pupil wrote:

> Every Thursday evening, at 8:15, many of the children in our class listen to the Standard Symphony Program, with their parents. The first time we were asked about it, we found that nineteen children heard the program. The next week there were twenty-eight out of a class of forty-two who listened in.[34]

An evening program, "The Standard Symphony Hour," which aired over KPO, had been singled out for public approval by Lee de Forest years earlier.[35]

This educational and cultural use of radio certainly must have reminded Herrold of those happier days of old, when playing concert music from his San Jose station was what started his interest in broadcasting in the beginning. While an Oakland school official's letter praising Herrold for his audio-visual work was found among his papers, probably the one he saved and treasured the most was a letter from Lee de Forest. It had been 25 years since de Forest had used Herrold's daily "concert music" at his booth at the Panama Pacific Exhibition. Now de Forest was writing on March 22, 1940, to ask Herrold for particulars about his "early work at that San Jose station, which I understand you founded in 1909" adding, "As you doubtless know, I began my radio telephone work in 1907...." Herrold's reply eminently satisfied the inquirer because six months later on September 7, 1940, it was "Lee de Forest Day" at the San Francisco World's Fair on Treasure Island. At the banquet of the Veteran Wireless Operators Association, where he was being honored, de Forest said:

> Very appropriately, the re-birth of my earliest broadcasting began here on the Pacific Coast when, during the Panama Pacific Exposition, pioneer station KQW at San Jose maintained regular transmissions which were daily heard in the Palace of Liberal Arts. That station, KQW, can rightfully claim to be the oldest broadcasting station of the entire world....[36]

KQW Joins CBS

While Herrold never lived to see it, the day was coming when New York would not only learn of his "first station" claim, but a major radio network would salute him with a great celebration and carry congratulatory messages from major capitals around the world.[37] It all began in the early 1940s when the Columbia Broadcasting System thought of establishing a strong flagship station in San Francisco. CBS set in motion a series of decisions which led to the network finally acquiring and owning the world's first broadcasting station. However, it would take ten years for this to happen, and the network had no idea it was buying such an historic property. What started CBS on the road toward purchasing KQW in 1949 was its desire ten years earlier to secure a clear channel frequency, enabling it to boost its power to 50,000 watts. CBS had been using KSFO as its San Francisco affiliate since January 1, 1937, and initially proposed acquiring it, provided the station's frequency could be moved to a clear channel position and qualify for a great increase of power. This seemed possible in early 1941 when CBS thought it had an agreement between KQW and KSFO to trade positions on the radio dial, allowing CBS to assume the San Jose station's clear channel frequency. But when CBS offered to buy KSFO and was turned down by the station owners, CBS decided to drop KSFO as its affiliate and make KQW its

San Francisco affiliate, which it did on January 1, 1942. The transfer was completed when the CBS program was switched from the KSFO transmitter to that of KQW at one second past midnight and listeners heard the network cue, "This is C-B-S, the Columbia Broadcasting System," followed by the local announcer intoning, "K-Q-W, San Francisco–San Jose, owned and operated by the Pacific Agricultural Foundation of California."

Part of the complicated background to this story was told by *Tide* magazine, which explained that KSFO in 1941 was principally interested in getting FCC approval to operate a powerful shortwave station from San Francisco and broadcast programs overseas to the entire Pacific area:

> A few days after KSFO got its short wave grant, KQW got permission from the FCC to expand from 5,000 watts to 50,000 watts on the long wave band. At this point the proceedings got complicated. CBS announced that effective January 1, [1942] it would use KQW to cover the San Francisco area instead of KSFO. Then KSFO itself applied for a domestic power increase from 5,000 to 50,000 watts. Whereupon the FCC called off its KQW grant pending consideration of KSFO's counter-claim.[38]

Herrold's original radio station was put on public display in downtown San Jose to celebrate the 50th anniversary of broadcasting. The reassembly of the old radiotelephone was done by Douglas Perham, who had heard Herrold on the air in 1909. The observance was cosponsored by KCBS and San Jose State College (Gordon Greb Collection).

When the United States was plunged into conflict on December 7, 1941, by the attack on Pearl Harbor, a final decision on this matter was put on hold. The FCC put a freeze on further proceedings. When the war was over, the commission took up the question again and its decision favored KSFO. By allowing KSFO to change its frequency from 560 kilocycles to 740 kilocycles, the station could increase its power to 50,000 watts and perhaps regain its affiliation with CBS. The construction permit allowing KSFO to do this was issued in 1948, and was slightly modified in 1949 requiring KSFO to operate with a directional antenna, using one transmission pattern in the daytime and another pattern at night. But for reasons which did not exist ten years earlier but came into existence because of new opportunities opening with television, KSFO decided to abandon this plan and allowed its application to lapse. As radio historian John F. Schneider explains:

> After lengthy hearings, the FCC granted the power increase.... However, the management of KSFO began to have doubts about the future of AM radio, and were putting all of their money into their new television station, KPIX. Negotiations were re-opened with CBS, and the result was that KSFO gave up its claim for the 740 dial position, in exchange for the CBS-TV network affiliation for San Francisco.[39]

This meant the way was opened for CBS to acquire KQW, change its call letters to KCBS, and make it the network's major West Coast station in San Francisco.

KQW: War News Center

When KQW became a CBS affiliate in 1942, the United States had suffered the sneak attack on Pearl Harbor just weeks earlier and was plunged into war against the Axis powers in Europe and the Japanese empire in the Pacific. CBS at the time was looking west across the Pacific and expanding its news division capabilities to cover the Far East from San Francisco. This was noted in the local press. "Columbia's increased activity in this area includes establishment of a 'listening post' here, set up immediately after the outbreak of war to listen in to foreign programs and translate and analyze the news for rebroadcast," according to the San Francisco *Call Bulletin*.[40] When it made KQW its affiliate, CBS also purchased a controlling interest in the station, acquiring more than one third of the shares of the Pacific Agricultural Foundation, Ltd. This financial clout enabled CBS to persuade Ralph Brunton to move KQW's studios into the more spacious and fashionable Palace Hotel on Market Street in San Francisco. It also made KQW its West Coast news headquarters for all reporting about the war against Japan. In 1942 CBS hired Don Mozley fresh out of University of Missouri journalism school and put him to work night and day as a San Francisco–based correspondent covering news from the Pacific. Recalling those days, Mozley said, "I had to prepare news for the 'CBS World News Roundup' at 5 A.M. and also at 10 o'clock at night. Everything we did was live. Recordings weren't allowed. We had a specially designed control board, something invented by Paul White (CBS news director), which enabled us to bring in reports from different correspondents by twisting a few knobs. He had one in New York and we had the other. It was quite a system." While entertainment came out of Los Angeles and Hollywood, Mozley remembered, "All war news from the Pacific came out of San Francisco. In fact, we broke the Japanese surrender 12 hours before anyone else." After CBS purchased KQW, Mozley joined the San Francisco station's staff, rose to news director, and led it into becoming one of the West Coast's most successful "all-news radio" stations.[41]

Radio Dispute Continues

The year 1945 was a time for joyous Americans to celebrate, because World War II was over, both in Europe and in the Pacific. KQW carried the news of the final allied victories to California listeners everywhere. But that same year on the home front, California's pioneer station was to learn its quarrel with KDKA was still going on.

Alerted to the fact the radio industry was going to honor KDKA with a big 25th birthday celebration in November, Ralph Brunton got his managers and staff together to do something about it. They decided that on November 10, 1945 — as the industry saluted KDKA's so called first broadcast — KQW would respond by telling the world how broadcasting really got its start in San Jose in 1909, 36 years distant, not 25 years as the eastern establishment had claimed. The West Coast station would do its own special, half-hour radio dramatization honoring the station's founder, Charles D. Herrold, in what would be called "The KQW Story." "It was quite an assignment," recalled the program's writer, director, and producer, Roy Grandey, when interviewed in 1996:

> I was given several files and there must have been the equivalent of about 50 pages that would go into a press book. They were articles about instances of what happened from those days — the early days — a lot of different biographies of Doc Herrold and so forth.... There was no controversy in the research material at all. It was very straightforward ... this pioneer did it![42]

With the files of information handed him by McCarthy, it was no problem for Grandey to script "The Story of KQW" in a dramatic fashion.[43] He asked radio engineer Paul Smith to think of ways of reproducing unique radio sound effects, not only by replaying old fashioned gramophone recordings of "In the Shade of the Old Apple Tree" and "Listen to the Mocking Bird," but also by putting the sound of an old spark gap radio transmitter on the air, reproducing the sharp, high or low pitched sounds of code — the distinctive dit-dah-dits — to open the show. Grandey selected all the members of the show's cast himself. He chose Don Victor as his associate director. As the script called for a dozen or more roles, four actors had to do clever voice changes: Dick Ellers, Herb Ellis, Dick Glyer and Jack Webb. Two staff announcers shared narration chores, as well as the opening and closing. They were the baritone voices of Clarence Cassell and Ken Ackerman. Sound effects were Don Creed's responsibility.

Choosing his actors carefully, Grandey gave the principal role of "Doc" Herrold to Jack Webb, a versatile young actor with a deep voice who would later would become a highly successful and well-paid Hollywood writer, producer and actor. He originated a police detective series *Dragnet*, which aired first on network radio and later became a coast to coast television favorite. It starred Webb himself as the program's L.A. police investigator, Sgt. Joe Friday. Grandey recalled, "When we went through our reading on the show, Jack said, 'What are you giving me here — this line about a water-cooled microphone. That's phony!' So I explained to him that microphones in the old days couldn't run for very long at a time. They had to be allowed to cool down." Grandey told Webb that Herrold actually invented a water-cooled microphone. Many years later, Grandey said he was listening on his car radio when he heard Webb's voice in a "sound bite" from the 1945 radio show, talking about a water-cooled microphone. "And a chill went down my spine," said Grandey. "It was the obituary for Jack Webb" being broadcast on a December 23, 1982, newscast.

While "The KQW Story" dramatized how Herrold became America's first broadcaster, starting in 1909, it also saluted other pioneer radio stations for what they had contributed, as follows:

- Aug. 20, 1920—8MK, Detroit, now WWJ, began its daily operation.
- Nov. 2, 1920—KDKA, Pittsburgh, inaugurated election returns.
- July 2, 1921—KDKA aired the first sports program (Dempsey-Carpentier fight).
- 1922—WEAF, New York, did the first commercial.
- 1923—President Harding used radio in St. Louis for a three-station hookup.
- 1924—National political conventions were heard for the first time on a network.
- 1926—The National Broadcasting Company was organized.
- 1927—The Columbia Broadcasting System was formed with 16 stations.
- 1928—Hoover delivered his acceptance speech from Palo Alto on 107 stations.
- 1931—A complete New York Metropolitan Opera was aired for the first time.
- 1933—President Roosevelt broadcast his first fireside chat.
- Dec. 7, 1941—Radio flashed news of the Japanese sneak attack on Pearl Harbor.
- Nov. 10, 1945—Radio celebrated another anniversary.

Scriptwriter Grandey provided one more dramatic moment. Earlier in the week a KQW technician had been sent to Herrold's Piedmont home. He took along a cumbersome recording apparatus in order to transcribe comments by KQW's founder. Given a microphone to talk into, the 70-year-old Herrold's words were etched onto a revolving 16-inch acetate disk and then taken back to the KQW studios to be used as the dramatic ending of "The KQW Story." Thanks to engineer Paul Smith, the entire half-hour KQW anniversary program, which had gone out live, was saved on another large disk. It was preserved by means of an electrical transcription—tape recording did not exist at the time—and it was taken by Smith with him to San Francisco State College when he left radio to teach there. The entire program can be heard today because it has been dubbed onto recording tape. This program preserves the only known recording of Herrold's voice, in which he is heard to say[44]:

> I am gratified and happy to speak to you on this occasion. Station KQW has gone far beyond my dreams. I am particularly proud that the dream we had for radio as an entertainment medium has materialized. Radio has indeed outgrown its infant clothes. I am happy to have been the first man to broadcast radio entertainment on a regular schedule.[45]

They Became Stars

Before networks such as NBC and CBS centralized their programming facilities and consequently began locating most of their production work in New York City and Hollywood, it was common for networks to originate programs almost anywhere in the country. In the 1920s and '30s, it was not unusual for local and regional stations with the talent and ideas to reach out to national audiences from their home studios. Enterprising radio station managers found it was often possible to interest sponsors in multi-station broadcasts if the linkage gave them a wider audience, without too much additional cost. They simply connected a host of transmitters by means of long line telephone facilities. So local programs in Detroit or Chicago or San Francisco soon were heard nationally on a network. These arrangements were ballyhooed as "hookups" and announcers would introduce them by intoning, "We take you now to———!" or "Take it away———!" to emphasize that they were switching from place to place.

Those words also gave important clues to waiting engineers, who needed to know exactly when to activate "on the air" switches and join their stations to the network. Thus it was a common practice in the late 1920s and early '30s for a number of national programs to come from grassroots America. Once a show proved popular locally, it was no problem for imaginative radio executives to set up a chain or go to an established system to give this particular program a larger audience and greater advertising. Many of the greatest shows went before local microphones before hitting the big time. Good examples of these were Chicago's *Amos 'n' Andy*, Detroit's *The Lone Ranger* and San Francisco's *One Man's Family*. A few regional networks—like the Don Lee Network on the West Coast, with which KQW was affiliated in the early 1930s—also were formed. In the early days of networking, there was such a plethora of original, live programming coming from local regions that the broadcasting industry was behaving in much the same manner as minor and major league baseball—promising talent played for local audiences before being brought up to play on a grander scale before fans on the national scene.

One example of this happened at the Herrold station. In 1915 two San Jose school boys, Al and Cal Pearce, became acquainted with Herrold when they sold newspapers outside his station at the corner of South First Street and San Fernando. Discovering they could sing and play the ukulele, he invited them up and let them entertain from his station in the Garden City Bank building. This encouraged the lads to try radio in San Francisco, where they succeeded as regulars on KFRC's Blue *Monday Jamboree* and *Happy-Go-Lucky Hour,* which were highly popular regional programs. Then the boys got their big break in 1933, when NBC put them on their own coast-to-coast NBC network series, which they originated from the West Coast, succeeding with national audiences as *Al Pearce and His Gang.*[46] Years later Al Pearce recalled, "In 1916 I sang on KQW. We were trying to demonstrate that radio could be heard 'overseas.' I sang, 'Hello, Hawaii, How Are Yuh?' In those days we pronounced Hawaii 'Huh-why-yuh.' The only one that picked us up was the USS *Sherman* 50 miles off shore!"[47]

Another actor who got his start with KQW a few years earlier than Jack Webb, was Raymond Burr, who became famous in the starring roles of *Perry Mason* and *Ironside* and had numerous other parts in dozens of Hollywood movies. In an interview with a newspaper columnist, Burr chuckled fondly over memories of having once served as a staff announcer at the San Jose station and teaching for a time at San Jose State College. "I had done 5,000 radio broadcasts and 20 plays before I started in motion pictures," said Burr, who was a big man with a resonant voice.[48] More than a handful of network programs and original talent came out of the San Francisco Bay region, thanks to opportunities provided by stations like KQW, KFRC, KPO, KGO, KSFO, KLX, and KROW, beginning in the late 1920s and early '30s. Others among the great radio and television stars who began their illustrious careers in San Jose, Oakland, and San Francisco were:

- Morey Amsterdam (comedian, *Al Pearce and His Gang*)
- Raymond Burr (*Perry Mason* and *Ironside*)
- Carmen Dragon (composer/conductor, *Railroad Hour* and *Baby Snooks Show*)
- Howard Duff (actor, title role of *Sam Spade*)
- Ralph Edwards (emcee/producer, *This Is Your Life*)
- Mark Goodson (co-producer, *Hit the Jackpot* and director *Stop the Music*)
- Merv Griffin (vocalist, *Freddy Martin Band*)
- Eddy Howard (vocalist and band leader, *Eddy Howard Show*)
- Art Linkletter (emcee, *House Party* and *People Are Funny*)
- Don McNeill (emcee, *The Breakfast Club*)
- Tony Martin (vocalist, *Burns & Allen Show* and screen actor)
- Carlton E. Morse (creator/producer, *One Man's Family* and *I Love a Mystery*)
- Barry Nelson (radio-television actor, *My Favorite Husband*)
- Al Pearce (emcee and comedian, *Al Pearce and His Gang*)
- Hal Peary (comedian, *The Great Gildersleeve* and *Fibber McGee and Molly*)
- Alvino Rey (guitarist and band leader)
- Robert L. Ripley (newspaper cartoonist, *Believe It or Not*)
- Vera Vague (comedian, *Bob Hope Show*)
- Lu Waters (jazz musician and bandleader),
- Doodles Weaver (comedian-singer, *The Spike Jones Show*)
- Pat Weaver (executive producer NBC's *Monitor* and network president)
- Meredith Willson (composer/conductor, *The Big Show*, *Burns & Allen*, and creator of stage and screen musical, *The Music Man*)

Herrold Gone, KQW Reborn

With Federal Communications Commission approval, KQW was purchased in its entirety by the Columbia Broadcasting System in 1949, its call letters changed to KCBS, and its licensed location moved to San Francisco.[49] No longer would a radio engineer be required to be on duty at the transmitter in the south bay giving hourly or half-hourly station breaks, saying, "This is KQW, the CBS station in San Jose, with studios in San Francisco." To take charge of the operation, network headquarters in New York sent Arthur Hull Hayes to the city by the Golden Gate as general manager and Jules Dundes to head up its sales department.[50] In time each of these men would return to New York and each would rise to the presidency of the CBS radio network in turn. In 1959 the network applied to have the station's transmission power expanded to 50,000 watts and the main transmitter moved from its old location 50 miles south in San Jose to a more modern, up-to-date multi-tower antenna complex at Novato (Marin County), about 25 miles to the north. When interviewed by a graduate student years later, longtime San Jose broadcaster Ruth Poindexter Fish recalled that in 1947 KQW's sales office was located in the same building as KLOK's, which was 40 W. San Antonio, San Jose. She also remembered when Lee Kopp was the only man left in the San Jose office and became the station's transmitter operator. Kopp was the last radio engineer to man the KQW transmitter in San Jose before it was moved north by CBS.[51] The new transmitter was ready for operation in Marin County in 1951.[52]

Broadcasting's Forgotten Father

A few years earlier, on July 1, 1948, a tired old man died quietly, alone, unsung and unrecognized, in a rest home in Hayward, California. The death certificate carefully filled out by his attending physician said the event took place at 11: 45 A.M. and that the patient had been suffering from a weakened heart and damaged liver. His occupation was "electrical engineer."[53]And when arrangements were made to take the body to the Oak Hill Cemetery in San Jose for burial in the family plot, Pastor Sands of the First Baptist Church "was asked by a local mortuary to conduct graveside services for a virtually unknown man." He arrived to find about a dozen people, none of whom he knew save one, the deceased himself, whom the First Baptist minister recognized as the man who had founded broadcasting's first station, KQW, of San Jose. As recorded by the church historian, the pastor thought to himself: "What an irony to discover that the deceased, aged 73 years, was Professor Dr. Charles David Herrold."[54]

9
Herrold: Lost and Found

> *Is there a way of providing a criterion of the prematurity of a discovery other than its failure to make an impact? Yes, there is such a criterion: A discovery is premature if its implications cannot be connected by a series of simple logical steps to canonical, or generally accepted, knowledge.*
>
> Gunther S. Stent, *Scientific American* (1972)[1]

Fifty years after regular broadcasting began in San Jose, California, the significance of this event, for all practical purposes, had been lost to history. By 1959 Herrold's San Jose station was owned by the Columbia Broadcasting System, its studios centralized in San Francisco, and its call letters changed to KCBS. The network knew little or nothing of the station's pioneer origins. When CBS learned ten years later of its West Coast station's historic background from San Jose State College professor Gordon Greb, the network decided the time was ripe to sponsor a celebration of its 50th birthday.

A major effort was made by KCBS to publicize its origins. There were network radio broadcasts from San Francisco and San Jose, major dinners and tributes from Bay Area and national broadcasting industry leaders, including CBS radio's president Arthur Hull Hayes, and a parade of bands and organizations through downtown San Jose. Worldwide publicity was also given to the event, including salutes from CBS correspondents stationed in London, Paris, Tokyo, and New York, congratulations from radio personality Arthur Godfrey from Hawaii, comedians Amos 'n' Andy in Hollywood, and other famous entertainers. Early day radio pioneers contacted Professor Greb and contributed new testimonials and other evidence. Greb's findings were summed up in an article published in the 1958-59 winter issue of the *Journal of Broadcasting*, which carried the original title of "The World's First Broadcasting Station," but which Editor Robert Summers renamed "The Golden Anniversary of Broadcasting" as he planned to recognize it as a significant "first station find" in his preface to the article.[2]

Although news of the event was spread widely through wire stories carried by the Associated Press and United Press and advertising in trade journals like *Broadcasting* magazine, it was ironic that many of the residents of the city of San Jose itself never knew it was happening. Both the *San Jose Mercury* and the *San Jose News* were shut down by a strike, preventing coverage of the event in the local dailies. Despite this setback, hope was high that broadcasting the event on radio itself would attract attention regionally, statewide and nationally, finally giving Herrold the recognition he deserved.

A Lost Story Surfaces

The rediscovery of Charles D. Herrold's importance to radio happened almost by accident. It occurred because of a visit to a San Jose Museum one day in the mid–1950s by a radio reporter in search of a news story. At the time Gordon Greb was news director of radio station KSJO and seeking local feature stories when he was shown an old microphone by San Jose city historian Clyde Arbuckle. When the curator casually mentioned that it came from a 1909 San Jose radio station, Greb thought he must be mistaken. He could not imagine a radio station operating prior to KDKA. Hadn't historians accepted 1920 as the year radio broadcasting began? Young Greb was almost certain something was amiss in Arbuckle's claim and asked to see other exhibits.

For years the National Association of Broadcasters (NAB) had been recognizing 1920 as the beginning of broadcasting. It had endeavored long ago to sort out claims made by several stations. None of them were from San Jose. It finally was fairly well accepted that the Westinghouse station KDKA in Pittsburgh, Pennsylvania — which called itself both the "first" and the "oldest" station — had initiated radio broadcasting when it relayed election news to a small audience on November 2, 1920. That pioneer station also had held the first commercial radio license issued by the U.S. Department of Commerce and Labor.

After World War II, Greb himself believed KDKA was America's first station when he wrote and produced a radio documentary *This Is Radio* honoring the Westinghouse station on its 27th birthday. After Army service, Greb became program supervisor for KTIM, San Rafael, and in November 1947 he saluted KDKA in a broadcast presented to a potential three million listeners in the San Francisco Bay Area. When he scripted and produced this 30-minute dramatization, using local actors and talent, Greb joined hundreds of other radio stations across the nation in celebrating broadcasting's birthday. He had no idea there was another claimant station less than 25 miles away. The fact that KQW in San Francisco had celebrated its 36th birthday two years earlier with its own radio documentary was something he hadn't known. Greb was on duty in the U.S. Army when it was broadcast in 1945 and had not heard KQW's claim. He, together with most people in radio, accepted what he read in the few trade journals and history books of the time that KDKA apparently predated them all.

Seeking Pioneer to Honor

It wasn't until after Greb took a teaching position at San Jose State College in 1956 that he found it necessary to review Herrold's claim that he was the "father of broadcasting." What led him to revisit Clyde Arbuckle's San Jose museum was a relatively minor project which Greb decided to undertake shortly after being named faculty adviser to the campus chapter of Sigma Delta Chi, the professional journalism society. Greb and his students were drawing up a list of candidates to be honored for their achievements in journalism. Knowing his professional journalism society regularly erected historic plaques honoring newspapermen like Benjamin Franklin and William Randolph Hearst, the professor's plan was to select someone who had contributed to San Jose's early journalism and to place a historic marker on the spot where it happened. In 1941, the Society of Professional Journalists (Sigma Delta Chi) started selecting and honoring sites significant to the history of journalism. Most of its honorees came from the print media, but seventeen years later the thought occurred to broadcaster Greb, "Why must the person come from the print media? Why not broadcasting? Why not radio?" Looking into the matter he learned "the site may be the location of a newspaper, magazine, or broadcast facility ... or place of a person whose acts were significant in the evolution and welfare of journalism."[3] Thus the professor decided to investigate historian Arbuckle's claim that there had been a radio station operating in San Jose as far back as 1909.

As the fall term began in 1958, the topic of the proposed project came up and led to an agreed upon strategy. The professor and his students initiated a plan to check out the local station's claims from A to Z, starting with whatever evidence could be found in local libraries and museums. The goal was to verify the claim that the city had an unsung, overlooked broadcast pioneer. Since Greb had classes to teach, he began by checking sources at San Jose State library first, and at the same time sent one of his students, Anthony Taravella, to meet with Arbuckle and ask him to document his earlier assertions. Tony had volunteered to assist his professor in the project, thinking the search was going to be a quick assignment, and never realized it would become a task that would continue for weeks, months, and years. After tracking down historian Arbuckle, quizzing him thoroughly, and being shown files on the early day San Jose radio station, Taravella rushed back to campus, declaring, "Professor, I think what Arbuckle showed me is true and the man who started this station in 1909 deserves recognition. I think you should see for yourself."

Confirming the Story

While Tony was off campus, Greb was carefully perusing library books, looking for any mention of Herrold's pioneering work. Initially, he found nothing to indicate there was a broadcasting station in San Jose station prior to World War I. Then, pulling a small, grayish book off the shelf and flipping it open, Greb found what he had been looking for—confirmation in print of Herrold's work *The First Quarter Century of American Broadcasting* in a 374-page book by E.P.J. Shurick. In this early survey of America's radio development, which Shurick published in 1946, Herrold was credited for his contribution in Chapter One, where Shurick said:

> Out in California, a Dr. Charles Herrold in 1907 read in a New York newspaper about Dr. Lee De Forest who transmitted music over the wireless.... It became an inspiration for him to take part in a science which challenged man's imagination.... Within a year he hung out a shingle which read, *The Herrold Radio and Engineering College.* From this school he began his own experiments with the wireless transmission of voice and music. In 1909 he made his first successful broadcast, and three years later started regular programs [on] ... his station in San Jose, which later was to become of national importance under the call letters KQW.[4]

Turning to *History of Radio to 1926*, by Gleason L. Archer, which had been published in 1938, Greb this time was left disappointed. He searched through the entire Archer book only to learn that this radio historian seemed totally unaware of Herrold and his work. However, the appendix to Archer's book did confirm that Herrold was on the air when radio had its sudden rise. The San Jose station was included on the list of the few stations which were licensed in the early 1920s.[5] The principal problem Archer tried to resolve in his book was KDKA's claim against rival station WWJ, Detroit, as both stations were squabbling over which was on the air first in 1920. The fulcrum of the quarrel concerned a few weeks difference between WWJ's "first" test broadcast in August 1920 and KDKA's "first" election night transmissions in November the same year. Because the latter continued on a regular schedule, Archer accepted the election night broadcast by KDKA on November 2, 1920, as the official beginning.

Many Pioneers, Many Unknown

Herrold's station was not the only one that was overlooked. Other contenders were for some unknown reasons overlooked as well. Some were listed in Archer's appendix, but remained unrecognized for their pioneer achievements for many years to come. In reproducing the Department of Commerce's *Radio Service Bulletin* of May 1, 1922, Archer showed KDKA was at the head of the list of 218 stations actively "broadcasting market or weather reports, and music, concerts, lectures, etc." Although KQW in San Jose did appear among the listed stations, Herrold's operation was lost in the crowd, unrecognized for its 1909–1917 and 1919–1922 history. By this time there were 45 stations in California, including more than a dozen in the San Francisco Bay Area. While KQW was first noted in the *Bulletin* published in January 1922, there were also three other San Jose stations licensed to broadcast in 1922—KSC in San Jose, which was put on the air by O.A. Hale & Co.; station KJJ in Sunnyvale, an operation of the Radio Shop; and KLP, Los Altos, of Collin P. Kennedy Co. None of those early licensees survived whereas KQW did. What Greb needed was more radio history prior to the 1920s. But where should he look? Where would he find further, detailed and documentary evidence of Herrold's pioneer work? Archer spoke to this problem in the preface to his book in 1939:

> Despite the fact that radio broadcasting began less than eighteen years ago, great confusion has arisen as to essential details of its beginning. Human memory is unreliable. Contemporary records, usually undated as to year or month, on paper that disintegrates in a decade, filed without regard to value, become perishable sources of information. Kaleidoscopic changes have occurred in the industry, the leaders of which have been too busy making history to give much thought to its preservation. There is a need of settling controversial problems of historical nature while many of the pioneers of radio are still living.[6]

Historian Opens Files

When Greb returned to historian Arbuckle, who opened his files to the professor, it was like providing Greb with a mariner's compass pointing the way to information about the early days of San Jose radio. Greb now had directions to take and he took them. Foremost among the pertinent documents in Arbuckle's files was a contract signed by Charles D. Herrold on December 17, 1931, and Fred F. Wells, allowing the latter to serve as both biographer and manager to commercially exploit the pioneer broadcasting activities of "the father of radio broadcasting" by a variety of

Author Gordon Greb holds the original Herrold microphone at the San Jose History Museum that started his quest for the full Herrold story in 1958. His search ultimately involved the local college, which is today San Jose State University, KCBS and the CBS radio network, scholarly journal editors and librarians, and finally Mike Adams, co-author of this book (Gordon Greb Collection).

means. According to the agreement, which was supposed to last two years, Wells was to set up stage presentations for Herrold and arrange lectures, advertising, writings, plays, book sales and other activities. Wells died within a year of the agreement and apparently never completed any of these assigned tasks, but he did interview Herrold and began preparation of an article or book for publication, which was entitled "Who Is the Father of Radio Broadcasting?" It was never finished and remained an unpublished manuscript of several pages about Herrold's radio work, which somehow Arbuckle had acquired and had kept safe in his files.[7] While brief, incomplete and badly in need of editing, this typescript was a beginning. It provided a rough outline of what Herrold believed he had accomplished. Arbuckle also had some old radio equipment, including an original water-cooled microphone.

Records kept by Herrold himself, Greb thought, would be the most valuable documents of all, detailing what he did, when, where, and why. "Somewhere there must be a treasure trunk of documents," Greb imagined. "If only I could find them, my problems would be over." What, he wondered, had happened to Herrold's personal records—his personal papers, correspondence, research, notes, experiments, clippings, radio logs, photographs, and publications, including newspaper and magazine articles? Learning from Arbuckle that Herrold had passed away in the late 1940s, but without any particulars as to time and place, the next logical step was to locate Herrold's heirs, maybe his widow, and if she were gone, perhaps a living son or daughter. Thumbing through the pages of the San Jose and other Bay Area telephone books, Greb was frustrated that none of the individuals by the name of Herrold who answered the phone had ever heard of Charles David Herrold. After an hour of dialing one Herrold after another with negative results, he finally quit this tactic and tried to think of what else to do. Why not try phoning the radio station itself? Herrold's old station KQW was still on the air, now broadcasting from San Francisco with its new call letters of KCBS, so perhaps it would have Herrold's records.

Station's Origins Revealed

When the station's switchboard operator answered, Greb decided to go the top and asked to talk to the general manager, whom he supposed would be the most knowledgeable person at the station. A voice answered: "Hello. Maurie Webster here. What can I do for you?" After explaining that San Jose State intended to honor the station and its founder as one of the first in the nation, Greb asked whether he could see records of KCBS's history and whether they went back to the year 1909. There was an astonished gasp at the other end of the line as the manager caught his breath—the fact he was running a pioneer broadcasting station was news to him. What emerged from the ensuing conversation astonished them both and they agreed to work together to uncover the facts of this station's origins. Both were eager to learn more.

Although he had been chief executive of a CBS-owned and -operated station in San Francisco barely more than one year, Maurie Webster had a long and broad background in radio broadcasting on the West Coast. Having been promoted to the Northern California post after a distinguished career at CBS headquarters in Southern

California, Webster was a veteran announcer, producer, researcher, engineer, publicist, salesman and administrator. He started in radio in 1932 in Tacoma, Washington, and rose to the top managerial assignments, including supervising the Navy's communications school at Harvard during World War II. Yet Webster was surprised that he had never heard of Charles David Herrold. Nor did he know until Greb called that he was in charge of a pioneer station. It seemed unbelievable that the history of KCBS went back to San Jose nearly 50 years ago. "We'll look for those records and if they're there, we'll find them," he promised Greb. "Broadcasting in 1909? That goes back a long, long time but we'll get busy and try to find them. I'll have Evelyn Clark get back to you."

Evelyn Clark was the station's public relations director, who phoned to say, "Good news! Several old staff members actually remember Herrold. We've found a note in our files that Mrs. Herrold is now remarried and her new name is True. She was living in San Jose when she last visited here. As for old records, we have only a few, nothing back to 1909, but we'll keep looking." It turned out that Evelyn was a journalism department graduate of the University of California and had been in the same class as Greb at Berkeley, although neither knew each other at the time. Neither of them also knew that one of Herrold's radio telephones had been set up and operated on the Berkeley campus in pre–World War I days, an interesting sidelight they would find out about later but would be overshadowed by what Greb would suddenly discover in San Jose.

Herrold's Records Found

Greb's search for the widow True (formerly Mrs. Herrold) now turned to scanning names in the San Jose telephone book. He began dialing everyone with the name True until finally he got the answer: "Yes, I'm Herrold's son. Mother changed my name when she remarried." It was Robert R. True, 44, son of Charles and Sybil Herrold. He was born in San Jose on September 4, 1914, and was now a city fireman. Wasting no time now that he was this close to a primary source, Greb got True to agree to be interviewed, picked up his notebook and recording machine, and was on his way! Yes, said True, as he invited his visitor in, he had a large collection of materials dealing with his father's radio work and would be glad to share them. When the son came down the stairs from the attic he was not carrying the treasure chest Greb had imagined, but an assortment of large cardboard boxes, one stacked atop the other. "Here they are," he said matter-of-factly. "Nothing's organized but it's all there. It'll take time, however, to find out what you want." Herrold's son had preserved his father's original papers, the greatest wealth of information yet. Altogether there were photographs, personal letters, notarized statements, clippings, contracts, patents, and even motion picture film showing Robert as a baby, crying into a radio microphone weeks after he had been born.

After days and weeks of frustrated hunting, finding this wealth of information was the realization of Greb's dream. In his eagerness to do everything right, Greb hooked up his recording machine and began describing each item contained in the boxes. Then, realizing there was too much to read at one sitting, Greb got permission to borrow what he considered the most important items, identified and itemized them, signed a note assuming full responsibility for their safekeeping, and promised to return them later. Greb was glad that this documentary evidence had at last been located, but he was extremely worried about the risk of these valuable records being kept in cardboard boxes. So he decided not to take newspaper clippings, magazine articles, and secondary materials and sought only original documents. Staying up late at night to read this valuable material, he realized it not only needed to be carefully preserved but also made known to the world. There was enough here to be written up in a scholarly article.[8] He began taking notes and weighing what to do next. The following day he sought to have the material copied. As photocopying machines were not readily available at the time, Greb had to order photographic negatives and prints made of precious originals in the journalism department's photo lab.

Now there were so many things to do it was no longer a simple project. Material evidence was beginning to pile up. What had hitherto been hard to find was now building and multiplying. That frustratingly blank wall of ignorance was changing into a huge waterfall from which great streams of information began to pour. Finding the Herrold papers opened up dozens of new promising leads, including a myriad of other people who knew something about Herrold's work — some dead, some living — but contacts which needed to be followed up.

SJS Professor Knew Herrold

Within the next few days, Greb found himself busy talking by telephone to more and more informed sources. Much to his surprise they were, in some cases, only a few steps away on campus or a short walk down the street. One close immediate source was Robert True's mother, who, it turned out, was still living in San Jose and whom Greb was determined to interview as soon as possible. However, someone even closer was Professor Harry M. Engwicht of the college's engineering faculty. Not only had Engwicht been Herrold's student in his College of Engineering and Wireless in downtown San Jose, but he also knew all about radio, being a "ham" himself. Licensed as an amateur radio operator (W6HC) when he was a young man, Engwicht was now serving as director of the Pacific Division of the American Radio Relay League (ARRL), a national association of amateur radio operators. From first-hand knowledge he easily confirmed Herrold's pioneering work and provided names of other former students and old radio amateurs he thought Greb should contact, which led eventually to dozens of eyewitness testimonials.

The most startling fact Greb learned from Engwicht was that Herrold's original radio equipment still existed and had been preserved by a private collector. The man who had saved it was Douglas Perham, an experienced, old time radio experimenter who had met Herrold when he was constructing wireless equipment in Palo Alto a few years before World War I. As Perham was a newly turned antiquarian, he intended to reassemble Herrold's old arc telephone system and display it with other artifacts

Museum founder and collector Douglas Perham was a radio pioneer in his own right. He knew all about Herrold's broadcasts in 1909, and obtained the inventor's technology for the Perham museum, circa 1959 (courtesy Perham Foundation Electronics Museum).

of the broadcasting history at a private museum. Perham not only had many pieces from Herrold's broadcasting machine but he also had an extensive file of materials on its operation, including radio logs, photographs, reports, and other materials kept by one of Herrold's assistants, E.L Portal. In answer to Greb's question, "What do you consider to be Herrold's contributions to radio broadcasting?" Perham unhesitatingly replied, "He was the first man to operate a radio broadcasting station."

Herrold's Wife Remembers

Secure in the knowledge he was now on the right track, Greb turned next to the person who must have played one of the most important roles in the Herrold story, Herrold's wife, Sybil M. True. She remarried in the mid–1920s and was now a widow, living in downtown San Jose. She spent an evening reminiscing about her ex-husband and early radio, telling how she probably was the first woman to do a regularly scheduled radio program. She recalled entertaining an audience of amateurs on her "Little Hams" program every Wednesday night before World War I, playing phonograph records borrowed from a local store. She told what kind of man Herrold was, saying, "He wanted always to share his honors with someone else. He was more than fair. He always was seeking perfection in the development of the radiotelephone and he worked very long hours. It was his life." Sybil had been a young girl in 1914 and now her voice brought the past alive, making it real with word pictures of the people and places she knew long, long ago. "You must find Ray Newby," she advised, as he had been Herrold's closest assistant in the earliest days of Herrold's school and wireless experiments.

By this time Greb was swamped. Working night and day over Christmas vacation, he saw problems ahead as he tried to pursue dozens of leads. With permission to use the telephone, photo laboratory, publication office, office space and other college services, Greb assembled a committee of student and faculty volunteers. KCBS had also become fully engaged and agreed to underwrite some of Greb's minor research expenses.

Assistant Recalls 1909

When Greb finally located Herrold's assistant Ray Newby in Stockton, California, and called him, he asked, "Can you verify Herrold's early day broadcasting?" Newby's immediate response was, "I was there in 1909 when he made his first broad-

Ray Newby, world's first disc jockey, proved he knew how to use a modern microphone and spin records on visiting the college radio studios in 1959. He was guest of honor at a dinner, parade and plaque celebration marking the Golden Anniversary of Broadcasting (Gordon Greb Collection).

cast." Since Newby was an eyewitness to the 1909 experimental transmissions, Greb realized he had to see Newby in person as soon as possible. He took student Anthony Taravella along, drove to Newby's Stockton home early in 1959, and recorded a lengthy interview on audiotape. Years later, in 1978, he returned to put Newby's recollections on sound film. Assisted by a student television crew provided by SJS professor Clarence Flick, Greb again visited Newby and did a videotaped interview with him for a television documentary.[9] Newby was able to identify documents, dates, photos, and incidents which recalled the excitement of Herrold's successful experiment.

By now KCBS was using its 50,000 watts of power to assist in the search for primary witnesses. The station asked listeners to call up if they knew of anyone connected to early day broadcasts. Soon Greb was in touch with more than a dozen old timers. One of them was Herrold's former assistant, Claude Kenneth Sanders, an automobile dealer in Turlock, California. He was shown alongside Emil A. Portal operating Herrold's 1912 radio station in a photograph. Because he was still a licensed amateur radio operator, Greb was able to interview Sanders on short-wave radio before going to see him in person. In the weeks and months that followed, Greb talked to dozens of other former listeners, announcers, entertainers, and students. Greb conducted interviews with Ira L. Smith, former KQW program director; Robert Stull, former student and business associate; and Joe Cappa, one of Herrold's former students.[10]

De Forest Salute

In February Greb flew to Los Angeles to interview one of radio's great pioneers, Lee de Forest. The professor was met by a CBS radio news crew and taken to de Forest's home in North Hollywood where a lengthy interview was recorded. It was edited at KNX and transmitted immediately to KCBS for use that evening in a radio newscast. De Forest said if Herrold's station was still on the air "it deserves to be congratulated—first with the spark, then with the arc and finally with the oscillating tube." Greb then took the original reels home as source material for his article.

Lee de Forest and Douglas Perham hold three of the inventor's original radio tubes. De Forest claimed to be the "Father of Radio" but credited Herrold with having founded America's first radio station. This photograph was made circa 1959 (courtesy Perham Foundation Electronics Museum).

Golden Anniversary Planned

Because 1959 marked the 50th anniversary of Herrold's first broadcast, it was agreed there should be a celebration which was announced at the San Francisco Press Club. Joint planning had brought together creative minds from the college, the station and the network. Professor Greb's campus chapter of Sigma Delta Chi took the lead in making the college's preparations, appointing 16 students to carry out various assignments.[11] SJS President John T. Wahlquist felt the college ought to join in the celebration since some of the earliest KQW broadcasts had originated on the campus and KQW's story had been documented by one of his faculty members. Webster thought of getting the U.S. Post Office to issue special stamp honoring Herrold but there wasn't time to get it done. When asked to participate, radio broadcasters throughout Northern California willingly joined in; for example, managers from 12 Bay Area radio stations founded before 1926 attended a luncheon sponsored by the San Francisco Downtown Association and Advertising Club, in addition to carrying news of the event on their stations. So many ideas were generated by the college, the station and the network that the entire program of activities lasted for more than a week, March 28–April 3, 1959.

On March 20, U.S. Senator Thomas Kuchel saluted the radio anniversary in a speech published in the *Congressional Record.* A few days later KCBS got a letter of congratulations from the White House, relayed by President Eisenhower's Press Secretary James C. Hagerty. At the state capital in Sacramento, the California State Senate passed a resolution commemorating the event and joined Governor Edmund G. (Pat) Brown in paying tribute to San Jose as the birthplace of broadcasting. Proclamations declaring April 3, 1959, to be the official 50th anniversary of broadcasting were issued by both Mayor Christopher of San Francisco and Mayor Solari of San Jose. And all across the nation listeners heard about the 50th anniversary on the CBS radio network. Altogether KCBS plugged its big event with 201 spot announcements, ran full-page ads nationally in *Broadcasting* magazine, took out five quarter-page ads in San Francisco daily newspapers, and aired 19 television spots on the local Westinghouse-owned San Francisco station KPIX. With San Jose papers on strike, local radio stations were vital in informing residents of the South Bay. Lowell Pratt handling public relations at the college prepared publicity and announcements. In addition, a radio documentary called *The Story of Broadcasting* was written by student Tony Taravella, produced and narrated by Greb and distributed free of charge for airing on independent stations nationally by the CBS organization.[12]

Original Station on Display

Museum curator Doug Perham reassembled the original Herrold station and put it on exhibit at its original site, the lobby of the American Trust Company, First and San Fernando streets, which previously was known as the Garden City Bank Building. At its historic marker dedication, the reconstructed Herrold station was not more than a few feet away from the ceremonies honoring it. From the time he left Stockton High School in 1902, Perham, who was a radio pioneer in his own right, had been interested in saving radio history for posterity. "I began doing this when I was young man working with Cyril F. Elwell and Lee de Forrest in Palo Alto," the 74-year-old curator told Greb. "Although I was only a handyman, I'd save stuff emptied into waste baskets because I thought what they were doing was important." This interest led Perham to amass a valuable collection of electronics artifacts, including rare Edison light bulbs, early de Forest radio tubes, and other technical apparatus. He put all of it on exhibit at his New Almaden Electronics Museum. Fifty years after working in radio, Perham learned that San Francisco radio KFRC had invested in a new, modern transmitter and was going to discard the old one. When told he could have it for his museum, Perham, then in his 70s, personally loaded it on a truck with help from his wife Connie and transported it away. In this way Perham obtained equipment from the original Herrold radio station and valuable papers pertaining to its operation from onetime employee E.A. Portal. Eventually he willed everything to a nonprofit Perham Foundation, which opened a new electronics museum at the Los Altos Foothill Community College.[13] While the Perham Museum was forced to close its doors at Foothill College a few years later due to a revenue shortfall from 1978's Proposition 13 tax cuts, the Perham Foundation carefully put its keepsakes in storage and made plans to display them again when a new museum was ready.[14]

In 2003, the Perham Foundation transferred its large collections to History San

Professor Greb (center) holds pencil and pad to interview former Herrold College radio alumni who came to see the old arc radio at its original site. Those present at the 50th anniversary celebration included Ira L. Smith, Terry Hansen, Ken Sanders, Ray Newby, Maurice Dee, Harry Engwicht, and Gene Wilson. Representing KCBS and the CBS network were Larry LeSeur, news correspondent; Arthur Hull Hayes, network president; Maurie Webster, network vice president; Ralph Story, television star; Mitch Miller, musical director; and KCBS staffers like Ken Ackerman, Don Mozley, Lee Kopp and employees not in the San Francisco studios. The 1959 observance was co-sponsored by KCBS and San Jose State (Gordon Greb Collection).

Jose, where it is being carefully catalogued and displayed. Included in that collection is the Herrold arc technology, and the papers and technology of Lee de Forest, both California radio broadcasting pioneers.[15]

Stars Celebrate 50th at Dinner

It wasn't until formal functions got underway that the organizers realized the 50th anniversary celebration was going to be a tremendous success. San Jose State College, for example, attracted far more people to the campus than they expected on

Friday, April 2, 1959, when the college's journalism society, Sigma Delta Chi, put on its annual "Deadline Dinner" to honor the occasion. Students sold so many tickets to the banquet that the newly opened cafeteria was filled to capacity, attracting more than 400 people for a program of entertainment that lasted nearly six hours, 6 P.M. till 12 midnight. Led by student chapter president Jim Curry and dinner chairman Bill Knowles, the group persuaded CBS radio president Arthur Hull Hayes to come west for the celebration with a planeful of CBS celebrities, including network stars Mitch Miller, Ralph Story, and Larry LeSeur. Although the head table was extended to accommodate the notables, there was such an overflow of prominent people in attendance that many well-known celebrities were scattered throughout the audience. Dave McElhatton, emcee, declared the V-shaped head table, "the first stereophonic speakers table I've ever seen."[16] Giving added life to the anniversary was 79-year-old Rudolf Friml who entertained at the piano, playing his own musical compositions which some radio listeners may have heard on the San Jose station 50 years earlier. When CBS foreign correspondent Larry LeSeur got up to the microphone, to review radio's 50-year-old history, this 30-minute portion of the dinner program was aired by KCBS as a live broadcast to its audience and other CBS affiliates.[17]

Big Parade and Dedication Ceremony

At nine o'clock the next morning, Saturday, April 3, two young men from San Jose State College took the first awkward steps that began radio's big anniversary parade through downtown San Jose. Marching side by side, journalism students Jerry Nachman and Hugh McGraw carried a banner reading "Golden Anniversary of Broadcasting," making it a time that these marchers and the crowds watching along South First Street would long remember. The students led a procession of vintage automobiles, marching bands, colorful floats, prancing horses, and sleek new convertibles carrying dignitaries. They halted at the reviewing stand at South First and San Fernando streets, where master of ceremonies Ralph Story officiated at the dedication program and interviewed San Jose Mayor Solari, Arthur Hull Hayes, Al Pearce, Ray Newby, Gordon Greb, and Mitch Miller in a 9:30 to 10 o'clock broadcast that morning. Then the historic plaque honoring the "World's First Broadcasting Station" by SDX (Sigma Delta Chi; also known as the Society of Professional Journalists) was ceremoniously placed on the American Trust building, the original site of Herrold's College of Wireless and Engineering. The celebration then moved to San Francisco, where hundreds of business executives, advertising professionals, and journalists honored KCBS at a luncheon that day and a dinner gathering of national figures called a "CBS All-Star Night," featuring from the CBS radio network Ralph Story, Arthur Hull Hayes, Larry LeSeur, Mitch Miller, and Earl "Fatha" Hines that night at the San Francisco Press Club.

Following the big 1959 celebration and for years afterward, KCBS management was forever seeking new ways to keep the public informed of its radio heritage. Starting with Maurie Webster and continuing with successive managers, KCBS began incorporating its pioneering status into ongoing advertising and publicity. As a station that favored news and interviews, KCBS had the opportunity to question several pioneer broadcasters in the early 1960s, one of them being C.L. McCarthy, former KQW owner. When the tape-recorded interview was over, general manager Webster made certain a copy was deposited in the oral history collection at Columbia University. Also by order of Webster, KCBS was now regularly crediting Charles Herrold as its 1909 founder whenever the station signed on or off the air. He had learned this was the daily practice at KQW in 1920s in fulfillment of a contract Herrold had made with the First Baptist Church, and he wanted it continued in the future. When Webster was promoted to network headquarters in New York City in 1961, Jules Dundes succeeded him in San Francisco and continued the policy of promoting KCBS as the preeminent pioneer station. "When I came back to KCBS in '61," said Dundes, "San Francisco was still a strong radio market. KSFO was number one with it strong personalities and middle-of-the-road music. KFRC and KYA had the rock audience. We continued to develop more informational programming and KGO got into that later. KABL had its good music format. Radio did well in San Francisco."[18]

In 1964 Dundes decided to call attention to the station's origins again and got its staff writers and editors searching for new information to add to the old. This resulted in the publication of an updated 17-page booklet, which included new information and photographs.[19] In talking about Maurie Webster in New York, Dundes told professor Greb that the former KCBS manager was still eager to inform the world that radio broadcasting originated in California. "What Maurie still wants to do," said Dundes, "is persuade CBS to exhibit Herrold's old radio station in the lobby of its new building." Webster even arranged for Ray Newby to be a mystery guest on the popular CBS quiz show *I've Got a Secret*. The panelists were stumped in trying to guess Newby's original occupation on the program of June 28, 1965. Newby found them amazed when he told them, "I was the world's first disc jockey" and then explained that "back in 1909 old 'Doc' Herrold and I put the first radio station on the air and I spun the records." Before he was has done, audiences not only knew that the station was still on the air but that its call letters were KCBS.

Herrold Forgotten Again

By 1970 it was KDKA's time to celebrate its 50th birthday. Once again the old Herrold station was forgotten in the well organized broadcast industry-sponsored celebration, which regarded KDKA's election night broadcast on November 2, 1920, as the starting date for radio. Seeing that many members of the National Association of Broadcasters were not cognizant of broadcasting's origins in California, Greb wondered what more he could possibly do. Perhaps Herrold deserved a book based on a major effort to collect more new evidence. He began a search for funding in 1970, seeking a grant that would enable him to visit distant libraries, museums and archives, record interviews with more early day radio pioneers, and review all "first station" claims for a book. Hoping CBS might underwrite such a project, he presented his proposal to Maurie Webster in New York, who offered to approach the network.

When the reply came, the news was not good. CBS had no educational grants to make that year and even if it did, the network tended to favor private schools and colleges rather than state-supported schools. Since Greb taught at a public institution, he was out of luck. Fortunately a small grants program at San Jose State College finally came to his support. Thanks to the Sourisseau Academy, a funding organization established in the history department, Greb was awarded $390 on December 10, 1974, for the purpose of collecting and preserving the Charles David Herrold papers. This enabled him to have them photocopied and bound into books, which he then donated to such repositories as the Library of Congress, Bancroft Library at U.C. Berkeley and San Jose City Library. While this made a limited edition of *KCBS: Broadcasting's First Station* available to a small number of library scholars, Greb worked out a plan for wider dissemination by also using the grant to put everything he had gathered on microfilm. When a short time later two interested researchers on the East Coast asked Greb to produce evidence substantiating Herrold's claim, he was able to comply by directing a nearby microfilm company to fill their needs.

"First" Question Debated

In 1971 a national organization, the Speech Communication Association (SCA), arranged a debate to try to settle the question "Who Was First on the Air — KCBS, KDKA, WHA or WWJ?"[20] Each station was invited to make its case on December 29 that year before the association members at the SCA's national convention in San Francisco. Professor Lawrence W. Lichty of the University of Wisconsin–Madison served as moderator, trying as best he could to maintain peace amongst the spirited arguers. Each claimant was vigorously represented by a champion. Gordon Greb, San Jose State College journalism professor argued for KCBS; Joseph Baudino, Westinghouse senior vice president made the case for KDKA; Harold B. McCarty, retired radio station manager, represented WHA; and Edgar B. Willis, University of Michigan speech professor argued for WWJ. When the dust had cleared, everyone shook hands and parted perhaps better informed, but no vote was taken among members of the audience. No one knew who had won — the answer was left in the air.

Recognition Sought Again

In 1972 interest in the Herrold story was revived by an out-of-town radio executive who had recently taken charge of a San Jose radio station. He was Bill Spendlove, the newly-named manager of station KLOK. Not only was Spendlove widely respected as a broadcast executive, having made his station number one in the ratings in Northern California, but he also belonged to all the major advertising and media organizations in the San Francisco Bay Area. When he saw the plaque on the American Trust Company stating that San Jose was the birthplace of broadcasting, he could not believe it. His immediate reaction was to ask, "Why don't more people know about this?" It ought to be known all over the world, he thought. Contacting Greb to see the evidence, he became convinced that the City of San Jose should imprint all of its outgoing mail with the slogan "San Jose: Birthplace of Broadcasting." He and Greb together approached the City Council with that proposal, getting its members to agree that if the Herrold claim were officially recognized by an industry group like the National Association of Broadcasters, the city would consider doing it. A radio committee was organized under the auspices of the Chamber of Commerce.

To win support the San Jose City Council authorized sending Greb and Spendlove as official representatives of the city to the spring convention of the National Association of Broadcasters in Chicago to make their case. The result, however, was a disappointment. Although CBS was contacted and promised to endorse the effort, New York executives were really more concerned about radio's future than its past. Their star radio performer, Arthur Godfrey, aging and facing competition from television, was retiring from broadcasting and making his last radio appearance at the Chicago convention. Thus CBS wanted to focus its publicity on Godfrey, not Herrold. Although the petition for Herrold's recognition was politely received, it was never actually presented to the NAB membership. Professor Greb was taken to the CBS-arranged press conference in a basement room of the hotel where he made the claim and was photographed shaking hands with the NAB president. However, none of the pictures or statements at the news conference were released nationally. It was a CBS-controlled, in-house exercise.

The network allowed KCBS to carry the story but was not prepared at the time to do more than that. All that NAB members ever learned about the San Jose claim was from a small story and photo which appeared in the organization's house organ later on. Again, Herrold never got a proper hearing. The following year the Broadcast Pioneers presented KCBS with its coveted Mike Award, the first CBS-owned station to receive it. This gave the station the same recognition as that given to KDKA, Pittsburgh, and WWJ, Detroit, some years earlier. However, neither Broadcast Pioneers nor National Association of Broadcasters were wanted to arbitrate the case. Despite this reluctance, there now appeared on the scene two radio historians—one from industry and the other from academia—who decided to look at all the evidence for the purpose of doing a scholarly paper on the problem. They began investigating who did what and when in radio, hoping to settle once and for all who deserved to be honored, looking especially at the claims raised by KCBS, KDKA, WHA, and WWJ, and to publish their findings.

New Scholarly Interest

In 1975 Westinghouse executive Joseph E. Baudino contacted Gordon Greb at San Jose State College. He told Greb he was researching early radio with Professor John M. Kittross and needed to verify Herrold's claims of being first. Greb knew what to do. He ordered copies of all the microfilmed Herrold documents mailed to these East Coast scholars immediately. In a phone conversation with Greb, Baudino, in Washington, D.C., also wanted to know how he could locate Joe Cappa, Ray Newby, and Robert Stull. He needed current addresses and telephone numbers in order to interview them. Then in August 1972 Baudino flew to San Jose to meet with Greb, search the newspaper morgue of the *San Jose Mercury*, and see as many former Herrold acquaintances in person as he could find. He succeeded in meeting Joe Cappa and recorded a 42-minute interview, in which he questioned his recollections of exactly when Herrold got his station back on the air after World War I. The original Baudino interview of Cappa was placed in Broadcast Pioneers Library and a copy was given to Greb. When he located records of several Herrold radio patents in the U.S. Patent Office, Baudino generously had copies made and mailed them to Greb. His research also took him to files of the Smithsonian Institution where his quest ended. Incorporating new and old data, he co-authored an article with Professor Kittross which was published in the Winter 1977 issue of the *Journal of Broadcasting*, "Broadcasting's Oldest Station: An Examination of Four Claimants." With respect to San Jose's place in broadcasting history, the authors concluded: "Herrold did operate the first radio broadcasting station in the United States, but this does not mean that KCBS, even with its many years of service, can claim to be the oldest station on the air" because of a gap in its continuous program service.[21]

California Historic Marker

Now that these scholars had decided KCBS was the first station and KDKA the oldest, the task of recognizing Herrold got a bit easier. On November 5, 1982, the State of California officially declared San Jose to be the site of the first broadcasting station in the world. The city was authorized to erect California Registered Landmark No. 952 at the exact location in downtown San Jose, corner of South First and San Fernando streets, where Herrold had made his very first radio broadcast.[22] A historical society dedicated to preserving California history, the ancient and honorable order of E Clampus Vitus, whose local chapter historian James M. Arbuckle prepared the petition, assembled the evidence, and got it recognized.[23] Arbuckle got valuable assistance from Claudia Jurmain, curator of the San Jose Historical Museum, who helped collect the evidence, and Janet Gray Hayes, chairman of the Redevelopment

This "50th Anniversary of Broadcasting" commemorative plaque was placed at the site of Herrold's original radio station in 1959 by co-sponsors KCBS and Sigma Delta Chi, the journalism society chapter at San Jose State Univesity (then a college) (Gordon Greb Collection).

Admiring the plaque placed where broadcasting began in 1909 were (left to right): professor Gordon Greb, who originated the idea; composer Rudolf Friml, whose music was heard on the station in 1912; and Dr. John T. Wahlquist, college president. They were photographed at the 50th anniversary celebration of broadcasting in 1959 (Gordon Greb Collection).

Agency, who organized support from recognized leaders. The original building had been torn down but San Jose Mayor John McEnery, who conducted the plaque laying ceremony, announced that the historic marker would be placed in a prominent place on the new building, which soon would be built there. Today the plaque can be seen alongside the SDX historic marker placed there in 1959 by the Society of Professional Journalists. The building, formerly the Garden City bank and the location of the Herrold station, is now called the Knight-Ridder building, home of this large national media company, parent of its local affiliate, the *San Jose Mercury News.*

New Professor and New Plans

Because San Jose State University is located close to the central city, the historic plaques honoring Herrold are sometimes seen by faculty and students walking downtown. When Mike Adams joined the SJSU faculty in 1989 to teach radio and television, he came steeped in broadcasting history, having recently produced a five-part

PBS TV series on antique radio called "Radio Collector," based on data supplied by amateur radio enthusiasts, reading of old magazines and books, and contacts with collectors of radio memorabilia. When Adams ran into Herrold's claim, he was not convinced, thought it less than believable, and couldn't take it seriously without verification. Colleagues at the university told him he could find the evidence in local museums, libraries, and various publications. After investigation he came to believe that San Jose indeed was the birthplace of broadcasting but nobody outside the San Francisco Bay Area seemed to know about it.

Believing the Herrold story would interest a wider audience if told on television, Adams decided to do a documentary. He contacted researcher Greb, descendants of Herrold, early radio survivors and everyone who could supply him with materials. With a small grant from the Perham Foundation and his university, donation of time and energy by numerous volunteers, students and friends, and the production facilities of the local public television station, Adams did on a shoestring budget what ordinarily might have cost $100,000. For one tenth that amount and 15 months of hard work, Adams produced an hour-long TV documentary, *Broadcasting's Forgotten Father.* With a film crew, composed largely of student trainees who accompanied him everywhere he went with Radio-TV-Film department gear, Adams interviewed key witnesses, questioned radio experts, visited original sites, and finally demonstrated on film exactly how Herrold's San Jose radio station operated. Audiences saw Adams doing what Herrold did, running the controls of an odd-looking, cone-shaped radiotelephone transmitter and playing music from a phonograph into a Herrold-invented microphone. They also saw motion picture film of baby Robert Herrold crying into a microphone, held in the arms of mother Sybil, the world's first female disc jockey, taken in 1914. Adams was about to show the world how radio broadcasting really began.

Herrold Story on Television

In September 1994 the video documentary, *Broadcasting's Forgotten Father: The Charles Herrold Story* was completed and aired on KTEH, the San Jose PBS television station. It was distributed to the Public Broadcasting System over its satellite network and offered free of charge to those PBS stations that wished to carry it.[24] Before the premier broadcast was aired, KTEH arranged a gala celebration, inviting guests to meet the program's producer Mike Adams amidst the "old town" atmosphere of San Jose Historic Park. Guests included surviving radio pioneers, contributing scholars, various leaders from near and far, Adams' production staff, and supporters from the community and college. The event was accompanied by an official proclamation from the mayor of San Jose calling the celebration "Charles Herrold Day." Thanks to advance publicity generated by the station, numerous newspaper readers learned of its showing, some read reviews of the show, and *TV Guide* gave it a "Best Bet" listing for the day the show actually aired. According to the Neilsen Company, which issues widely regarded audience measurement ratings, the program was watched in nearly 50,000 homes throughout the country on the night of its release. While a large number, the total potential audience could have been greater. It was reduced because PBS had scheduled another historical documentary the same night. People at home had to choose one or the other, the story of broadcasting on KTEH by Mike Adams or another equally interesting documentary on San Francisco's KQED by producer Ken Burns. However, according to a survey, neither of them beat the commercial stations stations. The number one and two rated shows that Monday evening were ABC's *Monday Night Football* and the CBS comedy show *Murphy Brown*. But unlike the earlier CBS-sponsored *Golden Anniversary of Broadcasting* in 1959, which suffered when both San Jose daily newspapers were shut down by a strike, the Herrold TV program got full and favorable coverage that day in the *San Jose Mercury News*, whose circulation was not interrupted. As it turned out, the Herrold story was shown on public television stations in New York, Boston, Sacramento, Philadelphia and many other cities around the country. "The audience for this historic documentary was small," Adams admitted afterward, "but I did get a response. So I know some people cared."[25]

Alliance Formed

While working together on the television documentary and gathering new information about Herrold, producer Adams established a close relationship with then-retired Professor Greb and they realized they had strong interests in common. They both loved radio, liked to write and teach, and were highly interested in the history of broadcasting. So Adams and Greb agreed to collaborate on a book. Before beginning their association, Adams forewarned his colleague, "Some critics tell me your 1959 celebration was a 'booster event' for San Jose, and that CBS used you and your college students for commercial purposes. The network wanted merely to attract listeners, sell advertisers, and make money. I don't know whether reputable critics really buy that point of view but whatever you and I do, it must be accepted by modern-day scholars and the broadcasting industry as factual, unbiased and true." Greb agreed with Adams's scholarly objective but replied, "That sort of criticism usually originates with someone looking for a way to discredit Herrold. It won't change the facts about what he did. When you find evidence that something important happened in history, people need to be told. KCBS and the college didn't sponsor the 50th anniversary for reasons that were strictly commercial. Town and gown should work together to enlighten the public. Since knowledge of history needs to be taught, using the classroom is not enough. Let us use advertising and publicity to help in that process. Without engaging the mass media, what happened in San Jose in 1909 will remain in the dustbin of history." Even though they had slightly different points of view, both agreed further research was needed to put Herrold's work into a national perspective. They asked themselves, "Why isn't Herrold more widely known after years of research, which included coast to coast broadcasts on the CBS Radio Network, national attention in professional and academic journals, and network exposure in a PBS documentary? Is there a 'Holy Grail' of radio history somewhere which we ought to seek?" The decision was made to obtain research funding in order to travel to several East Coast repositories of broadcast and radio history.

The Perham Foundation Electronics Museum, the major funding source for the PBS documentary, advanced money for a research project in the summer of 1995. Professor Adams spent a week at the Antique Wireless Association (AWA) archives near Rochester, New York, looking at the very complete library of early wireless documents. Later his colleague Gordon Greb flew east to join him in Washington, D.C. In New York assistance was given Adams by the late Bruce Kelley, who in 1951 founded and began to collect a world-renowned archive. Adams next went to the main branch of the New York Public Library to search the most complete microfilm collection of periodicals anywhere. The goal was to find out what others knew about broadcasting history and how those who wrote it knew it. Did all the information about early radio come from articles in periodicals like *Scientific American*? Was the story of broadcasting to be found in the hundreds of stories in the dozens of daily newspapers? Could it be possible that only the wealthiest broadcasting entities had the resources to preserve what is commonly accepted as the history of the technology and programming of radio? What was in the Library of Congress, the Broadcast Pioneers Library, and the Writers Project books which were published during the Depression?[26]

Clark's Radioana

As it turned out, most broadcast historians writing between the 1930s and the 1950s got much of their information from the Radio Corporation of America. Just as CBS was attempting to gather and disseminate its version of history in 1959, the Radio Corporation of America had collected and preserved and promoted its history with extreme care since its start in the 1920s. This great corporation employed and housed an archivist named George Clark. Until Clark's death in the late 1940s, the Clark Collection at RCA was the largest and most complete compilation of all things electronically transmitted from 1900 to 1950. It was well-organized and documented. It included the personal recollections of Fessenden, de Forest, Conrad and other early radio experimenters, most of whom were based in the Eastern part of the country. The collection was now housed in the Archive Center of the Smithsonian Institution, where Greb and Adams spent a week studying in the summer of 1995. By careful perusal, they gathered and copied about 900 pages of original, first-person radio history. The Clark collection was invaluable to historian Gleason L. Archer when he completed the substance of his seminal work in the mid–1930s, and the Clark documents are unarguably the best extant collection of East Coast radio and broadcast history. Most scholars would probably agree that it is a fair representation of broadcast history, although admittedly important parts of the story are missing. George Clark was one individual, charged by RCA with collecting whatever he thought was important. Because his work was a New York–based operation, located at the financial and administrative center of network broadcasting, Clark was well placed to leave as his legacy an outstanding collection of radio's development in the East for the first half of the 20th century.

Did the Clark archives mention Herrold? Yes, some mention of him can be found there, including copies of his Arc Phone patents, but nothing about Herrold was highlighted for particular attention, lost in a bulk of materials lacking perspective or comment. By subscribing to all the major newspapers and clipping any article about radio, Clark had saved in his collection a few articles from the *Oakland Tribune* and the *San Jose Mercury*, including the previously mentioned 1912 story in which a reporter visited the Herrold radio station during a broadcast. It described how the students were taking requests for phonograph records, which is today one of the characteristics of radio. But certainly overwhelmed by his historical mission, it appears unlikely that Mr. Clark ever bothered to read these stories, let alone put them into any perspective.

A Final Tribute

Because it was a new medium and outside the traditional scope of academic attention, scholarly interest in radio history was slow in developing. Perhaps if more digging had been done earlier, credit would have been given sooner to those who deserved it. That Herrold's work did reach across the country occasionally and that some accounts of it were, in fact, preserved in the extensive Clark collection, means the fact of Herrold being unknown for many years was not entirely his own fault. We should applaud those early historians who did indeed uncover Herrold's work and gave him credit for his extraordinary accomplishment in their books, such as the Federal Writers' Project of 1939, whose history *California* discussed Herrold's 1912 broadcasting in San Jose and E.P.J. Shurick, whose 1946 book, *The First Quarter-Century of American Broadcasting*, paid heed to Herrold's 1909 broadcasting.[27] We should be especially thankful, too, that Herrold was assisted over the years by some dedicated individuals who collected and saved important stories, papers, letters, records, and artifacts about his early pioneering station — people like Ray Newby, Harry Engwicht, Douglas Perham, Joseph Cappa, Ira L. Smith, Kenneth Sanders, Emil Portal, Fred C. Hart, Fred F. Wells, Clyde Arbuckle, Ralph Brunton, C.L. McCarthy, and others who strove to secure Herrold's place in history.

When radio bestowed its final honors on the living Charles Herrold in a documentary aired by KQW from San Francisco, San Francisco, on November. 10, 1945, he appreciated being remembered. In his last words to a radio audience from the station he founded, said

> I'm gratified and happy to speak to you on this occasion. Station KQW has gone far beyond my dreams. I'm particularly proud that the dream we had for radio as an entertainment medium has materialized. Radio indeed has outgrown its infant clothes. I'm happy to have been the first man to have broadcast radio entertainment on a regular schedule.

Both claimants, KCBS and KDKA, are now owned by a multi-billion dollar corporation, Infinity Broadcasting, and the effect that this control may have on the relative positions of these stations in radio history is unclear.[28] Infinity Radio, which is

Viacom's radio division, operates over 180 radio stations in the nation's largest markets, which include the two pioneer stations in San Francisco and Pittsburgh. Perhaps the court of world opinion in the final analysis will consider each case plausible and favor them both. Whatever the story of broadcasting turns out to be, we hope that future historians will have the wisdom of Solomon, the insights of Einstein and the compassion of Mother Teresa when the time comes for them to have the final say.

10

Case for First Broadcaster

> *There must be a process by means of which some individual or class can make a living out of promoting inventions. If the inevitable risks of a technical change are centered too closely about those people who originally make the change, and there is not counter-vailing means to protect these entrepreneurs, no one will dare take the risk.*
>
> Norbert Wiener, *Inventions* (1993)[1]

We think that Herrold, when he was alive, should have been recognized as a genius.[2] Since his accomplishment failed to make him rich or famous during his lifetime, it leaves us with an important question: Why is it that Charles D. Herrold is not better known as America's first broadcaster? If our book achieves anything at all, it should help to explain why this resourceful inventor — the first man to serve audiences using a radio station — has been overlooked. There are probably a number of reasons which explain this conundrum, ranging from the philosophical to the practical, for history not only arises from human activity but the vagaries of time and place, such as who won a war, who benefited from clever public relations efforts, and the very intellectual skills and weakness of everyone involved. Certainly Herrold himself is responsible for not having done a number of things to ensure his place in the history of radio. Clearly any belief that his success and his reputation were insured by securing patents on his radiotelephone was misplaced. It also did not help his cause that in getting publicity for his accomplishments in local San Jose newspapers, he rarely sought or got attention on a national scale. It would have helped Herrold immeasurably if he had published articles on his pre–World War I radio work in widely-circulated scholarly professional or trade journals. This absence reconfirms what a number of graduate students are told, which is simply "publish or perish."

There is another reason for Herrold's obscurity as an original radio broadcaster — he was too early. When Herrold put his ideas into practice, the technical and social conditions necessary for them to succeed were not yet in place. While witnesses have testified that the quality of his on-the-air broadcasting was amazingly clear, understandable, and sought after by those equipped with receivers to hear it, the prewar Herrold station was composed of cumbersome, primitive, and elementary components, compared to what the vacuum tube radio would soon bring. Being interested in invention, Herrold was undoubtedly talented and bright when it came to making his instruments work, but he didn't realize until it was too late that he needed political acumen as well as a natural aptitude for invention to survive in the world of business. While he himself seemed well informed about wireless developments in the outside world, including progress in his chosen field of interest, he barely thrust himself into it nationally and not energetically enough until late in life, after others had staked out their claims.

Herrold the Educator

If we had been able to ask him "What do you do for a living," our best guess is that Charles Herrold probably would have answered that he was the head of a technical college specializing in using and developing wireless and the radiotelephone. What would be the significance of such an answer, if we can assume that is what it would be? Obviously it would have meant a great deal more in the early part of the 20th century when the majority of the population never thought of seeking higher education, or even a technical education, for that matter, as most people did not consider a college education necessary for the lives they expected to lead. Few in those days finished high school. Only a small percentage of young men and women ever visited a college campus or heard a professor give a lecture, and the fact that Herrold spent three years at Stanford University, studying astronomy, physics and engineering was remarkable for the time. In 1895, anyone going to college for three years was unusual.[3]

Those who obtained academic credentials stood out and so did the institutions they attended. Reputations for excellence extended not only to individuals but to the colleges and schools themselves. A hierarchy of prestige existed then and still exists today. At the top we usually find such famed research institutions as Harvard and Yale in the eastern United States, and Stanford and the University of California in the west. In the middle are the so-called teaching institutions and four-year state universities, followed by the two year community colleges. At the lowest tier are the thousands of trade and technical schools, usually above the high school level, which teach a wide range of skills and train practitioners from electricians and auto mechanics to secretaries and office clerks. Thus Herrold's reputation as an educator, especially in terms of the kinds of people who knew him and with whom he associated, was largely influenced by the fact he chose the technical-vocational field as his principal field of interest. If where a person works is a predictor of a person's influence and prestige, it can be argued that Herrold's place in this academic aristocracy did not confer upon him much prestige and importance largely because he chose to stay outside it and gave up any benefits which continuing contact with higher education could have given him.

Compared with other radiotelephone specialists of his day, Herrold probably would have held his own in a discussion with experts in this field. But he hardly stands out as the best educationally prepared and most qualified person who was conducting experiments and research in this particular area. Lee de Forest, the son of a college president, undoubtedly would have won such a contest hands down. He stands apart from the major developers of radio broadcasting as he completed both his undergraduate and Ph.D. degrees at Yale University. None of de Forest's contemporaries were as well-qualified academically as he was. Another quick learner both inside and outside the classroom was Reginald A. Fessenden. Even though he was egotistical and impatient with his intellectual inferiors, Fessenden rose in the ranks of academia because of his demonstrated knowledge of science and mathematics, not because he carried to the position any prestigious college degrees. He had gone to college but never graduated. As for Frank Conrad's educational preparation, he benefited more from being with the right employers at the right time rather than academic preparation. He was, in truth, a self-educated radio expert who quit school at 16, learned electrical engineering as a Westinghouse employee and was awarded an honorary doctorate by the University of Pittsburgh in 1928 to acknowledge his contributions to KDKA and his numerous radio patents.

Unlike the self-assured de Forest or Fessenden, Herrold seems to have been left slightly uncomfortable with his incomplete academic credentials. Although he left Stanford University before completing his own undergraduate degree, he allowed himself to be called professor by the students he taught both in Stockton and San Jose. He may even have believed that by founding the Herrold College of Wireless and Engineering, he was entitled to award himself a degree. Almost from the start, his young wireless enthusiasts began addressing him as "Doc" out of their respect for his superior knowledge and the way he demonstrated it in his laboratory and classroom. Newspaper reporters began referring to him as a doctor in their stories and soon no one bothered to ask where his doctorate came from. In official correspondence in later years, Herrold added several engineering degrees and titles to his signature. On business stationary and in advertising, he identified himself as "Dr." Charles D. Herrold with a degree in electrical engineering. None of this was true.

Inspired by Students

What probably led Herrold to create and keep his broadcasting station on the air was the fact that he was the head of a trade school and was an old-fashioned American pragmatist. Applying knowledge in a practical fashion rather than focusing purely on theory and research, which he probably would have done at a major doctorate-granting institution, worked in many ways to his advantage. Because his students were keenly interested in wireless as a hobby, Charles Herrold saw it was to his advantage to allow them to spend countless hours using his wireless telephone station to entertain themselves and their friends. Using volunteer student help expanded his operating staff at little or no additional cost. Today the energetic enthusiasm of students involved in a broadcasting operation not only assists professors in their teaching but often leads them in new and fruitful directions in their own research.

They sometimes stimulate mentors to explore new pathways to knowledge. We have experienced this and know how the enthusiasm of young people can inspire teachers in the quest for technical inventions or creative programming. We learned this after being engaged for several decades as faculty advisors to our university's radio station. This stimulus can occur at any institution like that of the California State University system which gives most of its students on-the-job training to earn their radio broadcasting degrees, unlike the more research-oriented universities.

Herrold's school attracted the kind of individuals to whom the practical application of broadcasting appealed even though they never took courses in the subject matter of "broadcasting" per se. Despite the fact that Herrold's students set up and demonstrated his radiotelephone in 1916 on the Berkeley campus of the University of California before World War I, radio broadcasting seemed to have interested few if any faculty members there when these demonstrations took place. Herrold's radiotelephone was not even known to the University of Wisconsin which was pioneering a wireless service of its own about the same time. Consequently, Herrold's principal influence in Northern California was in attracting the enthusiasm of youth wherever he could find it, because his San Jose trade school was where excited youngsters could study wireless as well as learn and practice everything Herrold could teach them about radio broadcasting. Early newspaper accounts tell of Herrold's students playing recorded music for their friends regularly from the San Jose station, taking requests over the telephone for those wanting particular phonograph recordings, reading stories from the local newspaper, and in general, carrying out all the activities that continue to define radio broadcasting today. The San Jose station was not only educational but fun to operate.

Beginning of College Radio

As Herrold's San Jose station attracted student operators from its opening in 1909, which was years ahead of other school, college and university stations, it can be said that Charles Herrold was the single most important American educator to set the stage for what eventually became college radio. Underscoring this influence of college educators on early radio was a finding by University of Wisconsin Professor Robert W. McChesney, who said

> Although still largely overlooked in the mass communications literature, these nonprofit broadcasters are now recognized as the "true pioneers" of U.S. broadcasting, who were, as one of the leading radio engineers of the period observed, "at the start of things distinctly on the ground floor."[4]

Nonprofit stations sprang up by the hundreds to help pioneer radio's popularity in the early 1920s, the majority of them affiliated with a college or university. Approximately two-fifths of all radio stations on the air in 1925 were nonprofit operations. The fact that most of them got squeezed out in years that followed by profit-seeking entrepreneurs wanting their frequencies on the dial is another story.[5]

Herrold apparently believed, and said so in later life, that something as visible as entertaining young local amateurs and their parents with wireless music was a good way to promote his school. Another reason for the Herrold College to be involved in radio broadcasting as a promotional activity was that the act of being "on the air" and speaking or playing music that could be picked up on your friend's radio made attending Herrold's school a popular place to be. Just as a growing number of American colleges nowadays consider student evaluations valuable in granting promotions or tenure to professors, the fact that Herrold kept his students keenly interested and happy helped him a lot. When students learned how enjoyable it was to study radio at Herrold's College, newcomers followed their curiosity to the Garden City Bank building, signed up for courses and soon supplied Herrold with a steady stream of new paying customers. While Herrold was never properly credentialed academically, he nevertheless was an extremely successful teacher, a bright, self-taught subject matter specialist, popular with nearly all of his students because they were tremendously eager to learn wireless and radio. The success of Herrold's school and radio station was due, in part, to the fact that the wireless instruction was connected to the laboratory, which was constantly seeking ways to improve the radiotelephone. While few radio station operators dared put advertising on the air in the early 1920s, Herrold was, in fact, advertising his school every day he was on the air, starting with his first transmission in 1909. He not only was selling radio to the public but he was providing a first-class course of learning to whomever signed up. At his own school and during an earlier position at Heald's College of Mining and Engineering, he trained hundreds of students in practical aspects of wireless operation and the electrical theory necessary for a better understanding of radio as it existed prior to World War I. And because of the three years he spent at Stanford, he apparently knew enough to be an effective educator at the vocational and mechanical level. Therefore, the question can be asked: Would Herrold have attempted or even been permitted to experiment in the less than theoretical, less than serious, less than scientific broadcasting of music and entertainment had he been a professor accustomed to the more formal type of graduate education environment that Lee de Forest must have experienced at Yale? Probably not.

Herrold the Man

Herrold was unique. He was one of the few experimenters—de Forest, among others—who would think of putting his station on the air daily to send phonograph music to an audience using the wireless, which you'll recall from earlier chapters, was primarily the province of amateurs or those engaged in it for commerce or the safety of life and property. To describe how those personality traits that defined Herrold the man might have piqued his interest in broadcasting will require a bit of speculation based on the available evidence. Young Charles was shaped by a father who was an inventor. That time spent watching his dad in his shop obviously interested the young boy for he identified himself as an inventor as early as high school. His mother was said to be public spirited and cultured. It was from her that Charles learned the habits of a Victorian lifestyle, and through her was schooled in the arts and letters. We suspect that it was partly because of his mother that Herrold grew up to be the polite and mannered and cultured gentleman his acquaintances described him to be. He was also a musician, a fair piano player by all accounts, and like Lee de Forest, may have believed that some of this musical knowledge and enjoyment should be passed on to an audience.

There is continuing evidence that Herrold had a sense of personal responsibility and tried to be an informed and active citizen in his various communities of residence. As a child growing up in Iowa he helped save his schoolmates by warning them of a storm. In Stockton, he spent time near the Delta, talking with divers until he was able to invent devices which allowed them to see better under water. Later, he helped to save students and faculty at his school during a flood, and in correspondence with his mother he told how he had attended the local town council meeting to exhort the city fathers to do something about flood control. Later, while at his San Jose school, he spent weekends camping with his students, together building several cabins in the nearby mountains. He was handy with tools, a trait of which his father would approve, and it was said by his students that because of his mechanical and electrical skills, Charles Herrold was known as a "hands-on" instructor. He taught and lived his life by example.

There was also a sad, insecure part of Herrold's life. As a man in his 30s, he eagerly courted and married Sybil May Paull, a young woman barely 17 years of age. Between them they had two children. In later years Sybil spoke well of Charles as a gentleman and inventor, but Herrold apparently was unable to establish a good balance between work and family. If Herrold found it necessary to spend every day and night at the college, one would think he would have been home weekends with his family. Not so. Weekends he gave to his students as rest and relaxation in the form of wireless camping trips. There was only one area in which Herrold seemed to pay attention to his young wife. He turned her into a radio personality after their marriage in 1913 and encouraged her to obtain and program music, the Wednesday night "Little Hams" program. However, this form of attention wasn't enough. In the mid–1920s Sybil took the children and left Charles for another man, Henry True. Rather than turn the musical programming experience of her youth into an exciting career in radio broadcasting, she chose to help run her new husband's dry cleaning store.

Herrold remarried in 1926, soon after his divorce from Sybil. Not much is known about his second wife, whose name was Belle Coleman. There is no evidence of this marriage beyond a single newspaper article detailing an on-air live wedding ceremony, and the script of the wedding in Herrold's personal papers. Was it real? The authors have not been able to confirm or deny that a wedding ever took place. Of course, from this another conclusion can be offered: If Herrold was a person for which the entertaining of the public was important, whether by music or drama, as in the case of his apparently staged "radio wedding," then perhaps he did have the sort of needy personality that drives people to be on the air. Both authors have spent many years behind the radio microphone, enough years to know that there is a type of individual who seems to gravitate toward broadcasting to an audience. Charles Herrold may have possessed this trait. According to friend Clyde Arbuckle,

Herrold was a compelling storyteller as well. Radio was a natural outlet for this inclination.

As a good citizen, Herrold believed from the beginning that broadcasting should serve the needs of the public. He showed this trait by helping people to build radio receivers and placing a dozen receivers in a downtown music store. He did this before and after the war. And when he grew short of funds in the mid–1920s, he made every effort to keep his station in the forefront of public service, but failed to make a profit. He then tried to establish KQW as a municipal station in San Jose in 1922 and after this idea was rejected, he sought support from local community leaders in the Exchange Club. Finally, church leaders of the First Baptist congregation decided to keep the station on the air. Even though Herrold was later forced to become a salesman for commercial radio in Oakland, he continued, as detailed in his booklet on radio advertising, to promote high ethical and public service standards for sponsored broadcasting.

Although Herrold spent nearly all of his middle and later years living alone in the hills of Oakland, he was socially active and stayed in touch with people in the radio business and old acquaintances in the broadcasting community until he had to reduce much of this activity because of advancing age. It is noteworthy that Herrold had several careers in radio: first, as a pioneer and experimenter in the very early days; second, as the founding father of the first station and as a station owner before and after World War I; third, as a commercial radio salesman in the late 1920s; and fourth, as an on-air entertainer when he was a radio storyteller in the early 1930s. By 1930 he began to work diligently to secure his legacy as the "Father of Radio Broadcasting," writing the very bold "court of public opinion" letter in 1932 which was published in the major daily newspaper of his area, the *Oakland Tribune*. With help from a friend, he began work on his autobiography, hoping to have it published. From time to time, he assisted KQW in its attempt to gain national attention and official pioneer status for the station, which culminated in a gala 25th anniversary broadcast in 1934.[6] After each of these attempts to gain recognition failed, there was nothing more that Herrold personally could do to gain national recognition. By the mid–1930s he was out of ideas and energy. Nearing 65, he became a janitor at the Oakland shipyards during World War II, and throughout the rest of the 1940s there is very little evidence that he was involved in any radio activity, save for the occasional speech before local amateur radio clubs and his small involvement in the earlier-mentioned 1945 history of KQW documentary.[7] To the authors, it appears that after 1935, when he turned 60, he just seemed to have run out of energy and to have accepted anonymity.

Herrold the Inventor

Although Herrold obviously spent thousands of hours trying to invent a system of wireless telephony which would be accepted by the larger scientific community, he apparently labored for nothing. The first Herrold patent was filed on April 21, 1913.[8] Based on correspondence between Herrold and the N.W.T.&T lawyer, it was obvious that the company believed that Herrold's system could have a Poulsen infringement problem, and there ensued a long dialogue with patent attorney George Strong on how to describe the uniqueness of his oscillator and how to differentiate his system now called an "oscillating spark" from that of others like the Poulsen "active arc." While his system looked like an arc with its carbon and copper electrodes, critical differences were claimed. Herrold referred to a university laboratory demonstration he witnessed in 1913 comparing "six de Forest air arcs burning in series and six Poulsen arcs burning in an atmosphere of gaseous hydro-carbon" to show that his own system was different.

Herrold tried hard to present a learned analysis in favor of his own invention. He concluded that the radiation from his own "oscillating spark in liquid" was the best system so far. In defending his oscillating arc, he noted defects in others. Herrold claimed that Poulsen used a powerful blow magnet to attempt to change the arc into an oscillating spark, with the result that its arc roared and hissed. That, said Herrold, meant it could not be used as a telephone. The difference between his own "oscillating spark" method and Poulsen's was that his competitor's arc was a spark ball which was

> composed of dissociated particles from liquid and electrodes and not a true arc of incandescent vapor. A true arc in gas or under liquid (in gas bubble) has greater brilliance but higher conductivity than an "Oscillating Spark in Liquid." It is very difficult to maintain a true vapor arc steadily for any length of time under any liquid, without fluctuation when shunted with a condenser and inductance. It will almost certainly change to a spark with wonderful increase in radiation. A true oscillating spark (free from all arcing tendencies) is more adapted to the production of rapid oscillations than an "active arc" of true vapor; no matter in what medium.[9]

Herrold apparently believed that if an arc burned in an atmosphere of gas like Poulsen's, it was an arc, but when burned under water, it was an "oscillating spark." Throughout 1912 and 1913, Herrold, in both official and unofficial references to his oscillator, referred to it variously as oscillating spark and arc. Perhaps even then he believed that there was a significant difference. However, the evidence now suggests that he knew perfectly well that his self-credited oscillator was, in fact, an arc transmitter. He would concede this fact in his later patents by only using the term arc in referring to his own system. Certainly by 1914, Herrold began using the term "arc fone" to describe his own device. We conclude here that Herrold, while a bright and committed inventor and a skilled mechanical person, had not actually invented a unique system of his own when he stumbled into broadcasting. Lacking the depth and breadth of scientific background necessary, as well as the requisite luck or insight needed to be an original contributor to technology, Herrold nevertheless refused to give up and kept on trying to come up with something new. Without ever admitting it, Herrold had actually adapted the principles of the Poulsen arc to make a transmitter capable of transmitting voice and music. Perhaps his incomplete engineering education led him to believe he could develop a system that was new. Through that continuing belief, radio broadcasting was born.

While ample evidence that Herrold did indeed take out patents on a radio telephone exists, the use of which led to his developing America's first radio broadcasting station, his case for recognition would have been easier to make if important confirming records had not been lost. Perhaps through naiveté or innocence, Herrold entrusted valuable documents to a researcher who did not return them. The researcher died before his manuscript was finished, and executors of the dead man's estate never returned what was borrowed. In a letter to Ira Smith in 1930, Herrold wrote, "Years ago at the request of the late Col. Dillon I turned over a lot of exhibits, pictures, records and a book of valuable pictures which were to be incorporated in his books and also used in presenting my credentials at the two Institutes (IEE and IRE). After his death all these were lost...."[10] Other valuable records of the Herrold station and his experiments were lost in a fire: "My laboratory in the Santa Cruz Mts. was burned nearly two years ago with a lot of my boxed and stored records and letters." On Oct. 1, 1930, he wrote, "My files were burned with my laboratory some time ago."[11]

To evaluate Herrold's radiotelephone from a technical and legal point of view, we contacted William Byron, an authority on wireless technology.[12] Byron, a retired electrical engineer, wrote several articles for the *AWA Review* on arc technology. We asked Byron, who specialized in arc-based telephony, to read all the original Herrold patents and render an opinion on their technical soundness. Herrold received at least five patents between 1914 and 1916, but none were ever challenged because the arc system encountered obsolescence by the 1916 invention of the superior oscillating vacuum tube transmitter. According to Byron's analysis Herrold's patents certainly would have been challenged if they had infringed on any useful device. Herrold's system was of too low a power to be a competing system. According to Byron, "Had Herrold initiated a power-escalation program he would have been stopped very quickly, simply because the maximum efficiency of arc generators is just 50 percent. He could have not maintained an arc under liquid at the power level of a kilowatt, certainly not ten kilowatts. Both sparks and arcs were operated at hundreds of kilowatts but not on frequencies above the LF range. The highest-powered transmitters in the world, up to the thirties, were arc systems, and they were manufactured by the Federal Telegraph Company."[13] These arc generators created a continuous wave capable of transmitting messages in code, not telephone. But more important, even those considering a patent challenge would not have wasted their money after the Great War. With the rapid demise of spark and arc as a carrier of radiotelephone conversations concurrent with the quick acceptance of the vacuum tube as an oscillator for speech, it would have been, as the lawyers say, a moot point.

Byron concludes his analysis of Herrold the scientist:

> It is very easy, having considerably more technical knowledge and the benefits of one hundred years of technical advancement and hindsight, to second-guess people such as Charles Herrold. It is my opinion that he had just about as much technical "savvy" as had most non-professional people of his day. He and many others of the era had considerable talent with respect to machine work and mechanics in general, and many had their own tools, lathes included, which enabled some very fine work. His efforts and applications were devoted to what I would call "peripheral" apparatus. He, along with many, many other practitioners, didn't truly understand how the systems worked. He had enough capability to assemble a transmitter and to modulate it. His most important contribution, in my opinion, was the organization and production of probably the very first scheduled radio broadcast![14]

An analysis of Herrold's oscillating arc showed that it worked well enough to do what its inventor claimed. This was confirmed by another study of Herrold's technology by engineering professor James P. Rybak of Mesa State College, Colorado. His study of the Herrold "arc phone," which appeared in a publication read by radio specialists, concluded that it had the requisite design to serve as radio station for its time.[15]

Herrold the Broadcaster

What did Charles Herrold finally claim he had accomplished? That he was the earliest person ever to provide continuous broadcasting of entertainment and information, pre-announced and directed toward a known audience. This is what we call radio, which stems from the radiotelephone. It is not, however, the cellular phone.

To properly consider broadcasting, one must first put the term into perspective. The evidence suggests that the early radiotelephone experimenters and inventors probably became broadcasters by accident. They unintentionally attracted small groups of listeners as they endeavored to perfect the wireless telephone, hoping it would replace the Bell telephone. Fessenden was a musician, Terry a farm news enthusiast, de Forest an opera devotee, and Herrold a multi-talented pianist, music lover and headmaster of a wireless trade school. Finally, as a prelude to licensed broadcasting, Conrad used the phonograph as an audio source for his government-authorized 1919 Signal Corps tube transmitter experiments. But none of them was farsighted enough to know they were laying the foundation of a great communications industry.

If broadcasting is understood to mean what we see or hear on television and radio today, how was it defined during Herrold's time? There are two answers to this. The first is that broadcasting originally designated a single message sent from a single transmitter — say a land station — that was intended to be received by a group of ships belonging to a single company or a single flotilla. So it would seem that the term broadcasting as applied to electronic communications has always meant a single sender and more than one intended receiver. But the term evolved into something different by 1920s. This is when RCA historian George Clark decided to make up his own definition of broadcasting to better allow historians to pinpoint the first broadcast. Clark believed, and others concurred, that in order to qualify as a broadcast, a program had to be intentionally designed to entertain, persuade, or inform an audience, it had to be pre-announced, and it had to be listened to by a "citizen" audience. Current analysis now questions the adequacy of Clark's definition, which today seems arbitrary. The fault with Clark's definition is that it defines "audience" too narrowly. Clark's definition tosses away far too much — all of Herrold's pre-war broadcasting, all of Terry's public service transmissions to Minnesota farmers, and all that De Forest accomplished, including his 1916 broadcast schedule in New York. What does it matter that these early radio audiences were composed of commercial wireless or naval operators, amateurs, homemade set builders and hobbyists? Fascinated because people around the city of Pittsburgh bought receivers advertised by a department store in the fall of 1920 and tuned in to hear KDKA's election night broadcast, Clark mistakenly believed that this was the first time the American people heard broadcasting. He was unaware that average citizens had been listening to broadcasts from Herrold, Terry, Clark and others long before 1920. Maybe they couldn't go to the store to buy a radio set, but they had various means to get them. We know he was wrong, because men like Herrold had helped average citizens make their own sets to listen to his station as far back as 1912.

There is a fallacy in Clark's reasoning even when applied to the postwar period when radio gradually became popular. Homemade sets were required even to hear KDKA or WWJ as nearly all ordinary people did not have "store-bought" receivers even for their first broadcasts. Few members of the general public could buy off-the-shelf radio receivers in the very early years of the 1920s because these easy-to-use receivers were mostly in the design stage even then. Hobbyists were still the major source of supply for anyone wanting to tune in. Based on a study of the major radio periodicals between 1920 and 1923, it was found that the vast majority of listeners was still building their own sets, or listening to programs on sets built by their hobbyist and amateur friends and families. Even the term "radio broadcast" was not commonly used at the time, as the term "radio concert" and even "wireless concert" continued to appear in the popular literature of the 1920-1923 period. The written evidence from 1909 to 1917 indicates that both Herrold and de Forest used the terms "radio," "arc phone" and "wireless concerts" interchangeably. Even though sets used to receive radio broadcasts were built by hobbyists, many in the audience were "citizens" with no technical understanding, but rather a curiosity to listen on receivers built by friends and family. So the Clark definition falls short of historians' needs. It is flawed largely because it defines "audience" too narrowly. Radio broadcasting got its start long before 1920 and only a blind acceptance of Clark's point of view would make it otherwise.

Can we not agree on a proper definition of broadcasting today? Are modern historians still bound by the constraints of a "citizen audience"? We believe the answer is obvious on the surface. We find a growing consensus among telecommunication historians that broadcasting to audiences in America began well before 1920. Anyone interested would be well advised to consult the authoritative works of Erik Barnouw, namely, his three-volume set on the history of American telecommunications first issued in 1966, and *Stay Tuned* (2002), the one-volume history by Christopher H. Sterling and John M. Kittross first issued in 1978 and still one of the most widely respected and comprehensive studies available today.[16] Each of these historians recognizes and includes mention of Charles Herrold. Thanks to their scholarship, more is known about Herrold's proper place in radio history and what really happened during the "lost years of broadcasting."

By 1925 nearly all of the early pioneers who had experimented in the pre-war years sought recognition as early broadcasters. De Forest, Fessenden, Terry, Conrad and Herrold each wanted to be recognized for his prewar efforts. Only a careful reading of American radio history can reveal those who were pioneer broadcasters and those who were not. The overwhelming evidence is that Herrold led them all in what was truly a race for the radiotelephone. In the beginning, "voices" and "music" heard over the airwaves were picked up by accident. Radiotelephone experimenters largely ignored these amateur audiences from the start. But Charles Herrold thought differently. Seeing that his 1909 experiments got an unexpected response, he immediately recognized that "voices and music" were attracting potential students for his school and he kept it up. Thus airing "concerts" was done on a regular schedule in order to get and hold an audience of customers, which is not far different from today. Herrold's programming gave listeners something they wanted to hear, on a preannounced schedule, and often publicized in the newspapers. On discovering his 1909 audience, Herrold lost no time in instituting weekly "wireless phone concerts" and then putting them on the air daily. He publicized this activity with a notarized statement in a national publication in late spring 1910. Given the responsibility of providing daily technical activities for hundreds of eager young men, it is the authors' thesis that his and his students' broadcasting of the popular music of the day to an audience of their friends, families and possible future students was something Herrold did early enough and long enough to be the first man to do so. It was the cauldron from which broadcasting emerged, Charles Herrold–style.

Herrold in Perspective

We believe the time has come to recognize that Charles Herrold was an early and important but overlooked broadcaster. He was the first to start a radio broadcasting station and the first to broadcast entertainment programming to an audience on a regular schedule, but Herrold entered the 1920s without the resources to continue his dreams or to realize his legacy. He could not afford to rush to the United States Commerce Department to be the first licensed broadcaster, he was not the inventor of the vacuum tube radiotelephone; and he had neither the money nor the connections that would allow him to become an important part of the new radio era. At the beginning of the 1920s, as other stations got on the air using the new tube technology, Herrold had to find a practical way to support himself and his family by selling radio parts. It was a far cry from how his radio broadcasting had begun. At the start of the 20th century, Herrold, like many others was working hard for success—he was, in this fact, radio's everyman. Striving along with a handful of others to unlock the secrets of the early wireless telephony, Herrold represented a generation whose work ultimately benefited the whole world and revolutionized the communications industry, but in the end profited few, if any of them, for what they gave.

There is also irony in the Herrold story. In the often rancorous debate over who was the first broadcaster, there has been a longtime rivalry between Pittsburgh's Westinghouse station (KDKA) and the station that evolved out of Herrold's work on the West Coast (KQW/KCBS), which was eventually acquired by CBS. As these contenders sought recognition for their unique position in broadcasting history, there was no resolution of their differences for three-quarters of the 20th century. However, the new millennium brought about a change of ownership of both stations and there is now a chance to resolve the problem. Westinghouse, which led America into the great 1920s radio revolution with KDKA, was acquired by the Columbia Broadcasting System on December 1, 1997, and was made part of the CBS broadcasting empire with headquarters in New York City. Then, not too long afterward, CBS was swallowed up by Viacom, which meant that both stations now were part of the same conglomerate, the Infinity Broadcasting Corporation. Since both stations now had the same owner, Viacom was in a key position to determine whether to recognize the pioneer claims of each station—that KDKA is, in fact, the "oldest station" and that KCBS, is the "first station." Whether bringing these contenders under a single ownership roof will end the controversy remains to be seen. Of course, history, as seen by researchers and scholars, will make the final judgment about which station was first but the new corporate ownership now can play an important role in influencing that final decision by how it adjudicates the case itself.[17]

We conclude that Herrold was the first individual to have accidentally stumbled onto the activities of what is now accepted as radio broadcasting. The strongest evidence: a reiteration of this early reference to what is today considered one of the activities of broadcasting, an innocent but matter-of-fact advertisement in a 1910 catalogue of the Electro Importing Company of New York.[18] In order to show how useful wireless parts bought from the Electro Importing Company were, both assistant Ray Newby and Herrold went to a Santa Clara County notary public to swear out statements that testified to their success with the company's "one inch coil and Ericsson Dust microphone." The first three of these notarized statements testify to long distance radiotelephone transmission records between Herrold's San Jose school and government stations at Mare Island and the Farallon Island. But it is in this final and prophetic notarized statement written by Herrold and dated June 1910 that this earliest reference to Herrold being truly engaged in broadcasting is found: "We have given wireless phone concerts to amateur wireless men throughout the Santa Clara Valley."

Evolution of the Theory of Evolution

It is not unusual for great people to be lost in history. According to recent scholarship, there is a body of evidence in favor of a distinguished scientist named A.R. Wallace who may have come up with the theory of evolution before Charles R. Darwin. Yet Wallace is hardly known to the general public today and Darwin is acclaimed as originator of the theory of evolution. What is not generally known is that for many years Darwin had been working on a theory of evolution, which he told only to close friends, realizing it was controversial. Because his concept was not published, Darwin was surprised one day to be asked to review a similar theory submitted to him by a natural scientist working in the East Indies, A.R. Wallace. At first he thought he should give Wallace's work preference and hold back his own, but Darwin's friends prevailed upon them both to present their papers jointly to the Linnaean Society of London. Later both papers were published in the group's *Transactions* in 1858. Soon afterward Darwin earned a reputation and created a sensation largely because he went on to publish his theory in 1859 in *The Origin of the Species*. Wallace virtually disappeared.[19]

Evolution of a Verdict

Herrold believed his case for recognition would be won if he could make his case fully and fairly to the public. He was willing to let the people decide; he considered them to be a fair-minded jury if they heard all the facts. It is obvious that what Herrold needed years ago was a book. If his work had been presented earlier, there would be no need for it now. The story of the origins of broadcasting, which Herrold began to prepare, was never finished. Thanks to his efforts to collect and preserve important documents, however, it paved the way for what we have been able to present here. An assortment of friends and associates did what they could to make his work known over the years. They laid the foundations for what we know today and made it possible for what we have been able to offer here. Since Herrold said he was content to rest his case with the world court of pubic opinion, we hope this book reveals what needs to be known and will assist in bringing to a proper conclusion a case which should have been won in favor of Herrold by all the proper evidence long ago.

Notes

Acknowledgments

1. Webster, Hayes, and Dundes each managed KCBS at one time or another. Several talked with Greb more than once. Example: Maurie Webster was first interviewed by Greb in San Francisco in 1958; next, in the 1960s and '70s when he was a CBS executive in Manhattan, and finally, as a retiree in upstate New York in 1995. The authors have tried to cite the time and place of every formal interview throughout the book.

2. Each Special Collection is identified by letter, as follows: Mike Adams Radio Collection (A), George H. Clark Radioana Collection (CRC), Columbia University Oral History Collection, New York (C), Gordon Greb Radio Collection (G), Herrold Papers (H), Jim Kreuzer Collection, New York (K), BMI Imaging Systems (BMI), Perham Foundation (P), San Jose State University (SJS), Smithsonian Institution (S), Stephen True Collection (T).

Preface

1. *Wireless and Electrical Cyclopedia* (New York: Electro Importing Co., 1910) 122. This 1910 wireless parts catalogue of the Electro-Importing Company, New York, used notarized statements from users of its wireless parts. Herrold was one such individual, and apparently his novel use of their spark coil to broadcast music was a selling point, thus the notarization implying that a respected local authority had verified his claim. In the beginning wireless enthusiasts had to build their own transmitters and receivers to listen to two-way communication between ships and shore stations. The broadcasting of entertainment, the wireless concert, to an audience was rare.

2. The year 1920 has been celebrated by the National Association of Broadcasters as the beginning of radio's widespread use and popularity principally because the Department of Commerce began issuing the first commercial licenses then. Gleason L. Archer's history of radio (1938) also led to the acceptance of 1920 because for many years there was no generally known evidence to the contrary.

3. Gordon B. Greb, "The Need for Radio Research Now." Mass Media Section, Western Speech Association Convention, Palo Alto, California. 28 Nov. 1959. (G)

4. *Oakland Tribune*, 4 July 1948.

5. Gordon B. Greb, "Golden Anniversary of Broadcasting," *Journal of Broadcasting* 3:1 (Winter 1958 59) 3–13.

6. Greb's interview with Ray Newby, audiotape and typescript, Stockton, California, 9 Jan. 1959. (A) (C) (G)

7. KQW was purchased by the Columbia Broadcasting System in 1949, had its call letters changed to KCBS, was relicensed to San Francisco and increased its signal power to 50,000 watts.

8. Hans Fredrik Dahl, "The Art of Writing Broadcasting History," *Gazette*, 24:2 (1978) 134.

9. Asa A. Briggs. *The History of Broadcasting in the United Kingdom*, which covers the period 1896–1974, is a work of five volumes published by the Oxford University Press, London: *The Birth of Broadcasting* (1961), *The Golden Age of Wireless* (1965), *The War of Words* (1970), *Sound and Vision* (1995), and *Competition* (1995).

10. Guglielmo Marconi and Henry M. Dowsett in the 13th edition of the *Encyclopedia Britannica* in 1926 credited the Poulsen arc generator

with helping to develop wireless telephony from 1906 onward. In 1908 Majorana used a heavy current liquid microphone to transmit speech from Rome to Sicily. In 1909 the Colin-Jeance arc apparatus in Toulon contacted a French cruiser 100 miles away. In 1912 the Vanni liquid microphone with an arc transmitter carried speech from Rome to Tripoli. However, no European established a regular broadcasting schedule at the time. See "Wireless Telephony" in Clifton Fadiman (ed.), *The Treasury of the Encyclopedia Britannica* (New York: Viking, 1992), 197–98.

11. While special museums and collections have been funded to gather and preserve early TV and radio programming, it would be rare indeed to find any audio recordings of broadcasts going back to the first days of wireless and the radiotelephone. See "Museum of Broadcasting" news article in *Broadcasting* (15 Nov. 1976) 54.

12. Newby's recollections confirmed much of what Herrold had in his private papers, which were made available to Greb by Herrold's son Robert True in 1958 preceding the interview. (G)

13. Robert was given his stepfather's surname (True) when his mother, Sybil, remarried.

Chapter 1

1. Alexis de Tocqueville, J.P. Mayer, editor, and George Lawrence, translator, *Democracy in America* (New York: HarperPerennial, 1988) 11.

2. Hugh G. Aitken, *The Continuous Wave: Technology and American Radio, 1900–1932* (Princeton: Princeton University Press, 1985) 12.

3. Aitken, 538–547; and *Miracles in Trust* (Los Altos, California: Foothill Electronics Museum, 1964) 2.

4. Joseph Laffan Morse, ed., *Universal Standard Encyclopedia* (New York: Unicorn abridgment of Funk & Wagnalls, 1954) 4079.

5. The most startling example of historical oversight was the long delayed recognition of inventor Johannes Gutenberg, who is acknowledged by most historians today as having been the father of mass communications. Although Gutenberg was the first European to use movable printing type in 1450, his accomplishment went unrecognized for 300 years. It wasn't until 1760 that Cardinal Jules Mazarin found a Latin edition of the Bible, printed at Mainz, Germany, in his own private library and looked into the history of how it came to be. It was his attention that finally put Gutenberg's name in the history books, even though subsequent research has turned up other European printers who may have used movable type before Gutenberg. But Gutenberg, who published the Bible, still dominates the literature because no one has been able to find evidence supporting the others. Perhaps even for printing the records are irretrievable, and it is too late to know the whole truth. When vital records are lost, there is insufficient evidence to support what happened.

6. E.P.J. Shurick, "Radio Firsts," University of Oklahoma, 8 Mar. 1946: 3. See also his *The First-Quarter Century of American Broadcasting* (Kansas City: Midland Publishing Co., 1946).

7. Samuel E. Moffett, "The Age of Wireless Miracles," *Saturday Evening Post Reflections of a Decade, 1901–1910* (Indianapolis: Curtis Publishing Co., 1980), 133.

8. Ray Stannard Baker, *American Chronicle: Autobiography* (New York: Charles Scribner's Sons, 1945) 85.

Chapter 2

1. Gernsback, editor and publisher of *Modern Electrics*, traced the beginning of radio to 1887, the year Heinrich Hertz's experiment at Kiel, Germany, confirmed the radio wave theory of English scientist James Clerk Maxwell. Hugo Gernsback, "50 Years of Radio," editorial, *Radio-Craft*, March 1938.

2. Simple definition of a broadcaster: someone who intentionally seeks to attract an audience by transmitting something of interest to listeners regularly.

3. Portions of this chapter previously appeared in a journal published by the Antique Wireless Association, Inc., of Bloomfield, N.Y. Mike Adams, "The Race for the Radiotelephone, 1900–1920," *The AWA Review* (1996) 10:78–149. see: http://www.antiquewireless.org.

4. The Puskas brothers in Budapest, Hungary, first conceived of a wired entertainment service in 1881 and put it into operation for telephone subscribers in 1887. See David L. Woods, "Semantics versus the 'First' Broadcasting Station," *Journal of Broadcasting*, 11:3 (Summer 1967) 199–207.

5. Edward Bellamy, *Looking Backward: 2000–1887* (Boston, Houghton-Mifflin Co., 1888) 89–90.

6. It should be noted that Alexander Graham Bell used "loud speaking telephones" in good-sized lecture halls for his demonstrations. *New York Daily Graphic*, March 1877, 1.

7. William Peck Banning, *Commercial Broadcasting Pioneer: The WEAF Experiment, 1922-1926* (Cambridge: Harvard University Press, 1946) 3–4, 10–11, 32–34.

8. A copy of a reprint of an editorial cartoon by Robida with notations by Clark from the George H. Clark, "Radioana Collection, 1880–1950," Washington, D.C.: National Museum of American History, Smithsonian Institution.

9. *Ibid.*
10. Antony Askew, "The Amazing Clement Ader," *Studio Sound,* Sept. 1981: 44–46.
11. Askew, 44–46.
12. "Telephon-Hirmondo in Budapest," *Collier's,* 9 Dec. 1933. No author specified.
13. The subscription service originated by the Puskas brothers continued in Budapest to the year 1936. David L. Woods, "Semantics versus the 'First' Broadcasting Station," *Journal of Broadcasting,* 11:3 (Summer 1967) 205.
14. A.P. Morgan, *Wireless Telegraphy and Telephony Simply Explained* (New York: Munn and Co., 1913).
15. Clark Collection, Smithsonian. This article was not attributed or identified other than by date. Clark clipped articles from newspapers and magazines, handwriting in the margin the name of the newspaper and date of the article, but rarely the page number.
16. Rainey T. Wells testified he was a witness to Stubblefield's demonstration of radio in 1892. Thomas W. Hoffer, "Nathan B. Stubblefield and His Wireless Telephone," *Journal of Broadcasting,* 15:3 (Summer 1971) 317.
17. "Telephone Without Wires," *St. Louis Post-Dispatch,* 12 Jan. 1902.
18. R. Lochte, R. and R. McGaughey, "Nathan B. Stubblefield: Kentucky's First Broadcaster," paper, Broadcast Education Association, Las Vegas, Nev., April 1993.
19. Hugh G.J. Aitken, *Syntony and Spark,* (Princeton, N.J.: Princeton Univ. Press, 1985) 211–212.
20. "Murray, Kentucky, the Birthplace of Radio," *Kentucky Progress,* Mar. 1930.
21. Aitken, 211–212.
22. The "limited distances" of aerial conduction is a fact well known. However, as one examiner points out, "ground conduction becomes intertwined with certain other related phenomena in the developing telephone technology." Elliot N. Sivowitch, "A Technological Survey of Broadcasting's Prehistory, 1876–1920," *Journal of Broadcasting,* 15:1 (Winter 1970-71), 4.
23. Victor H. Laughter, *Operator's Wireless Telegraph and Telephone Book* (Chicago: Frederick J. Drake, 1909) 61.
24. The Poulsen arc transmitter and the wireless company built around it, Federal Telegraph, became the basis for the development of the modern electronics industry in what is now known as Silicon Valley.
25. Fessenden biography, *Electrical Experimenter,* Jan. 1917.
26. Fessenden bio. 1917.
27. John S. Belrose, "Fessenden and the Early History of Radio Science," 15th Annual Alexander Graham Bell Lecture, McMaster University, 1992.
28. R.A. Fessenden, "Recent Progress in Wireless Telephony," *Scientific American,* 19 Jan. 1907.
29. *Ibid.*
30. *Ibid.*
31. Greg Stec, "Fessenden: He Made Radio Talk," *Media History Digest,* 14:1 (1994): 41–50.
32. Stec, 41–50.
33. R.A. Fessenden, letter to S.M. Kintner, 29 Jan. 1932. (CRC)
34. Fessenden's device was made to his specifications by the General Electric Co. It is erroneously thought that he used an Alexanderson alternator. Hugh G.J. Aitkin, *The Continuous Wave: Technology and American Radio, 1900–1932* (Princeton: Princeton University Press, 1985).
35. G.H. Clark, "The Fortieth Anniversary of Broadcasting," unpublished document, 1946. (CRC)
36. H. Hallborg, memo re: Fessenden Co., 19 Dec 1946. (CRC)
37. William Mayer, Jr., "Development in Wireless Telephony," *Modern Electrics,* Feb. 1909.
38. "Poulsen Wireless Telephone," *Scientific American,* 6 June 1908.
39. Alfred N. Goldsmith, *Radio Telephony* (New York: Wireless Press, 1918).
40. *Ibid.*
41. "The Story of Count Majorana," Rome, Italy: *Antique Radio News,* 1993: 22–29.
42. Domenico Ravalico, *Radiotelephony,* Editori, Lirrai della Real Casa, S. Lattes and Co., 1920.
43. Earl W. Daniels, "Early Examples of Broadcasting," Jan. 1934. (CRC)
44. Hugh Enochs, "The First Fifty Years of Electronics Research," *The Tall Tree: The Story of Palo Alto and Its Neighbors.* Palo Alto, Calif.: Chamber of Commerce for History Association, 1:9 (May 1958): 8. (A) (G)
45. Cyril Elwell, "Autobiography" (unpublished), 1943. (CRC)
46. Lee de Forest, *Father of Radio* (Chicago: Wilcox and Follett, 1950). Also see: http://www.leedeforest.org
47. "Story of Lee de Forest," *Electrical Experimenter,* Dec. 1916, 561; Lee de Forest, *Father of Radio* (Chicago: Wilcox and Follett, 1950).
48. Hugh G.J. Aitken, *The Continuous Wave: Technology and American Radio, 1900–1932,* (Princeton, N.J.: Princeton Univ. Press, 1985) 162–249.
49. "Story of Lee de Forest," *Electrical Experimenter,* 561.
50. It can be argued that de Forest was a pragmatist here, too, contending that he used opera music simply as a program source for testing his transmitters at his High Bridge laboratory.
51. Lee de Forest, "Milestones in Radio History," *Radio World,* 1929.

52. Herbert J. Meneratti, letters to G.H. Clark, 1948. (CRC)

53. *Ibid.*

54. "Prospectus of the Radio Telephone Co, de Forest System," company advertising brochure (May 1907), unattributed and found by the authors in the Clark collection. (CRC)

55. Lee de Forest transmitted voice and music from the Metropolitan Opera House: the *New York Globe, New York Times, New York Commercial*, and *Modern Electrics*, Jan. 1910.

56. *Ibid.*

57. Lewis, *Empire*, 84.

58. Was de Forest surprised to learn the San Jose station was broadcasting daily and influenced to do the same when he returned to New York? The authors can't agree. Greb believes it was likely. Adams thinks not.

59. Patrick Robertson, *The Book of Firsts* (New York: Clarkson N. Potter, Inc., 1974) 145.

60. Around 1912 in Palo Alto, de Forest had made his radio tube perform as an amplifier and later sold it to the American Telephone and Telegraph Company as an amplifier of transcontinental wired phone calls.

61. "Election Returns Flashed by Radio to 7,000 Amateurs," *Electrical Experimenter*, Jan. 1917: 650.

62. *Ibid.*

63. "Air Will Be Full of Music Tonight," *New York Sun*, 6 Nov. 1916.

64. *New York Sun*, 6 Nov. 1916.

65. "Election Returns," *Electrical Experimenter*, 650.

66. Lee de Forest, letter to Charles Herrold, 22 Mar. 1940.

67. Lee de Forest, *New York World*, radio ed., 1929.

68. John F. Schneider, "Early Broadcasting in the San Francisco Bay Area: Stations That Didn't Survive, 1920–25," Schneider's web site: http://www.aa.net/~jfs, 3–4.

69. De Forest letter to Herrold.

70. Victor Appleton (Stratemeyer Syndicate pseudonym), *Tom Swift and His Wireless Message* (New York: Grosset and Dunlap, 1911).

71. After 1912 many radiotelephone stories appeared in the public press: "A New 100 Watt Wireless Telephone," *Electrical Experimenter*, July 1915; "Aids Wireless Telephony," *Detroit Free Press*, 29 June 1913; "Conversations and Music by Wireless," *Illustrated World*, Dec. 1915; "Eagle Men use Wireless Phone," *Brooklyn Eagle*, 19 June 1913; "Famous-Barr Installs Wireless Phone Music," *St. Louis Post-Dispatch*, 26 Oct. 1913; "Fined for Testing New Wireless Phone," *New York Evening Sun*, 23 Oct. 1913; "Fined for Wireless," *New York Journal*, 24 Oct. 1913; "Human Voice Heard 700 Miles by Wireless Phone," *Savannah News*, May 1913; "May Talk Soon from Europe to America," *New York World*, 17 Nov. 1912; "Perfects Wireless Telephone System," *Brooklyn Standard-Union*, 17 Oct. 1912; "Receives Wireless Telephone Messages with the Aid of Auto," *Los Angeles Examiner*, 29 Sept. 1912; "San Jose Inventor Claims Perfect Conversation with Santa Barbara," *San Jose Mercury-Herald*, Feb. 1913; "To Extend Wireless Phone," *New York Times*, 6 Mar. 1913; "Trinity Men's Club Hears About Wireless," *San Jose Daily Mercury*, 16 Jan. 1913; "Two-Way Wireless Phone Between Rome and Paris," *New York Times*, 6 Mar. 1913; "University of California Doing Good Radio Work," *Electrical Experimenter*, Apr. 1914; "Wireless Telephony is Near at Hand," *Little Rock Gazette*, 2 Nov. 1913; "Wireless Talk Across The Atlantic," *Boston Transcript*, 22 Nov. 1913; "Wireless Telephones," *Omaha Herald*, 10 Oct. 1913; "Wireless Telephone," *Macon* (Ga.) *Times*, 30 Oct. 1913; "Wonders of The Wireless Phone," *Savannah News*, 10 Jan. 1914.

72. "California Youth Invents Radiotelephone System," *Electrical Experimenter*, Apr. 1917: 891.

73. "Wireless Talkfest Planned," 1915. an.

74. Lewis, *Empire*, 104–07.

75. Sarnoff, 1920.

76. Archer, Gleason L. *History of Radio to 1926*. (New York: American Historical Society, Inc., 1938).

77. Louise Benjamin, "In Search of the Sarnoff 'Radio Music Box' Memo," *Journal of Broadcasting and Electronic Media* (Summer 1993) 38: 325–335.

Chapter 3

1. Ray Stannard Baker, *American Chronicle* (New York: Charles Scribner's Sons, 1945), 85.

2. Charles Herrold's mother, who had moved to Illinois with her family as a young girl, could trace her roots to pioneer settlers of the lower Mississippi Valley and was the daughter of the first white woman to live there. She was such an attractive woman that her Southern origins did not dissuade widower Herrold, who was a Civil War veteran and Union Army officer. He proposed and married her. Since he had led troops against the Confederacy as an officer, he was called "Captain" by his friends and neighbors afterward. For most of the 29 years of his working life, he was engaged in the mercantile business. Stephen True, *Herrold Family Genealogical Research*, unpublished, San Jose, Calif., 1992. (T)

3. Charles D. Herrold, letter to R.S. Gray, San Francisco, Calif., 1928. (G)

4. When Herrold's forebears crossed the Atlantic from Germany, they carried a dignified

old name to America and recorded it prominently where they settled, in the county of Westmoreland in the state of Pennsylvania, 50 miles east of Pittsburgh. The lineage of the Herrold family has been traced to 1616 in the village of Wurttemberg, Germany. In researching his ancestry, grandson Stephen True found eight generations identifying themselves as Herrold, including his grandfather, who was born Charles Herrold in 1875. Furthermore, he discovered the family name had evolved from Hoerold to Harrold to Herrold. (T)

5. George H. Herrold, *Autobiography* (unpublished, 1964) 29, 32, 38, 58–59. (T)

6. Eugene T. Sawyer, *History of Santa Clara County* (Los Angeles: Historic Record Company, 1922) 1293–1294.

7. Sawyer, 1293–1294.

8. *Ibid.*

9. Charles D. Herrold, "A Winter Hothouse," "The Blizzard, Uncle Charley and the Children," "The Ghosts of Herrold Manor," autobiographical radio stories, 1932–34. (T)

10. Regarding his neighbors' interest in their house, Herrold said, "I recognized the brown faces as those of my Indian friends who lived in a double teepee just outside of town. They were Chief Running Rabbit and his squaw, his son, Swift Foot, and his little daughter, known at school as Ethyln, but at home as Moon Flower. I insisted that it would be discourteous not to invite them in, since the Chief had never been in our home. Hanna Lusk, my great-grandmother, then 93 years of age, also insisted that it would be wrong not to invite them. So father went out through the storm door and told them to come in. It was the first time that the Chief and his family had ever been the guests of a white man in his own teepee. My father made the Chief feel at home, and mother, who did not like Indians, thawed out enough to make the poor squaw welcome." Charles D. Herrold, radio stories, 1932–34. (T)

11. Charles D. Herrold, radio stories, 1932–34.

12. *Ibid.*

13. *Ibid.*

14. Clyde Arbuckle, *History of San Jose* (San Jose: McKay Publishing, 1982) 386–392.

15. Sawyer, 1293–1294.

16. George H. Herrold, Autobiography, 29, 32, 38, 58–59. (T)

17. Herrold studied with a Lick Observatory astronomer named Campbell. George H. Herrold, letter to author Greb, 21 Mar. 1959. (G)

18. Arbuckle, *History*, 386–392.

19. Charles D. Herrold, letter, *Oakland Tribune*, 11 Mar. 1932. (G)

20. Charles D. Herrold, address, Commonwealth Club, San Francisco, 1928. (G)

21. Records show he attended Stanford for three years, 1895–1898. Stanford University Registrar's Office, letter to Gordon Greb, 15 Apr. 1972. (G)

22. Sawyer, 1293–1294.

23. George H. Herrold, letter to author Greb, 14 January 1959. (G)

24. Sawyer, 1293–1294.

25. Fred C. Wells, *Charles Herrold, Pioneer Radio Broadcaster*, authorized biography, unpublished, San Jose, 1932. (A)

26. Wells, unpub. bio., 1932.

27. Different wavelengths have different characteristics. For a more detailed scientific analysis, see President's Communications Policy Board, *Telecommunications: A Program for Progress* (Washington: Government Printing Office, 1951), 22.

28. Some believe Bellamy's idea of radio may have been inspired by the Puskas brothers in Budapest, Hungary, who began entertaining telephone subscribers linked to a central unit as early as 1877. See Dave Woods, "Semantics versus the 'First' Broadcasting Station," *Journal of Broadcasting*, 11:3 (summer 1967).

29. *Ibid.*

30. *Ibid.*

31. Charles D. Herrold, letter to mother, Stockton, 31 March 1907. (T)

32. Herrold, letter to mother, 1907. (T)

33. Clyde Arbuckle, interview with author Adams, video, San Jose, 1991. (A)

34. Erik Barnouw, *A Tower in Babel* (New York: Oxford University Press, 1966) 34–35.

35. George H. Herrold, letter to the author Greb, San Diego, 21 Mar. 1959 (G)

36. Sybil True, interview with author Greb, audio, San Jose, Calif., 2 Jan. 1959. (C) (G)

37. Sawyer, 1293–1294.

38. Robert True, interview with author Adams, video, Cool, Calif., 1992. (A)

39. True video, 1992.

40. There is an extensive photographic record of Charles, his son and his students camping in the woods while experimenting with wireless. Most of what is known personally about Charles D. Herrold during this time with his family was passed down from Sybil to Robert's son, Stephen, the Herrold family historian. (T)

41. Stephen True, interview with author Adams, video, Los Angeles, Calif., 1992. (A)

Chapter 4

1. Joseph Epstein, "What made Alexander Graham Bell invent the telephone?" *The New Yorker*, 13 Apr. 1998, 70.

2. Fred C. Wells, *The Work of Charles Herrold, Pioneer Radio Broadcaster*, authorized biography, unpublished, San Jose, 1932. (A) (Also

available at one time in Clyde Arbuckle's files at the San Jose Historical Museum.)

3. Charles Herrold, letter to Lee de Forest, 25 Mar. 1940. (G)

4. Ray Newby, interview by Gordon Greb, audio, Stockton, Calif., 9 Jan.1959. (G) (C)

5. "Wireless Telegraph to be Demonstrated," *San Jose Daily Mercury*, 25 July 1909.

6. "Spark" referred to a spark transmitter, which was used to send out code. It contained a coil or transformer, a spark gap, a capacitor, a helix and a sending key. An operator activated telegraph keys to send out dots and dashes on the smaller sets. Harold S. Greenwood, *A Pictorial Album of Wireless and Radio, 1905–1928* (Los Angeles: Floyd Clymer Publisher, 1961) 47.

7. Charles Herrold, untitled typescript on Herrold College of Engineering stationery (circa 1920s), 1. (G)

8. Charles Herrold, business history interview, typescript, 1922. (A)

9. Ray Newby, interview with author Greb, video, Stockton, Calif., 1978. (G) (SJS)

10. Charles D. Herrold, "90 Miles with a One Inch Coil," *Modern Electrics*, 10 Oct. 1910: 380

11. Newby video, 1978. (G) (SJS)

12. Newby video, 1978. (G) (SJS)

13. Charles D. Herrold, "Experiments on Ground Antenna with their Relation to Atmospherics," *Radio Amateur News*, July 1919: 11–13, 44–45.

14. Cyril F. Elwell began experimenting with a radiotelephone in Palo Alto in 1907. Others on the West Coast included William Dublier, of Seattle, whose work in 1910 was headlined: "Wireless Telephones for Spokane," in a story predicting his invention would "revolutionize telephoning." Dublier later visited Herrold in San Jose to discuss purchasing "an arc fone" and witnessed a demonstration. Another newsmaker was Earl C. Hanson, of Los Angeles, 19, who in 1912 sent a wireless "voice" message on a spark coil transmitter to a receiving set in a car. Similar attempts to develop the radiotelephone for two-way communication were being undertaken by various experimenters across the nation before World War I. None came close to being radio broadcasting. See "Wireless Telephones for Spokane," *Spokane Inland Herald*, 20 Nov. 1910; Hackett/Dublier papers, Jim Kreuzer collection, New York; "Local Boy Invents 'Radio Car'," *Los Angeles Examiner*, Mar. 1912.

15. Hugh Enochs, "Electronics Research Community Develops Around Stanford Laboratories," *The Tall Tree: The First Fifty Years of Electronics Research* (Palo Alto: Chamber of Commerce, 1958), 8–9.

16. Responding to Lee de Forest by letter on 25 Mar. 1940, Herrold wrote, "I never employed a Poulson [*sic*] arc in broadcasting...." (G)

17. Douglas Perham, who was employed as a mechanic by Cyril F. Elwell at the Poulsen Telegraph and Telephone Company in Palo Alto, 1909–12, heard Herrold's San Jose station 1909–1912. He told author Greb, "Charles D. Herrold was the first man to establish a broadcasting station. How do I know? Because I heard him." Interview with Douglas M. Perham by Gordon Greb, typescript, 3 Jan. 1959 (G). For further information on Perham in Palo Alto, see Enochs' *The Tall Tree*, op. cit. 6–7.

18. Newby video, 1978. (G) (SJS)

19. Newby audio, 9 Jan. 1959. (G) (C)

20. Newby video, 1978. (G) (SJS)

21. Thorn Mayes, *Wireless Communication in the United States*, East Greenwich, R.I.: New England Wireless and Steam Museum, 1989, 201–208.

22. Newby video, 1978. (G) (SJS)

23. Newby video, 1978. (G) (SJS)

24. Charles D. Herrold, letter, *Oakland Tribune*, 11 Mar. 1932.

25. Charles D. Herrold, letter to Lee de Forest, Oakland, Calif., 25 Mar. 1940. (A) (G)

26. "Radio 12 Years Ago and Today: San Jose Station One of First to Give Program," *San Francisco Chronicle*, 30 Mar. 1924: Sunday magazine section.

27. "Concert by Wireless Telephone a Success," *San Jose Herald*, 22 Jul. 1912.

28. *Ibid.*

29. The correct spelling was Fairmont, not Fairmount, but both spellings are found in various Herrold-related documents.

30. "Trinity Men's Club Hears About Wireless," *San Jose Mercury-Herald*, 16 Jan. 1913.

31. "San Jose Inventor Claims Perfect Conversation with Santa Barbara," *San Jose Mercury Herald*, Feb. 1913.

32. "Tests of Wireless Phone Successful," *St. Paul Pioneer Press*, 13 Oct. 1913.

33. Call letters came into use after 1912. The wireless telephone of NWT&T identified itself as SJN ("San Jose Telephone") and it operated under Herrold's supervision in the Garden City Bank building. When Herrold broadcast entertainment, usually at night, he used 6XE or the call letters FN. Baxter was PH. See G.E. Baxter letter to Marconi Co., 3 Jan. 1913. (A) (G)

34. When Robert J. Stull was manager of the Herrold College (circa 1920), Herrold began typing a summary of his work, saying, "On the Ruins of the old McCarthy Co. was built the National Wireless Telephone and Tel. Co., which commenced work on arc sets with the idea of getting around the Poulson [*sic*] patents." He added, "Jahnke undertook this work" and it failed. So Herrold said he gave NWT&T what was needed with his arc.

35. H.L. Rodman, "The Janke Arc," *Pacific Radio News*, May 1921: 329.

36. George M. Davis, notarized affidavit, 30 Apr. 1933. (A) (BMI) (G)

37. "San Jose California and San Francisco Linked by Radio Telephone," NWT&T press release, July 1912. (A)

38. NWT&T press release, July 1912. (A)

39. "Naval Wireless Telephony on the Pacific Coast," *Modern Electrics*, Mar. 1912: 873

40. Charles D. Herrold and assistants, exchange of telegrams, Point Arguello, Calif., San Francisco, Calif., and Mare Island, Calif., 1–13 Sept. 1913. (A) (G) (BMI)

41. Charles D. Herrold, "National Wireless Telephone and Telegraph Company report on instruments and accessories in situ at government and demonstration stations," 1913. (A)

42. Herrold, NWT&T report, 1913. (A)

43. Doug Perham, Clyde Arbuckle and Joe Cappa told author Greb they heard Herrold broadcasting regularly. Example: When Ray Newby was asked whether the station experimented "every day," he answered: "Oh, yes—almost any hour of the day or night—sometimes all night. We would be testing and experimenting and adjusting and trying new adaptations of Herrold's ideas." See Ray Newby interview by Gordon Greb, audiotape/typescript, Stockton, Calif., 9 Jan. 1959, and "Concert by Wireless Telephone a Success," *San Jose Herald,* 22 July 1912. (G) (C)

44. "University of California Doing Good Radio Work," *Electrical Experimenter*, Apr. 1914, 183.

45. Historian John M. Kittross has suggested to the authors that this particular NWT&T work by Herrold, while admittedly not broadcasting, makes him a worthy pioneer in developing person to person wireless telephony since he was in the forefront of cellular phone and PCS development.

46. *Electrical Experimenter*, April 1914.

47. James A. Hestwood, letter to NWT&T, 3 Feb. 1913. (A) (G) (BMI)

48. To say that Herrold had "hundreds, if not thousands of listeners" is an estimate. Licensed commercial and amateur operators were on the increase. Hobbyists, too, who subscribed to wireless publications called up Herrold after hearing his programs on their home receiving sets. Herrold knew he had a sizeable audience from regular, steady feedback.

49. Legal evidence and other notarized documents offered in Herrold's court case against NWT&T, 1912–1913, are from courthouse records in San Jose. See also Herrold's personal papers. (A) (G)

50. Charles D. Herrold, letter to NWT&T, 15 Nov. 1912; and Herrold and E.A. Portal, affidavit, 19 Nov. 1912. (A)

51. Charles D. Herrold, response to NWT&T, 14 Feb. 1913. (A)

52. Herrold response, 4 Feb 1913. (A)

53. Herrold response, 4 Feb 1913. (A)

54. Charles D. Herrold, collection of affidavits, 13 Feb. 1913. (A)

55. Charles D. Herrold, affidavit, "Important Inventions in the Art of Radiotelephone," 18 Apr. 1913. (A)

56. J.B. Young, affidavit, 11 Aug. 1913. (A)

57. Attorneys whose names appear on Herrold's patent applications are G.H. Strong and John A. Nairsmith.

58. The telephone microphone patent was issued jointly to C.D. Herrold and E.A.B. Portal on Dec. 21, 1915.

59. Charles D. Herrold, collection of affidavits, 13 Feb. 1913. (A)

60. *Herrold v. NWT&T*, S. Clara Co. Sup. Ct., case 21282, commenced 17 Dec. 1913, dismissed 7 June 1915.

61. Charles D. Herrold, "Report on the Golden Matter," 11 Nov. 1912. (A)

62. Herrold was employed by the company "from early in 1912 till late in 1913," according to a NWT&T official. See George M. Davis, notarized affidavit, 30 Apr. 1933. (A) (BMI) (G)

63. Herrold, report, 11 Nov. 1912. (A)

64. Charles D. Herrold, "Report on the Golden Matter," 11 Nov. 1912. (A)

65. To be a "demonstrator" meant that Herrold was putting his arc phone at the service of NWT&T.

66. William Morris Herrold, conversations at the Hof Brau, 28 Oct. 1913. (A)

67. W.W. Hanscomb, letter to R.B Wolverton, radio inspector, 6 Jan. 1914. (A) (G) (BMI)

68. F.G. Schmidt, letter to W.W. Hanscomb, 16 Feb. 1914. (A)

69. *Herrold v. NWT&T*, S. Clara Co. Sup. Ct., case 21282, commenced 17 Dec 1913, dismissed 7 June 1915.

70. The Consumer Price Index, 1915–1999, shows that one dollar spent in 1915 would require $16.30 today, according to the Bureau of Labor Statistics, U.S. Department of Labor. *World Almanac 2000* (Mahwah: N.J., 1999), 112.

71. NWT&T contract with Herrold, 22 June 1912, S. Clara Sup. Ct. records.

72. *Herrold v. NWT&T*, case 21282.

73. Victor Anzini, deposition, S. Clara Co. Sup. Ct., Feb. 1914. (A)

74. The trial, of course, was about a narrow contractual issue, but the authors speculate that had the improvements to the arc fone technology been major, and had they satisfied the NWT&T as to their commercial viability, it seems likely that the company would have agreed to pay Herrold any sum he requested.

75. "Rival Engineer Testifies," *San Jose Mercury-Herald*, 4 Apr. 1915.

76. Herrold, letter, 15 Nov. 1912; and Herrold-Portal, affidavit, 19 Nov. 1912. (A)

77. Herrold, letter, 15 Nov. 1912; and Herrold-Portal, affidavit, 19 Nov. 1912. (A)

78. NWT&T, response to Herrold's claim, S. Clara Co. Sup. Ct., Nov. 1912. (A)

79. Herrold, letter to NWT&T, 15 Nov. 1912. (A)

80. *Herrold v. NWT&T*, S. Clara Co. Sup. Ct., case 21282, commenced 17 Dec. 1913, concluded 7 June 1915.

81. This NWT&T loss was only a beginning. During two decades of experimentation, Herrold said he invested every cent of his inheritance into developing arc technology and lost it all — a total of $80,000 — when it became obsolete by 1920. "Forum" (Letter to the Editor), *Oakland Tribune*, 11 Mar. 1932.

82. As head of an electrical engineering college, Herrold may have concluded he had the authority to grant the Ph.D. and E.E.E. to himself. He undoubtedly would have relished the honor of receiving an honorary degree from an accredited college or university.

83. "Words are the counters of wise men, and the money of fools," said Thomas Hobbes, English philosopher, who wrote that by nature man's life was a war: "solitary ... nasty, brutish, and short." See Tryon Edwards (ed.), (New York: Standard Book Co., 1961), 739.

84. John Locke, unlike Hobbes, believed in man's natural goodness and defended the individual's right to life, liberty and property, protected by a social contract. See Louis Kronenberger (ed.) *The New Dictionary of Thoughts* (Boston: Little, Brown and Co., 1971), 464.

Chapter 5

1. Jerry Flamm, *Good Life in Hard Times* (San Francisco: Chronicle Books, 1977).

2. Hugo Gernsback, *Radio for All* (Philadelphia: J.B. Lippincott, 1922) 168.

3. George H. Clark, "Radioana Collection, 1880–1950," Washington, D.C.: National Museum of American History, Smithsonian Institution.

4. *San Jose Times Star*, 12 Feb. 1913: 1.

5. "Concert by Wireless Telephone a Success," *San Jose Mercury-Herald*, 22 July 1912.

6. *Wireless and Electrical Cyclopedia* (New York: Electro Importing Co., 1910) 122.

7. Letter from Simpson Reinhard to Gordon Greb, Feb. 22, 1959. (G)

8. Ray Newby interview, audio, with Gordon B. Greb, Stockton, Calif., 1959 (G), and its typescript, Columbia University Oral History Collection (C). Also Newby interview, video, with author Greb, Stockton, Calif., 1978 (G) (A) (SJS), Herrold Papers, Perham Foundation, San Jose. (A)

9. Gordon B. Greb, "The Golden Anniversary of Broadcasting," *Journal of Broadcasting*, 3:1 (Winter 1958-59): 3–13; Franklin Smith, "Oldest Station in the Nation," *Journal of Broadcasting*, 4 (Winter 1960): 40–55; Joseph E. Baudino and John M. Kittross, "Broadcasting's Oldest Stations: An Examination of Four Claimants," *Journal of Broadcasting*, 21:1 (Winter 1977): 61–83; John M. Kittross and Christopher H. Sterling, *Stay Tuned: a Concise History of Broadcasting* (Belmont, Calif.: Wadsworth Pub., 1978 and 1990); Erik Barnouw, *A Tower in Babel: Vol. 1, A History of Broadcasting in the United States* (New York, Oxford Univ. Press, 1966).

10. Newby interviews with author Greb, audio, 1959, and video, 1978. (G)

11. "Is Wireless Telephony a Fact?" *San Jose Mercury-Herald*, 8 July 1912.

12. "Concert by Wireless Telephone a Success," *San Jose Mercury-Herald*, 22 July 1912.

13. *Mercury-Herald*, 22 July 1912.

14. Charles Herrold, interview on KQW, San Jose, 1932, Herrold Papers. (G) (A)

15. Newby interviews with author Greb, audio, 1959, and video, 1978. (G)

16. Newby interviews, 1959 and 1978.

17. Sources for the Herrold Papers are letter-coded in endnote 2 of the Acknowledgments.

18. Dr. Robert Summers was the editor of the *Journal of Broadcasting* who urged author Greb to submit his findings.

19. *Ibid.*

20. Joseph Cappa, letter to author Greb, Alamo, Calif., 16 Feb. 1959. (G)

21. George M. Davis, notarized affidavit, San Francisco, 30 Apr. 1933. (G) (A)

22. Robert J. Stull, Herrold Laboratories publicity release, San Jose, 1922. (A)

23. *Pacific Radio News*, San Francisco, 1919–1922.

24. Dick Partsch, Tommy Reed and Robert Stull, "Testing of a Radio Telephone," unpublished bachelor of science thesis (Berkeley: University of California, 1916). Noted by Herrold in 1919 article in *Radio Amateur News* (Vol. I, No. 1) 12.

25. Robert Stull, interview with author Greb, audio, Fullerton, Calif., 5 Aug. 1965. (G) (A)

26. Robert Stull, letter to author Greb. (G)

27. Terry Hansen, sworn affidavit, 2 Nov. 1930. (G) (A) (T)

28. "Former San Jose Boy Now Foremost Expert in Radio," *The World*, 1922.

29. Clyde Arbuckle, interview with author Adams, video, San Jose, 1992. (A)

30. Newby interviews with author Greb, audio, 1959 (G) (A) and video, 1978. (G) (A)

31. Sybil Herrold True, interview with author Greb, audio, San Jose, 1959. (G) (A) (C)

32. Sybil True, interview with Greb, 1959. (G) (C)

33. Stephen True, interview with author Adams, video, Cool, Calif., 1992. (A)

34. Connie Perham, interview with author Adams, San Jose, 1992. (A)

35. Marconi's first name was Guglielmo, not William. "Marconi at Exhibition," *New York Eagle*, 7 Mar. 1914.

36. Espencheid Papers, select correspondence. Archives Center. Smithsonian Institution. (S)

37. Charles Herrold, letter to Ray Newby, 17 Dec. 1945. (G) (A)

38. Herrold, KQW interview, 1932. (G) (A)

39. Charles Herrold, interview, "KQW, the Pioneer Station of the World," KQW press release, 1929. (A)

40. Sybil True, interview with Greb, 1959. (G) (A) (C)

41. Stephen True, interview with Adams, 1992. (A)

42. Herrold, KQW interview, 1929. (G) (A)

43. Anonymous witness, interview, "KQW, the Pioneer Station of the World," KQW press release, 1929. (A) (T)

44. Newby interviews with author Greb, audio, 1959 (G) (A) (C) and video, 1978. (G) (A) (SJS)

45. Charles Herrold, letter, *Oakland Tribune*, 11 Mar 1932.

46. An early term for television was "radio with pictures."

47. Stull, publicity release, San Jose, 1922. (A) (T)

48. Charles Herrold, letter to Lee de Forest, 25 Mar. 1940 and Herrold letter to Ray Newby, 17 Dec. 1945. (G) (A)

49. Fred F. Wells, "Who is the Father of Radio Broadcasting: Lee De Forest or Charles Herrold?" unpublished authorized biography, 1932. (A)

50. According to most historians, a proper definition of "broadcasting" must contain at least three key elements: It is (a) radio communication (b) regularly intended for (c) the public. For a more complete and detailed analysis, see Christopher H. Sterling and John M. Kittross, *Stay Tuned: A Concise History of American Broadcasting*, (Belmont: Wadsworth Publishing Company, 1978) 13.

51. "Talks by Wireless while San Jose Sleeps," *San Jose Times Star*, 12 Feb. 1914: 1–2.

52. "Early in 1912 I installed a receiving set with 24 telephone receivers in a local music store so that their customers could hear the wireless telephone music." Letter to Lee de Forest from Charles Herrold, 25 Mar. 1940. (G)

53. Fred F. Wells, "The Work of Charles Herrold, Pioneer Radio Broadcaster," unpublished, 1932. (A)

54. Herrold Papers, "KQW, San Jose, California: The Pioneer Broadcasting Station of the World," unpublished six-page typescript, undated, 2.

55. "Rites Tuesday for Pioneer Oakland Radio Engineer," *Oakland Tribune*, 4 July 1948.

56. Newby, interview with author Greb, 1978. (G) (A) (C)

57. Sybil True, interview with author Greb, 1959. (G) (A) (C)

58. Robert True, interview with author Adams, 1992. (A)

59. Charles Herrold, correspondence with Lee de Forest, collected 1940–1942. (G) (A)

60. Ron Gordon, interview with author Adams, video, San Jose, 1992. (A)

61. Edward Altenbach, interview with author Adams, Oakland, 1992. (A)

62. Newby, interview with author Greb, 1978. (G) (A) (C)

63. Christopher H. Sterling and John M. Kittross. *Stay Tuned: A Concise History of American Broadcasting* (Belmont: Wadsworth Publishing Company, 1978) 53–58.

64. "Election Returns Flashed by Radio to 7,000 Amateurs," *Electrical Experimenter*, Jan. 1917: 650.

65. "Wireless Music Christmas Day," *San Jose Mercury-Herald*, 22 Dec. 1916.

66. "Concert by Wireless Heard by 300 People," *San Jose Mercury-Herald*, 26 Dec. 1916.

67. *Mercury-Herald*, 26 Dec. 1916.

68. "A Wireless Concert," *San Jose Mercury-Herald*, 25 Dec. 1916.

69. "Pistol Shot by Wireless as Old Year Goes," *San Jose Mercury-Herald*, 31 Dec. 1916.

70. Harry Engwicht, letter to author Greb, 1959. (G)

71. "Wireless Plants Must Come Down," *San Jose Mercury-Herald*, 16 Apr. 1917: 1.

72. "German Officers in Tijuana," Associated Press, 3 Mar. 1917.

73. Clinton de Soto, *Two Hundred Meters and Down*, American Radio Relay League, 1936.

74. "Local Boy Who is to be First-Class Govt. Electrician," *San Jose Mercury-Herald*, 15 May 1917.

75. Charles Herrold, letter to R.S. Gray, 30 Oct. 1928. (G) (A) (BMI)

76. Herrold letter to Gray, 30 Oct. 1928. (G) (A) (BMI)

77. Robert True, interview with author Adams, 1992. (A)

78. Herrold letter to Gray, 30 Oct. 1928. (G) (A) (BMI)

79. Records of U.S. Department of Commerce; licensing of wireless operators began in 1913.

80. U.S. Department of Commerce, *Commercial and Government Radio Stations of the United States* (Washington, D.C.: Government Printing Office, 1920).

81. Gordon B. Greb, correspondence with

Federal Communications Commission, 27 Jan. 1959. (G) (A)

Chapter 6

1. *Webster's Guide to American History* (Springfield: G. & C. Merriam Co., 1971) 410.

2. Ray Newby letter to Gordon Greb, 29 Mar. 1971 (G) and Newby interview, audio, with Greb, 9 Jan. 1959. (G) (A) (C)

3. Joe Cappa, letter to Gordon Greb, 14 Apr. 1971. (G)

4. On July 11, 1919, the U.S. President directed that all radio stations should be returned to owners by March 1, 1920, and amateurs were authorized to return on Oct. 1, 1919. Christopher S. Sterling and John M. Kittross, *Stay Tuned: A Concise History of American Broadcasting* (Belmont: Wadsworth Publishing Co., 1978), 52.

5. Herrold said he resumed broadcasting "immediately after the war." Hostilities ceased Nov. 11, 1918, but the armistice was signed June 28, 1919. Witnesses verify he was testing in 1919 and on the air by 1920; namely, Robert Stull ("He also had his arc and by that time a few tubes....") Joe Cappa ("I helped Prof. rebuild his arc.") and Ray Newby ("His station was in my building.") See also Joe Cappa, letter to Gordon Greb, 12 Feb. 1968. (G)

6. Fred C. Wells, "The Work of Charles Herrold, Pioneer Radio Broadcaster," (unpublished) 1932. Herrold Papers, Perham Foundation, San Jose. (A)

7. Herrold may have begun test transmissions as early as 1919, but there are no documents showing the exact date. He is reliably said to have resumed broadcasting in 1920, according to more than one witness.

8. "Prof had erected a one wire Marconi antenna at the garage on South First Street. He was putting out a signal, but it did not have the carrying power of his old umbrella antenna." Joe Cappa letter to Greb, 12 Feb. 1968, 2. (G)

9. Joe Cappa said he distinctly heard both Herrold in San Jose and de Forest in San Francisco "on the air" in 1920. Cappa letter, 12 Feb. 1968. (G)

10. Herrold Laboratories (half-page advertisement), "When Using V.T.s –," *Pacific Radio News* (June 1921), 386.

11. Besides offering a product for sale from Herrold Laboratories in his monthly advertisments, Herrold also promoted his call letters—KQW, 6XE and 6XF. Pacific Radio News, Jan., Mar., and July 1922.

12. Clyde Arbuckle, *Clyde Arbuckle's History of San Jose* (San Jose: Memorabilia of San Jose, 1986) 387.

13. Virtually all stations in 1921 and 1922 were operated as a side line, "seeking publicity, fun, or prestige in the community." Christopher H. Sterling and John M. Kittross, *Stay Tuned: A Concise History of American Broadcasting* (Belmont: Wadsworth Publishing Co., 1978), 63.

14. Herrold stations are identified by his name instead of call letters in Eugene T. Sawyer, *History of Santa Clara County, California: Biographical Sketches* (Los Angeles: Historic Record Co.) 1922.

15. There are several examples of pioneer stations using experimental licenses for broadcasting as late as the 1930s. Examples: (1) station W2XR, which later became WQXR, New York and (2) station 6XAM, which finally became the Warner Bros. station KWBR, Oakland, Calif. *Radio* (April 1922) 17.

16. Robert Stull, interview with Gordon Greb, audio, Fullerton, Calif., 5 Aug. 1965. (G)

17. Herrold got 6XF (March 1920) several weeks ahead of Dr. Conrad's 8XK (April 1920). The call letters told that the station was in a radio district, 6; that it was experimental, X; and was given out alphabetically, F.

18. Herrold station 6XF is seen in this photograph, taken Feb. 1921 (month and year visible on calendar). (G)

19. Fairfield, a student of Herrold's, later became chief of the Electronics Instrument Branch, NASA, Ames Research Center, Moffett Field, Calif. Leonard J. Fairfield, letter to Ray Newby, 6 July 1965. (G)

20. Charles D. Herrold typescript for R.S. Gray, Commonwealth Club [of San Francisco] Sub-Section Radio, preparatory to talk (circa 1928). (G)

21. The term CW (continuous wave) commonly referred to vacuum tube transmitters which came into widespread use in the 1920s.

22. *B.C.R.C.*, [San Francisco] Bay Counties Radio Club newsletter, Oakland, Calif., Oct. 1921. (G)

23. While modern radio engineers have a much better understanding of it today and use a more precise definition, CW was a shorthand way of describing "voice" transmissions at the time. See its original definition in Austin C. Lescarboura, *Radio for Everybody* (1922) 24–38.

24. *B.C.R.C.*, [San Francisco] Bay Counties Radio Club newsletter, Oakland, Calif., Oct. 1921.

25. According to government records, KQW was relicensed for three months on Dec. 5, 1922, then for one year on March 5, 1923, and every three months in 1924. It transmitted at 360 meters or 485 meters in 1923, providing "entertainment and weather," and in 1924 changed to 240 meters (1260 kilocycles). See Charles D. Herrold, letter of 19 Oct. 1930. (G)

26. *Radio,* 17 Apr. 1922, 17.

27. *Radio*, Dec. 1922, 36.

28. *Radio*, 17 Apr. 1922.

29. Ray Newby interviews with author Greb, audio, 1959 (C), and video (SJS), 1978. (G) (A)

30. Robert Stull interview, 5 Aug.1965. (G)

31. Joe Cappa, interview with Gordon Greb, audio, Alamo, Calif., 20 Mar. 1959. (G)

32. Jerry Flamm, *Good Life in Hard Times: San Francisco's 20s and 30s* (San Francisco: Chronicle Books, circa 1977), 41–42.

33. "Who Will Ultimately Do the Broadcasting?" *Radio Broadcast*, April 1923, 523–526, in Lawrence W. Lichty and Malachi C. Topping, *American Broadcasting: A Source Book on the History of Radio and Television* (New York: Hastings House, 1975) 125–28.

34. "San Francisco Wireless Lecture," *San Jose Mercury-Herald*, 9 Jan 1922.

35. "KQW Fetes 26th [*sic*] Birthday in Big Show," *San Francisco Chronicle*, 15 Jan. 1934.

36. "Monthly Broadcasts of Radio News," *Radio*, Feb. 1922, 33.

37. "S-J Radio Club Hears an Interesting Address," *San Jose Mercury-Herald*, 5 July 1922.

38. "Wireless Phone Progress Shown," *San Jose Mercury-Herald*, 9 Mar. 1922.

39. Saratoga Blossom Festival Radio Concert Program, 1 and 2 Apr. 1922. (G)

40. "Exposition Gets Radio Wizard," San Jose newspaper clipping in Herrold Papers (May 1922). (G)

41. "Commercial Club Backs Radio Plan," *San Jose Mercury Herald*, 29 Apr. 1922 and "Experts Laying Plans for City Broadcasting Outfit," *San Jose Mercury-Herald*, 30 Apr. 1922.

42. *Radio*, July 1922, 33.

43. *San Jose Mercury-Herald*, 16 Apr. 1924.

44. *Action*, First Baptist Church newsletter, San Jose, Calif., 6 Dec. 1978.

45. Fred C. Hart and Ira L. Smith, interview at KCBS, audio, San Francisco, 19 Apr. 1962 (C)(G)

46. Charles D. Herrold, letter to Ira L. Smith, 1 Oct. 1930. (G) (A)

47. Hart and Smith interview, 19 Apr. 1962.

48. Harry T. Saine, who installed KQW's new transmitter, was its chief technician for 12 years. Harry T. Saine, letter to Sigma Delta Chi, San Jose State College, 30 March 1959. (G)

49. Radio programs of the 1920s are listed in J. Fred MacDonald, "Index to Radio Programs," *Don't Touch That Dial: Radio Programming in American Life, 1920–1960* (Chicago: Nelson-Hall, 1991) 389–397.

50. Charles D. Herrold, "Sales Power of The Radio in Advertising," *Advertising by Radio*, (KROW, Oakland, Calif.) 30 Aug. 1930. (A) (G) (T)

51. Herrold, "Sales Power," KROW, 30 Aug. 1930.

52. Herrold, 30 Aug. 1930.

53. Arbuckle, *History of San Jose*, 387.

54. Bob Hill, "Wireless Radio, KQW and F.B.C.," *Action*, 6 Dec. 1978.

55. Hart and Smith interview, 19 Apr. 1962.

56. Hart and Smith.

57. Hart and Smith.

58. Herrold Papers: *San Jose Evening News* series of articles ending March 27, 1926, by R.L. Burgess, "KQW Making San Jose Known All Over West," "Herrold, Famous Expert, Defends KQW," and "These Articles KQW Alibi"; and by City Editor Jack Wright, "Interest in Radio Quiz Is High," "Kennon Answers Charges," "KQW Suggestions," and "Nothing Brilliant Is In These KQW Suggestions."

59. Hart and Smith interview, 19 Apr. 1962.

60. Warren F. Hodges, interview by Gordon Greb, telephone recording, 15 Feb. 1999.

61. *San Jose Evening News*, series by R.L. Burgess and Jack Wright, ending 27 Mar. 1926.

62. Hart and Smith interview, 19 Apr. 1962.

63. *San Francisco Chronicle*, 15 Jan. 1934.

64. Herrold's 1948 death certificate named his former wife as "Sybil True Hendrickson," which is not known to be her correct last name.

65. "Move to Oust Herrold, 'Father of Radio,' As Director of Local KQW," *San Jose News*, 15 Nov. 1926.

66. "Move," *San Jose News*, 15 Nov. 1926.

67. Herrold left no contracts or papers explaining his dealings with the Exchange Club.

68. "Move," *San Jose News*, 15 Nov. 1926.

69. Hart is said to have had between 31 and 42 publications. *San Jose Mercury-Herald*, 16 Nov. 1926.

70. "Vital KQW Meeting To Be Held Tonight," *San Jose Evening News*, 22 Nov. 1926.

71. "C.D. Herrold to Lose Job With Radio KQW," *San Jose Mercury-Herald*, 16 Nov. 1926.

72. "Solution of KQW Problems Near," *San Jose Mercury-Herald*, 26 Nov. 1926.

Chapter 7

1. Austin C. Lescarboura, *Radio for Everybody* (New York: Scientific American Publishing Co., 1922) pp. iv–v.

2. Frederick Lewis Allen, *Only Yesterday: An Informal History of the 1920s* (New York: Harper & Row, 1931).

3. Gleason L. Archer, *History of Radio to 1926*, (New York: The American Historical Society, Inc., 1938) 138n.

4. WWJ and KDKA have long disputed which should be called the first commercial station on the air with regular daily programs. The facts are these: On Aug. 20, 1920, the *Detroit News*

began broadcasting from its plant with a de Forest "radiophone" (8MK) which eventually got the call letters WWJ. On Nov. 2, 1920, Westinghouse, using licenses which ultimately became KDKA, began broadcasting election returns, continuing radio work originated by employee Frank Conrad (8XK) in 1919. The National Association of Broadcasters supported WWJ's claim when asked to adjudicate. See the web site for station WWJ: www.wwj.com; and Mitchell Charnley, *News by Radio* (New York: The Macmillan Co., 1948) 3.

5. KDKA Public Relations Department, "History of Broadcasting and KDKA Radio," in Lawrence W. Lichty and Malachi C.Topping, *American Broadcasting* (New York: Hastings House, 1975) 103.

6. Charles D. Herrold, letter to Lee de Forest (25 March 1940); and "#2 Mr. Gray. Subject: War Activities of Herrold" (undated typescript). (G)

7. Erik Barnouw, *A Tower in Babel* (New York: Oxford University Press, 1966) 55.

8. Susan J. Douglas, *Inventing American Broadcasting 1899–1922* (Baltimore: Johns Hopkins University Press, 1987) 246.

9. In later years as a Colombia University professor, Armstrong proved his genius by inventing frequency modulation. (FM)

10. This rising popularity of radio in the 1920s is the reason so many observers failed to see broadcasting's origins actually predated this period and why so little research has been focused on the period 1899–1922. See Susan J. Douglas, *Inventing American Broadcasting 1899–1922* (Baltimore: Johns Hopkins University Press, 1987) xx.

11. Letter to Merle Sterns from sister Birdie in New Jersey, 12 May 1922, donated to the Perham Foundation. (A) (G)

12. Archer, *History* (1938) 141.

13. Trevor Williams, *A Short History of Twentieth Century Technology, 1900–1950* (New York: Oxford University Press, 1982) 313–314.

14. Paul Schubert, *The Electric Word: The Rise of Radio* (New York: Macmillan Co., 1928) 214.

15. Lescarboura, *Radio for Everybody* (1922) 91.

16. Schubert, 194–195, 212.

17. "Radio Investment Traps," *Literary Digest*, 8 July 1922, 25.

18. Schubert, 222.

19. Bruce Bliven, "How Radio is Remaking Our World," *Century*, June 1924.

20. *Radio Broadcast*, May 1922.

21. John Spaulding, "1928: Radio Becomes a Mass Advertising Medium," *Journal of Broadcasting*, 8:1, 31.

22. *Radio Broadcast*, Apr. 1922.

23. "San Jose's Charles Herrold was the principal West Coast exponent of wireless entertainment in the 1920 era." Elliot N. Sivowitch, "A Technological Survey of Broadcasting's Prehistory, 1876–1920," *Journal of Broadcasting* 15: 1 (Winter 1970-71).

24. *Radio*, Apr. 1922, 17.

25. *Radio*, Dec. 1922, 36.

26. John F. Schneider, "The San Francisco Radio Dial," online: http://www.adams.net/~jfs/early.htm.

27. Christopher H. Sterling and John M. Kittross, *Stay Tuned: A Concise History of American Broadcasting*. (Belmont: Wadsworth Publishing Company, 1978) 83.

28. The 1921 listing by the Radio Service did not include several "Special Land Stations" from its edition of June 15, 1919. *Commercial and Government Radio Stations of the United States, June, 1921* (Washington, D.C.: Radio Service, Bureau of Navigation, Department of Commerce, 1921).

29. In 1920 Lee de Forest played an important role in helping put a Detroit station (WWJ) on the air and that same year he also opened his own station in San Francisco (California Theater), which was an ambitious effort but with a short history. He is listed in government publications with licenses 2XG in New York, 8MK in Detroit, and 6XC in San Francisco.

30. 8XK was relicensed to Conrad in April 1920. *Bureau of Navigation Bulletin*, 1 May 1920 ed., Archer, 199.

31. David W. Kraeuter, *A Biography of Frank Conrad* (Washington, Pa: Pittsburgh Antique Radio Society, 1990).

32. Frank Conrad and W.W. Rogers. Interview with George Clark. Smithsonian, 1940. (GRC)

33. Conrad and Rogers. Interview, 1940.

34. Kintner, Davis, and Williams. Testimony before the FTC. Smithsonian, 1934. (GRC)

35. Kintner, Davis, and Williams. Testimony, 1934.

36. "8XK, Pittsburgh," *QST*, Sept. 1920.

37. Alan Douglas, *Radio Manufacturers of the 1920s* (New York: Vestal Press, 1991).

38. Conrad and Rogers. Interview, 1940.

39. Conrad and Rogers. Interview, 1940.

40. Frank Conrad, letter to George Clark, Smithsonian, 29 Sept. 1937. (GRC)

41. "Pittsburgh's KDKA Tells Story of How Radio Has Survived," *New York Times*, 15 May 2001, A1.

42. "[A number of] feats predated Frank Conrad's transmissions in Pittsburgh in 1921 [*sic*], which are conventionally taken as representing the birth of broadcasting in the United States." Hugh G.J. Aitken, *The Continuous Wave: Technology and American Radio, 1900–1932* (Princeton: Princeton University Press, 1985) 470.

43. The Marconi Company station at Chelmsford, England, began experimental voice and music transmissions in January 1920 but suspended service

in November 1920 when its transmissions were said to be "interfering with radio communication to aircraft and ships." Patrick Robertson, *The Book of Firsts* (New York: Clarkson N. Potter. Inc., 1974) 146.

44. Luke F. Lamb, et al., *Wisconsin Public Broadcasting: Seventy-Five Years of Service* (Madison: Park Printing House, 1992), 5.

45. Harold A. Engel, "WHA, Wisconsin's radio pioneer," *Badger History* (Madison: State Historical Society of Wisconsin) March 1949.

46. C.M. Jansky, Jr., "The Beginnings of Radio Broadcasting," (remarks) honoring Dr. Earle M. Terry at WHA Family Dinner at the University of Wisconsin, 24 Nov. 1958. (G)

47. Jack Pearson, "World's Oldest Radio Station," *Exclusively Yours* (The Patten Company, Inc., 161 West Wisconsin Ave., Milwaukee, Wisconsin 53203, March 1987) 40:5, 8–15.

48. Remarks by C.M. Jansky, Jr., at a dinner on 24 Nov. 1958 and at the dedication of WHA's historic marker.

49. Werner J. Severin, "WHA, Madison: Oldest Station in the Nation," paper, Association for Education in Journalism, Madison, Wis., 1977, 12. (G)

50. Pearson, "World's Oldest" (illustration of marker), p. 9.

51. Lee de Forest, *Father of Radio: Autobiography of Lee de Forest.* (Chicago: Wilcox and Follett, 1950), 356.

52. Mitchell V. Charnley, *News by Radio* (New York: Macmillan, 1948), 1.

53. Joseph E. Baudino and John M. Kittross, "Broadcasting's Oldest Stations: An Examination of Four Claimants," *Journal of Broadcasting*, 21:1 (1977), 74–76.

54. Charnley, 1–5.

55. See WWJ Detroit's web site on the Internet for its history: http://wwj.com/history.

56. Lee de Forest, letter to Charles Herrold, 22 March 1940. (G)

57. *Pacific Radio News*, July 1920 and June 1921.

58. John F. Schneider, "Early Stations in San Francisco," online: http://www.adams.net/~jfs/early.htm.

59. See that Herrold's printed radio schedule, which he handed out to fairgoers, included Rock Ridge. (G) (A)

60. "Radio as You Ride," *Literary Digest*, 11 Nov. 1922: 28.

61. Christopher H. Sterling and John M. Kittross, *Stay Tuned: A Concise History of American Broadcasting* (Belmont: Wadsworth Pub. Co., 1978) 62.

62. John F. Schneider, "Stations That Didn't Survive, 1920–25," online, http://www.adams.net/~jfs/kre.htm.

63. Schneider, "Didn't Survive," ibid.

64. Schneider, "Early Stations," ibid.

65. *Radio*, Feb. 1922.

66. Edward Sarno, "The National Radio Conferences," *Journal of Broadcasting*, 13:2, 189–202.

67. Sterling and Kittross, *Stay Tuned* (1978) 85, 107–108.

68. Marvin Besman, "The Zenith-WJAZ Case and the Choas of 1926-27," *Journal of Broadcasting*, 14:4, 423–440.

69. Philip T. Rosen, *The Modern Stentors* (Westport: Greenwood Press, 1980) 11.

70. Robert W. McChesney, "Conflict, Not Consensus: The Debate over Broadcast Communications Policy, 1930–1935," in William S. Solomon and Robert D. McChesney. *Ruthless Criticism: New Perspectives on U.S. Communication History* (Minneapolis: University of Minnesota Press, 1993) 229.

71. *San Jose Evening News*, 18 Aug. 1925.

72. Since KDKA continues to claim to be the "oldest" and "first" station in America, the pioneering work of Herrold, 1909–1917, is largely unknown to the establishment press. Yochi J. Dreazen, "Pittsburgh's KDKA Tells Story of How Radio Has Survived," *Wall Street Journal* (15 May 2001) A1.

Chapter 8

1. *San Francisco Chronicle*, 30 Mar. 1924.

2. Bob Hill, "Wireless Radio, KQW, and FBC," *Action* (First Baptist Church of San Jose) 6 Dec. 1978, 2. (G)

3. *San Jose Mercury-Herald* 1 Dec. 1926.

4. *San Jose Evening News*, 1 Dec. 1926.

5. Fred C. Hart and Ira L. Smith, interview at KCBS, audiotape, San Francisco, 19 Apr. 1962. (C) (G)

6. The elusive Herrold was seldom at home at No. 10 Abbott Drive, Piedmont, when city census takers called. As a consequence he rarely is listed in Oakland city directories. However, because he used the Piedmont address regularly on his stationery, we know he always lived there.

7. *Monthly Publication* (San Francisco: Commonwealth Club of California) Nov. 1928, 184. (G)

8. Charles D. Herrold, letter to Ira L. Smith, 1 Oct. 1930. (G)

9. *Santa Cruz Sentinel* 19 Apr. 1930.

10. Charles D. Herrold, letter to Fred J. Hart, 12 July 1930. (G)

11. *Advertising by Radio* (bi-monthly journal) KROW, Oakland, Calif., 30 Aug. 1930. (G)

12. *KQW: For God and Country*, San Jose: KQW publication, 1930. (G)

13. *KQW: For God and Country.*

14. Ira L. Smith, letter to Charles D. Herrold, 30 Sept. 1930. (G)

15. Herrold letters were turned over to author Greb by Ira L. Smith for safekeeping and were made part of the Greb radio collection to be placed in a public library at an appropriate time. Smith-Herrold correspondence in Gordon B. Greb, *KCBS: Broadcasting's First Station* (San Jose: San Jose State Univ., photocopied ltd. ed., 1973). (G)

16. H.P. Davis, "The Early History of Broadcasting in the United States," in *The Radio Industry: The Story of Its Development*, as told by leaders of the industry to the students at the Graduate School of Business Administration, George F. Baker Foundation, Harvard University (Chicago & New York: A.W. Shaw Co., 1928).

17. "Decade of Broadcasting Observed at Station KDKA, Pioneer Station of the World, in Special Radio Program," undated news clipping from the files of Ira L. Smith (circa 1930). (G)

18. Sergeant Wells had served in France with the Seventh Battalion of the First Canadian Division, surviving a gas attack at Ypres. He was severely wounded in the second attack and lost an arm.

19. Fred F. Wells, *The Work of Charles Herrold, Pioneer Radio Broadcaster*, authorized biography, typescript unpublished, San Jose, 1932. (A)

20. Wells, *The Work of Charles Herrold*, 1932.

21. Wells, *The Work of Charles Herrold*, 1932.

22. Charles D. Herrold, letter to editor of "Forum," *Oakland Tribune*, 11 Mar. 1932.

23. The *San Francisco Chronicle* called it the 26th anniversary, but it was 25 years in the broadcast interview.

24. *San Francisco Chronicle*, 15 Jan. 1934.

25. "Radio Growth Marked With Hectic Days," *San Francisco Shopping News*, 15 Sept. 1947.

26. Fred C. Hart and Ira L. Smith, interview at KCBS, audiotape, San Francisco, 19 Apr. 1962. (C) (G)

27. Ruth Poindexter Fish, interview by Edwin C. Crouch, San Jose State University, 1981 (typescript). (G)

28. Howard Neikirk telegram and reply by RCA, New York, 7–8 May 1935. See George H. Clark Radioana Collection, Smithsonian Institution. (G)

29. George H. Clark, "RCA Radio History Archives" (papers), Washington, D.C.: Smithsonian Institution, collected by RCA's historian during his lifetime, 1881–1956.

30. Tom Lewis, *Empire of the Air: The Men Who Made Radio*. (New York: HarperPerennial, 1993) 112.

31. Young Greb at age 12 may have met Herrold at KTAB, Oakland, in 1934 when the author was a child actor on an adventure serial, *Rusty, the Boy Aviator*. He was introduced to a tall, genial old man outside the Oakland studios who was a radio storyteller. Greb now believes it was Herrold himself.

32. Polk's *Oakland City Directory*, 1935.

33. Young reviewer Greb was ten years old when he conducted this radio audience survey. Gordon Greb, "Standard Symphony Hour," *Whittier School Snap* (mimeographed publication) Oakland, Calif., Feb. 1932, 13–14. (G)

34. Greb, ibid.

35. Tom Lewis, *Empire of the Air: The Men Who Made Radio* (New York: HarperPerennial, 1993) 241.

36. Lee de Forest, address to radio association, Treasure Island, San Francisco, 7 Sept. 1940. (Ralph Brunton files, Atherton, Calif.).

37. CBS Vice President and KCBS Manager Maurie Webster letter to NAB Executive Harold B. Fellows, 26 Jan. 1959. (G)

38. *Tide*, 15 Dec. 1941.

39. John F. Schneider, "The History of KQW/KCBS San Jose/San Francisco, California," online: http://www.adams.net~jfs/KQW.htm.

40. *San Francisco Call Bulletin*, 1 Jan. 1942.

41. Don Mozley, interview with Gordon Greb, phone, audiocassette, Kentfield, Calif., 8 Apr. 1995. (G)

42. Grandey got into radio in Seattle, Washington in 1934, when a University of Washington radio broadcaster teaching on campus spotted his talent for script writing. After graduation, Grandey became chief writer of *Seattle Streets* (a take-off of *The March of Time*) and then joined his former instructor at CBS (KNX) Hollywood, where networks began buying his scripts. For a short time he was a Pacific Northwest radio executive and then a station manager in Alaska. When KQW needed a scriptwriter, Grandey applied and McCarthy brought him to San Francisco. Roy Grandey, interview with Gordon Greb, audiocassette, San Mateo, Calif., 5 Dec. 1996. (G)

43. Roy Grandey, "Story of KQW" (San Francisco: KQW radio script and audiotape of broadcast) 10 Nov. 1945. (G)

44. Grandey, "Story of KQW" 10 Nov. 1945.

45. Charles D. Herrold, "Story of KQW," (San Francisco: KQW disc recording) 10 Nov. 1945. (G)

46. Jerry Flamm, *Good Life in Hard Times* (San Francisco: Chronicle Books, circa 1977), 36–37.

47. Terrence O'Flaherty. "Are Yuh Listenin'?'" *San Francisco Chronicle*, 7 Apr. 1959.

48. Ron Miller, "Raymond Burr was…" *San Jose Mercury News*, 14 Sept. 1993.

49. In 1949 the Palace Hotel on Market Street in San Francisco became the new business and studio location of KCBS, not San Jose.

50. Parke Blanton, *Crystal Set to Satellite: The Story of California Broadcasting: The First*

Eighty Years (Sacramento: California Broadcasters Association) 1987, 40.

51. Edwin C. Crouch, "Station KLOK: One Woman Remembers San Jose Radio in the 1940s" (unpublished graduate paper) 21 Apr. 1981; and Lee Kopp, interview with Gordon Greb, 19 Apr. 1995. (G)

52. Schneider, "KQW/KCBS..." online: http://www.adams.net~jfs/KQW.htm.

53. On the death certificate, Herrold's former wife was listed as "Sybil True Hendrickson" which the authors think is in error because they found no evidence Sybil True used Hendrickson as a last name either by consent or marriage.

54. Bob Hill, *Action*, San Jose: First Baptist Church (newsletter) 6 Dec. 1978. (G)

Chapter 9

1. Gunther S. Stent, "Prematurity and Uniqueness in Scientific Discovery," *Scientific American*, Dec. 1972.

2. Gordon B. Greb, "Golden Anniversary of Broadcasting," *Journal of Broadcasting*, 3:1 (Winter 1958-59) 3–13.

3. Historic sites honored by Sigma Delta Chi since 1941 are listed in a directory published annually for its members.

4. Shurick, E.P.J., *The First Quarter-Century of American Broadcasting* (Kansas City: Midland Publishing Co., 1946).

5. See the four-page correction/addendum sheet bound into the Arno Press (1971) edition of Archer's book, originally published by the American Historical Society (1938).

6. Gleason L. Archer, *History of Radio to 1926* (New York: The American Historical Society, Inc., 1938) preface.

7. The contract was mainly unfulfilled because of the untimely death of Wells. According to a clipping (undated) saved by Herrold from the *Oakland Tribune*, Fred F. Wells, known as "Doc" Wells, died in 1932 at 1634 Grove Street, Berkeley, Calif. He was past state commander of the Disabled American Veterans. His survivors included his wife, Mrs. Ruth Wells and one daughter, Patricia.

8. Robert E. Summers, "A New 'First' Station," *Journal of Broadcasting*, 3:1 (Winter 1958-59), 1–2.

9. This videotaped Newby interview was conducted by Gordon B. Greb for San Jose State student Jack Ashworth's TV documentary which subsequently was used for classroom instruction and was later incorporated into Adams' PBS documentary. (A) (G) (SJS)

10. Greb donated copies of these recorded interviews to the oral history collection at Columbia University.

11. Among those providing valuable assistance to Greb in carrying out the project at San Jose State College were Kenneth Roed, assistant professor, who was co-adviser to Sigma Delta Chi, and professors Dwight Bentel, Dolores Spurgeon, Pearce Davies, Charles Kappen, and Lowell Pratt. Sixteen college journalism students helped carry out 50th radio anniversary responsibilities. They were Jim Adams, John Adams, Joe Crow, Corky Dannenbrink, Dave Elliott, Phil Geiger, Robert Kauth, Bill Knowles, Jerry Nachman, Bill Phillips, John Salamida, George Skelton, Anthony Taravella, Gene Tyler, J.P. Vanettinger, and Bob Wilson. They are credited in "SDX Slates Top Program to Honor KCBS Anniversary Celebration," SDX Deadliner Newsletter (Dec. 1958).

12. Evelyn Clark memo, 2 Feb. 1959, *Radio KCBS: 50 Years of Broadcasting* (San Francisco: KCBS, Apr. 1959).

13. The Perham Foundation was incorporated in California in 1959.

14. Perham left Palo Alto 1912, founded radio station WJAM in Iowa, and returned to California in 1928. Hugh Enochs, "Electronics Research Community Develops Around Stanford Laboratories," *The Tall Tree: Palo Alto and Its Neighbors*. Palo Alto: Chamber of Commerce, May 1958.

15. The Perham Foundation is at www.perham.org

16. Signatures of 50th anniversary dinner attendees were collected on a sign-up sheet, which is preserved by author Greb. Some personages like *Oakland Tribune* publisher Joe Knowland, for example, had to sit in the audience because the head table already was filled with VIPs. (G)

17. The entire six-hour dinner program was recorded on reel to reel tape by Walt Fox and Glen Pensinger of the SJS Audio-Visual Department.

18. Parke Blanton, *Crystal Set to Satellite: The Story of California Broadcasting: The First Eighty Years* (Sacramento: California Broadcasters Association, 1987) 40.

19. *KCBS: The Original Station: A 55-Year Pioneer in Tune with Tomorrow* (San Francisco: CBS) 1964.

20. John M. Kittross and Joseph E. Baudino, "Broadcasting's Oldest Station," *Journal of Broadcasting* 21:1 (Winter 1977), 61–83.

21. Kittross and Baudino, *Journal of Broadcasting* 21:1 (Winter 1977), 72.

22. California Historical Landmark No. 952 was placed at South First and San Fernando streets, San Jose, site of the "first radio station in the world," on Apr. 3, 1984.

23. James Arbuckle, club historian, who was unrelated to city historian Clyde Arbuckle, initiated the project.

24. Mike Adams' 1994 TV documentary *Broadcasting's Forgotten Father*, has been available for purchase from the Perham Foundation.

25. In an ironic twist, the program's airing on PBS was publicized in nearly every Northern California media outlet but it got little mention on KCBS. The TV documentary was largely a biography of Herrold, not the station.

26. See also bibliographies assembled by Christopher Sterling and Don Godfrey's *Reruns on File: A Guide to Electronic Media Archives* (1992).

27. Federal Writers' Project. *California* (American Guide Series, 1939) 117 and E.P.J. Shurick, *The First Quarter-Century of American Broadcasting* (Kansas City: Midland Publishing Co., 1946) 10–11.

28. Viacom was a $20-billion communications giant in 2001, controlling broadcast and cable television, radio, outdoor advertising, and online operations. The corporation owned and operated CBS, MTV, Nickelodeon, VH1, BET, Paramount Pictures, Infinity, UPN, TNN (The National Network), CMT (Country Music Television), Showtime, Blockbuster, and Simon & Schuster.

Chapter 10

1. Norbert Wiener, *Invention: The Care and Feeding of Ideas* (Cambridge: MIT Press, 1993) 9.

2. "If an individual commands no reputation, and thus is unrecognized, then it is not possible for him or her to claim status as a genius." Dean Keith Simonton, *Origins of Genius: Darwinian Perspectives on Creativity* (New York: Oxford University Press, 1999) 5.

3. Among notable Californians who dropped out of college were Jack London, who studied briefly at the University of California at Berkeley, and John Steinbeck, who never finished Stanford University.

4. Robert W. McChesney, "Conflict, Not Consensus: The Debate over Broadcast Communications Policy, 1930–1935" in William S. Solomon and Robert W. McChesney (editors), *Ruthless Criticism: New Perspectives on Communications History.* Minneapolis: University of Minnesota Press, 1993, 223.

5. McChesney, 224.

6. Herrold's station obtained national recognition from Sigma Delta Chi (now known as the Society of Professional Journalists) in 1959 and official recognition from the California State Landmarks Commission in 1984. Both placed historic markers honoring the site of "world's first broadcasting station" at First and Market streets, San Jose.

7. Herrold's job as a janitor was related by Herrold's grandson —family researcher Stephen True.

8. C.D. Herrold, *Oscillator for Wireless Transmission*, No. 1,096,717 granted May 12, 1914.

9. Charles Herrold, letter to N.W.T. &T attorney, 1914. (A)

10. Herrold, letter to Ira L. Smith, 5 Sept. 1930. (G)

11. Herrold, letter to Smith, 22 Sept. 1930. (G)

12. William J. Byron was educated at Carnegie Institute of Technology (EE) and at Michigan State University (physics). Born in 1923, he took an early interest in wireless, was an amateur operator for 40 years, and has been a lifetime member of wireless organizations (AWA, SOWP, and ARRL). His principal occupation has been that of a nuclear energy reactor-safety instrumentation and control design engineer. He was last associated with Princeton University, five years before retirement.

13. William Byron, "An Analysis of Herrold's Radiotelephone System," (unpublished) prepared especially for authors Greb & Adams. (A)

14. Byron, analysis for Greb & Adams.

15. Professor James P. Rybak, an electrical engineer and professor of mathematics and engineering at Mesa State College, Grand Junction, Colorado, analyzed the technology of Herrold's radiotelephone in "Forgotten Pioneers of Wireless: Part 4 — Charles D. Herrold" *The Old Timer's Bulletin*, (Aug 1998) 39:3: 20–24.

16. Dr. John M. Kittross, professor and radio historian, believes broadcasting should be defined as "an announced or publicized regularly and frequently scheduled service to the general public of entertainment and information" and believes it is significant that the Communications Act of 1934 stated that broadcasting goes "to whom it may concern" openly and freely. Statements made by John M. Kittross in 1999 correspondence with Greb and Adams. (G) (A)

17. Resolution of the controversy remains for the future. KDKA — licensed in 1920 —continued to proclaim itself as the "oldest" and "first" station as recently as 2002. See its Internet home page. KCBS — the station Herrold founded in 1909 whose service was interrupted during World War I — says it may not be the "oldest" but believes steadfastly that has always been America's "first" station. See the "History" page of the KCBS web site.

18. This reiterates what the authors said earlier about *Wireless and Electrical Cyclopedia* (New York: Electro Importing Co., 1910) 122. For that discussion, please see the Preface and Chapter 5.

19. *Universal Standard Encyclopedia*, 2245–2246.

Bibliography

Special Collections

The Herrold Papers are located as follows: Original photos, memorabilia and paper documents are with grandson Stephen True and author Gordon Greb; microfilmed copies of the papers are in the Library of Congress; photocopies and microfilm of many the papers and copies of the photograph collection are in the possession of the authors and at the Perham Foundation Electronics Museum in San Jose; original audio and video tape interviews are with the authors; a select number of audio tapes are in the Columbia University Oral History Collection.

Each source is letter-coded in the bibliography and endnotes as follows:

(A)	Mike Adams Radio Collection
(BMI)	BMI Imaging Systems (microfilm company)
(C)	Columbia University Oral History Collection, New York
(CRC)	Clark Radioana Collection (Smithsonian Institution)
(G)	Gordon Greb Radio Collection
(H)	Herrold Papers
(K)	Jim Kreuzer Collection, New York
(P)	Perham Foundation
(SJS)	San Jose State University
(S)	Smithsonian Institution
(T)	Stephen True Collection

General

Aitken, Hugh G.J. *The Continuous Wave: Technology and American Radio, 1900-1932.* Princeton: Princeton University Press, 1985.

_____. *Syntony and Spark: The Origins of Radio.* New York: John Wiley, 1976.

Appleton, Victor (Stratemeyer Syndicate). *Tom Swift and His Wireless Message.* New York: Grosset and Dunlap, 1911.

Arbuckle, Clyde. *Clyde Arbuckle's History of San Jose.* San Jose: Memorabilia of San Jose, 1986.

Archer, Gleason L. *History of Radio to 1926.* New York: American Historical Society, 1938.

Baker, Ray Stannard. *American Chronicle: Autobiography.* New York: Charles Scribner's Sons, 1945.

Baldwin, Neil. *Edison: Inventing the Century.* New York: Hyperion, 1995.

Banning, William Peck. *Commercial Broadcasting Pioneer: The WEAF Experiment, 1922–1926.* Cambridge: Harvard University Press, 1946.

Barnouw, Erik. *The Sponsor: Notes on a Modern Potentate.* New York: Oxford University Press, 1979.

_____. *A Tower in Babel: A History of Broadcasting in the United States to 1933.* New York: Oxford University Press, 1966.

Bellamy, Edward. *Looking Backward: 2000–1887.* Boston: Houghton-Mifflin, 1888.

Blake, G.G. *History of Radio Telegraphy and Telephony.* London: Chapman and Hall, 1928.

Blanton, Parke. *Crystal Set to Satellite: The Story of California Broadcasting; The First Eighty Years.* Sacramento: California Broadcasters Association, 1987.

Breeden, Robert L. *Those Inventive Americans.* Washington, D.C.: National Geographic Society, 1971.

Buxton, Frank, and Bill Owen. *The Big Broadcast: 1920–1950: The Complete Reference Work.* New York: Avon Books, 1973.

Cardwell, Donald. *The Norton History of Technology.* New York: W.W. Norton, 1995.

Charnley, Mitchell V. *News by Radio.* New York: Macmillan, 1948.

Clarke, Donald, ed. *Great Inventors & Discoveries.* London: Marshall Cavendish Books, Ltd., 1978.

Csida, Joseph, and June Bundy Csida. *American Entertainment: A Unique History of Popular Show Business.* New York: Watson-Guptill, 1978.

De Forest, Lee. *Father of Radio: The Autobiography of Lee de Forest.* Chicago: Wilcox and Follett, 1950.

Douglas, Susan J. *Inventing American Broadcasting 1899–1922.* Baltimore: Johns Hopkins University Press, 1987.

Enochs, Hugh. *The Tall Tree: Palo Alto and Its Neighbors.* Palo Alto: Chamber of Commerce, May 1958.

Fadiman, Clifton, ed. *Treasury of the Encyclopædia Britannica.* New York: Viking Penguin, 1992.

Federal Writers' Project. *California.* American Guide Series, 1939.

Flamm, Jerry. *Good Life in Hard Times.* San Francisco: Chronicle Books, 1977 (circa).

Flehr, Paul D. *Inventors and Their Inventions.* Palo Alto: Pacific Books, 1990.

Greb, Gordon B. *KCBS: Broadcasting's First Station.* (ltd. ed.) San Jose: San Jose State University, 1973.

Greenwood, Harold S. *A Pictorial Album of Wireless and Radio, 1905–1928.* Los Angeles: Floyd Clymer Publisher, 1961.

James, Peter, and Nick Thorpe. *Ancient Inventions.* New York: Ballantine Books, 1994.

Kuhn, Thomas S. *The Structure of Scientific Revolutions.* Chicago: University of Chicago Press, 1962.

Lehrburger (Larsen), Egon. A *History of Invention.* London: J.M. Dent, 1969.

Lescarboura, Austin C. *Radio for Everybody.* New York: Scientific American Publishing Co., 1922.

Lewis, Tom. *Empire of the Air: The Men Who Made Radio.* New York: HarperPerennial, 1993.

Lichty, Lawrence, and Malachi C. Topping. *Broadcasting in America: A Source Book of Radio and Television.* New York: Hastings House, 1975.

Lochte, Robert. *Kentucky Farmer Invents Wireless Telephone! But Was It Radio? Facts and Folklore about Nathan Stubblefield.* Murray, KY: All About Wireless, 2001.

Lyons, Eugene. *David Sarnoff.* New York: Harper and Row, 1966.

Maclaurin, W. Rupert. *Invention and Innovation in the Radio Industry.* New York: Macmillan, 1949.

McChesney, Robert W. *Telecommunications, Mass Media and Democracy: The Battle for the Control of U.S. Broadcasting, 1928–1935.* New York: Oxford University Press, 1993.

Meyer, Jerome S. *World Book of Great Inventions.* New York: World Publishing Co., 1956.

Morse, Joseph Laffan, ed., *Universal Standard Encyclopedia.* New York: Unicorn (abridgment of Funk & Wagnalls), 1954.

Newhouse, Elizabeth, ed. *Inventors and Discoverers: Changing Our World.* Washington, D.C.: National Geographic Society, 1988.

Rosen, Philip T. *The Modern Stentors: Radio Broadcasters and the Federal Government, 1920–1934.* Westport: Greenwood Press, 1980.

Saturday Evening Post Reflections of a Decade, 1901–1910. Indianapolis: Curtis Publishing Co., 1980.

Schubert, Paul. *The Electric Word: The Rise of Radio.* New York: Macmillan Co., 1928.

Shurick, E.P.J. *The First Quarter-Century of American Broadcasting.* Kansas City: Midland Publishing Co., 1946.

Simonton, Dean Keith. *Origins of Genius: Darwinian Perspectives on Creativity.* New York: Oxford University Press, 1999.

Solomon, William S., and Robert W. McChesney, eds. *Ruthless Criticism: New Perspectives on Communications History.* Minneapolis: University of Minnesota Press, 1993.

Sterling, Christopher H., and John M. Kittross. *Stay Tuned: A Concise History of American Broadcasting.* Belmont: Wadsworth Publishing Company, 1978; 2nd ed., 1990.

Strebeigh, Fred. "Messages by Wireless" in Newhouse, Elizabeth L., ed., *Inventors and Discoverers.* Washington, D.C.: National Geographic Society, 1988.

Tuchman, Barbara W. *The Proud Tower.* New York: Macmillan, 1966.

Weber, Robert J., and David N. Perkins. *Inventive Minds: Creativity in Technology.* New York: Oxford University Press, 1992.

Wiener, Norbert. *Invention: The Care and Feeding of Ideas.* Cambridge: MIT Press, 1993.

Williams, Trevor I. *The History of Invention.* New York: Facts on File, 1987.

_____. *A Short History of Twentieth Century Technology, 1900–1950.* New York: Oxford University Press, 1982.

Unpublished

Barrett, Dick. Letter to Gordon Greb, 19 June 1995. (G)

Baxter, G.E. Letter from P. H. to Marconi Co., 3 Jan 1913. (H)

Certificate of Death. Charles D. Herrold, No. 051087, filed at Alameda County Coroner's Office, Alameda County Records Office, Oakland, CA, 6 July 1948; deceased 1 July 1948.

Crouch, Edwin C. "Station KLOK: One Woman Remembers," *San Jose Radio in the 1940s*. San Jose State University (paper) 21 Apr. 1981. (G)

Davis, George M. Notarized affidavit, 30 Apr. 1933. (G) (H)

Fairfield, Leonard J. Letter to Ray Newby, 6 July 1965. (G)

Greb, Gordon B. "The Need for Radio Research Now." Mass Media Section. Western Speech Association Convention. Palo Alto, California. 28 Nov. 1959. (G)

Herrold, Charles D. Business history interview. typescript, 1922. (A) (H)

_____. Letter to R.S. Gray of the Commonwealth Club, Sub-Section Radio. "Subject: War activities of Herrold." Undated. (G)

_____. "Material Requested by the Santa Cruz 'Sentinel,'" 19 Apr. 1930. (G)

_____. "Sales Power of the Radio in Advertising." *Advertising by Radio*. Oakland: KROW 30 Aug. 1930. (G)

Rybak, James P. "Forgotten Pioneers of Wireless: Part 4—Charles D. Herrold." Typescript of submission. *The Old Timer's Bulletin* (Aug. 1998) 39:3; 20–24. (G)

Saine, Harry T. Letter to Sigma Delta Chi, San Jose State College, 30 Mar. 1959. (G)

"San Jose California and San Francisco Linked by Radio Telephone." National Wireless Telephone and Telegraph press release, July 1912. (H)

Sarnoff, David. "Sales of Radio Music Box for Entertainment Purposes." Memo. 31 Jan. 1920. (C) (S)

Shurick, E.P.J. "Radio Firsts." University of Oklahoma. Paper. 8 Mar. 1946. (G)

Stanford University Registrar's Office. Letter to Gordon Greb. 15 Apr. 1972. (G)

True, Stephen. 1926 wedding program radio script. (A)

Wells, Fred F. *The Work of Charles Herrold, Pioneer Radio Broadcaster*. Authorized biography, unpublished. San Jose, 1932. (P) (H)

Interviews

Recorded by Gordon B. Greb with each of the following:

Cappa, Joe. Audiotape, Alamo, Calif., 20 Mar. 1959. (C) (G)

De Forest, Lee. Audiotape, Los Angeles, Calif., 14 Feb. 1959. (C) (G)

Kopp, Lee. Phone, audiocassette, San Jose, Calif., 19 Apr. 1995. (G)

Grandey, Roy. Audiocassette, San Mateo, Calif., 5 Dec. 1996. (G)

Hodges, Warren F. Phone, audiocassette, Chico Calif., 15 Feb. 1999. (G)

Mozley, Don. Phone, audiocassette, Kentfied, Calif., 8 Apr. 1995. (G)

Newby, Ray. Audiotape, Stockton, Calif., 9 Jan. 1959 (C) (G)

_____. Video, Stockton, Calif., 1978. (SJS) (G) (A)

Smith, Ira L. Audiotape, San Jose State College, 5 Mar. 1959 (C) (G)

Stull, Robert. Audiotape, Fullerton, Calif., 5 Aug. 1965. (C) (G)

True, Sybil M. Audiotape, San Jose, Calif., 2 Jan. 1959 (C) (G)

Recorded at KCBS studios with the following:

Greb, Gordon, with Scott Beach. Audiotape, San Francisco, 23 Feb. 1962 (G)

Hart, Fred C., and Ira L. Smith. Audiotape, San Francisco, 19 Apr. 1962. (C)

Government Publications

United States v. Zenith Radio Corporation, Docket No. 14257, 14 Apr. 1926.

Department of Commerce. Bureau of Navigation. Radio Service. *Radio Stations of the United States*. Washington: U.S. Government Printing Office, 1 July 1916. ed.

Selected Serials

Action (newsletter)
Advertising by Radio (bimonthly)
American Review of Reviews
BCRC (newsletter)
Broadcast Reporter
Commonwealth Club Monthly
Electrical Experimenter
Gazette
Journal of Broadcasting
Journal of Broadcasting and Electronic Media
KCBS: The Original Station (booklet)
Literary Digest
Modern Electrics
New England Wireless and Steam Museum

Radio
Radio Amateur News
Radio Broadcast
Radio KCBS: 50 Years of Broadcasting (booklet)
Scientific American
Tide (company magazine)

Newspapers

References to Herrold's radio work:

"Wireless Telegraph to be Demonstrated." *San Jose Daily Mercury*, 15 July 1909.
"Concert by Wireless Telephone a Success." *San Jose Herald*, 22 July 1912.
"Wireless Pest: 'Oh, You Beautiful Doll'..." *San Francisco Examiner*, 6 Sept. 1912.
"Trinity Men's Club Hears About Wireless." *San Jose Mercury-Herald*, 16 Jan. 1913.
"San Jose Inventor Claims Perfect Conversation with Santa Barbara." *San Jose Mercury-Herald*, Feb. 1913.
"300 Mile Talk by Wireless Telephone." *San Francisco Call*, 13 Feb. 1914.
"Phones 300 Miles Away Without Any Wires." *San Francisco Examiner*, 13 Feb. 1914.
"Tests of Wireless Phone Successful." St. Paul Pioneer Press, 13 Oct. 1913.
"Talks by Wireless While San Jose Sleeps." *San Jose Times-Star*, 12 Feb. 1914.
"Wireless Music Christmas Day." *San Jose Mercury-Herald*, 24 Dec. 1916
"A Wireless Concert." Editorial. *San Jose Mercury-Herald*, 25 Dec. 1916.
"S. J. Parents Hear Wireless Lecture." *San Jose Mercury-Herald*, 9 Jan. 1922.
"Harding to Takes Up Radio." *San Jose Mercury-Herald*, 9 1922.
"Herrold Laboratories." Advertising. *Pacific Radio News*, Jan., Mar, June, July 1922.
"Wireless Phone Progress Shown...." *San Jose Mercury-Herald*, 9 Mar. 1922.
"Commercial Club Backs Radio Plan." *San Jose Mercury-Herald*, 29 Apr. 1922.
"Experts Laying Plans for City Broadcasting." *San Jose Mercury-Herald*, 30 Apr. 1922.
"S. J. Radio Club Hears An Interesting Address." *San Jose Mercury-Herald*, 5 July 1922.
"Monometer Boys to Be on KQW Tonight." *San Jose Mercury-Herald*, 16 Apr. 1924.
"First Broadcasting in History of World Was Done in This City." Part I, *San Jose Evening News*, 18 Aug. 1925 and "Work of Prof. Herrold Laid Radio Foundation." Part II.
"Radio 12 Years Ago and Today: San Jose Station One of First to Give Program." *San Francisco Chronicle*, 20 Mar. 1924: Sunday magazine section.
"Forum." Letter to the Editor. *Oakland Tribune*, 11 Mar. 1932.
"KQW Claims Oldest Radio Station Title." *San Jose Mercury-Herald*, 31 Oct. 1939.

Related work by others:

"Local Boy Invents 'Radio Car.'" *Los Angeles Examiner*, March 1912.
"Wireless Telephones for Spokane." *Spokane Inland Herald*, 20 Nov. 1910.

Microfilm

"Charles David Herrold Papers," and "Papers on the Origin of Radio Broadcasting in San Jose, CA: 1909." Collected papers donated by Prof. Gordon B. Greb, Sept. 1975: BMI Imaging Systems, 1115 E. Arques Ave., Sunnyvale, CA 94086.

Internet Resources

The author's web site: http://www.charlesherrold.org
Lee de Forest Website: http://www.leedeforest.org (also author Adam's site)
Antique Wireless Association website: http://www.antiquewireless.org
John F. Schneider's Bay Area radio history web site: http://www.aa.net/~jfs
Guide to radio history: http://www.antiqueradio.com

Index

www.ingramcontent.com/pod-product-compliance
Lightning Source LLC
LaVergne TN
LVHW081258100826
845148LV00005B/908